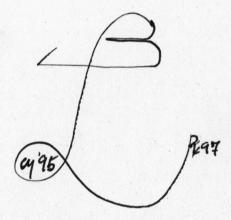

WORD WATCH

WORD WATCH

The Stories Behind the
Words of Our Lives

ANNE H. SOUKHANOV

A HENRY HOLT REFERENCE BOOK

Henry Holt and Company ■ New York

Henry Holt and Company, Inc.
Publishers since 1866
115 West 18th Street
New York, New York 10011

Henry Holt® is a registered trademark
of Henry Holt and Company, Inc.

Published in Canada by Fitzhenry & Whiteside Ltd.,
195 Allstate Parkway, Markham, Ontario L3R 4T8.

Library of Congress Cataloging-in-Publication Data
Soukhanov, Anne H.
Word watch: the stories behind the words of
our lives / Anne H. Soukhanov.—1st ed.
p.   cm.—(A Henry Holt reference book)
Includes index.
1. English language—New words—Etymology.   I. Title.   II. Series.
PE1574.S68 1995   94-39799
422—dc20   CIP

ISBN 0-8050-3564-8
ISBN 0-8050-4544-9 (An Owl Book: pbk.)

First published in hardcover in 1995
by Henry Holt Reference Books.

First Owl Book Edition—1996

Designed by Paula R. Szafranski

Printed in the United States of America
All first editions are printed on acid-free paper.∞

1   3   5   7   9   10   8   6   4   2
1   3   5   7   9   10   8   6   4   2 (pbk.)

The definition of *obstetrician's hand* on page 92 from *Dorland's Illustrated Medical Dictionary*, page 731 (Philadelphia: W. B. Saunders, 1994), is reprinted by permission.

The lines from Richard Cohen's November 7, 1993, column titled "Cursive, Foiled Again," on page 125, are © 1993, Washington Post Writers Group. Reprinted with permission.

Letters to the editor previously published by *The Atlantic Monthly* and quoted at various entries are reprinted by permission of that publisher.

Personal correspondence to the author from named readers of the "Word Watch" column are reprinted by permission of the writers.

To the memory of
Ivan Michaelovich Soukhanov, Ph.D.,
soldier, scholar, mentor, friend, and parent,
who understood the words in many languages, but most of all
understood the meaning of the word *understanding*.

July 30, 1903–April 18, 1989

Contents

Foreword

In an essay she wrote in the 1920s Virginia Woolf described with a sense of marvel the act of coining a new word. It is, she wrote, "as if thought plunged into a sea of words and came up dripping."

Very few of us, to be sure, will ever have that experience firsthand. The countless thousands of distinct English words that we will write and speak in the course of a lifetime are almost universally a given. As individuals we may come upon them newly, but the discovery is a personal affair, not one that belongs in the annals of language; the words themselves, after all, have in most cases been in existence for years—for decades if not centuries. That phrase "in most cases" is important, however. For it is also true that in our lifetimes new words come into being, impelled by new conditions that finally demand to be given names. To be made aware of these new words as they begin to find a place in the common vocabulary is not exactly the experience Virginia Woolf described. But there is an undeniable wonder to it nonetheless.

New words are the birth certificates of change—change in attitudes, in mores, in human relations, in technology, in the social and economic landscape, in the natural world. It was with that thought in mind—the conviction that a column devoted to new words and terms would also, in effect, be a column that offered snapshots of our rapidly evolving world—that the editors of *The Atlantic Monthly* approached Anne H. Soukhanov with the idea of writing the regular feature that would come to be known as "Word Watch." The choice of Soukhanov was both happy and serendipitous. Was there any group of people, we asked ourselves, who made it their business to track words that were attempting to enter the language—and kept records of citations which would indicate whether those attempts were succeeding? The answer: dictionary makers, of course. A call across town to Houghton Mifflin, the publisher of *The American Heritage Dictionary*, got the editor in chief herself on the line. Yes, said Anne Soukhanov, she had just this kind of information in her voluminous files. Yes, she would be free for lunch at the Parker House. And yes—this was a few days later—yes, she would be delighted to give the column a try.

That was in the spring of 1986. Anne's work first appeared in the July 1986 issue, under the headline "Words Received" on the magazine's Almanac page. That space proved too confining. The fact is, there was much more to say about the many new words and terms that Soukhanov came up with—for instance, *gold-collar worker* ("an employee in a brain-intensive business") and *airy-fairy* ("an intellectual, especially one in the diplomatic corps")—than we were providing room for. The solution was obvious. In January of 1987 we inaugurated "Word Watch," and it has been appearing on the last page of *The Atlantic Monthly* ever since.

"Word Watch" was an immediately popular feature. *The Atlantic Monthly* is a reader's magazine, and so it is perhaps not surprising that a column about words should have found in our readers a receptive audience. But a large measure of the column's success was Anne's quirky erudition and relentless diligence. A typical phone conversation with Anne might begin with her saying, "Hi, I'm hot on the heels of *grapho-therapy* and I've got a call in to a professor of industrial psychology at Ohio State." Our criteria were stringent: to be the subject of a "Word Watch" column, new words and terms had to show real signs of gaining acceptance—had to show that they were in fact needed. No nonce words need apply. Occasionally Anne would have to break the bad news about a particularly fetching new word that unfortunately seemed to be going nowhere: "I'm afraid we've been able to find just the one cite for it. This one isn't going to make it." More often she could report that not only was a new word or term making rapid inroads into common usage but that it had achieved a status sufficient for inclusion in the next edition of *The American Heritage Dictionary*. Anne was able to make such a determination because even as she turned out "Word Watch" month after month she was also shepherding that new edition toward publication—an extraordinary undertaking, as anyone who has been involved in the making of a dictionary can attest. *The American Heritage Dictionary of the English Language*, *Third Edition* was published in 1992 to widespread acclaim. How Anne managed to fulfill her responsibilities as editor in chief while also conducting "Word Watch" investigations into obscure linguistic nooks and crannies ("I haven't given up on a Bulgarian connection for *playtza*, but the Yiddish angle is looking stronger—I'm waiting for the editor of *The Great Yiddish Dictionary* to get back to me") was a continual source of mystification and amazement.

She did have help—from readers. One measure of the success of any magazine column is the quality of the mail received. Anne's has been voluminous and intelligent, and in many cases the writers have been able to give the lexicographic enterprise a much-needed assist by amplifying the information that she herself was able to dig up. Even when correspondents have written to take exception—and it seems to be a characteristic of people interested in words that they are ready at the drop of a hat to do so—they have used tones that rarely exceed moderate militancy. "May I respectfully question the origin of the word *bazuko* given by Anne H. Soukhanov in your February issue?" one writer began. The letters, together with Anne's replies, which have run frequently in the Letters to the Editor section of the magazine, represent a virtual extension of the "Word Watch" column itself. For reasons of space many of the letters about "Word Watch" cannot be published, but I happen to know that Anne has replied personally to every one of them.

Many of Anne's admirers hoped that with *The American Heritage Dictionary* behind her, she would finally gather the hundreds of words discussed in "Word Watch" over the years and place them between the covers of a book—a book that was as much a work of recreation as of reference, a book that was as much about our society as about our words, and a book that revealed, as we watched Anne Soukhanov go about her task, what a lexicographer's job entails. And now she has.

Meanwhile, the English language shows no disinclination to assist new coinages into currency. There is still a "Word Watch" column to produce and (ahem!) a deadline to meet. The material for volume two is fast a-piling.

—Cullen Murphy, Managing Editor, *The Atlantic Monthly*

Acknowledgments

gratitude *noun*, expression of appreciation for benefits received: "He who receives a benefit with *gratitude* repays the first installment on his debt" (Seneca).

THE STORY: The word *gratitude* occurs only 22 times in a rather famous study of word frequency; the pronoun *I*, by contrast, occurs 25,932 times in the same study. Let me then increase the frequency of occurrence of *gratitude* by using it to acknowledge just a few of the many mentors and friends who, over the years, have made this record of the words of our lives possible. It is their training of me, their wise counsel, their encouragement, and their personal example that must be mentioned.

Deepest thanks go to Harold T. Miller, who taught those of us who worked with him that if you can't do it right, don't bother doing it at all. Simply put, Mr. Miller represented *rectitude*, a word and a trait rarely encountered today. Thanks in equal measure extend to David R. Replogle, who, in three corporate environments, has given me outstanding opportunities in lexical and general-reference publishing. The same must be said of Robert M. Landis, Esq., who understood fully and supported unstintingly the editorial process. And Henry Bosley Woolf bestowed the greatest gift: instruction in the art and craft of lexicography.

To my loyal friend Cullen Murphy, Managing Editor of *The Atlantic Monthly*, this writer owes exactly as much. He conceived the idea of a column about new words of social import, invited me to write it, edited it personally in its early years, and, along with another former colleague, Nan

Talese, urged me to write this book. Amy Meeker, Associate Editor at the magazine, and Amy Levine, Assistant to the Editor of *The Atlantic Monthly*, now edit and fact-check the column with that very special touch all authors want but rarely get. Given the caliber of Cullen Murphy and his staff, it was no surprise that *The Atlantic Monthly* won the National Magazine Award for General Excellence in 1993.

Into a third very special group fall other loyal friends and respected colleagues; namely, William Safire and his assistant Jeff McQuain of the *New York Times*, who have ever been ready to put in a good word, in good times and in bad. The award-winning publicist Sandra Goroff-Mailly taught me how to explain our complex language with simplicity, style, and humor. More than that, she's my best friend.

My agent, Bert Holtje, and my editor, Kenneth Wright, believed in and championed this book. If you like the book, thank *them* for bringing it to you.

Every author wants an excellent publisher, and in Henry Holt and Company this author has found one. Special thanks go to Lisa Goldberg, assistant managing editor, for her careful attention to every detail during production of this book.

Every author wants and needs the support of family. For over twenty-five years my husband and two sons have given me that. What more can be added? My *gratitude*, that's what.

WORD WATCH

Introduction: Let the
Words Speak for Themselves

Tell me how much a nation knows about its own language,
and I will tell you how much that nation cares
about its own identity.
—John Ciardi

With mathematical exactitude the poet states the premise on which the arguments posed by the 365 words in this book are based and from which the conclusions about their social significance are drawn.

Language is people: the human comedy and tragedy. The history of English, then, is also a panorama of the living, loving, joking, cursing, arguing, poetizing, working and playing people, who, in their tens and hundreds of millions, in a score of lands and across fourscore centuries, have shaped and reshaped our native tongue into what it is.

—Robert Claiborne

The language historian identifies the nature of the individual and collective human forces that shape the national identity and, at the same time, the people's most precious communicative medium—their language.

If language is people in the sense articulated by Claiborne, it is a bellwether of the times in which they reside. The stories behind key words of our

2 · WORD WATCH

era together constitute a sociolinguistic chronicle of the times of our lives. For better or for worse, the dictionary editor is a chronicler of the people's beliefs, thoughts, actions, and behaviors.

Word Watch: The Stories Behind the Words of Our Lives chronicles aspects of the national character and the acts of the people who forge it, by presenting the stories behind the words examined since 1986 in my column "Word Watch," published by *The Atlantic Monthly*. The mission of the column has always been to examine new words with meanings not clearly apparent to sophisticated readers. More than that, however, the words have to make a statement about the direction in which society is evolving. Grouped into thirteen chapters by subject category, the words from the column—in addition to material appearing for the first time here—do just that. Reading through the list shows you what we have done, what we have not done, and what we ought to have done. Claiborne's human panorama is revealed word by word, chapter by chapter, in no uncertain terms. A critic once wrote of "Word Watch" that it "is like a canoe trip down the raging river of words. . . . The words . . . haven't been entered in the dictionary yet. They're raw, hot, new to the tongue, and beg to be read out loud." Taking Susan Trausch's cue, let's delve into a representative sampling:

affluenza. dance with (the) wolves. walk the cat back. firp. myc. LUG. rug-ranking. granny dumping. divorce jewelry. Divorceware. smoodge. Sovok. Wall in the Head. Begin amputation. Waldheimer's disease. Schindler defense. Colombian syndrome. Dirty Harriet Syndrome. Kojak Liberal. atomic mafia. isopraxism. ISO-9000. HIV roulette. blood culture. genocide pop. Lake Wobegon effect. imeldific. street triage. WASP Rot Syndrome. Xer. Generation E. zero-parent. agita. insurance technician. Paris Lip. newszak. softgel. Stephanopouli. schmooseoisie. thermagation. toy food. Urban Yoga. teledildonics. digital money. half-Cab. drive-by hatred. glading. constant whitewater. anticipointment. decession. corporate concierge. kata tataki. keh. beeper boy. beeper gun. 24/7. ghost rider. grease-trap theory. bomb blanket. Iraqi manicure. 16th republic. White Iraqi. grassy knollism. Xerocracy. blaff. gastroporn. appliance garage. Spinnish. mersh. paper curtain. pipe a quote. nacul. quux. fuzzy elevator. virtual office. pharming. skycar. suitcase car. land yacht. Bosnywash. FlashBake. Exerlopers. black-water rafting. river rider. egoboo. 'zine. undertoad. Boweryphone. off the grid.

A rumbustious lot, these and the rest of the words: They are variously robust, argumentative, querulous, quirky, rollicksome, cheerless, déclassé, defamatory, pitiful, courageous, and sometimes downright alarming. Rarely are they literary. Several words, deriving from various chapters, are the addends constituting the sum of our behaviors in the last decade. No question about it: *zero-parent*, in chapter 1, "The Times of Our Lives, the Words of Our Lives," represents a new generation at risk. Used as an adjective to modify *children*, *kids*, and *family*, this term denotes at least 2.8 million U.S. children with no parents because of death, desertion, drugs, or imprisonment. They are, in effect, children without a country. In *our* country, a country fixated on family values. Close behind the *zero-parent* children hovers the *squeegee kid*, who, in the six-year interim between his first appearance in *The Atlantic Monthly* and his reappearance here, has undergone a structural linguistic shift from *kid* to *man* The *squeegee kid* of the eighties, now the *squeegee man* of the nineties, makes a strong statement about the state of our cities, a problem that the *Kojak Liberals*, but not those suffering from *WASP Rot Syndrome*, must address—and fast.

To some, the decade of the eighties was a *serious* time. After all, that period gave us a new sense of self-importance and a new sense of the word itself—this one referring to all the good things serious money can buy: *serious* wine, a *serious* car, even *serious* fun. The eighties, often called the "*Bonfire of the Vanities*" decade, also brought us *affluenza, boomerang babies, laughism*, and *non-ism*. All these remain with us today, in a time of regression if not outright *decession*, one in which members of the new *anxious class* fear for their jobs even while gainfully employed in a work environment now called *constant whitewater*. As I write this, in December of 1994, in a period the Berliners call "Between the Years," in a period I call "Between the Centuries," we may write yet another new meaning of *serious*: at no time since perhaps 1914 has the world been so dangerously fluid, with institutions and rules long observed dissolving in midair between the centuries like the grin of the Cheshire cat. In an era of major medical advances, our private lives have been changed forever by the specter of AIDS, a situation that has generated a whole new vocabulary of sexual negotiation explicated at the entry for *HIV roulette*. In the nineties, with health-care reform at the top of many people's watch lists, the *insurance technician* looks over your doctor's shoulder and engages in Monday-morning quarterbacking. In an era now virtually divested of the threat of mutual nuclear destruction, an *atomic mafia* is reputedly at work in Eastern Europe—its mission being to black-market to interested buyers nuclear weapons and matériel from stockpiles in the former Warsaw Pact countries. In countries of the Balkans where some battlefield commanders are alleged to be convicted criminals, the so-called *Colombian syndrome* is the dynamic. At home, a *decession* has gone on, bringing with it a new kind of business English—one characterized by verbs such as "reinvent," "re-engineer," and "outplace." In looking to the future with a strong sense of the past ten years, we might characterize our feeling as *anticipointment*. Certainly that term is apropos on the global economic front, in personal terms voiced by those in the Japanese workforce who have suffered *kata tataki*, and by the *karoshi widows* of men who have worked themselves to death ("industrial accidents" is the term of art used by the Labor Ministry there), not to mention the U.S. *cross-functionals* who must perform the tasks once done by their now laid-off colleagues. And the *16th republic* of the former Soviet Union, a term denoting the 40 million officers, soldiers, and their dependents of a virtually unemployed military-industrial complex, has strategic, security, and economic-political implications reaching far into the twenty-first century. (This *16th* of the former fifteen republics ranks by population as the third-largest, only after Russia and Ukraine in size and potential power.)

This short list captures the essence of the acts of man and the times of man in the eighties into the nineties. The fabric of our lives is shot through with the strands of violence, disintegration of established norms, disease, and economic problems on the broadest of scales. Reading the stories behind the words of the eighties will illuminate the inevitability of what was to come; reading those behind the words of the nineties will provide a sense of what lies ahead.

Though we live in serious times, we as Americans have always seemed to temper seriousness with levity. *Word Watch* may give you *agita* in your "panza," but offsetting that are the funny, quirky surprises that characterize American English and those who speak the language. At *duh*, surely *the* interjection of the eighties, you'll find out how I almost entered a nonexistent, phantom word in my column. And you'll get the whole megillah on *mahosker*, a meaty, beefy word that's very New York. The *wallyos* and *garmentos* compete with the *firps* for your attention. A reader from Calgary, Alberta, the "geographic center of winter" in North America, has his say at the entry on *winter-beaters*, a.k.a. *rat cars*. The subculture of language aficionados who collect words with double *u*'s is exposed at the hacker's term *quux*. *Velcroid*,

Twinkie, and the verb *Exxon* and its mate *Goodyear* are but a few examples of the Goo Goo Clusters of trademarks taking on figurative lives of their own in a country increasingly dominated by business, pop culture, and the electronic media. And, if Diana Vreeland's grandson was right when he said to *Vanity Fair* last year, "My grandmother is no longer a person. She's an adjective—as in 'This paper-white narcissus is very Diana Vreeland,'" then the issue of renaming things and people by plutographic use of the names of the rich, the famous, and the infamous is revealed at the verb *Rembrandt*, the adjective *imeldific*, and the noun *georgi*, where you can learn how to *marcos* and how to *barbara*. But beware of *Bernies* carrying *georgis*.

Each chapter is introduced by a list of the words discussed in it, so that you can read through them (aloud if you like) and decide at the outset whether or not to take your canoe down a particular river. Regardless of your choices, don't miss *airy-fairy* in chapter 13, a word now used to mean a rather vague, impractical British foreign-service officer. It, like the story of *sunbeam*, a word given us by Alfred the Great, focuses our attention on history, and in so doing, evokes the verse of England's most influential poet. More than that, however, *airy-fairy* conjures the image of a language that always surprises, never stands still, baffles us with an unrequited love, sometimes shrouds itself in mystery, and bespeaks the fleetingness of life.

Claiborne's living, loving, arguing, cursing, poetizing words have come alive for me during twelve months of self-imposed incarceration with them. They've been *aquarunning*, *kickboxing*, *fitness walking*, *Exerloping*, *Flash-Baking*, *Exxoning*, *extreme skiing*, *heli-hiking*, *paintballing*, *practical shooting*, *black-water rafting*, and *mudwalking* through my mind. What is more, certain terms that capture the preeminent concerns of the nineties and beyond have taken on spiritual identities of their own and are watching as I put pen to paper right now. A *squeegee kid* now grown into a *man* is busily washing the windows of my study, attempting to seize and hold my attention. A *narcokleptocrat* from the *narcokleptocracy* that rules sectors of banking, law, government, and commerce stands in a corner discussing, with a *postconviction expert*, his chances of getting into *Club Fed* as opposed to Atlanta Federal Penitentiary. At the door, controlled by cellular-phone-equipped modern *Fagins*, *beeper boys* stand with *beeper guns*, possibly contemplating a *home invasion*, in this, a small city not yet Thinsulated with a $50,000 *hydraulic bollard* or *Lazy Tongs*. On the sofa sit the children without a country—the *zero-parent* kids, to whom I have been trying to explain the meaning of "family values." It is to the *zero-parent* children, for whom we may have to construct a network of orphanages reminiscent of those built in the late nineteenth and early twentieth centuries after flu, TB, and diphtheria epidemics had killed their parents, that the words written by our society and contained in this book are dedicated.

Note: Cross references at the ends of some entries lead you to entries elsewhere in a chapter or in other chapters. To find those entries, turn then to the detailed index beginning on page 411. All entry words (i.e., words that are the subjects of discussion and appear in the text as boldface headwords) are entered in boldface in the index as well.

1

The Times of Our Lives, the Words of Our Lives

affluenza
beyond risk
boomerang baby
brain spa
chien zone
clutter buddy
cocooning
couch people
coyote
crash and burn
curb cut
CWASP
dance with (the) wolves
dink
dis
divorce jewelry
domo
dracontologist
duh
Edge City
elevator surfing
emotional literacy
firp

food insecurity
fruppie
full Cleveland
gerbil tube
gimme cap
granny dumping
halter-top briefs
HIV roulette
hotsy-potatsy
imeldific
intentional community
Lake Wobegon effect
lambada
late decider
mad-dog
mamou
mutual child
NIMBY
non-ism
outlaw party
over-the-counter student
penturbia
populuxe

Saturday school
serious
Shelter-Pak
sippy
skinship
skosh
snide (*noun*)
spillite
squeegee kid
street triage
superfluous father syndrome

swive
tract mansion
vogueing
wallyo
WASP Rot Syndrome
white-bread
wigger
Xer
zero-parent
zoomer

A book is like a quarrel:
One word leads to another,
and may erupt in blood or
print, irrevocably.
—Will and Ariel Durant,
A *Dual Autobiography*

Life needs a good editor.
—Alberto Manguel

In this great big *mamou* of a chapter, one word certainly does lead to another: where else could you begin with *firp*, move into *yog*, study *jantakinzillion*, and end up with the Peace Corps in Paraguay—all in a single discussion? That's English for you; that's life for you.

Though the text has been edited, the times of which these words are signs have not been touched up. In a powerful splash of linguistic *spillite*, the words of chapter 1 illuminate these raw, unedited times—on the streets, in the schools, in the family, even in the *chien zones*. In the spotlight are the CWASPS, the *dinks*, the *domos*, the *fruppies*, the *sippies*, and the *zoomers*, who, in one huge *outlaw party*, *vogue* across the pages, *elevator surfing* to the end of the twentieth century. Along the way, they encounter that segment of the population predisposed to *dis* and *mad-dog* others; they beat a hasty retreat to the safety of the *gerbil tubes* that insulate, insulate, insulate and separate, separate, separate. The attire of choice might be *full Cleveland*, *halter-top briefs*, or a *gimme cap*. Whether they be *wigger* or *wallyo*, the words of our lives—some with a lot of *snide*—fairly erupt into print, sometimes drawing blood.

The majority of the words in chapter 1 just happen to be associated with the tensions derived from the sharp contrastive elements and contradictions in today's society: the widening divide between the haves and have-nots, the unity and disunity of the family, the driven self-absorption of the eighties and the unfocused resentment and angst of the *nones* and *Xers* of the nineties.

Joining *squeegee kid* and *zero-parent* are other terms expressive of the neediness in our world. Here come the *couch people*—the almost homeless who may end up fully homeless, living in *Shelter-Paks* or undergoing *street triage*. Standing in line at the schoolhouse door are the *over-the-counter students* who could become classed as *beyond risk* kids in the age of an at-risk generation in need of courses in *emotional literacy*.

In the family setting, parents of *boomerang babies* suffer from the *crowded-nest syndrome* and abet the *kept-kids phenomenon*, all the while trying to engage in *cocooning*. And the aforementioned *dinks* are fast losing ground to the *reassembled family*. Couples adorned with *divorce jewelry* often produce a *mutual child*. When the going gets rough in at-home eldercare situations, *granny dumping* can and does take place. *Granny dumping* is, yes, disgraceful. It is named by a slang expression whose register is entirely equal to the disgrace it identifies. Equally appalling is the euphemism *food insecurity*: many independent elderly people suffer from it.

While the *affluenti* of the eighties *marcosed* their way into *imeldific tract mansions*, the phenomena of *affluenza* and *non-ism* became apparent in some of their offspring. Many of these children are dubbed the *Xers*—also called with derision *slackers*. *Generation X* (and the conflicting views surrounding it) is discussed at some length at the entry *Xer*.

In terms of the *Xers*, line 73 from Horace's *Ars Poetica* is apropos:

> *Men ever had, and ever will have, leave*
> *To coin new words well suited to the age,*
> *Words are like leaves, some wither ev'ry year,*
> *And ev'ry year a younger race succeeds.*

This "younger race," the *Xers*, have already expressed themselves in a sometimes sleery language (yes, that's *slur* plus *sneer*), with the compound *air family* a signal example. The tension and resentment between the generation called X and the baby boomers is palpable. It is a situation that bears careful watching.

Other expressions coined to suit our age are to be found within the main entries of this chapter. A few worth naming here are: *clutter clinic, recovering clutterer, Frankenstein syndrome, topper-outer, divorce frame, muppy, causeway crowd, bridge and tunnel people, emotional divorce, sleeper effect, positive taillight sign*, and the adjective *yo*. You don't like the sound of them? Wish they had been edited out? Hate the pervasive use of *syndrome*, as in *superfluous father syndrome*? Resent the use of *honkey tube* for *gerbil tube*? Object to *wigger*? Here's my answer, in the words of Derek Walcott, who said it best: "To change your language you must change your life."

affluenza *noun*, **1.** an array of psychological maladies such as isolation, boredom, passivity, and lack of motivation engendered in adults, teenagers, and children by the possession of great wealth and the advantages such wealth affords: "In America . . . there is a widespread disease called *'affluenza'* where [*sic*] people lavish the latest . . . toys on their children as a substitute for talking to them" (Universal News Services Limited, February 13, 1992). "[A] significant number of our most privileged citizens lead lives of chronic anxiety, depression and underemployment. There is even a catchy name, *affluenza*, for the various pathologies that afflict the rich" (*Psychology Today*, April 1989). **2.** new dietary, social, and general-health problems created in developing countries by the introduction of Western habits, food, products, and addictions: "Dr [Margaret] Ashwell [science director of the British Nutrition Foundation] made a special reference to diet in the developing countries and described the disease *'affluenza.'* 'It's the combination of affluence and influenza—the western world sneezing some of its bad things over developing countries,' she said. 'Smoking, cola, fast food and bottle-feeding are taking their toll in these countries'" (*Press Association Newsfile*, October 7, 1989).

THE STORY: *Affluenza* was characterized by one media source as an eighties disease. Far from it. A review of the evidence accrued electronically since November 1986, when this blend first appeared in my "Word Watch" column, revealed forty-seven citations for the word, citations spanning a fourteen-year period, with several in the nineties. Far from going the way of whooping cough and typhoid fever, *affluenza* is, in the words of Ralph Minear, the coauthor of *Kids Who Have Too Much*, a "social epidemic." Private counseling programs are available for those so afflicted. What is more, *affluenza* has acquired a synonym: *rich kids syndrome*.

Citations for *affluenza* go back at least to 1979, with an early example derived from an October 25, 1979, *Washington Post* article in which the writings of Ann Beattie are discussed: "[Another newspaper refers to] the people she writes about, usually disenchanted orphans of *Affluenza*, as The Beattie Generation."

A former director of the C. G. Jung Institute in San Francisco, who, contrary to some suggestions, is not the coiner of *affluenza*, said in an August 25, 1993, interview that the word is a "shorthand term" coined by a senior colleague of his. The Institute's former director had studied the effects of great inherited wealth on youngsters and the ways by which young people can be damaged by receiving too much too soon. (The results of his privately circulated report summating the study drew press attention in 1984.) In the 1993 interview, he pointed out that *affluenza*, often considered offensive and not in use technically, has no synonym in the technical literature.

The second sense of the word, referring to developing countries, is an apt metaphorical extension illustrating how derivative, highly specific secondary meanings of words can evolve. This second sense shows that, on the edge of the twenty-first century, we as Westerners, no matter how well-meaning, are still bearing undesirable "gifts" to cultures ill-prepared to deal with them. See also *WASP Rot Syndrome*.

beyond risk *adjective*, relating to or being a highly troubled youth who may be a chronic truant, a runaway, a drinker, or a drug user, or any of the above, but who has the inner potential to change for the better, given intensive supervision and intervention by trained young caseworkers: "Young Caseworkers Ride Herd on '*Beyond Risk*' Teens: . . . The youths they supervise are enrolled in Choice, a program that focuses intensively on youngsters '*beyond risk*,' . . . but not so hard-core as to be beyond hope. . . . They try to contact each child three to five times a day" (*Washington Post*, March 16, 1994).

THE STORY: Like it or not, the phrase *beyond risk* is adjectival, and so it is labeled to reflect that function. Given the crisis of children in this country, one can be fairly certain that over the passage of time, *beyond risk* will coalesce into a hyphenated form like its predecessor *at-risk*.

Caseworkers are on the job sixty to seventy hours a week imposing upon these youngsters basic supervision, an understanding of expectations and personal accountability, acceptance of and adherence to a curfew, the relinquishment of drugs and alcohol, the avoidance of crime, and good study habits. Over all, the *beyond risk* kids are made to realize that the choices are theirs and theirs alone. See also *zero-parent*.

boomerang baby *noun*, a gainfully employed young person, typically a college graduate, who chooses to return home and live indefinitely with his or her parents, for reasons of greater financial security. Also called *boomerang child; boomeranger; boomerang kid*: "The *real* social commentators of our times, namely cartoonists like Gary Trudeau and comics like Bill Cosby, are already using these young adults as fodder for their humor. And, of course, as they did with 'yuppies,' the 'me generation,' and 'dinks,' the experts have already given the phenomenon a name—*boomerang babies*" (Hatfield, Mass., *Valley Advocate*, August 15, 1988). "If you have a *boomerang child* at home—or if you are one—you're part of the nation's steady adaptation to a lesser standard of living" (Jane Bryant Quinn, *Washington Post*, April 18, 1993).

THE STORY: Here's a term with staying power. It's still a viable item in society's lexicon because of the deteriorating economy. According to the March 1987 *Current Population Reports*, more young adults were then living at home with their parents than at any other time since World War II. A full 52.2 percent of the men and 33 percent of the women aged twenty to twenty-four were, at that time, living in the parental abode or were having their food and shelter parentally underwritten. In their book *Boomerang Kids* (1987), Jean Davies Okimoto and Phyllis Jackson Stegall observed that the cost of living had escalated by 267 percent since 1970, the purchasing power of the dollar had plummeted by almost 300 percent over the same period, and entry-level salaries had failed to keep pace with housing costs; thus *boomerang kids*, many trying to pay off college loans, were strapped for cash. According to Allan Schnailberg, a professor of sociology at Northwestern University, parents who try to do too much for their children have contributed to *boomeranging* too. Kids who have never learned how to confront and solve problems often react to them by retreating—in this case, creating for the parents what is called the *crowded-nest syndrome*.

In order to foreclose on the *boomerangers*, some parents in the nineties are downsizing their homes: they move, for example, from houses to smaller condominium apartments with fewer bedrooms. Other parents actually pay rent for their adult children in order to avoid the *crowded-nest syndrome*. In so doing, they have created the so-called *kept-kids phenomenon*. And *phenomenon* is indeed apt: in her article, Jane Bryant Quinn pointed out that approximately "11 million twentysomethings have yet [in 1993] to give up their childhood rooms." She went on to say that in the nineties, about 34 percent of the *boomerangers* are classed as students. Most of the rest are young single people staying at home until they marry or accrue enough money to buy their own homes. Quinn explained that nowadays young men marry at about age twenty-six; young women, at about age twenty-four; or four years later than the young adults of thirty years ago. Of the twentysomething *boomerangers*, nearly half the singles are still living at home with their parents as opposed to only 3.6 percent of the married ones. This situation redefines for *boomeranged* parents the pop-culture imprecation "Get a life!" Egad, kids, get an apartment! See also *dink, Xer.*

brain spa *noun*, a New Age therapeutic facility in which clients are subjected to soothing and stimulating visual and aural effects, generated electronically, in an effort to induce relaxation, euphoria, and "synchronicity" of the brain, a state that is purported to reduce stress, enhance self-esteem, and improve problem-solving ability: "For the last 14 months Mr. [Randy] Adamadama . . . has presided here at the Universe of You, Marin County's first *brain spa*" (*New York Times*, October 27, 1988).

THE STORY: *Brain spa* clients, many of whom interrupt their workdays for treatments, recline on lounges and listen through earphones to a mix of New Wave music and sounds from nature while wearing goggles that flash kaleidoscopic patterns before their eyes. This equipment, known as the Synchro-Energizer, was invented by Denis E. Gorges. It coordinates light and sound to create a "harmonic" in much the same way a conductor leads an orchestra.

Though Gorges admitted that he isn't sure exactly how the Synchro-Energizer works, the concept of the *brain spa* seems to be gaining in popularity: twenty *brain spas* that use Synchro-Energizers have opened in the United States, as have facilities in Japan, Spain, and Germany. Adamadama "hopes such *brain spas* will become a sort of McMeditation, doing for brain function what fast-food franchising did for hamburgers. 'You park your car, you run in, you get your anxiety released,' he said of his operation. 'Every shopping center should have one'" (Springfield, Mass., *Union-News*, 1988).

chien zone *noun*, an area in a city in which dogs may be walked and in which they may relieve themselves: "Pressed to action at last by an outraged citizenry—at least, those who aren't dog owners—officials announced a fine of $100 per offense and the creation of a 40-man dog doo police. Critics quickly attacked, . . . while one city council member suggested that what Paris needs are 'chien zones'" (Washington Post, August 2, 1992).

THE STORY: Deep doo-doo may be defined as the twenty tons of the stuff that have been known to repose on the streets of Paris at any one time—an olfactory, if not a public-health, problem, particularly in summer. (Rome has its cats; Paris, its dogs—dogs have resided there since medieval times, when they were relied upon to keep the wolves away from the inhabitants' doors.)

Chien zones would contain dog pollution, as the problem is called. Some cities have them, and they're modeled after the pet rest areas sometimes to be found as adjuncts to interstate highway rest stops here in the United States. In the meantime, the wise thing to do is to purchase a big package of cani-wipes and a pooper-scooper, and admit the obvious: it's a dog's life out there.

clutter buddy *noun*, one who supports another person in sorting and discarding accumulated personal possessions: "An opera singer . . . returned to her Manhattan apartment, vowing to 'de-clutter.' She telephoned her *clutter-support buddy* a week later to say that, for the first time in some years, she had glimpsed the top of her coffee table. . . . The bookcase, buried under sheet music . . . came into view the next week. Again, she phoned her *clutter buddy* to report progress" (*Chicago Tribune*, May 10, 1992).

THE STORY: The anticlutter movement of the nineties—thought by some to be a reaction to the acquisitiveness of the eighties—is manifest in *clutter clinics* held at some universities, adult education classes in *clutter management* (which have produced some 200,000 *clutter graduates*), *clutter hot lines*, and *de-clutter guidebooks*. At the top of the list of the five most popular courses offered by First Class, a Washington, D.C., adult education center, is—you guessed it—"Conquering Clutter" (*Washington Post Magazine*, "Hit List," Sunday, October 10, 1993).

What does all this really say? According to some experts, it says obsession. (Consider those who squirrel away wire tie-twists, old rubber bands, and empty margarine and ice-cream tubs.) It also says emotional attachment. (Consider the closets across the country that are stuffed with old prom and bridesmaid dresses.) It says umbilical attachment to the past. (Consider the box full of keys to houses one hasn't lived in for twenty years or longer.) It says anxiety about the future. (Consider the often-heard statement, "If there's a war or another depression, we might need that manual typewriter or that moth-eaten fur coat.") Most chronic clutterers tend to be people on the go, not couch potatoes.

Recovering clutterers advise others to start their own recoveries small: in trying to kick the habit, clean a small area—even if it is only twelve inches square—keep that area clean, and only then go on to another spot. They also advocate giving oneself frequent—and disposable—rewards along the way. After all, Rome wasn't dismantled in a day.

cocooning *noun*, retreating into the privacy of one's home during leisure time instead of traveling on vacations, dining out, attending the theater, or shopping in person, used as a means of insulating oneself from what is perceived as a harsh, unpredictable outside world. This socioeconomic trend is believed to represent an attempt by many people to gain more control over their lives: "At the moment, there's a trend . . . toward control. A part of that trend has a name: 'cocooning.' It's very complex, but basically it involves building a shell of safety around yourself, so you're not at the mercy of the unpredictable world" (Faith Popcorn, *The New Yorker*, July 7, 1986). "The harassments of daily life . . . have driven people to *cocooning*. They have gone to ground in their dens . . . to keep at bay the modern world, the discontinuities of which have produced a longing for tradition" (George F. Will, *Washington Post*, June 11, 1987).

THE STORY: In early 1986, Faith Popcorn, founder of BrainReserve, a Manhattan trend-analysis firm, identified as *cocooning* this phenomenon, the characteristics of which include soaring sales of VCRs and CD players, increased popularity of BarcaLoungers fitted with stereo headphones, an upsurge in home deliveries of take-out food, increased shopping by catalog, a lack of interest in domestic and international travel, and a fascination with time management. The word and the trend are still in play in the nineties.

Cocooning in the sense identified by Popcorn is formed from either the verb or the noun *cocoon* used figuratively. Such figurative use of the verb was found in the September 8, 1982, issue of the *Christian Science Monitor*: "Cocooning you in your own little music world, they [Walkman radios] leave you free to walk, run, cycle, or drive at will." This citation, antedating the trend spotted and named four years later by Popcorn, is an example of how the English language resonates in response to the changing behavioral patterns and interests of its speakers. Since the eighties, derivative forms of *cocooning* have been spawned: for example, *cocooner* appeared in a March 17, 1991, headline in *Publishers Weekly. Cocoony* and *cocoon-friendly* also exist.

couch people *plural noun*, homeless families who, because of a shortage in low-income housing, drift from place to place, living temporarily with friends or relatives, and often sleeping on their hosts' couches or floors: "According to some estimates, 100,000 families in New York City are *couch people*" (*New York Times*, June 20, 1987).

THE STORY: In what might be called "Notes from the Underground of the Eighties and into the Nineties," *couch people*, a compound formed in the manner of *boat people*, has emerged to denote what *Times* reporter Suzanne Daley called "the hidden homeless." These are the people who have not yet resorted to the shelter system but who are likely to end up there, said Daley. She pointed out in her story that the term *couch people* was being used regularly as a descriptor by advocates for New York City's homeless.

Days in the lives of the *couch people*, up to 200,000 of whom are children, are stressful and frightening: They may live anywhere from a day to several years on the couches or floors of anyone willing to give them shelter. Many of them lose their possessions to thieves or they relinquish them to their hosts in payment for shelter. *Couch people* live in constant fear—fear of their surroundings and fear of the welfare hotels. See also *over-the-counter student*.

coyote *noun*, a roving firefighter who is dispatched, often for days at a time, to remote, usually serious, forest fires in order to bring them under control: "Like the scraggly creature that lives a bare subsistence in the wild, *coyote* crews are left in the fire zone to sleep when they can and continue to fight the fire" (*Boston Globe*, August 20, 1986). "They also decided to establish 'spike camps' close to the fire lines and dispatch . . . *coyotes*, who hike 2 or 3 miles to remote areas of the blaze, dig out lines all day with hand tools and then camp where they can" (United Press International, August 26, 1986). —*verb*, to dispatch (firefighters) to battle remote blazes: "'You can't *coyote* people too many shifts,' said Leland Singer, a fire information officer. 'It's exhausting and stressful. You have to bring them out and feed them good meals'" (*Boston Globe*, August 20, 1986).

THE STORY: This relatively new meaning of the noun *coyote* and the emergence of a verb appeared in general sources in 1986–87, when forest fires were raging in parts of the United States.

In yet another noun usage, *coyote* has come to mean a person who escorts illegal aliens across the border from Mexico into the United States, usually for a high fee, often robbing or even attacking them in the process. In this usage, *coyote* exhibits transference of meaning from that which is animal to that which is human, adding to it decidedly negative connotations and denotations. Other examples are *wildcat(ter)* (a speculative oil driller or miner, or a striker), *mule* (an illegal narcotics courier), *mole* (a double-agent-in-place within a government), and *chicken hawk* (a pederast).

The verb *coyote* joins a veritable zoo of other such verbs formed from pre-existing nouns, of which these are but a few examples: *cat, buffalo, bug, bull, dog, fish, fox, goose, horse, mouse, rat, snake, squirrel, turtle* (a verb familiar to all rag sailors), and *wolf. Mongoose* and *tsetse fly*, however, show no signs of making the list. See also *eeling* at *black-water rafting* and the verb *kangaroo* at *kangaroo care*.

crash and burn *idiom,* **1.** to fail utterly, as in politics, sports, or personal relationships, usually in a highly public manner: "When [Senator Gary] Hart *crashed and burned*, most of his people caught on somewhere else in a matter of weeks" (*Washington Post*, November 11, 1987). "O'Grady . . . proved his guts . . . when he *crashed and burned* 17 times before finally qualifying for the [golf] Tour four years ago" (*Sports Illustrated*, January 19, 1987). **2.** to fall asleep from utter exhaustion: "'When I come home,' [executive Nancy Spears-Wade] said, 'all I want to do is *crash and burn* on the couch at 7 P.M.'" (Springfield, Mass., *Union-News*, December 1, 1987).

THE STORY: Idioms are notoriously difficult to trace, and this one, the history of which is still unresolved, puts etymologists, or word historians, into a tailspin. *Crash and burn* reflects the combined influences over time of aviators' lingo, the counterculture of the sixties, and the language of sports, including that of skateboarders and dirt bikers, the latter of whom published a magazine called *Crash and Burn*. A study of ten years' worth of citations revealed numerous occurrences of this idiom in the contexts of air and auto accidents. An early metaphorical use in the general press appeared in a May 22, 1978, *Washington Post* story: "The Sonics were on a tear, the arena exploding with noise, and the Bullets were no longer speeding. They were *crashing and burning*." (Still other evidence indicates that college students used the idiom to mean utter academic failure.) The second sense, referring to sleep, exhibits traces of the slang sense of *crash*, prevalent in the sixties, "to find lodging or shelter, as in a crash pad; to go to sleep." But all these strands are relatively recent.

After *crash and burn* was discussed in my May 1988 "Word Watch" column, a fully loaded mail train pulled in. One letter out of a multitude came from a former member of the U.S. Army Air Force during World War II. In it the writer provided details of his own torments aboard a B-24 Liberator, perhaps best described by novelist Ernest Gann as "a collection of spare parts flying in loose formation, with an evil nature all its own." My correspondent said that of the many ditties sung about missions aboard this aircraft, the following one, to be sung to the tune of "Bless 'Em All," but with substitution of "the eff word," contains what may be the genesis of *crash and burn* in its unitary meaning of today.

> *If ever I'm up in a Bee Twenty Four*
> *And don't know which way to turn,*
> *As I grab my bag and head for the door,*
> *I'll punch the button marked Spin,* Crash and Burn.

This theory, by the way, is supported by Robert L. Chapman, whose *New Dictionary of American Slang* labels the idiom "*Army.*"

The phrase was still being used in the early fifties in naval flight training as the final two words of the complete sequence "stall, spin, *crash* and *burn*," according to a letter from Robert Heinecken, a pilot so trained. In his letter he pointed out that the "'stall' and 'spin' maneuvers [were] practiced regularly as part of one's training but the '*crash and burn*' parts were to be avoided. Perhaps this explains why those two words remain in the language [as a unit] and continue to carry the figurative meaning of a *visible* failure." Heinecken went on to say that "these four words *stall, spin, crash* and *burn* were part of a drinking song sung to the tune of 'John Brown's etc.' and were shouted in staccato fashion for emphasis. . . . Because the 'stall' and 'spin' problems are associated mostly with propeller-driven aircraft . . . I suspect the full four-word term . . . originated during World War II."

If *crash and burn* really does go back to the Second World War (if not to the First, when planes were beginning to be used in combat), it certainly continued in use during the Vietnam War. Another letter, this one from Roger A. Brooks, informed me that he had encountered it in 1971 during twenty-six grueling weeks of Army Infantry Officer Candidate School at Fort Benning, Georgia. Brooks's tactical officer was a Cobra gunship pilot with 164 Vietnam combat missions under his belt. This tac officer used *crash and burn* in the literal sense with respect to choppers that had gone down in the jungles around An-loc and Hué, but he "also applied the term to . . . what he thought would happen to many of us as we attempted to survive the . . . curriculum of the Infantry OCS program." When an officer candidate failed to make it through any of the curriculum "panels," or particularly the dreaded, most difficult, twenty-fourth week of the course, "it was said of him that he '*crashed and burned.*'"

curb cut *noun*, a pavement slope leading from a sidewalk to a street that permits people in wheelchairs, and others, such as Rollerbladers and cyclists, to move easily from sidewalk to street and back without having to negotiate a curb: "Throughout history, people with physical disabilities have been isolated. . . . In America, thousands are fighting to gain access. For example, for the blind, it's a question of braille in elevators. For those in wheelchairs, it's ramps or *curb cuts*" (*Parade*, January 12, 1986).

THE STORY: This citation named a structural pavement feature that we were familiar with but had no technical term for. It alerted the editors of *The American Heritage Dictionary of the English Language, Third Edition* that inclusion of the term was called for. *Curb cut* gained entry in the edition, published in 1992. Things have not been as easy for disabled people themselves, however. Recall the difficulty of a disabled passenger at Dulles International Airport in the early nineties: he had to crawl without assistance up the stairs of an aircraft. The battle for better access is clearly not won—the unkindest cut of all.

CWASP *noun*, an affluent Irish Catholic professional person, such as a physician or an attorney, who appreciates his or her position in society and the rise to it but who is not overly concerned with ethnicity: "*CWASPs* are defined by their business or professional status. . . . But they have an added aura. They may lapse into 'Danny Boy' at private get-togethers on March 17, but they don't venerate that sort of gunk. Basically, they'd rather be sailing" (*Boston Business*, Summer 1986).

THE STORY: *CWASP* was coined in 1986 by Maureen Dezell of *Boston Business* magazine. In its first appearance in "Word Watch," I labeled it an acronym, and that's what it was back then: its letters stand for Catholic White Anglo-Saxon Protestant—a puckishly oxymoronic creation, to say the least. Since then, various pronunciations have been advanced for the word, some being [see-wasp], [kwasp], and [qua WASP], where the *qua* means "in the character or capacity." Having a unitary pronunciation and having displayed plural use, the word is certainly moving into the noun zone; hence the label here. It shows no signs of going the way of *radar*, *snafu*, and *scuba*—acronyms that took on lowercase style on their way to noundom. Let's face it: because of its spelling, a lowercased *cwasp* would look just like a typo formed by an operator hitting the *c* key when keying in that other, well-established word *wasp*. CWASP has already generated *CWASPdom*, yet another sign of staying power.

CWASP is interesting for other reasons. For one thing, it's a Boston coinage. For another, it is "not a term of deracination," in the words of Gregg Singer of the Center for English Language and Orientation at Boston University. In a letter to the editor of *Boston Business*, published in the Winter 1986 issue of the magazine, Singer differentiated *CWASP* from terms like *Afro-Saxon* and made the point that *CWASP* was instead a term of "reracination." Said Singer, "That is, a CWASP is not a CWASP because he or she is less a Catholic but rather by virtue of being more like a Protestant." See also *WASP Rot Syndrome*.

dance with (the) wolves *idiom*, to repudiate self-centered, greed-directed values as part of a spiritual, moral, and ethical rebirth: "He's the man who discards his corrupt white man's values and takes on those of a primitive but more soulful culture in closer harmony with the Earth. He's the man who *dances with wolves*, the natural man, the new Green hero of the '90s. . . . His values are repudiated, assassinated. When he recovers, he is a man of the '90s. Metaphorically, he learns to *dance with the wolves*" (*Washington Post*, November 3, 1991).

THE STORY: It's not unusual for English to take book titles and accord them figurative meanings with or without change in the written form. *Jekyll and Hyde*, after Robert Louis Stevenson's *Strange Case of Dr. Jekyll and Mr. Hyde*, is an example of the first kind; Mary Wollstonecraft Shelley's *Frankenstein* and Joseph Heller's *Catch-22* are just two among many of the second kind. Similarly, movie titles have moved into the general parlance with meanings of their own. Important instances of this pop cultural cross-pollination are *Rambo*, *Star Wars*, *Fatal Attraction*, *Top Gun*, and *Home Alone* (as in *home-alone* kid). And psychothriller author Jonathan Kellerman has a character in one of his novels call another character a "Phantom of the Opera."

It is less usual for a movie title to form the root of an idiomatic phrase, as is the case with the Kevin Costner movie *Dances With Wolves*. Here we see our very first example of what may become an important idiom of the nineties: it appeared in a *Washington Post* article by Hal Hinson entitled "Hollywood's New Hero—Stars Warm to the '90s: No More Mr. Ice Guys."

Whether the locution *dance with (the) wolves* becomes part of the idiomatic fabric of English depends upon the degree of wide, sustained use it achieves over time. Should a noun like *wolf-dancer* evolve in the manner of *arm-twister*, *backslapper*, and *hairsplitter* from the preexisting idioms *twist* (someone's) *arm*, *slap* (someone's) *back*, and *split hairs*, that will be one sign of possible staying power. But in the end, it will be the users of the language, responding to societal change (if there is any), who will determine the longevity of *dance with (the) wolves*. See also *wolf ticket*.

dink or **DINK** *noun*, a childless, two-career couple: "Just because they're *dinks* doesn't mean they're better educated or better placed in the work force. . . . A *dink* couple can consist of a blue-collar husband and a wife employed in a secretarial position. But, between them, they make substantially more than the average family income" (*Los Angeles Times*, February 8, 1987).

THE STORY: *Dink*, which began its linguistic career in 1982, gained widespread currency during the last few months of 1986: it was formed from Double Income, No Kids. It may originally have been spelled *DINC*, where the C represented Children. Since that time, *dink* has become a full-fledged noun. Its coiner is unknown; however, some evidence indicates people in advertising and demographics may be responsible. It is, of course, unrelated to *dinky*, just as it is unrelated to other preexisting *dinks*—one of which is a two-page insert in a full-size newspaper, and others of which are vulgar or offensive words.

Dinks in the socioeconomic sense have certain distinguishing characteristics: the women usually retain their maiden names, the couples are very career-oriented, one spouse—typically the husband—cooks the meals, and they usually own property in upscale locales. Tom O'Sullivan, an advertising executive who is quoted in the *Los Angeles Times* citation, adds that "*dink* is just a great word. . . . It's like a good dirty joke. It makes it from coast to coast in seconds."

Dink, however, may go into eclipse now that we are in the uncertain nineties. A citation from the March 11, 1992, issue of the *Houston Chronicle* forbodes the demise of the *dinks*: "Amy Barr, director of the Good Housekeeping Institute, said the home and the American family defined as *Dinks* households . . . are rapidly being redefined as *Ikts* (infants, kids, teens)." All this relates closely to the *boomerang baby* phenomenon and the lifestyle of the *Xers*.

The abode of the nineties is now being called the hearth of the *reassem-*

bled family, which may include parents, grandparents, *mutual children*, children of previous marriages, grandchildren being raised by the grandparents, and *boomerang children*. By its very constituency, the family of the nineties closely resembles that of the nineteenth century, defined as follows in *An American Dictionary of the English Language*, by Noah Webster, revised and enlarged by Chauncey A. Goodrich, 1855: "the collective body of persons who live in one house, and under one head or manager; a household, including parents, children, and servants, and, as the case may be, lodgers or boarders." All of which proves the adage: What goes around, comes around. See also *domo, fruppie, NIMBY, sippy, zero-parent*.

dis *verb, slang*, to exhibit disrespect toward: "The victim, according to detectives, made the mistake of irritating Nuke at a party. 'He *dissed* him,' Sergeant Croissant said, using the street term for acting disrespectfully" (*New York Times*, November 15, 1987). "Queen Elizabeth II returned to London yesterday after a week of being *dissed* during a visit to Cyprus. . . . Jeering nationalists almost drowned out a ceremony. . . . Demonstrators called her 'Killer Queen.' . . . (*Washington Post*, October 25, 1993).

THE STORY: *Dis* is closely associated with the so-called MTV Generation, rap, youth culture, and, of course, the 'hoods. Certainly a lot has happened to the verb *disrespect* because of these forces since the time of its first attested appearance in 1614, seventeen years before emergence of the noun.

One might reasonably assume that *dis*, a clipped form of this verb, would never gain entry into a reputable dictionary. But consider first what has happened in the case of the similarly formed *sus* or *suss*, a British slang word that has crossed the Atlantic and has worked its way into the *Supplement* to the *Oxford English Dictionary* and into *12,000 Words*, a supplement to *Webster's Third New International Dictionary*. The noun *sus*, abbreviated from *suspicion/suspicious* or from *suspect/suspected*, with the derivation depending on contextual use, goes back to the mid-1930s. It can mean "suspicion of criminal behavior" or "a criminal suspect." It has sustained wide attributive use by the British in locutions such as *sus law, sus case*, and *sus charge*. The verb, now most often spelled *suss* and going back only as far as the mid-1950s, can mean "to suspect (someone) of a crime," "to feel that an event is likely to occur; surmise," or, in combination with *out*, "to size up" and "to discover the truth about; figure out."

Citations for the noun and verb are to be found in *Vanity Fair*, the *Los Angeles Times*, *People*, *The Economist*, and the *Manchester Guardian Weekly*, with this one from the October 10, 1987, issue of the *Financial Times* typical: "When we were 'jung and easily freudened,' we had the inveterate gambler *sussed* out: he was a self-punishing neurotic who played in order to lose." Another indicator of the staying power of *suss* is the existence of the adjective *sussy*, "suspicious."

Dis is similar in its formation to the unexceptionable *sub* from *substitute*. *Suss* is similar to *igg*, taken from *ignore* by African-American jazz musicians in the urban North of the 1930s. See also *mad-dog*.

divorce jewelry *noun*, wedding jewelry from a failed marriage that is melted down by the owner and then reworked into new pieces: "The Orange, Calif., jeweler dispenses goggles and blowtorches so clients can rid themselves of bittersweet memories by melting their jewels. 'Some people get an emotional release by destroying a symbol of misery,' [the jeweler Ken Olson] says. The melted wedding rings or anniversary pins are remade into *divorce jewelry*" (*USA Weekend*, July 8, 1990).

THE STORY: Olson is the coiner of this new term—fashioned in the manner of *estate jewelry*—according to an article in the July 26, 1989, edition of the *Chicago Tribune:* " 'It was a joke at first,' Ken Olson said. " 'Just in conversation. I recall a gal bringing in a bunch of stuff to me the first week we were open. She was getting a divorce, so (I said), We'll make a *divorce ring* for you. It was no pre-planned strategy.' "

Preplanned or not, the idea hit a niche market: at least eight other jewelers in Orange County began to offer the same service, though some don't allow their customers to take the jeweler's torch in hand themselves for reasons of safety. Some *divorce jewelry* is an amalgam of multiple failed marriages. Clients seem to be motivated toward meltdown for economic as well as psychological reasons. A related term is *divorce frame*, a narrow picture frame in which to display one's own image in wedding finery sans the image of the ex. See also *Divorceware*.

domo *noun*, a professional person, typically aged thirty to thirty-nine, who markedly downscales his or her career in order to perform more meaningful work and experience a higher quality of life than can be sustained within the stressful, regimented structure of the corporate workplace: "Downward mobility among fast-track careerists might be to the '90s what the lust for material wealth was to the '80s, despite the failing economy. Former 'yuppies are now '*domos*' . . . as we enter 'The Flee Decade'" (Hatfield, Mass., *Valley Advocate*, September 24, 1990).

THE STORY: If *dink*, *NIMBY*, and *zoomer* were symptomatic of the ethos of the eighties, the noun *domo*, originally an acronym formed of *d*ownwardly *m*obile *p*rofessional, may be a key word of the nineties. The *domo* trend, presaged perhaps by the *cocooning* observed in the mid-1980s, is being seen among thirtysomethings with well-paid partners and considerable savings of their own. A few years ago, the press reported on superwomen who *stressed out*, *topped out*, and then *dropped out*, rather than contending with the double bind of a demanding career and equally demanding family responsibilities. What makes the *domos* different from the *topper-outers* is that men have joined the exodus. See also *fruppie*, *dink*, *NIMBY*, *sippy*.

dracontologist *noun*, one who studies the possibility of the existence of giant lake-dwelling creatures, such as huge serpents: "The sighting reports collected by the *dracontologists* are fairly consistent: when more than a hump was visible above the water, witnesses described a long, thick neck, a large head like a snake's or a horse's, and a steady movement through the water as if the creature had a motor, or fins or flippers underwater" (*Boston Globe*, October 12, 1986).

THE STORY: *Dracontologist* is derived from *dracontology*, a word coined by a friar at the Benedictine abbey St.-Benoit du lac on the shores of Lake Memphremagog. In this international lake, which straddles the border between Vermont and Quebec, alleged sightings of a creature similar to the fake Loch Ness monster have occurred. According to Jacques Boisvert, president of the International Society of *Dracontology*, the word *dracontology* is formed from the Greek word *drākon*, "large serpent." On December 3, 1984, the Office de la langue française du Gouvernement du Québec accepted this neologism as a legitimate word, spelled *dracontologie* in French.

A similar neologism, one that some folks in Dallas, Texas, are concerned with, is *cockroachologist*. This ologist collects the bugs, trying especially to garner large specimens: "Mr. [Michael] Bohdan and Mr. [Ron] Shapp are challenging local residents to produce the largest cockroach in Dallas. 'The response has been mind-boggling,' said Mr. Bohdan, who calls himself a *cockroachologist*. 'Everyone in Dallas is thinking cockroach'" (*New York Times*, June 30, 1986).

duh *interjection*, used to express great indecision, hesitation, contempt, or displeasure: "There they find—*duh*—a pudgy redneck sheriff, ornery cowboys just itching for a fight, the works" (*Washington Post*, December 12, 1980). "I had Donna Mills on 'The Tonight Show' . . . and she says, 'I was just voted one of the 10 sexiest women in America, and I don't know what that means.' Doesn't know what it means? I said to her, 'Take a guess. What do you think it means. *Duh* . . .' Give me a break" (Jay Leno, *New York Times*, November 22, 1987).

THE STORY: *Duh*, pronounced in a loud, drawn out, throaty tone, is often heard but rarely seen in print except in dialogue. It is certainly a more colorful interjection than, say, *uh*, *ah*, *hum*, *humph*, *hmm*, *mm*, or *eh*. *Duh*, like its kissing cousins *awww* (of comic-strip character "Goofy" fame), *hee-yuck* (I. Troll), and *dyuh* (Mortimer Snerd), has been on the scene for over fifty years. It was an essential element in the voice-overs for animated characters in the classic film cartoons. It moved in and out of popularity among American youths over the years; for example, it was popular among high school students during the sixties, and then came back in the eighties, as evidenced by the two citations shown here. During the eighties, *duh* also became a noun meaning "dud" or "dumb cluck," as in "He's a real *duh*."

But there is another story behind this story, and though embarrassing, it begs to be told at long last. In 1988 when working on *duh* for "Word Watch," I was excited over the possibility that it was moving into compound adjectival use (citations had turned up showing it as a predicate adjective). A key piece of new citational evidence was electronically generated from the text of a leading American business magazine. The citation rhapsodized about the wonderful "*duh*-free shopping" tourists could avail themselves of while in Rhodes. Terrific, thought I. I mean, like, you're on a cruise in the Aegean, right? You've got to buy your mother-in-law a gift, correct? When in port, you're in a hurry. You go into shop after shop overflowing with varied wares, and you go, "*Duh*. Whaddya think I'm gonna get her that she'll be crazy about? *Duh*." Ignoring the sprachgefühl bell screaming in my head, I decided that the form *duh-free* was linguistically unexceptionable and used the form in the manuscript for the column. Cullen Murphy, the careful editor at *The Atlantic Monthly*, did not share my view, however. He and I decided to obtain the in-print copy of the magazine story, and, much to our mutual horror, discovered that *duh-free* was a phantom word, a typo found solely in the computer database. The form seen on the hard copy was, of course, *duty-free*.

Edge City *noun*, an urban jurisdiction not officially structured or recognized as a city per se but having a large population, diverse ethnic elements, cultural and intellectual attractions, and highly developed business, shopping, and walking environments as well as residences: "Almost 100 more *Edge Cities* are about to hit critical mass. Only 12 percent of all Americans live in the old big cities the size of El Paso or larger" (*Washington Post*, September 29, 1991).

THE STORY: *Edge City* is the coinage of Joel Garreau, a senior writer at the *Washington Post*, and the author of *Edge City: Life on the New Frontier*. Garreau has identified what he calls "the new American urban place," typified by areas like Montgomery County, Maryland, and Fairfax County, Virginia, which abut Washington, D.C.; the Route 128 High Technology Highway area near Boston; and the O'Hare International Airport area near Chicago.

According to the coiner, almost 125 *Edge Cities* exist in the United States, "each of . . . them bigger than Memphis by any functional urban standards: tall buildings, bright lights, corporate headquarters, luxury hotels, fancy shops, even population. They far outnumber the 35 or so old urban cores of comparable size."

Whether or not *Edge City* becomes a fixture in the language depends largely on the future of these areas twenty years hence. After all, the coiner says, "*Edge City* . . . is the creation of a new world, being shaped by the free in a constantly reinvented land." See also *penturbia*.

elevator surfing *noun*, *slang*, climbing on top of an elevator cab and riding up and down, sometimes jumping from that cab to a passing cab. Also called *Action*; *elevator action*; *piloting an elevator*: "A college freshman fell to his death in a sport called '*elevator surfing*,' a little-known but dangerous practice that plagues high-rise buildings" (*Chicago Tribune*, March 16, 1990).

THE STORY: The term *elevator surfing* is formed in a manner similar to six other *surfing* compounds: *bodysurfing* (riding waves to shore without a board), *windsurfing* (sailboarding), *sky surfing* (hang gliding), *shoulder surfing* (stealing access codes by peering over the shoulder of the user), *car surfing* (riding on the roof of a moving car), and *channel surfing* (flipping TV channels).

Elevator surfing, a fad on some college campuses, came to national attention in 1990 when a University of Massachusetts *elevator surfer* was killed doing it. Although most citations for the term are dated 1990, this deadly game has been a problem for years in high-rise dorms, according to officials quoted in the *Los Angeles Times* of March 18, 1990. Participants either push the emergency "stop" button between floors and pry the doors open to climb on top of a cab or they climb through the ceiling emergency hatch.

Other fads on campuses are *stair diving*, in which stairwells are greased with a slippery substance, enabling students to dive or slide down them; *bar golf*, in which students make the rounds of various drinking establishments, apartments, or fraternity houses (also called *holes* because there are typically nine of them), all the while drinking enough at each *hole* to make *par*; *power keg*, a contest in which the imbibers are required to drink constantly because the beer-keg tap remains open until the keg's entire contents have been consumed; and *cow tipping*, a game popular on some rural campuses in which groups of students locate cows that are sleeping upright and then push the unsuspecting bovines over, at the same time attempting to evade the inevitable manure. See also *shoulder surfing, trawler.*

emotional literacy *noun*, the knowledge needed by young people to understand the nature of stress and violence and to control their emotions, especially in the nonviolent resolution of disputes: "With teen-age suicides, homicides, and pregnancies increasing, some educators have begun to give courses in 'emotional literacy'" (*International Herald Tribune*, March 7, 1992).

THE STORY: First there was *computer literacy*. Then came *Cultural Literacy*, the title and central thesis of a 1987 book by E. D. Hirsch, Jr., a professor of English at the University of Virginia, with *Cultural Literacy* denoting knowledge of the common stock of people, places, sayings, happenings, and ideas essential for literate communication. Next came still more *literacy* compounds such as *geographic literacy*, a phenomenon remarked upon by Usage Panel Chair Geoffrey Nunberg in a usage note in *The American Heritage Dictionary of the English Language, Third Edition*: "Recently, the meanings of the words *literacy* and *illiteracy* have been extended from their original connection with reading and literature to any body of knowledge."

Such is indeed the case with *emotional literacy*—a term whose very existence is a sad commentary on our times and our failures in the family and society. Courses on this subject, which can be tailored to the needs of kindergarteners through high schoolers, teach life-coping skills that ought to be taught in the home but usually are not. Students are encouraged to reveal and come to terms with the everyday violence and stress they personally experience, by means of role-playing, art therapy, oral discussion, and essays.

According to Nancy Goldstein, a community coordinator for a Washington, D.C., nonprofit organization that gives workshops on violence prevention, "Some violence is such a normal part of [fourth-graders'] lives that telling them there is an alternate way . . . just doesn't fit into their lifestyles" (*Washington Post*, March 25, 1992). See also *emotional divorce* at *mutual child*.

firp *noun*, *slang*, a person regarded with contempt or great derision; a jerk: "A white VW Golf with the top down had pulled up next to me. The blonde from the beach was behind the wheel. . . . 'You really the landlord? . . .' 'Sorry,' I said. '. . . I'm not in the real-estate business.' The blonde's face managed to turn ugly while retaining its beauty. 'What a *firp*! Told you, Mar [her companion], it was total bullshit!'" (Jonathan Kellerman, *Private Eyes*, 1992).

THE STORY: What a word and what a story. I first encountered *firp*, which has the same kind of burpy attraction as the verb *Bork*, while reading the novel by Kellerman, the California-based child psychologist and the creator of the Alex Delaware thrillers. At that time, I thought *firp*, like *buff* ("cool; terrific; handsome; well-built"), might be an example of California Valley Girl Speak. E-mail consultations with linguists, extensive database searches, forages through slang and other dictionaries, even requests for information from listeners during a National Public Radio (NPR) interview, yielded no other evidence of the use of *firp* in the English language.

The situation was even more interesting because Dr. Kellerman had used in *Private Eyes* still another mysterious word, *yog* ("a thug; a hit man"): "He actually paid out plenty to the *yog* who did the dirty work." I speculated dangerously that *yog*, for which no other evidence existed, might have been *goy* spelled backward or that it might have been a typo for *yob* (British slang for a skinhead or a hooligan formed by spelling *boy* backward). In desperation, I was driven to get in touch with Dr. Kellerman. The payback was stunning. In a letter to me dated February 16, 1993, the author said, "You couldn't find the words in question because I made them up. (That's the fun of fiction!)"

A similar instance involved the slang word *jantakinzillion*, "an indeterminately enormous number or quantity," formed in the manner of *zillion*, *gigantazillion*, and *bazillion*: "The creases [between the tiles on the floor of the Roanoke, Virginia, Regional Airport] are wicked on the little round tips on the heels of high-heeled shoes. Women are losing them by the *jantakinzillion*," wrote *Roanoke Times & World-News* columnist Ed Shamy on April 10, 1991. After a great deal of research and similar academic speculation with experts,

I asked Shamy about the word. He, like Kellerman, turned out to be the coiner. He created the word in April of 1991, but its antecedents are more complex. Shamy, who had served with the Peace Corps in Paraguay from 1980 to 1983, respelled the Guarani word *heta*, "many," into *janta*. (Guarani is the language of a group of South American Indians of Paraguay, Bolivia, and southern Brazil.) In the respelling process, Shamy substituted a *j* for the *h* and then added the *n* to the meaningless infix *-ki-* to make his new coinage more easily pronounced.

food insecurity *noun*, a condition of malnutrition and hunger, or the fear of it, seen in some members of the U.S. elderly population who are unable, at all times, to obtain the food essential to a balanced diet through nonemergency channels: "[A new Urban Institute] study determined that 2.5 million to 4.9 million elderly Americans suffered from *food insecurity*, about 40 percent of them with incomes above the poverty line. . . . The study reported higher levels of *food insecurity* among elderly renters, who had to pay for housing, than among homeowners, many of whom had paid off their mortgages" (*Washington Post*, November 17, 1993).

THE STORY: *Food insecurity*, formed on the structural pattern of the rather direct compound *job insecurity* and its antonym *job security*, is an example of superficially harmless, yet, in point of fact, pernicious euphemism. Euphemism the word comes from the Greek *euphēmismos*, "speaking well (of)." Euphemism the process has generated an entire sublanguage of English— one called by journalist Hugh Rawson, the compiler of *A Dictionary of Euphemisms and Other Doubletalk* (1981), "society's basic *lingua non franca* . . . [the] outward and visible signs of our inward anxieties, conflicts, fears, and shames."

More specifically, *food insecurity* is a consciously negative euphemism. It is negative because it diminishes the force of its tabooed synonyms, *hunger* and *malnutrition*. In so doing, it echoes society's ancient unease with things deemed shameful, loathsome, obscene, fearsome, or supernatural. (For instance, some peoples of the world avoided naming the bear; instead, they preferred to call it by such circularities as *glory of the forest*, *proud honey-foot*, *the eater of honey*, *the old one*, *the hairy one*, *the noise maker*, *the licker*, *the brown*, or *grandfather*.)

Food insecurity is also a conscious euphemism in that its use seems intentional in this, an era of depersonalization. By its very structure, the term focuses the reader's attention not on the life-threatening aspects of the condition and the role played by individuals and society in creating the condition, but on economic and bureaucratic factors. Conscious euphemisms, like *nose spasm* for *sneeze*, *hernia* for *rupture*, *sleep with* for *fuck*, *case* and *patient* for *corpse* (in the parlance of *funeral directors* but not *undertakers*), *Final Solution* and *ethnic cleansing* for *genocide* and *mass murder*, and *rearrangements* and *events* for *nuclear accidents*—all of them indicating denial big-time—form a codex of linguistic duplicity.

At the very root of all this lies ancient superstition, pervasive even at the dawn of the twenty-first century. The eminent language scholar George Harley McKnight put the situation into stark perspective some seventy years ago in his book *English Words and Their Background*: "Euphemism . . . leads to the avoidance of unpleasant words because of a supposed essential connection between the name and the thing named. . . . Contrary to the prevalent impression, . . . it is often to the survival in modern life of features of primitive superstition, rather than to an increase of delicacy attending civilization, that is to be attributed the euphemistic elements in modern speech."

fruppie *noun, slang,* a young upwardly mobile Jew who is religiously observant or newly observant, especially in Orthodoxy: "Rabbis, sociologists and marketing consultants say the number of *fruppies* is growing as Jewish baby boomers return to their orthodox religious roots after experimenting with and rejecting other lifestyles" (Springfield, Mass., *Union-News*, November 4, 1990).

THE STORY: According to Ann Levin, writer of the Associated Press story cited in the Massachusetts paper, the word *fruppie* derives from the Yiddish word *fromm*, "religious," and elements of *yuppie*.

One indication of the trend is the marked increase in the number of different kosher products available today. Lubicom, which sponsors the International Kosher Food Trade Show, says the number of such products rose "from 1,000 in 1977 to 20,000 [in 1990]. At the same time, sales ballooned from $290 million to $1.75 billion a year as companies from Coors beer to Pepperidge Farm have been awarded kosher certification." Another word in the set of interest in the nineties is *typpies*: "*Typpies*, tattooed young professionals, don't go in for the usual brightly colored, whimsical depictions of . . . dragons . . . and other images that recall late 1960s poster art. Instead, they're big on ethnic themes: Maori armbands, Celtic symbols and Egyptian fertility signs" (*Houston Post*, January 20, 1991). See also *dink, domo, NIMBY, sippy.*

full Cleveland *noun*, *slang*, a middle-aged male tourist to Florida who hails from the Midwest, has a sunburned pate, sports white patent-leather shoes, a white belt, white pants, and a colorful polyester shirt; *also*: the ensemble so worn: "'You get everything from Linda Evangelista, fresh from the Milan collections . . .' Ms. [Tara] Gilani [a Miami writer] said, 'to what I call a *full Cleveland*'" (*New York Times*, November 26, 1991).

THE STORY: *Full Cleveland*, designating certain members of the so-called white-bread, white-belt, polyester culture, is yet another item in the prolific arena of geographic, specifically urban, eponymy. It joins others in the set: *Buffalo wings*, *chicken Kiev*, *Aberdeen Angus*, *Canton crepe*, *San Francisco fog* (not the real thing, the *aerogel*), *Manhattan clam chowder*, *Bronx cheer*, *Denver boot*, *Acapulco gold*, *New York minute*, and *Lyme disease*.

Full Cleveland, like *playtza*, *winter-beater*, and *quux*, elicited a lot of mail from "Word Watch" readers when it appeared in the column in August of 1992. A correspondent from Oakmont, Pennsylvania, reported, in terms of the ensemble *full Cleveland*, which echoes the *full* as in *full dress uniform*, that on Pittsburgh daytime radio in the sixties and seventies, "aspiring humorists went out of their way to define '*full Cleveland*' carefully . . . [in] trying to promote Pittsburgh-Cleveland rivalry, while insulting people as best they could." And Lewis J. Poteet, an English professor at Concordia University in Montreal, wrote to me that "'*full Cleveland*' was also a term for a GM car with the motor entirely manufactured in Cleveland, where usually only some parts were made. Car fans believed that a '*full Cleveland* motor' was somehow more powerful or reliable than the others." In *Car and Motorcycle Slang* (1992), Lewis Poteet and his coauthor brother Jim Poteet define *full Cleveland* as "a used-car salesman wearing white tie, white belt, white shoes, [and a] plaid jacket."

gerbil tube *noun*, *slang*, a usually glass- or plastic-enclosed pedestrian air walk or overpass connecting two or more buildings for the sake of security. Also called *honkey tube*: "'Gerbil tubes* is the term used by one mayor I know to describe these glass bridges" (Robert Campbell, *Boston Globe*, October 2, 1988).

THE STORY: "If you want to live in New York, you've got to insulate, insulate, insulate," says a character in Tom Wolfe's *Bonfire of the Vanities*, referring to walling oneself off from the undesirable elements of the city. The pedestrian overpass, like the private elevator, the doorman, the limo and the taxi instead of the subway and the bus, the electronic security system, the multiple locks, the barred windows, the dog, and the guarded suburban enclave with *hydraulic bollards*, is simply another exponent of this type of social isolationism, or *armor-plated cocooning*.

In the piece excerpted above, Robert Campbell, the architecture critic of the *Globe*, went on to say that "another acquaintance has coined an even more vivid phrase for all such walkway systems. He speaks of 'the condomization of the American city.' Like sperm cells who [sic] mustn't be allowed either to spread disease on the one hand or generate life on the other, the pedestrians in the glass tubes are isolated from the world around them."

But how do those on the outside regard the trappings of those inside? A citation from the October 6, 1986, issue of *Newsweek* provides the answer: "Outside Presidential Towers, four new monoliths [in Chicago] holding 2,346 pricey apartments, ousted skid-row denizens wryly curse enclosed walkways between the towers as '*honkey tubes*.'" See also *hydraulic bollard, intentional community*.

gimme cap *noun*, *slang*, a cloth cap with a bill, decorated with a product logo or an organization name: "He received . . . an armadillo hat, a purple sweatshirt . . . and several *gimme caps*" (United Press International, February 27, 1986).

THE STORY: The *gimme cap* is at present an indispensable element in Bill Clinton's informal wardrobe. It derives its name from its use by various manufacturers and other groups as an advertising or public relations giveaway, according to George H. Haas, a senior editor at *Outdoor Life*, in an interview. *Gimme*, the slang contraction of *give me*, formed similarly to *wannabe*, came to be used as a modifier of *cap* by alteration of the oral request, "Gimme a cap," or "Gimme one of those," made by customers to dealers, particularly in farm and hunting equipment outlets.

Gimme has long been employed as a modifier in expressions such as *gimme game* and *gimme racket*, both of which mean "begging," and in *Gimme Girl*, which, in the Roaring Twenties, meant "vamp."

granny dumping *noun*, *offensive slang*, abandonment of an elderly person by relatives, a landlord, or a caregiver, typically by leaving the person along with a suitcase of essential personal effects in a hospital emergency room. Also called *elderly abandonment*; *packed-suitcase syndrome*: "*Granny dumping* is sweeping the US. . . . Couples unwilling to carry on caring for elderly relatives are abandoning them at the casualty departments of hospitals. Well scrubbed and neatly dressed, the elderly person will be deposited in the waiting room" (*The Times* [of London], December 2, 1991).

THE STORY: In the seventies and eighties, the terms *throwaway child* and *throwaway kid* gained wide currency as a result of family dislocations, drug addiction, alcohol abuse, and sexual promiscuity/abuse. Now comes a new, also highly disturbing phenomenon, this one associated with today's in-home and institutional eldercare, and caused, at least in the home setting, by the unremitting stress experienced by family caregivers.

Granny dumping is the term used by emergency room personnel, hospital workers, and even by advocates for the elderly. Citations for it surfaced at the end of 1990. This type of abandonment seems to be occurring most often in states like Florida, Texas, and California, where large retirement communities are found.

In one common scenario, the elderly person is brought under the guise of illness to a hospital emergency room by a nursing home attendant or a landlord. When the emergency staff is ready to release the patient, no one can be found to transport the person back to the residence. Inquiries to the responsible party reveal that the person's room or living space is no longer available. In other incidents, family caregivers have dropped off elderly relatives at hospitals with notes pinned to them, saying in effect, "Please take care of _____ ."

Toni Mitchell, M.D., the director of the Tampa General Hospital Adult Emergency Department, has called such incidents "the *positive taillight sign.* They roll them in the door and all I see is [*sic*] the taillights vanishing in the distance" (*Roanoke* [Va.] *Times & World-News*, November 29, 1991).

New York Times columnist Russell Baker captured the urgency of the situation when he used *granny-dump* in a piece dated April 2, 1992: "Contemplating the possibility of being *granny-dumped*, I wonder if our politicians might be numb to furies seething among Americans. Wake and look, gentlemen. There's trouble out here. People sleeping in the streets. . . . Millions with no medicine, no doctor. The desperate young are abandoning helpless, hopeless Granny." See also *drive-by hatred, moral panic.*

halter-top briefs *plural noun*, a woman's sleeveless upper garment constructed from men's knitted briefs: "You probably have no idea what *halter-top briefs* might be, but we predict that by Memorial Day, *halter-top briefs* will be seen on streets, in stores, and in shopping malls everywhere" (Donna Salyers, "Needlepointers," Springfield, Mass., *Union-News*, January 30, 1989).

THE STORY: "Sewing Hits *Atlantic Monthly*," said the Monday, June 26, 1989, "Needlepointers" column headline right after *halter-top briefs* became an item in the June "Word Watch." Donna Salyers, who turned out to be the coiner of the term for the thing itself, remarked thus: "Not often does the topic of sewing find its way into *The Atlantic Monthly*. The June issue, however, is a notable exception, wherein an article by this writer is quoted. . . . Yessiree, right there alongside heavy-duty stuff on subjects such as nuclear strategy, NATO, and cryopreservation (!?), is a dissertation on '*halter-top briefs*.' . . . How often, after all, is one's literary ability spotlighted in such an esteemed way?"

Halter-top briefs got into my column because it exemplified a fast-in, fast-out linguistic, if not sartorial, fad. Once in a while I can't resist delving into the patently ephemeral. Unlike *hot pants*, which came into style and then went out, coming back yet again, *halter-top briefs* stood little chance of getting into dictionaries.

Halter-top briefs are constructed in a resourceful way. Keep these instructions in mind if you're ever in a sudden bind: slit the crotch, sew the fly closed, and overcast the crotch opening and the leg holes with decorative edging. The crotch then will become the neck of your garment, with the leg openings accommodating your arms. The result is a close-fitting, sleeveless halter, the elastic waistband of which will fall to your midriff. The legholes-now-armholes will give you arm openings "with a high-cut racing style," said Salyers in her original piece. She added that "the fly front [if not sewn together] on the wearer's back makes an interesting conversation piece." A size Medium (34–36) pair of men's briefs will transform into a size Small halter top; a size Large (38–40) will become a size Medium for women. In the original piece, I said that unless the wearer can be called a Ten, she has no business picking up the scissors.

HIV roulette, *noun*, *slang*, unsafe sex. Also called *sexual roulette*: "Sex in the late 20th century, often known among singles as '*HIV roulette*,' is about to take a new turn" (*Los Angeles Times*, May 17, 1990). "Actually, a quick look at the statistics is a good cautionary guide for anyone who is playing *sexual roulette*: Approximately 1 million Americans—or one in every 250—are now infected with HIV, according to the CDC" ("*HIV Roulette*: The new odds. The risky plays," *Men's Journal*, June/July 1994).

THE STORY: The AIDS catastrophe, like the dawn of the Space Age and the Great Gender Shift in writing, has changed forever the language we speak. In the same manner, the epidemic of this STD (sexually transmitted disease) has changed radically the nature of private life in our times.

Now, as the AIDS epidemic moves into its second decade, 1 in 100 American males and 1 in 800 females have HIV—an increase of 130 percent from 1992 to 1993 in the number of those who contracted the disease via heterosexual relations.

In terms of the changing language as a reflection of the changing and increasing risks, we observe the emergence of a very businesslike language of sexual negotiation or transaction. A *Los Angeles Times* article some years back used some of the expressions common to this new language: *condom management strategy, condom-consciousness, sex negotiations, negotiating safe sex, effective birth control agreements,* and *voluntary safe sex compliance*. Add to that short list these from *Men's Journal: gauging your STD quotient, Western blot indeterminate test result,* and *serodiscordant couple* (a couple with one HIV-positive partner, one HIV-negative partner).

Etymologically speaking, *HIV roulette* was obviously influenced in its formation by *Russian roulette*, a term dating at least to 1917 and attested in print to the year 1937 by the *New Oxford English Dictionary. HIV roulette* is not the first extension of *roulette* to the sphere of reproductive matters, however. The *New OED* attests another, generally related, usage in the October 9, 1976, issue of *Lancet*: "Abusive parents are often the scarred survivors of generations of *reproductive russian roulette.*" See also *Colombian roulette* at *Iraqi manicure*.

hotsy-potatsy *noun, slang,* a sexually promiscuous woman; a tramp: "I'm no *hotsy-potatsy*" (Imelda Marcos, *Newsweek*, March 17, 1986).

THE STORY: *Hotsy-potatsy* is an example of a word-formative process called *intentional rhyming*. Intentional rhyming involves the juxtaposition of two rhyming terms, the first one usually an adjective, and the second, usually a noun. One word in the set is often used in an exaggerated or figurative way. Typical examples of intentional rhyming are *fat cat, gruesome twosome,* and *ooly-drooly*. The word *hotsy-potatsy,* now in the nineties often used to mean simply "one who is on the cutting edge, as a hot marketer," seems to blend part of the meaning and part of the sound of the noun *hot patootie* ("girlfriend"), which dates to the year 1935, with the rhyme of the adjective *hotsy-totsy* ("just right; satisfactory"), which dates to 1926. *Hotsy-potatsy* also seems to be formed partly by the process of *reduplication,* the repetition of an element within a word, often involving slight variation in the initial consonant or the medial vowel. Typical examples of reduplication are *footsie-wootsie,* *nasty-wasty, piggy-wiggy, poopsie-woopsie, popsy-wopsy,* and *itsy-bitsy.* A final word about *hotsy-potatsy:* if you say to-MAH-to, Gre-NAH-da, and po-TAH-to, you won't have any difficulty pronouncing *hotsy-potatsy.* See also *imeldific.*

imeldific *adjective,* ostentatiously extravagant to the point of vulgarity: "To call something '*imeldific*' would describe it as a shameless and vulgar extravagance" (*People,* April 28, 1986). "She'll need extra room for her crates of china, closets of clothes and collection of California pals. . . . Yes, it's been an *imeldific* eight years" (*New York Newsday,* November 15, 1988).

THE STORY: This eponymous adjective, used in *New York Newsday* to refer to Nancy Reagan, was coined by Imelda Marcos, The Eponym Herself, who must be brought onstage right now: "She did not merely arrive at the Manhattan court. She made an entrance. Limousines swept Imelda Marcos and entourage from her $1,800-a-day Waldorf Towers suite to her debut before Judge John Keenan. 'They will list my name in the dictionary,' said Imelda. '*Imeldific,* to mean ostentatious extravagance'" (*U.S. News & World Report,* November 14, 1988).

THE STORY: The Marcos Phenom just won't go away. The surname itself was genericized—by *Boston Globe* columnist Bella English, who wrote an entry for it on August 13, 1990—thus: "**marcos:** . . . behavioral disorder characterized by pathological spending of other people's money. (*I marcosed out with my parents' Visa at Filene's Basement last week.*) (*The S&L bandits are marcosing with our tax dollars.*)" It's generally unusual for a given name and a surname belonging to the same person to be separately eponymized. But then again, if one of the 3,000 pairs of shoes fits, ya just gotta wear it. See also *Rembrandt.*

intentional community *noun,* a self-sustaining town typically having its own police force, fire department, and other services, formed by a group of people who share values and interests. Also called *private town:* "[They] are creators of Ponderosa Village [Washington], a 1,000-acre '*intentional community*' whose residents hope to ensure their survival in the social upheavals they see on the horizon. They . . . are not survivalists, not a religious cult and not a commune" (Associated Press, July 31, 1988).

THE STORY: The term *intentional community* itself is not new: it has long been used to refer to nontheistic communities organized by Buddhists, and to monasteries and convents. Nor is *private town* new: for example, in 1895,

James Walker Tufts, the inventor of the soda fountain, founded Pinehurst, a *private town* in south-central North Carolina, now a privately owned resort. What is new is the trend among some people to "circle the wagons"—to seek isolated, well-protected areas in which to begin their lives afresh and avoid the chaos ahead.

A typical residence in such a community is modern and elaborate; amenities include a hot tub, an attached greenhouse, a satellite dish, solar heating and natural cooling, and a root cellar. Prospective residents are told that they must be able to conform to the community's principles of self-reliance and adhere to community goals. People who can work in nearby businesses and industries or can create their own jobs are in particular demand. See also *gerbil tube, hydraulic bollard, nacul, New York barricade, penturbia.*

Lake Wobegon effect *noun*, a misleading perception of progress in education caused by unanalytical study of and subsequent misinterpretation of statistical data: "The argument over the *Lake Wobegon effect* has turned nasty" (*New York Times*, May 10, 1988).

THE STORY: In 1988, John J. Cannell, M.D., of Beaver, West Virginia, observed widespread discrepancies between the academic performance of some of his young patients and their grade levels, irrespective of the fact that West Virginia, a state with one of the highest illiteracy rates in the country, had reported above-average student performance on standardized tests. Dr. Cannell formed Friends for Education Inc., a group that canvassed various state departments of education in order to determine the reason for this strange paradox. Eventually, Chester E. Finn, Jr., then an assistant secretary of the U.S. Department of Education, held a meeting with Cannell and representatives of the major testing services to discuss the issue. The test makers explained that their definitions of what constituted normal performance had been devised years before and that because schools were getting somewhat better, more and more students were exceeding the old norms. The outcome of this February 1988 meeting was, in part, the emergence of a new term, *Lake Wobegon effect*, derived from Garrison Keillor's fictional Minnesota town where "the women are strong, the men are good-looking and all the children are above average."

Other relatively new terms in which *effect* is an element are these, all of which are suggestive of changes in human behavior: *airport effect*, "expansion in the market for a heretofore local or regional product, such as Colorado's Coors beer, resulting from marked consumer demand for the product outside its locale or region of inception," a term used in October 1988 by *Business Month*; *sleeper effect*, "a fear of serious romantic commitment experienced by adults who are children of divorced parents," a term used by Judith Wallerstein in her book *Second Chances: Men, Women and Children a Decade After Divorce*; and *Passover effect*, "the ability to postpone one's death, as from a terminal disease, for about one week by sheer force of personal will," a term used by researcher David Phillips, a sociology professor at the University of California at San Diego, who, with Elliot King, reported a study of the phenomenon in the September 1988 issue of *Lancet*. See also *Nixon effect* at *hedonia hypothesis*.

lambada *noun*, **1.** an energetic, sexually suggestive close dance for couples: "Described as a kind of 'world-beat Dirty Dancing,' *lambada* has captured the attention of a '90s crowd fed up with the separateness of dancing to rock and house music" (*Christian Science Monitor*, February 2, 1990). **2.** the music for this dance, ultimately of Brazilian origin, now a quick-tempo combination of African, Caribbean, and European styles: "*Lambada* is a mix of Latin rhythms like Colombian cumbia, Dominican merengue, Argentinian tango and Brazilian samba ensembled in a new and contagious sound that invites people to the dance floor" (*Los Angeles Times*, November 18, 1989).

THE STORY: By the time I submitted this piece to *The Atlantic Monthly*, everyone in the country knew what *lambada* was, so we decided not to run it. Since 1989, the word has virtually died out in the media, a possible reason that it is not entered in most dictionaries (space is tight and lexicographers will more often than not sacrifice ephemera for words known to have staying power). *Lambada* does have an interesting history, so here it is: It is derived from the Portuguese verb *lamb(ar)*, meaning "to whip," plus the suffix *-ada*, meaning in English "-ade," which is used in loanwords from the Romance languages to mean "an action or a process," as in *cannonade*.

The dance, which originated in northwest Brazil, goes back at least to the 1930s, when it was all the rage in Rio. Then the dictatorial president Getúlio Vargas, concerned about the "immorality" of the dance, banned it. Nevertheless, it remained popular in nonurban areas, where a Caribbean influence had begun to permeate the musical accompaniment. Having briefly reemerged during the 1960s in Brazil, *lambada* emigrated to Europe in the 1980s, thence to its United States debut, continuing in popularity from the mid-1980s up to the early 1990s.

Similar to the tango or the foxtrot—from the waist up, that is—the *lam-*

bada is characterized by footwork involving one step followed by two quick steps. Its chief identifying feature is the *thigh straddle*: one partner places his or her upper thigh between the other partner's legs, thereby keeping both partners' hips tightly together as they dance. This close body contact, marked by erotic circling and rubbing of the hips, resulted in the dance being called the nineties' answer to safe sex. See also *vogueing*.

late decider *noun*, a college graduate, who, in midlife and midcareer, decides to become a schoolteacher. Also called *second-career teacher*: "*Late deciders* have forsaken a bevy of career paths for teaching. They are former attorneys and computer analysts, musicians and military officers" (*Washington Post*, April 14, 1991).

THE STORY: Only a few years ago, people were leaving the teaching profession by the thousands. Now it seems that many other people want to enter it. From 1985 to 1989, programs for career-switching college graduates certified 12,000 teachers. Although teacher salaries rose by about $4,000 in 1990 dollars since 1979, and teachers were paid an average of $35,104 in 1992–93, up 3.2 percent from 1991, money is usually not the deciding factor influencing these career switches. The key factors motivating the *late deciders* are concern about the quality of education in this country and a desire to improve it, a desire to put their life experience and expertise to good use in making a difference in the lives of students, and the challenge of bringing a new degree of creativity to the classroom.

School principals say that *late deciders* make excellent teachers, given their maturity. "'It's the wave of the future,' said Clark Dobson, assistant dean of education at George Mason University" (*Washington Post*). The state and city most often sought by already employed teachers? Connecticut, where the average 1993 salary was $48,918, and Hartford, where it was about $54,000.

mad-dog *verb*, *slang*, to stare coldly and fixedly at (another), taken to be a challenge to fight: "'He would ... *mad-dog* me and say names under his breath,' Mr. [Chris] Simmons [a seventeen-year-old African-American student at Palm Springs High School] said [of a Hispanic fellow student with whom he had had his first fight]. 'One day I got sick of it'" (*New York Times*, March 18, 1994).

THE STORY: The context is tension among members of various groups, not just between Hispanics and African-Americans in southern California public schools, but also between straights and gays on at least one university campus. One manifestation of the tension is staring, by whatever name one chooses to call it.

The roots of this street-language verb go back roughly 457 years to the noun phrase *madde dogge*. Since that early time, the noun phrase has become a full-fledged compound and undergone functional shift to a verb: Random House Reference Division editor Jesse Sheidlower points to his firm's earliest citation for it, taken from Léon Bing's 1990 book about Los Angeles street gangs, *Do or Die*, where a character says, "Why the hell didn't he just say not to *mad-dog* somebody?"

That being so, the term reflects the characteristics exhibited by canines affected with rabies, specifically the symptoms associated with the so-called furious stage. In this stage, the dog becomes "irrational and vicious," says Richard Asbury, DVM, who adds that the animal "adopts a stiff-legged gait" and has a deceptively "anxious" look, "pupils dilated." In all reality, the animal is "displaying stalking behavior, looking for trouble, displaying no fear."

If looks could kill, then staring, also called *stareism* by some wags, is a serious issue among some of today's youth. The December 20, 1993, Associated Press story headed "George Mason Issues 'No Staring' Gay Rule" makes the point, reporting that "in a leaflet handed out to students, George Mason University cautioned against offending gays and lesbians by *staring* at them or by keeping a physical distance during conversation."

Michelangelo Signorile, a contributing writer with *Out* magazine, informed me during a telephone interview in the early spring of 1994 that *staring* is a cultural thing often misunderstood by Americans. In Italy, for instance, men often stare at each other with no other motive in mind than admiration of another's appearance or attire, a look totally devoid of innuendo, he said. See also *laughism, dis*.

mamou *noun*, something very big or important, such as a key objective or a crucial maneuver fraught with risk: "It was becoming clear that we needed to do something bigger—much bigger. It was time for the big *mamou*. If we didn't pull something off and the industry continued to head south, Mesa was going to be in trouble" (T. Boone Pickens Jr., *Boone*, 1986).

THE STORY: *Mamou* in its extended sense is occasionally heard but rarely seen in print. It is possible that the extension in meaning is derived from *Mamou*, a Louisiana town renowned as the "Cajun Music Capital of the World" and the seat of the first and most authentic Mardi Gras. The town was immortalized as "the Big *Mamou*" in "La Chanson des Mardi-Gras," to wit:

> *Les Mardi Gras devient de tout partout;*
> *Mais principalement de Grand* Mamou

where the spelling in title and lyrics reflects exactly the people's usages. (And Crawfish Big *Mamou* is one of the gastronomic delights on the menu of Chef Paul Prudhomme's restaurant K-Paul's I Louisiana Kitchen. In a telephone interview in 1987, the chef's secretary confirmed that this usage was undoubtedly drawn from references to the town.)

But the ultimate origin of the word *mamou* is uncertain, and conflicting theories about it abound. The *Mamou Acadian Press* of September 18, 1986, stated that "there are many stories about the name MAMOU. One was the legendary Indian, Chief *Mamou*. It is certain that [the] vast prairie [in southwestern Louisiana, 25 miles wide and containing more than 1,200,000 acres] was known as *Mamou* Prairie as far back as the 1700s and that the Anglo-Americans called it the 'Mammoth Prairie' because of its immense size. And when the Frenchmen came they called it '*Mamou*' for mammouth."

There is also a line of possible connection between *mamou* and the French words *mammouth* for "mammoth" and *mamelou*, meaning "a person with sharply pronounced breasts," as in *un(e) gros(se) mamelu(e)*. Frederic G. Cassidy, Ph.D., the chief editor of the *Dictionary of American Regional English*, said in a letter to me that he was "pretty sure that *mamou* is French. The association with Cajun cookery would support this. To me, *mamou* is a hypocristic (baby-talk) variant of French *maman*, parallel to our *mama*, British *mummy*, etc. Used by adults, these terms of affection often become ironic or even satiric, as in our use of 'What a mama,' 'She's a *big* mama,' etc. The French do this too. . . . I'd easily dismiss *mammouth* and *mamelu*, which would make *big* redundant."

The word *mamou* is also used locally to denote the coral bean plant, *Erythrina herbacea*. According to R. Dale Thomas, Ph.D., director, Northeast Louisiana University Herbarium, a scholar who believes the word may have a Native American etymology, this plant, associated with Native American folklore and medicine, stands from three to five feet tall and has very large woody roots measuring five inches in diameter by five feet in length. The plant produces bright, dark red flowers on large spikes. Each flower yields a very hard bean pod. The seeds, which may be poisonous, are used in making rosaries.

mutual child *noun*, the offspring of a couple, one or both partners having been previously married and having children from the former marriage or marriages: "Parents planning the birth of a *mutual child* . . . ideally would have been married for at least five years, so stepparent and stepchildren would have worked out their relationships" (Springfield, Mass., *Union-News*, March 21, 1989).

THE STORY: *Mutual child*, used by Anne C. Bernstein, a professor of psychology at the Wright Institute in Berkeley, California, and the author of *Yours, Mine and Ours* (1989), joins other rather antiseptic terms, such as *domestic partner*, *displaced homemaker*, and *significant other*, used to characterize relationships of the eighties and the nineties.

Yet another term used by Bernstein in her book is *emotional divorce*, referring to a complete emotional break with a former spouse: "If an *emotional divorce* has not occurred, the children of the marriage can be caught up in conflict between their own parents, and that can make it much harder for them to accept the child of the marriage." See also *emotional literacy*.

NIMBY also **Nimby** *noun*, *slang*, a person who objects to the establishment in his or her neighborhood of projects, such as prisons, homes for the homeless, halfway houses, landfills, incinerators, and power plants, that are regarded as dangerous, undesirable, or unsightly: "'They are not screamers. They are *NIMBYs*,' [Leeta] Pistone says, referring to the derogatory acronym . . . which applies to groups that oppose projects in their own neighborhoods but don't mind seeing them elsewhere" (*Los Angeles Times*, March 29, 1987). "Home builders and city planners have a new name for an old enemy—the *Nimbys* . . . , those who want no construction that might disturb the character and real estate value of their neighborhoods" (*Forbes*, December 22, 1980).

THE STORY: Geopolitical-military *NIMBYism* probably reached its apex a few years ago when a U.S. general suggested that the dirty detritus of banned nuclear weapons be loaded into rockets and shot to the sun. Echoes of more localized *NIMBYism* resonate in the portless Long Island garbage barge and the so-called nuclear train plying the tracks of this country, seeking a dump site acceptable to nearby residents. Since the time that *NIMBY* first appeared in "Word Watch" (August 1987), the term, then regarded as an acronym, has transformed itself into a full-fledged noun and has gained entry in the third edition of *The American Heritage Dictionary of the English Language* (1992).

According to the September 1982 issue of *Nuclear News*, "A few years ago ANS [the American Nuclear Society] stalwart Walton Rodger coined the acronym *NIMBY* . . . to describe the modern national syndrome that urges the immediate rejection of almost any large construction project in any local area." His acronym is, of course, formed of the phrase *Not In My Back Yard*. In a May 8, 1987, *Chicago Tribune* story, Eric Zorn identified the characteristics of *NIMBYs* as individuals with "petitions in hand, veins standing out on neck." Zorn went on to point out that "as more and more people move to suburbia and the aging baby boom generation trades in its condos for colonials on cul-de-sacs, *Nimbyness* promises to flower. . . . *Nimbys* may well be to the last half of this decade what yuppies were to the first half." See also *CWASP*, *dink*, *domo*, *fruppie*, *sippy*.

non-ism *noun*, strict, broad-based self-denial, often seen as a radical reaction to prior overindulgence and as an attempt to gain control over one's life: "'The most virulent *non-ism* grows out of, or even coincides with, eras of easy money and indulgence,' said Dr. Stuart Ewen, a professor of communications at Hunter College" (*New York Times*, July 27, 1990). "A Boston psychiatrist has complained that his 24-year-old son is suffering from severe '*non-ism*.' . . . The young man looked at the chaos around him and . . . gave up drinking, drugs and caffeine, meat, sugar, dairy and wheat products and sex" (*The* [London] *Independent*, June 1990).

THE STORY: *Non-ism*, a nineties trend believed by some to be a direct reaction to the scandalous greed, the ecologic disasters, and the epidemics of sexually transmitted disease of the eighties, is practiced by people who are called *nones* (*non* in the singular). What is more, *non-ism*, the apotheosis of Nancy Reagan's "Just say no," may be the most recent manifestation of the puritanism that seems to remain a subtext to life in the United States.

Dr. Derrick de Kerckhove, a professor at the University of Toronto, says that "people are confused. . . . They don't know who they are, and they reckon with that by stating who they aren't." Defining who one is or what one wants is therefore undertaken by thinking and communicating in terms of opposites. If language is a reflection of the will, the interests, the conflicting ideas, and, yes, the obsessions of its users, then the results of a study that I made of words formed with the prefix *non-* are not surprising. In one small sampling of 1,094 printout pages averaging 37,000 occurrences of various *non-* prefixed words, 81 of those words, recurring with relatively high frequency, were found to be directly related to eight major categories of concern in twentieth-century life.

These words appeared in two broad contexts: matters of human behavior and matters of commerce. Here are the eight categories, along with typical words from each: substance abuse (*nonaddicting, nonalcoholic, nondrinking, nonsmoking, nonuser*); psychology (*nonadversarial, nonassertive, nonconfrontational, nonthreatening*); nutrition (*noncaloric, nonchocolate, nonfattening, nonsweet*); industry (*nonleaded, nonskid, nonstick*); medicine (*nonaspirin, noninvasive, nonpathogenic*); government/politics (*noncrisis, nonracist, nonradical*); ecology (*nonaerosol, nontoxic*); and personal life (*nonbetting, nongambling, nonflying, nonsexual*). Of the 81 terms, the most frequently occurring was *nonsmoking*, which appeared 759 times as an adjective modifying at least 74 consistently recurring nouns such as *trend, initiative, program; area, section; passenger, traveler; flight, bus;* and *ruling, policy, law.* See also *laughism.*

outlaw party *noun*, an illegal nightclub that operates only one night a week in frequently changing locations in an effort to avoid prosecution and to keep out unwanted patrons. Also called *moving club; outlaw club; warehouse party*: "The concept of an *outlaw party* is neither new nor native to New York. Los Angeles, for instance, has had '*moving clubs*' for a few years" (*New York Times,* April 14, 1989).

THE STORY: These are modern, mobile speakeasies, access to which is largely controlled by word of mouth. When a new location—an abandoned warehouse, an old dance hall, a rooftop, or even a former synagogue—is selected, handbills are printed and distributed among the faithful. A nominal cover charge, an unspoken dress code (some clubs accept leather and black but turn away jeans and loafers), and a reliable group of bouncers serve as admission and crowd control.

On a typical evening, usually from 11:00 P.M. to 4:00 A.M., a successful, popular *outlaw party* can draw 1,000 people, with another 300 to 400 denied access. One of the big attractions is *house music* or *house mix*, which can be anything from rap to a kind of disco pop with a strong beat. Patrons come to dance, drink at the cash bar, and socialize. As one devotee put it to the *Times,* the *outlaw parties* are "fun because they move around. . . . The crowd changes depending on where they are."

A related word is *causeway crowd*, barflies who traverse the bridges link-ing Miami Beach and the mainland in pursuit of cosmopolitan fun. Manhattanites refer to such recreational commuters as *bridge and tunnel people*, or *B&Ts*.

over-the-counter student *noun*, a late, unexpected enrollee, especially one at a public high school, who has failed to meet the entrance requirements of public schools with selective admissions policies: "[A certain high school has] traditionally been a dumping ground for . . . *over-the-counter students*, who register late and can't be placed elsewhere" (*New York Newsday*, December 14, 1989).

THE STORY: A typical *over-the-counter student* resides in the inner city, speaks English as a second language if at all, is several grade levels behind his or her peers, has personal difficulties, and registers for classes often as late as November.

Over-the-counter students create additional difficulties for already overcrowded schools beset with security and behavioral problems, communications and socialization troubles, and a shortage of teachers. For example, in 1988, 600 *over-the-counter students* enrolled at Wingate High School, in New York City, during the first two months of the fall semester, having come from places like St. Croix, Haiti, and the Dominican Republic.

According to a November 21, 1989, article in the *New York Times*, "60 percent will be gone before the school year ends, mostly because of changing family situations." The use of *over-the-counter* with reference to such students is undoubtedly influenced by *over-the-counter stock*, a security that does not meet the listing requirements of the New York or American Stock Exchange. See also *couch people*.

penturbia *noun*, a region of in-migration and opportunity within the United States, consisting of small cities and towns, new subdivisions, homesteads, and industrial and commercial districts interspersed with farms, forests, lakes, and rivers: "*Penturbia* is the caring conserver's ideal territory. Long-run growth will be greater in *penturbia* than anywhere else in the nation. Look for *penturbia* beyond the normal commuting range of the nation's central cities" (*American Demographics*, June 1987).

THE STORY: *Penturbia* was coined in 1986 by Jack Lessinger, a professor emeritus of real estate and urban development at the University of Washington (Seattle), who first used the word in his book *Regions of Opportunity*, published that year. In *American Demographics*, Lessinger provided his own story behind the word: "I call it *penturbia*, because it is the fifth [major in-migration] since the American Revolution." (The other four occurred between 1760 and 1789, when the Carolinas, Vermont, and New Hampshire grew at the expense of Virginia, Massachusetts, and Pennsylvania; between 1817 and 1846, when settlers flowed westward from New York to New Orleans via the Ohio and Mississippi rivers; between 1873 and 1900, when people moved to the great industrial centers such as Chicago and Minneapolis and to raw-material centers such as Seattle and San Francisco; and between 1929 and 1958, when the suburbs emerged at the expense of big cities and small towns.)

Characteristically, *penturban* centers experienced below-average growth in the years 1950–1970 and above-average growth in the 1970s. These *penturban* counties grew by 9 percent between 1980 and 1985, nearly double the national rate: Shelby County, Alabama; Amador County, California; and Grady County, Oklahoma. *Penturbia* is driven by a consumer called "the caring conserver," who prefers a simple yet somewhat cosmopolitan lifestyle, who guards and saves personal resources, and who rejects mass consumptive values: "To prevent runaway growth and conserve local resources, *penturbanites* demand judicious county planning," Lessinger has said. See also *Edge City*, *intentional community*.

populuxe *adjective*, of or relating to the decade from the mid-1950s to the mid-1960s, during which the affluent American middle class, stimulated by postwar economic prosperity, spent unprecedented sums on material possessions designed in pretentious poor taste: "In his . . . [1986] book [*Populuxe*], Thomas Hine dubs this period the *populuxe* decade. . . . 'People wanted to be known for their good taste,' writes Mr. Hine, 'but they also wanted to have great showy things that demonstrated that they had arrived. *Populuxe* is vulgar by definition'" (Michiko Kakutani, *New York Times*, October 29, 1986). —*noun*, the ethos and the styles of this decade: "*Populuxe* was the innocent, optimistic, glitzy celebration of America's great leap forward into Tomorrowland, under construction in 1954 by Walt Disney on the outskirts of Anaheim, Calif." (Karal Ann Marling, *New York Times Book Review*, November 9, 1986).

THE STORY: *Populuxe* promptly evokes images of push-button automotive gearshifts and soaring tail fins, masses of polished chrome, spike heels and tight sheaths, corrugated potato chips served with California dip, split-level abodes with Hollywood closets and rumpus rooms, and deluxe dinettes.

Appropriately enough, *populuxe*—a succinct descriptor of a collage of kitsch—is a portmanteau word, a synthesis of elements derived from the words *populism*, *popularity*, and *luxury*, with the *e* added not from *deluxe* as might be expected but merely "to give it class," according to the coiner, Thomas Hine, who is the architecture and design critic at the *Philadelphia Inquirer.* Sprachgefühl, the lexicographer's instinctive feeling for what is linguistically apropos or effective, tells me that *populuxe*, like *art deco* and *putting on the ritz*, is a term that is here to stay—at least in design circles.

Saturday school *noun*, a weekend disciplinary program for public high school students who frequently misbehave during weekly school hours: "For the first infraction, a student can be suspended from school for one day or be assigned to four hours of *Saturday school*" (*Los Angeles Times*, December 18, 1986).

THE STORY: *Saturday school* denotes a practice that has been in and out of use at least since the year 1915. It is intended to reduce markedly the rate of suspensions in student populations. It is again in force in many school systems in the United States. One school official in Irvine, California, said this about the advantage of *Saturday school* over suspension: "Kids who ditched school fell farther behind when we suspended them for being truant."

Students might be sent to *Saturday school* for any of various infractions, such as tardiness, truancy, failure to deliver classwork or homework, or the creation of a disturbance. *Saturday school* is useful in forcing students to make up missed work, according to proponents. In other cases, students undergoing this weekend detention are required, from seven or eight in the morning until noon, to clean school buildings and grounds.

Saturday school isn't all that bad, however. A Word Watcher of Lithuanian ancestry informed me that for over forty years the term has been used by European immigrants for schools that operate on Saturday mornings, often in church fellowship halls or rented school buildings, for the purpose of teaching youngsters their parents' and grandparents' native languages and the histories and cultural backgrounds of the countries whence the families came. Teachers may be parents or professional instructors who do the job pro bono or at minimal pay. Might *Saturday school* be an answer for those parents seeking to instill in their children ethnic and cultural knowledge not available in most schools, together with extra practice in foreign languages in public school districts where bilinguality is not encouraged?

serious *adjective*, of such quality as to appeal to the expert, the connoisseur, or the sophisticate: "Every *serious* kitchen needs at least one peppermill" (*Washington Post*, September 16, 1979). "'We're not making home computers. We're making *serious* computers'" (Kenneth Olson, president of Digital Equipment Corporation, *InfoWorld*, September 19, 1983).

THE STORY: Once in a while, a new sense of a preexisting word becomes the signature of a generational attitude. Such is the case with *serious*. *American Heritage* Usage Panel Chair and Stanford linguist Geoffrey Nunberg, Ph.D., observed at the time that "if something isn't *world-class* nowadays, it's most likely *serious*. The original source of the new use of *serious* was doubtless in the phrase *serious money*, but by now it's been extended to all of the things serious money can buy."

Some of these things are, according to thousands of citations pulled up and examined at the time, *serious* automotive aerodynamics, *serious* food, *serious* makeup and accessories, a *serious* pizza, *serious* desserts, a *serious* body, *serious* wine, *serious* pasta, even *serious* fun. A Mitsubishi commercial characterized a $20,000 car as "a *serious* luxury sedan at a price that is not too serious" (*New York Times*, August 21, 1987). And *Advertising Age* pointed out that cars such as the Datsun 280ZX and others identified by numbers and letters rather than by model names are "*Serious* Cars Designed by *Serious* Engineers (SC-DSE)."

The newer meaning of *serious* should not be confused with its established senses: "of great importance" (*serious* business), "deserving to be taken seriously" (*serious* music; a *serious* novel; *serious* doo-doo; a *serious* candidate), and "marked by or demanding considerable devotion, effort, care, or interest" (*serious* monogamy; *serious* tanning; *serious* skiing; *serious* partying; a *serious* correspondence).

Nunberg believed that *world-class* and *serious* were "the accolades of a generation who pride[d] themselves first and foremost with being discriminating consumers, who [could] evaluate everything as if it were a prospective purchase. Like the decade itself, the language of the Eighties [was] all business."

That being so, I can predict new sensemaking in the nineties. The adjective *major* is undergoing similar change. Consider this Macy's advertisement from the *New York Times* of August 15, 1993: "A Junior Shop with *Major* Attitude, Complete with Brass Buttons, Braiding & Bravado!" Nowadays it's no longer "big hair" for a bouffant do; it's "*major* hair," used by a *Washington Post* reporter in 1993 to describe Lynda Bird Johnson Robb's appearance.

Shelter-Pak *trademark*, used for a five-pound, full-length hooded and belted garment that doubles as a coat and a shelter, designed especially for homeless people: "The demand for *Shelter-Paks* on the street is overwhelming" (*New York Times*, February 29, 1992).

THE STORY: Trademarks aren't usually associated with a heightened sense of social consciousness, but this one is. Students in the Survey of Apparel course at the Philadelphia College of Textiles and Science have over the years developed special products for people with special needs, one of them being Braille blocks for sightless toddlers. In 1990, thirty students in the course combined individual prototypes and came up with a garment they jointly coined the *Shelter-Pak*.

During the design stage, the students interviewed homeless people, asking them what features would or would not be desirable. Undesirable: neon colors that attracted attention. Desirable: earth tones, such as tan, that were inconspicuous; and no closures, such as zippers, hooks, or buttons, that would restrain a victim under street attack from escaping quickly. One side of the *Shelter-Pak* is wool; the other, waterproof nylon. In warm weather, the *Shelter-Pak* can be folded into one of its own deep pockets and then carried like a backpack or used as a pillow.

In 1993, engineering students at Howard University, in Washington, D.C., organized a similar project. In teams that consulted with homeless people, they designed one-person shelter structures. One structure was a ten-pound inflatable tent made from bicycle tire inner tubes. Another looked like a giant Slinky covered with waterproof, insulating fabric. The students tested the efficacy of their shelters by spending below-freezing nights in them. "It makes you think of engineering as a people field," remarked freshman Trebus Smith to a *Washington Post* reporter who was investigating this, a new trend in student activism.

sippy *noun*, a financially secure consumer, aged fifty-five to eighty, having been married at least once and in good health, who is a member of a large segment of the senior population commanding 30 percent of the discretionary funds in the marketplace: "Seniors who feel left out in shopping centers now catering to . . . yuppies may take heart from the prediction of a sociologist who believes that '*sippies*' will soon control United States buying power" (*Boston Globe*, April 9, 1986).

THE STORY: The eighties were years during which such new coinages proliferated on the model of *yippy* and *yuppie*. *Sippies* was coined in the plural by

Dr. Lynette Milner of US International University. It was an acronym for senior *independent pioneers*.

A related word, *muppy*, has two meanings—the first, "a medical urban professional," and the second, "a maturing Baby Boomer living in the 21st century, specifically, one in the 35–54-year-old age group." Marissa Piesman, the cocoiner of *yuppie*, used *muppy* in its first sense in the January 9, 1984, issue of *People*: "In Boston there are a lot of *Muppies*—Medical Urban Professionals. Instead of talking about real estate . . . they talk DNA."

And the *Baltimore Sun* of May 5, 1986, used *muppy* in its second sense: "We suspect the new term to describe these maturing yuppies in the next century will be *muppies*. By the year 2005 . . . there will be a 40 percent increase in the number of *muppies* . . . who will be leasing BMWs, joining health clubs and sipping Chablis and nibbling Brie in their harborside condos." Well, maybe. The 40 percent sounds right, but given the far-reaching effects of today's recession, *decession*, or whatever-you-want-to-call-it, I suspect that some *muppies* may end up in the market for the ultimate Shelter-Pak. See also *CWASP*, *dink*, *domo*, *fruppie*, *NIMBY*.

skinship *noun*, in Japan, a state of empathy among people, especially the bonding of friends, business associates, or family members, developed through close, sustained interaction. Among family members, *skinship* is often expressed by affectionate physical contact, such as a mother's hugging of her child. In other settings, it is marked by friendship and cooperation: "Yataro Kawabata . . . said it was sad that the nation is losing the '*skinship*' of public bathing. . . . 'Young people don't have a chance to learn the social manners to be gained from bathing together'" (Associated Press, September 16, 1982).

THE STORY: *Skinship*, a behavioral term with no sexual connotations, is a Japanese coinage in English. It falls into a category of words called *waseigo*, literally translated "Japanese-manufactured language" (where *wa* means "Japanese," *sei* means "manufactured," and *go* means "language or words"), according to Jeremy Silverman, a business consultant who speaks Japanese fluently. *Waseigo* words, which are usually restricted in use to the Japanese culture, are often applied in ways that standard English terms are not. Although *skinship* is formed in a manner similar to *kinship*, the apparent meaning of *skin* (that is, empathy and bonding) is not established among native English speakers.

Other *waseigo* words are *OL* (for "office lady"), a secretary; *salaryman*, a white-collar worker; *nighter*, a nighttime baseball game; *pushcase*, a flip-top box, such as one for cigarettes; and *Christ one-piece*, a cassock (the final element of which means "dress" when standing alone).

skosh *noun*, a small amount; a little bit: "This is a well-plotted, economical thriller. Although the beginning is a *skosh* slow, [the author] picks up the pace" (*Los Angeles Times*, June 21, 1987).

THE STORY: For openers, I give you a poem to the editor of *The Atlantic Monthly*, written by Word Watcher Stephen R. Cohen of New York City and published by the magazine in March 1988:

> *To use "skōsh"*
> *May not be gōsh,*
> *Though I sé*
> *'Twill soon be passé.*
> *A dictionary entry's absurd*
> *For many a nonce word.*

Sorry, Steve. Although your rhyme and meter are right on target, your sprachgefühl is a *skosh* off. This word has sustained more than enough currency over the years to remove it from the nonce class and place it in the mainstream. It was entered and defined in the third edition of *The American Heritage Dictionary* in 1992, albeit with a slang label there. Pronounced [skōsh], it is borrowed into English from the Japanese word *sukoshi*, meaning "a tiny amount." Its use in English goes back at least to the Korean War, during which the UN and American armed forces picked it up. Eric Partridge, in his *Dictionary of Slang and Unconventional English*, recorded the use of *skoshi*, meaning "a little," in a citation dated July 1953. (The term could be a corruption of the Japanese word *sukoshi*. In GI lingo, *skoshi* was further corrupted to *skoshie*, meaning "few/little.")

Skosh came to prominence through its use by Levi Strauss in print and broadcast ads dating at least to 1977. The company sent me an audiocassette called "Jogger," in which *skosh* was used that year by a mature male jogger, who, while on a run, stops briefly to explain why he likes to run in Levi's: "I get just a *skosh* more room where I need it," he says. And a citation from Tom Clancy's *Red Storm Rising* illustrates a new, prepositional use of the word: "O'Malley didn't have enough fuel to pursue. 'Stand by, Romeo, we're coming in *skosh* fuel. Five minutes out.' 'Roger that, we'll be ready for you.'"

snide *noun*, slyly disparaging character, tone, or outlook: "'Of course,' says Dorothy Sarnoff, an image consultant in New York, . . . 'I changed him [U.S. Senator Robert Dole]. He was the best student I ever had. A nice, nice man. I took away his *snide*'" (*Life*, September 1987).

THE STORY: "You want more *ugly?*" That use and the noun use of *snide* are particularly interesting examples of functional shift, chiefly because the shift from adjective to noun rarely occurs in print. The *Oxford English Dictionary* does, however, record noun usage of *snide* as far back as 1885, when it meant "counterfeit jewelry; a base coin." Other senses meaning variously "a base, contemptible person; a swindler, cheat, or liar" and "hypocrisy; pretense; malicious gossip" go back to 1874 and 1902, respectively.

The shift from adjective to noun was discussed at some length by Hans Marchand in his book *The Categories and Types of Present-Day English Word-Formation: A Synchronic-Diachronic Approach*. Marchand explained that most such changes involve elliptical constructions where the substantive (the noun) is absent but can always be readily supplied, as in *advisory* (an advisory + *report*), *facial* (a facial + *treatment*), *spectacular* (a spectacular + *production, performance, show*, or *program*), *local* (a local + *citizen*), and *hopeful* (a hopeful + *candidate*). He pointed out that "some of these elliptic expressions have gained complete independence from their original full syntagma basis, as is the case with *musical*. The word is no longer thought of as a shortening of *musical comedy*, but has become a substantive in its own right."

Still other examples, called "de-adjectivals" by Sir Randolph Quirk, are *natural, final, regular, comic, roast, perennial, annual, monthly, weekly*, and *daily*. The noun *cool*, as in "Don't lose your *cool*," is another close equivalent to Sarnoff's *snide*. With apologies to Bette Midler, it's just so *jive!*

spillite *noun*, extraneous light that spills over from a brightly illuminated area, such as a tennis court or a swimming pool, into other areas, such as a private yard, where the illumination is not wanted: "He [the owner of a tennis court situated in his yard] hired . . . experts [during a neighborhood controversy] who testified . . . that they had reduced the lighting '5 foot-candles lower' than most [tennis] courts. The experts swore neighbors would experience 'no *spillite*'" (*New York Times*, January 29, 1988).

THE STORY: Advocates of simplified, or phonetic, spellings such as *lite, brite, nite*, and *tonite* must have rejoiced at the sight of *spillite* on the pages of the *Times*. Such simplified spellings have never gained wholesale acceptance as standard variants—*lite* beer and beef, *brite* Christmas balls, and lively *niteries* notwithstanding. The fact that *spillite* is being used in a context involving legal process may result someday in its being entered in law databases and dictionaries, all of which is a big step toward possible entry in future editions of general dictionaries. This has not always been the case with *brite*, *lite*, *nite*, and *tonite*, and others in the same class, the use of which is generally restricted to product development, trade names, advertising, and intentionally slangy contexts.

In the case of *spillite*, the word has its ultimate origins in the film industry, where it denotes the excess light created by lamps that often *spill* beyond the area called for in a particular shot: "The task of the director of photography is to combine and control a multitude of lighting considerations to create a seemingly natural setting. The instruments of his trade include 2 k's, skypans, HMI's, chicken coops and zip lights. And with the use of barndoors, flags, scrims and C stands he can direct and contain unwanted elements such as '*spillite*'" (Gilbert Prowler, Mission Hills, Calif., letter to the editor, *The Atlantic Monthly*, April 30, 1988).

squeegee kid *noun*, *slang*, an inner-city youngster who attempts, uninvited, and for a tip, to wash the windshield of a car stopped in traffic, typically at an intersection or during a traffic jam: "The trouble with *squeegee kids* is that they're essentially extortionists. They never ask if you want your windshield squeegeed. They just march up and do it. Then they hang around the driver's window, trying to guilt-trip you into paying them. . . . It's hard not to be sympathetic with the *squeegee kids*. They're poor. They live in a tough part of town. And at least they're not dealing crack" (*Washington Post*, April 28, 1989).

THE STORY: That was six years ago. The story today is this: the *squeegee kids* of the eighties have "grown up," in a manner of speaking, into what is now called, in the parlance of New York City, at least, the *squeegee men* (or *guys* or *beggars*), some being as old as forty-seven. The existence of the term *squeegee man* indicates that squeegeeing has become a career path for some practitioners of the eighties and that other people, driven by inner-city decay and a decaying economy nationwide, have taken it up in desperation.

On September 26, 1993, the *New York Times* said this: "The *squeegee men* who rise up across the windshield at stop lights may be among the most addiction-addled New Yorkers, but even they are noticing themselves being denounced in this season's mayoral campaign speeches as they hustle on the dank urban cusp between plain begging and outright intimidation." *Squeegee men* can be classed into three groups: burned-out addicts and alcoholics, who will usually retreat meekly when flagged off by irritated motorists; generally friendly people, who, if given the chance, will clean a grimy windshield effectively; and intimidators, who break or bend wipers, smear windshields with filth, and frighten motorists.

Back in 1989, I reviewed twenty-nine citations for *squeegee kid*. The evidence at hand indicated that the squeegee phenomenon began in Baltimore in 1985. The practice was dangerous for all. During the eighties, one youngster was run over by an eighteen-wheeler as he darted onto an expressway to do a window. New York City in the nineties could learn a bit from the Baltimore experience. Baltimore established specific sites, called *Squeegee Stations*, where the kids could operate in relative safety; this strategy also permitted the motorists a measure of choice, for signs reading "*Squeegee Kids Ahead, Move to Right, Contributions Accepted*" were erected near these newly licensed stations. The kids were issued ID cards with photos and numbers, and were given lessons in common courtesy. The strategy worked well with some, but not always with others, who moved their business back into traffic.

Clearly, the *squeegee kid*-grown-into-the-*squeegee man* is a matter of concern, especially to the so-called *Kojak Liberals* and others who will have to deal with the so-called *broken windows syndrome* of our urban society. See also *Kojak Liberal*.

street triage *noun*, a process for sorting the newly and the chronically homeless into groups, based on their likely benefit from concentrated care and training, especially in private shelters. Also called *creaming*: "*Street Triage*: A San Diego Shelter Feeds the Homeless with an Uneven Hand: For Newly Indigent, There Is Swordfish and Manicures; Others Get Soup and a Cot" (headline, *Wall Street Journal*, February 18, 1992).

THE STORY: *Street triage* seems to be catching on at some shelters across the country. The paradigm is St. Vincent de Paul Village in San Diego, California, run by Father Joe Carroll. This 500-bed facility is divided into two units, one with 300 beds that is reserved for the newly homeless who exhibit potential for reentry into productive society, and the other for the chronically homeless—the alcoholics, the drug addicts, the mentally ill. Newly homeless clients must be recommended by a church, a community group, or members of the shelter's staff. If accepted, these clients enjoy gourmet food, semiprivate rooms, round-the-clock access to the shelter, cable TV, beauty and barber services, plus required courses in such things as résumé writing and budgeting.

superfluous father syndrome *noun*, a complex of social, psychological, learning, emotional, and economic problems seen in children of fathers whose parental roles have been undercut or obviated, especially because of the loss of inner-city jobs and an increased reliance on welfare: "The *super-fluous' father syndrome* is creeping up the socioeconomic scale to embrace people who have never been out of work or on welfare" (William James Raspberry, *Washington Post*, March 9, 1994).

THE STORY: Strengthening the two-parent family is the key, it is believed by many, to erasure of the sociopsychoeconomic ills of the nineties, ills that portend tragedy in the society of the twenty-first century. Certainly, many children are not merely *at-risk* (a cliché that began in the eighties); they are now being described as *beyond risk*. According to Don E. Eberly, who has launched the National Fatherhood Initiative, and who spoke with Raspberry, "The correlation between the absence of fathers and every single social problem . . . is dramatic, absolutely dramatic. The rise in welfare dependency and the steep increase in child poverty are explained by the emergence of father-less households."

More frightening, even, is the growing cultural idea that fathers are marginally, if at all, important in the nurturing of children, an astonishing notion, indeed, when one considers that fathers in the nineties generally seem to want to play an active, nurturing role in the lives of their children, particularly when they realize their crucial role in the rearing and socializing of adolescent boys.

Eberly's colleague David Blankenhorn coined the term *superfluous father*, according to Raspberry. It is parallel in linguistic structure to the famous *superfluous man* of the nineteenth-century Russian novelist Ivan Turgenev. The term was popularized by his 1850 work *The Diary of a Superfluous Man*, which developed the theme of humiliated human dignity in a manner reminiscent of Gogol and Dostoyevsky.

The opposite number of *superfluous father syndrome*, one called the *Frankenstein syndrome*, emerged late in 1993. It denotes the test-tube impregnation of older women: "A 59-year-old British woman, who was artificially impregnated with eggs from a younger woman, gave birth to twins . . . , becoming the oldest woman on record to have a child. . . . The case 'bordered on the *Frankenstein syndrome*,' said Dr. John Marks, the former chairman of the British Medical Association's ethics committee. He added that the woman would be 69 when her children were 10 years old" (Associated Press, December 28, 1993). These two syndromes join several others, all relating to the family and all quite negative: *battered child syndrome, battered wife syndrome, battering parent syndrome,* and *sudden infant death syndrome.*

swive *verb,* to have sex with: "In the illuminist days of the Grand Tour, the British traveller abroad was aristocratic, typified by the brutish milord who *swived* chambermaids and made 'native' a pejorative term" (*The Independent* [London], January 11, 1991).

THE STORY: Jonathon Green's *Slang Thesaurus,* usually a fecund source for everything imaginable and unimaginable, lists 139 synonyms and idioms for *copulate. Swive,* however, isn't in there. Nor does *swive* appear in any of the four major American collegiate dictionaries. It does appear, labeled variously *obsolete* and *archaic,* in the *Oxford English Dictionary, Webster's Third New International Dictionary,* and the *Random House Dictionary of the English Language, Second Unabridged Edition.* It is of interest to watchers of the changing language because these temporal labels may have to be removed: the word seems to be undergoing a renaissance in usage. Four citations in addition to the one given at the outset have surfaced for *swive,* these appearing from 1978 to 1991 in the *Manchester Guardian Weekly,* the *Chicago Tribune,* the *New York Times,* and *National Review.*

The transitive sense of *swive* dates at least to 1386, when Chaucer used it in "The Miller's Tale." (The inflected forms of the verb are *swives, swived,* and *swiving.*) *Swive* goes back to the Middle English word *swiven,* which in turn came from the Old English term *swifan,* "to revolve, sweep, or wend." The agent noun, now spelled *swiver,* goes back to about 1440, when it was written *swywer.*

A citation for *swiver* surfaced in an August 31, 1978, article by Joseph McLellan in the *Washington Post* titled "John Barth for Semidemigodhood Society for the Celebration of Barthomania": "The final phrase (which apparently represents Barth's latest judgment on his unusual fan club) was intoned by the presiding officer, who is officially known as *Swiver-*in-chief. Other officers include the Tender of the Turnstyle, who does odd jobs, and the Keeper of the Eggplant, who keeps the nonbiodegradable eggplant, symbol of the society."

tract mansion *noun*, a luxury home measuring no less than 12,000 square feet, situated in an exclusive development. Also called *megahouse*; *spec house*: "The number of luxury-housing developments, subdivisions of 20 to 100 or more so-called *tract mansions* with prices approaching the $1 million mark, has sharply increased in the last several years" (*Washington Post*).

THE STORY: *Tract house*, a well-established English term, defined as "one of numerous houses of similar or complementary design constructed on a tract of land," connotes neither opulence nor great size. Specifically, when one contemplates a *tract house*, one does not immediately think of fourteen miles of interior wiring, a six-car garage, or an antique chandelier from the Vatican. On the other hand, *tract mansion* conjures visions of all this, and more.

According to a May 20, 1987, article in the *Wall Street Journal*, construction of *tract mansions* began in the early 1980s, when "the forces of new money and conspicuous consumption . . . united . . . to create a new breed of house that puts Tara to shame." These mansions, built in that decade by real estate tycoons even before buyers had been secured, reflected the taste and expectations of enormously wealthy people who believed that Colossal meant Arrival. A great number of *tract mansions* were bought by CEOs of huge corporations, by the corporations themselves as *company homes*, by successful entrepreneurs, and by other real estate agents. A typical *tract mansion* of the era was not contemporary in design; rather, the style varied from brick Colonial to Tudor to Mediterranean stucco to Gothic-cum-gargoyles. The mansions could have as many as five floors connected by elevators, not to mention grandiose staircases. Other popular accents were marble foyers; soaring cathedral ceilings; dining rooms equipped for banquet serving; living rooms the size of basketball courts; master bedrooms with his and her bathrooms and dressing rooms—each equipped with a fireplace and wine rack; and poolside spas with wet bars and waterfalls.

Some *tract mansions* came fully decorated and furnished, right down to the linen, china, silver, and crystal. But according to the *Wall Street Journal*, the real signature of the *tract mansion* was its use of antique accessories: the garbage disposal in one such house was embedded in an antique butler's table.

vogueing *noun*, *slang*, an ostentatious, stylized, posturing dance affected in imitation of the characteristic strutting moves and haughty gazes of runway models during fashion shows: "It's called *vogueing* and if you've never heard of it, you're not alone. It's New York. *Very* New York" (*USA Today*, March 30, 1989).

THE STORY: The now obsolete verb *vogue*, meaning "to play (someone or something) up or down," goes back to the year 1661; in the sense "to bring into or keep in vogue," it dates to 1687. The *-ing* form illustrated here, itself separately derived from the title of the fashion magazine *Vogue*, goes back only as far as the 1960s, when the dance was first observed in the Harlem clubs named for couture houses—clubs that first sprang up among young people as alternatives to street gangs. The art of the *voguer* in this context imitated the life and the persona of a greatly admired symbol such as a beauty queen or a high-fashion model.

The dance, described in a May 29, 1989, *People* story as "[a combination] of break-dancing bravado, Jane Fonda aerobics and the high-style gestures of a Christian Lacroix model elaborately posing on a runway to the beat of Madonna," enjoyed a resurgence in popularity in the mid-1980s, having been revived by African-Americans and Hispanics in the gay and transvestite uptown clubs. *Vogueing* then took to the downtown nightspots and was performed on certain television programs. It is performed by elaborately attired and coiffed teams called *houses*, these too named for couture establishments. At the time of the 1989 *USA Today* story, the phenomenon had not yet reached Los Angeles, according to David Depino, Tracks deejay and "senator" at the House of Extravaganza: "L.A.'s too far behind the times for this. You know, when it gets to L.A., it's already over." And at this writing, it's definitely over, just like the *lambada*.

wallyo *noun, slang,* a young man; a fellow, usually of Italian descent: "I swung open the heavy glass doors. Everywhere I looked was marble and the Great Food hush. I wanted to back out and get a steak and *pommes frites*, but it was too late. I had been seen by the *wallyo* and the madame in the black jeweled sweater" (Julie Baumgold, *New York*, November 2, 1987).

THE STORY: This colloquialism, often heard in communities with large Italian populations, is a phonetic respelling into English of the Neapolitan *guaglione*, meaning "street urchin; corner boy." (In the *New York* citation taken from an article titled "Mr. Peepers in Paris: Le Hot Center," *wallyo* referred to a Parisian wine steward, however.)

Although some etymologists point to the French *voyou*, "street bum; urchin," from *voie*, "street; road," as the root of *wallyo*, Luigi Ballerini, Ph.D., the director of New York University's Department of French and Italian, disagrees. Ballerini firmly believes, as do I, that the ultimate origin of *guaglione*—the source of *wallyo*—is the Latin *ganeo, ganeonis*, "a dissolute man; a frequenter of disreputable inns." If this is indeed so, then the linguistic process of *amelioration* has occurred during the word's development from Latin to Italian to English, for, according to Robert Chapman's *New Dictionary of American Slang* and other sources, *wallyo* is not used pejoratively. Rather, it is used affectionately, somewhat in the same manner as "young squirt." (Amelioration is the process by which a word originally having a pejorative or negative meaning takes on a positive or neutral meaning.) Ballerini has added that *"Guaglione"* is the title of a popular 1950s Italian tune in which a young man with a crush on a girl is discouraged from further pursuit of her because of his tender age, a factor that has rendered him more suitable for soccer than for romance, thence marriage.

Robert W. Creamer, formerly a senior editor at *Sports Illustrated* and an *American Heritage Dictionary* usage panelist, who went to school in Tuckahoe, New York, and to college at Fordham University, knew *wallyo* (also spelled *guaglio*) from those days in his life. In his circle of friends and acquaintances, it meant "buddy," "pal," or "guy," the equivalent of "Mac" or "Jack" in expressions like "Hey, *wallyo*! Which way to the subway station?" This usage parallels the use of *guaglio* in southern Italy, where it is applied— affectionately and familiarly—to grown men, and where it also means "waiter." In places like Basilicata (Lucania), Apulia, and Calabria, the phrase *Eiu, guaglio!*—in English, "Hey, boy!"—is used in calling a waiter to the table, with offense neither offered nor taken. All this came to me in a letter from Gregory McNamee of Tucson, Arizona, who "learned vernacular Italian in the rural province of Basilicata and embarrassed [himself] roundly in Rome by summoning a waiter so; the whole restaurant fell into a shocked silence like that in those annoying stock-brokerage ads, and service declined considerably" (personal correspondence, May 24, 1988).

Obviously, amelioration of the term has not reached Rome. Nor has it occurred in another Italian word commonly heard in English. That word is *ginzaloon*, and it is deemed offensive. Lexicographers often gang up queries to specialists, and so when I was studying *wallyo*, I asked Professor Ballerini to tackle *ginzaloon* at the same time. *Ginzaloon*, defined as "a tough street Italian," came to my attention in this citation: "There is still a trace of the *ginzaloon* in [the then–New York district attorney Rudolph] Giuliani" (Sergeant Michael Verde, quoted in the August 1987 issue of *Vanity Fair*). Ballerini feels sure that the first element of this word was derived from the ethnic slur *guinea*, perhaps via the forms *ginzo*, *guinzo*, which mean the same thing. "As for the suffix *-loon*," Ballerini said, "it is used either by analogy with *macaroon*, *pantaloon*, etc. (*pantaloon* being originally a mask of the Commedia dell'arte, and *pantalone*, meaning 'a braggart') or [it] is akin to the English *loon*, *loony*." English *loon* has had the meanings "a worthless person; a scamp," since 1490; "a man of low birth," since 1535; "a boy," since 1560; "a man; a chap," since 1590; and "a boor," since 1619. Though this historical progression of senses suggests that the English word is the source of the final element of *ginzaloon*, the real story still remains a mystery.

WASP Rot Syndrome *noun*, a distinct decline in the economic, political, social, and intellectual hegemony once enjoyed by America's privileged social class descended chiefly from the early European settlers, marked in the progeny of this class by a slow erosion of energy, ambition, accrued wealth, academic accomplishments, and social responsibility: "I have a confession: My family has a social disease. I call it *WASP Rot Syndrome*. . . . [K]nowing first-hand about *WASP Rot* is why the defeat of the handsome clubman George Bush did not surprise me" (Abigail Trafford, *Washington Post*, February 21, 1993).

THE STORY: *WASP Rot* as a malady without nomenclature came to my attention during the Christmas holidays of 1991 while in an affluent county in Connecticut. Over cocktails I (a WASP, the Russian surname notwithstanding) asked another WASP (a physician whose family has made a point of Thinsulating itself from every social disease except *affluenza*) if perchance he had heard about the recently unemployed two-career white-collar breadwinners in New Hampshire and Vermont who had had to resort to gravedigging that winter in order to feed their families, a news story of considerable significance in the New England area at the time. With an expression of total ennui and complete indifference, he murmured, "Oh. I hadn't heard." Since further imposition of the issue gained little or no reaction from him, I dropped the subject, but thought at the time, "There must be a word for people like you."

Then two years later came Abigail Trafford's *Washington Post* article titled "The *Wasp Rot* Chronicles: How the American Upper Crust Crumbled." Trafford is the coiner of *WASP Rot Syndrome* and the editor of the Health section of the *Post*. The citation for the syndrome that is given at the outset is the first occurrence of it in print. She first used *WASP Rot* in her 1982 book *Crazy Time: Surviving Divorce and Building a New Life*, now in its 1992 revised edition. In *Crazy Time*, the term appears with reference to the malady of a character named Austin van Elder: "Austin doesn't know what he wants to do. His father is an overbearing and unsuccessful stockbroker. His mother drinks. Despite the glamour of nannies and summer places, the family has *Wasp Rot*—the slow erosion of trust funds, Scholastic Aptitude Test scores and ambition." The *Founding WASPs* were judges, tycoons, and administrators, said Trafford; today's *WASP Rotters* prefer to be day laborers or drummers. Or they prefer simply to tune out of the stark reality of society in the nineties. Early WASPs sat on charity boards in the city, said Trafford; today's *WASP Rotters* prefer to live in cabins in the woods.

Several etiologies of *WASP Rot Syndrome* have been suggested by the coiner and others studying the phenomenon. Among them are the social exclusivity enforced by early-twentieth-century WASPs that precluded an infusion of new blood and new ideas; a slowly developing torpor that encouraged later generations to rely on the income from trust funds rather than generate new capital of their own; a rarefied snobbishness that served to validate the view that vocations such as politics are "dirty"; a self-absorption that quenched concerns about the problems of the needy, thereby obviating the WASPs' tradition of contributing actively to charitable causes; a deterioration of rectitude and attention to ethics that resulted in wimpish undirectedness; a denial of and disdain for the raw drive, bold ambition, and risk-taking characteristic of the *Founding WASPs*, combined with the emerging excuse that, in any case, the progeny would be incapable of matching or exceeding the successes of the ancestry; and finally, "the revolt of the WASP women" on whose talents, energies, and sacrifices the great successes of the old-line families once depended. See also *affluenza*, CWASP.

white-bread *adjective*, bland, homogenized, and conservative: "They believe in a strong defense, a robust anti-Communism, a two-fisted Israel, covert operations, a dismantling of minority programs, a skedaddling of feminism—a return to *white-bread* elitism" (James Wolcott, *Vanity Fair*, June 1987).

THE STORY: This adjectival extension of the noun *white bread* is similar to the familiar *meat-and-potatoes* (a *meat-and-potatoes* approach to diplomacy), *bread-and-butter* (*bread-and-butter* political issues), and *corn pone* (*cornpone* humor). It is also an example of the productivity of the word *white* in compounding: *white book*, *white-collar*, *white elephant*, *white heat*, *white list*, *white noise*, *white paper*, *white squire*, and *whitewash* are but a few familiar examples.

But *white-bread* is semantically closer to the newer *white-leather* (California's *white-leather* sofa crowd) and *white-belt* (an aging *white-belt* sales executive).

Employed as a freestanding noun, *white bread* in this figurative use by the *Washington Post*'s West Coast social critic still connotes the low roughage and negligible food value of the bread itself: "Well, the week after the Tower Commission report was released, I was . . . thinking: 'This Whole Iran Thing has gotten out of hand. What this country needs is a bit of my analytic style.' I figured America had been Feeling Good About Itself long enough; the *white bread* of a Positive Mental Attitude needed a bit of my yeast. The Beltway needed to tighten its belt" (Ian Shoales, *Washington Post*, June 7, 1987). An analogue to *white-bread* is, of course, *vanilla*, defined as "unoriginal, uninspiring, and unexciting" (*vanilla* software).

wigger also **whigger** *noun, offensive slang*, a young white urban teenager who identifies with the culture and affects the mannerisms of speech and style of the hip-hop generation. Also called *poser; wannabe; wannabe black; yo-boy:* "'They're black to be cool,' she [Traci Williams, an African-American teenager] says. . . . She limps around the asphalt, parodying the street strut affected by white kids she knows. 'I say, "Get out of my face, you're a *wigger*"'" (*Washington Post*, July 20, 1992).

THE STORY: The story surrounding *wigger*, simply put, is the MTV Generation's variation on the theme of the Jazz Age and, later, Motown. The culture and the voice of the *hip-hoppers* have been so powerful that some of the words associated with them have gained entry in *The American Heritage Dictionary of the English Language, Third Edition*. Examples are *'burb, 'hood, home boy, high-five, body popping, yo,* and *hip-hop* itself.

This is also a story about the power of rap, which has eclipsed many other genres in the youth culture. The story unfolded at a time when, according to the *Washington Post*, "the tension surrounding racial discourse burn[ed] at a high flame—the year of David Duke, Rodney King, and Sister Souljah." Conflicting reasons for the *wigger* phenomenon abound. From the kids we learned these things: African Americans are tough; they are good in athletics; they're good dancers. The whites are caricaturing them: they're raised in affluent, exclusive, exclusionary white suburbs and don't want to be thought of as wimps, so they affect hip-hop macho. From adult observers came these thoughts: The kids are becoming more multicultural. They *are* involved in caricature. MTV has penetrated forever the white, upper-class suburbs with the blunt messages of rap. Rap stars—black and white—are seen as symbols of virility. Some kids simply copycat their African-American friends. It's about Attitude.

All these diverse opinions notwithstanding, another phenomenon, this one linguistic, is in play here. It relates to the functional shift of the interjection *yo*, as seen in the noun compound *yo-boy*. This new adjectival use of *yo* is particularly apparent in a sentence from an interview with an unidentified girlfriend of a high school girl whose boyfriend is clearly a *wigger*: "'He's cute, but he's too *yo*'" (*Washington Post*).

Xer *noun*, a member of the generation born after 1960, especially a person who is between the ages of nineteen and twenty-nine, characterized variously as practical and hardworking; unsettled and bewildered; in constant need of stimulus and feedback because of constant exposure to myriad electronic media in childhood; and often skeptical of and discontented with the driven self-absorption of the previous generation. Also called *Baby Buster*; *Buster*; *slacker*; *twentysomething*; *Yiffie*: "*Xers* are obsessed with the houses they can't afford, and instead of engaging with the world, they retreat: either mooching off Mom and Dad or marginalizing themselves in . . . 'McJobs'—'low-dignity, low-benefit, no future' positions in the service industry" (*New York Newsday*, November 17, 1991). "Here come the *Yiffies*! The arrival of the *Baby Busters* in the work place is enough to make you want to live into the 21st century, just to see how it all turns out. . . . In 1980, the driven 'Yuppie' set the style. This time around, *Fortune* found not just new people—*YIFFies* are 'young, individualistic, freedom-minded and few'—but new attitudes as well" (Jim Wright, *Dallas Morning News*, January 20, 1991). "Let's examine a recent example of the ways the stereotype is used against the young: the cover of the February 1994 anniversary issue of the New Yorker. There, an archetypal *X-er*—a young, witless, bepimpled hip-hopper with ears pierced and a baseball cap on backwards—reads a handbill for a Times Square sex show. . . . The message: Seattle grunge bands, Beavis and Butthead and their friends have taken over American culture" (Douglas Brinkley, Education Review section, *Washington Post*, April 3, 1994).

THE STORY: "I wish I could tell you more about these purple-haired people that I expect you to take so seriously, but there is still a lot we don't know about them. And what we do know does not console [us]. It is a fragmented generation in just about every way," said McCann-Erickson vice-president and director of media services Karen Ritchie to the RAB board in the spring of 1992, quoted in the November 12, 1993, issue of *Radio & Records*.

I felt the same way when, as far back as the end of 1989, reporters began calling me, asking what I thought the name for the new generation of the twenty-first century would be. At that time, I dubbed it "The Brown Paper Bag Generation," very generic because the people it denoted had not yet displayed any identifying characteristics. As of this writing, critics still cannot seem to agree on a set of identifiers—characteristics or names. Two of the latest submissions, aside from *Generation X*, have been *The Angry Generation*—suggested by some George Mason University fans of the late Nirvana singer Kurt Cobain, whose 1994 suicide spoke for that generation's despair—and *The Blank Generation*.

Generation X, the most well known term because of its proliferation by the media, is the precursor of *Xer*. *Generation X* was used by Canadian public-opinion pollster Allan Gregg in a speech about the baby bust. In the speech, Gregg borrowed the name of Billy Idol's former band, Generation X. Idol most probably got it from *Generation X*, the title of a 1965 self-improvement manual for young adults by British educators Charles Hamblett and Jane Deverson. In one of the many small ironies involving language, X had originally been intended to refer to the children of the sixties; instead, it came to be used by those very children of their *own* kids.

It was left to Douglas Coupland, the Canadian author and cartoonist (aged twenty-nine in 1991), to use the term in a comic strip for a monthly business magazine. In the strip he depicted a generation trapped in dead-end jobs, resentful of the baby boomers, and believing itself a lot smarter than its elders. Coupland followed this up with a novel titled *Generation X: Tales for an Accelerated Culture* (1991). This novel, which tells of three friends marooned in Palm Springs, contains a glossary of terms used by or befitting *Xers* and their attitudes, some of them these: *bleeding ponytail* (an elderly baby boomer who longs for his hippy youth), *air family* (the false sense of community and esprit de corps in a conventional office environment), *veal-fattening pen* (a fabric-coated, easily disassembled office cubicle assigned to junior staffers in a corporate environment), and *down-nesting* (the growing trend of parents to move into smaller abodes to preclude return of their adult children—the ones aged twenty to twenty-nine in particular). Other terminology used by *Xers*, terminology that in and of itself self-defines their attitudes, are these, taken from "Trash That Baby Boom," an article by Ian Williams in the January 2, 1994, issue of the *Washington Post Magazine*, and you don't need definitions to catch the Zeitgeist: the *MTV Video Fight Syndrome, sullen, non-user-friendly, fatalism, boomers' hypocrisy,* the *Bryan Adams "Summer of '69" Syndrome,* maelstrom of video input, family dissolution, sensitive crap detectors, the *cultivation of the absurd, yeah, whatever,* and the *Christa McAuliffe Spring Break Syndrome.*

In an article titled "*Generation X:* The Truth Behind the *Baby Busters,*" John Parikhal, the CEO of Joint Communications, a consulting firm that specializes in custom market research, said in the October 22, 1993, issue of *Radio & Records* that the so-called *Xers* don't even think of themselves as a generation, that the name for them is basically a creation of the media, and that the choice of a name to begin with is nothing more than an attempt to continue the practice of labeling as "generations" all groups separated from one another by fifteen years—a naming practice popularized by such pre-existing terminology as *The Lost Generation, The Silent Generation,* and *The Beat Generation.*

Parikhal made the point that the members of the group at issue grew up, by and large, with two working parents, a factor that makes them seek "families by association," and makes them "family-hungry." They are also bereft of faith. As Ian Williams put it, "Have you ever lived in a time when you felt America was on the right path, heading in the right direction, with a wonderful future? With few exceptions, anyone born after 1960 cannot."

The entire generational period from 1961 to 1981, in which the *Xers* are a subclass, has been dubbed the period of the *Thirteeners,* also styled *13ers.* The terminology comes from the fact that this is the thirteenth generation after the American Revolution. Bill Strauss and Neil Howe, the authors of *13th-GEN: Abort, Retry, Ignore, Fail?* (1993), characterized the *Thirteeners,* and thereby the *Xers,* as follows: "*Thirteeners* see life from the outside in (results first, meaning later), rather than from the inside out, which is the Boomer habit. . . . *Thirteeners* also focus on the present because they have no idea what the future will bring. . . . Having grown up with one broken promise after another (families, schools, job markets), *Thirteeners* want only realistic commitments. . . . *Thirteeners* have had it with corporate bombast and bossy Boomers telling them what to do" (*New York Times,* September 26, 1993).

Clearly, there will be a conflict in future years between the members of *Generation X* and those who class themselves as *Generation E.* And until the boomers "release the choke hold they have on American culture" (Ian

Williams), that conflict will be tripartite. See also *boomerang baby*, *dink*, *Generation E*, *zoomer*.

zero-parent *adjective*, of, relating to, or being a family or child with parents who have been killed or jailed or who have simply disappeared: "With rare exceptions, two-parent families are good for children, one-parent families are bad, and *zero-parent* families are horrible" (William James Raspberry, *Washington Post*, August 8, 1990).

THE STORY: If you read that definition in vacuo, you might think that the children spoken of reside in a war- or revolution-torn area—Bosnia or Somalia, for instance. But not here. After all, this is America. It is therefore a terrifying indictment of American society that the term *zero-parent* was coined to denote young children in what was once known as the "Land of Opportunity."

It was even more terrifying to learn that, during the presidential election campaign of 1992, the nation's attention was being focused almost entirely on place-mat terms such as *family values*, on the definition of the very word *family*, and on the usage by then–Vice President Quayle of *Murphy Brown* as a generic descriptor of single mothers. All this, and more, while an entirely new generation of societal orphans was virtually ignored.

And here's the "more." Here's former First Lady Barbara Bush, speaking in August of 1990 at the Republican National Convention, defining for the nation the word *family*:

> We have met so many different families, and yet they really aren't so very different. As in our family, as in American families everywhere, the parents we've met are determined to teach their children integrity, strength, responsibility, courage, sharing, love of God and pride in being an American. . . . However *you* [emphasis as heard in the speech] define family, that's what we mean by family values. . . . You know, to us family means putting your arms around each other, and being there.

With apologies to Thomas De Quincey and to no other, listen thou, milady, to the sighs of orphans and drink the tears of the *zero-parent* children. In your speech; you conjured the image of tiny, spindly, underfed arms entwined. And in that speech, you defined not *family* or *family values* but the ethos that spawns *WASP Rot Syndrome*.

The March 30, 1992, issue of the *Daily Report Card* of the American Political Network, Inc., revealed the specific result of the *zero-parent* phenomenon, whose ultimate causes, as suggested in the definition, are drugs, alcohol, and murder: the emergence of "a new breed of American orphans," urban children who are, in effect, doomed to be shuttled endlessly in a state of dislocation to and from the homes of relatives, neighbors, and strangers. In fact, with at least 2.8 million children categorized by the U.S. Census Bureau as parentless as far back as 1980, the *zero-parent* family is now seen as replacing the single-parent family as "the emblem of social distress."

U.S. senator Daniel Patrick Moynihan predicted the acuteness of this problem in a paper written in 1989. He pointed out that the pervasive use of crack cocaine would have the same effect on the children of this country as the TB, diphtheria, and flu epidemics had in the past; that is to say, he predicted that by necessity, a special system of orphanages like those of the nineteenth and early twentieth centuries would have to be built in the twenty-first century or earlier in order to care for the *zero-parent* children. Today, some experts are recommending just that. First Lady Hillary Rodham Clinton stated in 1994 that the statistics on "our most vulnerable citizens," to use the words of a Carnegie Corporation report, outline an "appalling portrait of America's children," 30 percent of whom now have unmarried parents, 25 percent of whom live in poverty, and all of whom, to quote the April 25, 1994, issue of *U.S. News & World Report*, "have become the stuffed animals in the playpen of American politics."

An early lexical warning of this crisis appeared in the mid-1980s with the sudden emergence in print of the term *boarder baby*, for which sufficient citational evidence was accrued to warrant its entry in the 1992 third edition of *The American Heritage Dictionary of the English Language*. A *boarder baby* may be defined as "an infant, often the offspring of AIDS victims or drug addicts, who remains for weeks, months, sometimes up to a year or more, at the hospital of birth, awaiting placement in a home." A study commissioned by the Department of Health and Human Services, forwarded to Congress in November of 1993, reported that there are now 22,000 *boarder babies* in the United States. See also *WASP Rot Syndrome*.

zoomer *noun, slang,* a person, typically between twenty-five and thirty-four years of age or much older, who returns to college after an interruption to complete an undergraduate or graduate degree program: "The *zoomer* phenomenon has created a potential student body that hasn't been picked to the bone by aggressive recruiters and changing demographics. . . . *Zoomers* encompass a wide variety of backgrounds and motivations" (*Washington Post*, February 10, 1989).

THE STORY: Generational naming—*Xers, domos, dinks, NIMBYs,* for instance—has been a linguistic trend in the past fifteen years. Now comes *zoomer,* a word at the end of the alphabet but denoting people engaged in fast-paced catch-up ball. A major trend in college admissions has been the return of the adult, or nontraditional, student, with the number of traditional students, typically aged eighteen to twenty-two, sharply declining because of the baby bust of the late 1960s and 1970s. According to the *Washington Post,* 40 percent of the 10.6 million undergraduates enrolled in U.S. colleges were, in the eighties, older than twenty-five; of these, two thirds (or almost 3 million) were pursuing a degree after "graduatus interruptus."

Zoomers can be broken down into three major groups: young adults (aged twenty-five to thirty-four and constituting 56 percent of the whole), mid-career adults taking advantage of employee education assistance programs, and older adults or seniors whose familial responsibilities have been markedly reduced by *empty-nesting* and whose discretionary incomes permit them to return to academe. Reasons for their resumption of college-degree programs include a desire to compete more effectively for job advancement; career changes demanding further, more specialized, education (a sign of the times in the nineties); and the satisfaction of having the opportunity to finish something started earlier on in life. The *zoomers'* needs are being met by colleges in a variety of ways, including enhanced extension and continuing-education programs, independent study, life-experience credits in some curricula, telephone conferencing with professors, and more flexible class scheduling.

The word *zoomer,* most probably influenced in its formation by *boomer,* is a clipped phonetic respelling of and derivation from the word *resume.* See also *domo, Xer.*

2

The Words of
Our Disorders

acquired uncombable hair
adolescent medicine
agita
air epidemiology
Begin amputation
casino feet
emporiatrics
fifth disease
gephyrophobia
hedonia hypothesis
holiday heart
horrenderoma
insurance technician
isopraxism
jogger's paw
kangaroo care

lovemap
mouse terrorism
myc
neomort
off the grid
Paris Lip
pharming
pizza-cutter's palsy
'roid rage
softgel
Thucydides syndrome
universal reactor
urgicenter
wallet biopsy
white coat hypertension
Xenomouse

Words are the physicians of a mind diseased.
—Aeschylus (525–456 B.C.), *Prometheus*

Medicine is all the fashion . . . these days.
—Jean-Jacques Rousseau, *Émile* (1762)

A doctor saves lives—it's up to people to create lives
that are worth saving.
—Philip Gold, immunologist (1974)

If the "interest in disease . . . is only another expression of interest in life," as Thomas Mann put it in *The Magic Mountain*, then the language of medicine and malady, as it is touched briefly upon in this chapter, represents in its very expressivity the major issues and trends of our lives in these times.

Here we treat matters of the human psyche and behaviors: at *gephyrophobia*, for instance, no fewer than 176 other phobias could have been charted, with their very existence being an indicator of the angst that causes the *agita*. *Hedonia hypothesis*, a coinage representing the work of a Boston College neuropsychologist, explains in the blink of an eye the possible stress thresholds of Saddam Hussein, George Bush, Ross Perot, and Bill Clinton. *Isopraxism*, a phantom *-ism*, may represent some clues to the underlying cause of mass behaviors—the big migrations, the adoption of fads, the hysteria and the panics, and, yes, the violence. *Lovemap* explores the back alleys of human sexuality, and *white coat hypertension* explains, to me, at least, why I kicked and bit a nurse forty-four years ago in a country doctor's office (if Daddy had only understood the cause, I might not have been punished).

The chapter looks into some of the maladies associated with lifestyles—*holiday heart* and *'roid rage*. Even the dogs get their day at *jogger's paw*. Workplace-related maladies like *casino feet* and *pizza-cutter's palsy* are diagnosed, and the fad *Paris Lip* is defined for immediate posterity (for it may be liposuctioned from the language soon). A frozen-in-time section of the vocabulary of research and genetics is to be viewed at *mouse terrorism*, *myc*, *neomort*, *pharming*, and *Xenomouse*, where the main focus is really on the medical and genetic ethics of genetic engineering.

The affluenza of the twentieth century may have brought *adolescent medicine* to the point of board certification; if not only that, the drug culture and the threat of sexually transmitted disease helped. Add to this new subspecialty *fifth disease* and *kangaroo care*.

Thucydides syndrome sheds some light on the reasons for the plague of Athens, and *air epidemiology* represents a measure of the actuarial frustration among epidemiologists in tracking AIDS statistics. *Softgel* harkens to the tampering crimes of the eighties but shows that out of most negatives a positive polarity can emerge—in this case, a better way of configuring an oral medication.

On the eve of the twenty-first century in a world where the basics of public health either have not been achieved or have regressed to rudimentary stages, as in the former Soviet Union, the fearless traveler contemplating a foray to such climes might consider boning up on the *emporiatrician's* art—*emporiatrics*, the etymology of which is given in the words of the physician who hates the word—and was chiefly responsible for proliferating it.

Horrenderoma gives you a lexical CAT scan of a medical slang term associated with another scourge of American and world health—cancer. It, and *wallet biopsy*, have a sardonic edge unique to a field that has a daily rendezvous with death. Sometimes laughter is the best medicine, when all else fails.

But the single most expressive term in the chapter—expressive in its very bureaucratese—is the innocuous-sounding *insurance technician* . . . the term nobody in the health-insurance business wanted to talk to me about. Every patient entering a hospital needs to know what *insurance technician* means, in terms of managed care. This single term authenticates a point made a little more than thirty years ago by Emmett M. Hall, M.D., of the Royal Commission on Health Services in Canada: "As we examined the hundreds of briefs with their thousands of recommendations we were impressed with the fact that the field of health services illustrates, perhaps better than any other, the paradox of our age, which is, of course, the enormous gap between our scientific knowledge and skills, on the one hand, and our organizations and financial arrangements to apply them to the needs of men, on the other." His words might have been spoken by those attempting to reform health care and control health-care delivery costs in the United States in 1994–95.

Though Ibycus (fl. ca. 550 B.C.) was correct when he remarked, "You cannot find a medicine for life," especially in these complex, troubling times, you can, in this chapter, find a medical word-reminder of just about every major aspect or issue of the last decade.

acquired uncombable hair *noun*, a condition in which a patient grows coarse, dry, blond or light brown hair that stands straight out in a disorderly way and is impervious to attempts at grooming. Also called *spun glass hair* and technically *pili trianguli et canaliculi*: "Imagine if *every* day were a bad-hair day. That apparently is the case for a 39-year-old woman thought to be the first documented victim of '*acquired uncombable hair*'" (*Washington Post*, March 29, 1994).

THE STORY: As if we didn't have enough to worry about in terms of health. Here comes a new problem and a clutch of three new medical terms that name it. The culprit in the case is an antiandrogen named spironolactone, which the patient had been taking as a treatment for hair loss. (This drug is also sometimes used to elevate the body's potassium level.)

Conditioners didn't help, and neither did stopping the intake of the drug. Treatment with steroids was ineffective. The patient finally had to cut her hair off. In a more recent interview, her physicians stated that, in the manner of *congenital uncombable hair* (identified in 1973 and affecting kids aged three to twelve, with more than fifty cases identified), the woman's hair is finally beginning to show signs of normality.

adolescent medicine *noun*, the subspecialty of medicine that studies and treats the mental and physical maladies of young people aged twelve to nineteen, with a focus on counseling, education, diagnostics, and prevention:

"This November [1994], the American Board of Pediatrics will recognize the subspecialty when it offers the first board certification exam in *adolescent medicine*, testing doctors' skills at screening for and handling such issues as drug abuse, eating disorders and sexually transmitted diseases" (*U.S. News & World Report*, May 16, 1994).

THE STORY: If the problems articulated at *affluenza*, *boomerang baby*, *Xer*, and *glading* are indicative of some of the adolescent disorders of our time, is it any wonder that the American Board of Pediatrics has been moved to take action?

At this writing in the summer of 1994, 270 physicians had signed up for the board certification exams. Much of their practice will involve prevention through counseling and education; giving sexually active girls Pap smears; giving both genders advice about safe sex, abstinence, and contraception; providing diet control for overweight kids; and treating adolescent depression. Still other issues include smoking, alcohol, and teen pregnancy.

agita *noun*, acid indigestion: "No wonder Christopher Columbus sailed to America—why get *agita* with Alitalia?" (*ADWEEK*, October 7, 1985). "He wrote funny songs. . . . One was about cooking scungilli, or conch, an Italian delicacy. Another was about the . . . *agita* . . . that can afflict those who indulge in too much good Italian food" (*New York Times*, February 26, 1984).

THE STORY: This word, pronounced in English [ăj' ĭ-tə], is Italian-American, according to Luigi Ballerini, a professor of Italian at New York University. It was brought to my attention by a dictionary user who had heard it in New York City and felt impelled to call the office to learn more about it. Thanks to this alert word lover, *agita* not only made its way into "Word Watch," but it also gained entry in the third edition of *The American Heritage Dictionary of the English Language*, based on the citational evidence of its usage that was accrued over time.

An early citation derives from a March 31, 1982, article in the *New York Times* in which Arthur Perfall, a spokesperson for the MTA, is quoted thus: "Boring, maybe, but nice. . . . No running around, no *agita*. Nice." Another piece of evidence for *agita* is to be found in a song sung in Woody Allen's *Broadway Danny Rose*, wherein an Italian-American entertainer has the line "*Agita* in the panza," literally translated as "acid in the paunch."

Professor Ballerini believes that *agita* comes from the Italian *acidità*, a technical term meaning "acidity." Over time it was, he believes, transformed, with the *c* becoming a *g*, and the *-di-* dropping out altogether. Etymologists, however, believe that *agita* ultimately derives from the Italian verb *agitare*, "to agitate," itself coming from the Latin verb *agitare*, meaning the same.

In any event, the word has gotten into the Gulf Stream of American English, as these examples attest: "Enid is going to give them such *agita*! I would tell them to change their telephone number and not give her the new one" (Carol Burnett in the February 20, 1984, issue of *People*, forecasting events on the soap opera *All My Children*); "Sam Giancana might have gotten more *agita* from this princess than from the Feds" (*Forbes*, July 2, 1984).

Certainly, *agita* is a great word, a colorful word, and a word much more evocative than, say, *heartburn*, *colic*, *gripe*, *cardialgia*, *dyspepsia*, or *pyrosis*. The only close competitor with *agita* might be the rarely encountered technical term for *colic*—*tormina*—as in *tormina in the tummy*.

air epidemiology *noun*, study of the cause, distribution, and control of diseases in populations, based on suspect data or interpretations: "Some epidemiologists say the risk of one infected heterosexual passing the [HIV] virus to another in a single sexual encounter is between 1 in 100 and 1 in 1,000. But others dismiss the data on which it is based as flimsy. 'You've heard the term air guitar?' asked [Andrew] Moss [an epidemiologist at the University of San Francisco]. 'That's *air epidemiology*. I don't know how you can use that number usefully'" (*Washington Post*, November 17, 1991).

THE STORY: *Air* in jocular or ironic combinations has come a long way since its use by the English Congregationalist minister Edward Miall in an 1843 issue of his weekly, the *Nonconformist*: "An *air-built castle*, which dissolves away before the gaze of reason." In addition to *air guitar* and *air piano* (referring, of course, to when one pretends to play an imaginary instrument), we have *air kiss* (in which no actual contact is made), not to mention *air hook* (a dialect term for the human nose), *air pudding* (nothing at all to eat), *air hose* (a slang term for shoes without socks), and *air dance*—also called *air jig* and *air polka* (underworld and prison lingo for execution by hanging).

Spinning off from these usages are punning uses of *air* as a modifier in headlines, two examples being "*Air* Clinton: David Brock on the Travelgate Cover-Up," on the cover of the June 1994 issue of *The American Spectator*, where *air* presumably refers to air travel arrangements made in the White House Travel Office and to appearances as opposed to reality; and "*Air* Training: Tired of lacing your running shoes?" which introduced a short piece on the new Instapump Fury—running shoes that allow the wearer to control the fit by inflating them either with a pump button or with a carbon dioxide canister, written up in the June 1994 issue of *Details*. See also *air family* at *Xer*.

Begin amputation *noun*, surgical amputation of an extremity or extremities as a result of wounds caused by the high-velocity projectiles or pellets discharged upon explosion of a fragmentation or cluster bomb: "The Gaza Hospital is situated inside the Palestinian refugee camp. . . . Norwegian surgeon Dr. Hans Husum spoke about what is now being referred to as the '*Begin amputation*,' referring to wounds caused by . . . fragmentation bombs. 'I received a patient with what appeared like [*sic*] a bad wound on his foot; the skin on his leg looked fine, but underneath the muscles and bones were completely destroyed,' the . . . doctor said. 'I had to amputate his leg all the way to his knee'" (*Washington Post*, June 27, 1982).

THE STORY: The *Washington Post* citation marks the year in which this macabre medical eponym was coined by surgeons operating in Beirut, according to an article by Fawwaz Traboulsi published in the Spring 1988 number of *Granta*. Traboulsi remarked that 50 percent of all victims of cluster-bomb attacks undergo amputation surgery. The term derives its first element from the surname of the then–prime minister of Israel, Menachem Begin. *Begin amputation* is formed in the same manner as two other eponyms involving prime ministers: *Wellington boot* and *Gladstone bag*.

casino feet *noun*, pain, tenderness, and swelling in the feet and legs of people who stand immobile or nearly so for long periods: "Foot problems among workers and gamblers at . . . casinos are 'reaching epidemic proportion,' says [Dr. Leonard Hymes,] a podiatrist who calls the painful condition '*casino feet*.' . . . Actually, we could name this problem for anyone who stands in one place for a long time with very little movement,' he said. 'It could also just as easily be called *bank teller's foot*, *assembly line foot* or *security guard foot*'" (Associated Press, August 20, 1981).

THE STORY: *Casino feet*, best viewed from a vantage underneath gaming tables, is seen specifically in wait staff, dealers, and gamblers, whose feet and leg muscles become stressed from maintaining erect body positions over long periods. These long periods of standing adversely affect blood flow, causing the blood to pool. Phlebitis and varicose veins can result. Preventive measures and treatments include wearing sensible shoes, shifting one's weight from foot to foot, rocking back and forth on the balls of the feet, flexing the toes, walking around whenever possible, and, on breaks, sitting with the feet elevated.

Casino feet joins other medical terms that name conditions by combining one noun (the producer or the cause) with another noun (the physiological site or the effect); for instance, the familiar *trench foot, tennis elbow, golf arm, prizefighter ear, baseball finger, whiskey nose, jock itch, diaper rash*, and *motion sickness*, and the less generally familiar *immersion foot* (a condition similar to *trench foot*, seen in those who have spent long periods in water), *march foot* (painful swelling of the forefoot following excessive foot strain), *LA arm* (motorist sunburn on the forearm from getting caught in gridlocks on the sunny California freeways), *tennis toe* (a painful great toe associated with subungual hematoma, usually developing after a vigorous game during which shoes with protective tips are worn), and *holiday heart. Phantom hand* is yet another: it is an impression, a paresthetic feeling, that the hand is still attached to one's body after it has been amputated. Lexically, however, this one is slightly different: the *phantom* is not a cause or a producer of the condition; rather, it is merely a descriptor of the end result. See also *jogger's paw, 'roid rage.*

emporiatrics *noun*, the medical science that deals with the prevention, detection, and treatment of travel-related diseases. Also called *emporiatric medicine; travel medicine*: "Emporiatrics . . . seems especially likely to benefit US travelers to developing areas, as the enormous differences between home and foreign environments necessitate special measures to protect travelers' health" (*Journal of the American Medical Association*, June 24, 1983).

THE STORY: Given some of the major public health problems in places like the former Soviet Union, where outbreaks of cholera and even bubonic plague have been reported, *emporiatrics* looks to be a flourishing branch of medicine in the nineties. The word *emporiatrics* is formed from the Greek *emporos*, "traveler," and English *-iatrics*, "medical practice."

The person responsible for proliferation of *emporiatrics*, B. H. Kean, M.D., clinical professor (emeritus) of tropical medicine and public health, in the Division of International Medicine, The New York Hospital–Cornell Medical Center, revealed the long and interesting story behind this coinage in a letter to the editor of *The Atlantic Monthly* published in December 1990.

Dr. Kean opened by confessing that he has "always hated the term," but added that he felt "obliged to explain [his own] culpability." Dr. Kean went on with the story:

> The word came into being in 1954 . . . with a trip to the New York Public Library. That was the year that Somerset Waters, a travel consultant and adviser to President Eisenhower, and I created the Travelers Health Institute, for the purpose of getting to the bottom, as it were, of that ancient scourge of the accidental tourist, Montezuma's revenge, a.k.a. traveler's diarrhea. Our first official act was to order stationery; Waters felt that a letterhead with a proper logo was essential to our feeble fund-raising efforts. Besides, he reasoned, if there could be *pediatrics* for children, and *geriatrics* for old people, why not *emporiatrics* for travelers. . . ? I hated it. It reminded me of "emporium," the entrepreneurial euphemism for the musty, depressing corner drygoods store ubiquitous in the Midwest of my youth— wholly inappropriate. . . . But Waters was a stubborn man. He made a trip to the New York Public Library, where he charmed the resident linguistics expert into agreeing with him. Thus our new letterhead read, "Devoted to the Science of *Emporiatrics*." Convinced that the phrase was a real dud, but not beyond a little honest self-promotion, I used it in a few speeches and let the matter drop. Years later, while perusing *Dorland's Medical Dictionary*, my eyes stumbled on the term *emporiatrics*. . . . So much for a parasitologist's flair for language. *Emporiatrics* has become the widely used name for a whole subspecialty of medicine. Waters was the genius but, within medical circles at least, I usually get the credit.

Emporiatrics, which has markedly expanded in recent years in response first to the American trend toward vacations in exotic places and then to increased immigration into the United States, involves, at least for travelers, pretrip, on-the-trip, and posttrip services. An *emporiatrician* reviews the traveler's health records and assesses the person's physical condition before departure, provides information regarding potential health risks in the destination country, recommends preventive measures, and provides the appropriate inoculations. On-the-trip services include advice as to the location of qualified English-speaking physicians in the destination country, tips on management of disease during the trip, and warnings to avoid over-the-counter remedies. Posttrip services include treatment of any diseases acquired during the trip and followup screening.

fifth disease *noun*, an illness common chiefly among children aged five to fourteen, caused by parvovirus B19 and lasting one to three weeks, characterized by a lacy, fiery red, migratory facial rash, minor gastrointestinal or respiratory symptoms, and sometimes arthralgia. Also called technically *erythema infectiosum* and nontechnically *slapped cheek disease:* "The 1980's included the transmission of salmonellosis from chickens to eggs, the spread of Lyme disease, . . . the causal role of parvovirus in *fifth disease*, and the resurgence of sexually transmitted disease through sex-for-drugs activities" (*Public Health Report 1990*, November/December 1990).

THE STORY: Many years ago, this disease acquired two names in a development process involving three languages—German, French, and later, English. Its causative agent, however, was determined only after ninety-four years had passed from the initial naming. In 1889, the name *erythema infectiosum* was given to the disease by one G. Sticker, first noted in an article by him entitled "Die neue Kinderseuche in der Umgebung von Giessen (*Erythema infectiosum*)." Six years later, a French doctor, L. Cheinisee, coined the term *cinquième maladie eruptive*, or, in English, *fifth rash disease* (later shortened to *fifth disease*). The coinage is attested in an article by Dr. Cheinisee, titled "Une *cinquième maladie eruptive*: Le megalerytheme épidémique."

Choice of the numerative name was influenced by the existence of four other childhood diseases then regarded as clinically and epidemiologically distinct: scarlet fever (*first disease*), rubeola (measles, or *second disease*), rubella (German measles, or *third disease*), and epidemic pseudoscarlatina (Dukes' disease, or *fourth disease*). There is also a *sixth disease*, roseola. Though the modern medical literature no longer uses the terms *first* through *fourth* and *sixth disease*, *fifth disease* has persisted in usage in both medical and general writing, perhaps because of the difficulties some laypeople have in remembering and pronouncing the Latinate form assigned by Dr. Sticker.

Epidemics of *fifth disease* typically occur in late winter and early spring, according to the Centers for Disease Control. Two to three million cases of it are seen in school-age children in the United States each year. Although the disease is rather inconsequential in children, it can be problematic in adults, specifically those who have been immunocompromised or are pregnant. *Fifth disease*, which, in adults, can lead to painful arthritis, has also been associated with spontaneous abortion, stillbirths, and nonimmune fetal hydrops.

gephyrophobia *noun*, a fear of crossing bridges, especially high ones, rooted in a complex of fears involving water, driving, and heights, often seen in some motorists: "Raymond Friedman, a Los Angeles psychiatrist who specializes in psychological traumas, said *gephyrophobia* . . . is far more common than people think" (*New York Newsday*, November 30, 1990).

THE STORY: Though not new, *gephyrophobia* is rarely encountered in general print sources, and some *gephyrophobes* may not even know the nomenclature describing their fear. These terms are not entered in most medical and general dictionaries, even though bridge toll police will tell you that instances of crippling fear of bridges seem to be on the upswing among motorists. For instance, in 1991, no fewer than 993 terrified drivers—more than triple the number in 1987—willingly relinquished the wheel, allowing police officers to drive them across the Chesapeake Bay Bridge—all 4.3 miles of it. (Similar incidents occur daily on bridges all over the country.) According to toll police, some people crawl down onto the floors of their vehicles, put their heads between their knees, and whimper in terror. Truck drivers sometimes panic and just pull over. Even some retired commercial airline pilots have been known to balk at traversing huge, soaring spans such as the Bay Bridge.

Gephyrophobia, whose key constituent element identifying the thing feared is the Greek noun *gephyra*, meaning "bridge," is a malady controllable with medications and "talking therapy." Self-administered therapies are deep breathing, focusing the attention on nonmoving objects such as hood ornaments, and concentrating on keeping the vehicle within the lane markers while pretending the stretch is just a road, not the deck of a high bridge.

In terms of word development, the second key constituent element, the suffix *-phobia*, is just as interesting as the factors contributing to the malady so denoted. Derived from the Greek suffix of the same spelling and meaning as the ones we know in English, *-phobia* resembles—but surpasses—yet another suffix, this one *-ism*, in two ways: like *ism*, *phobia* has emerged as a freestanding noun, and, like *-ism*, the suffix *-phobia* is extraordinarily productive in the formation of other terms.

If the productivity of *-phobia* is a leading indicator of the state of our disorders, then it is also an exemplar of the people's creativity in coining new words. The following short list of phobias is a core, derived from a list of at least 176 such terms, excluding the other-*phobia* coinages that continue to emerge.

Phobia	Fear of/Aversion to
acarophobia	small insects
acrophobia	heights
agoraphobia	the out-of-doors
aichmophobia	pointed objects
algophobia	pain
androphobia	men; males
anthophobia	flowers
anthrophobia	people
anuptaphobia	being single
aquaphobia	water
arachibutyrophobia	peanut butter becoming stuck on the roof of one's mouth
asthenophobia	displaying one's emotions
atelophobia	imperfection in oneself
belonephobia	needles
bromidrosiphobia	body odors, real or imagined
catagelophobia	ridicule; criticism
centophobia	things new; new ideas
chrematophobia	money
chronophobia	time—seen in long-term prison inmates
clinophobia	going to bed
coitophobia	sexual intercourse
dementophobia	going insane
dermatophobia	skin; touching skin
dextrophobia	things on the right
dromophobia	wandering; travel
ecophobia	home
erythrophobia	blushing
euphobia	good news
feminophobia	women; females; things effeminate
genophobia	sex
hagiophobia	things holy
heliophobia	the sun

Phobia	Fear of/Aversion to
hemophobia	blood
herpetophobia	reptiles
heterophobia	straights
homophobia	gays
hygrophobia	liquids
iatrophobia	going to the doctor
kilobytophobia	computers; one's own computer illiteracy
levophobia	things on the left
linonophobia	string
macrophobia	prolonged waiting
necrophobia	death; corpses
nosophobia	sickness; disease
novercaphobia	one's stepmother
numerophobia	numbers
nyctophobia, scotophobia	darkness; the dark
ochlophobia	crowds
ophidiophobia	snakes
optophobia	opening one's eyes
peccatophobia	commission of sin
peladophobia	going bald; baldness
pentheraphobia	one's mother-in-law
pogonophobia	beards
pyrophobia	fire
spermatophobia	sperm or the loss of one's sperm
stenophobia	narrow spaces; caves
thanophobia	death
theophobia	the wrath of God
topophobia	performing onstage
tropophobia	change; moving; decision-making
uranophobia	heaven
vitricophobia	one's stepfather
xenophobia	strangers; outsiders
zoophobia	animals

Clearly, the only thing left to fear is fear itself, or perhaps the fear of pho-bias—in this case, *phobophobia*. With apologies to FDR, I refer you to *non-ism* and *quux*.

hedonia hypothesis *noun*, a hypothesis in neuropsychology holding that a negative hedonic state, such as stress, tends to increase a subject's eyeblink frequency and that a positive hedonic state, such as contentment or plea-sure, tends to decrease eyeblink frequency. Also called *hedonia-blink hypothe-sis*: "Joe Tecce, a neuropsychologist. . . , counts how many times candidates blink. The concept, . . . the *Hedonia Hypothesis*, is that the more stress or negative feelings you have, the more you blink. The more relaxed you feel, the less you blink" (*Boston Sunday Herald*, October 11, 1992). "In the blink of an eyelash, [Dr. Joseph J.] Tecce puts to work his *hedonia hypothesis*. . . . [He] has trained his . . . eyes on two statesmen caught in the crucible of world events, President Bush and . . . Saddam Hussein, who are locked in an eyeball-to-eyeball confrontation in the Persian Gulf. If Tecce's data are accu-rate, Saddam will blink first in the war of nerves" (*Boston Herald*, September 19, 1990).

THE STORY: If the eyes are the windows to a person's soul, then it might be said that study of eyeblink frequency is an indicator of the workings of a per-son's mind, especially when under stress. *Hedonia hypothesis*, which has been referred to by *Newsweek* and *USA Today*, among other general sources, first came to my attention in 1990. The term, which is related to *hedonics* (the branch of psychology that deals with pleasant and unpleasant conscious states and their connections with organic life), was coined in 1978 by Joseph J. Tecce, a professor of neuropsychology at Boston College. (Both *hedonia* and *hedonics* share the common Greek linguistic forebear, *hēdonē*, meaning "plea-sure.") The definition of *hedonia hypothesis* given here is based on Tecce's "Contingent Negative Variation (CNV) and Eyeblinks" found in a mono-graph titled *Psychopharmacology*, edited by M. A. Lipton et al.

In a 1989 issue of *Clinical Electroencephalography*, Tecce pointed out that "the finding of a stress-blink association has been called the '*Nixon effect*' since it was observed during Richard M. Nixon's speech of resignation [on August 8, 1974] as President of the United States." In videotapes of a Dan Rather interview with Saddam Hussein, Tecce determined that Hussein reg-istered 56 blinks per minute (BPM) when responding to a question about de-bating with George Bush and Margaret Thatcher; then, while listening to the translation of his answer, he registered a full 120 BPMs. And when asked about an impending conference with the UN secretary-general, Hussein's BPMs escalated to 128. Conversely, when Hussein was televised with a group of detained British schoolchildren, his BPM rate registered only 19–28. Bush's BPMs, on the other hand, were considerably lower: on August 8, 1990, when he announced U.S. troop deployments to the Middle East, the president registered only 20–22 BPMs. At an August 30 press conference, he exhibited 38 BPMs (troop deployment questions), 41 BPMs (the issue of a food embargo against Iraq), and 58 BPMs (questions about Soviet cooperation). The flurries of eyeblinks exhibited by Nixon and Hussein are described by Tecce as *eyeblink storms* (3 blinks or more per second), or *eyeblink bursts*. Possible causes of these episodes, aside from stress resulting from confrontation, are a sense of failure, audience-induced stress, speech (which itself involves increased cognitive effort), and environmental factors such as bright TV lights and room temperature.

Tecce's eyeblink analysis of the 1992 presidential debates held on October 11, 15, and 19 revealed that of the three candidates, Ross Perot exhibited conspicuously fewer BPMs than the other two: he averaged 7 BPMs overall in the three debates, with the highest blink response being 15 BPMs when commenting in the second debate on excessive health-care costs. His second-highest rate—14 BPMs—occurred in the first debate in reply to a question about most-favored-nation status for China in view of its human-rights violations. His third-highest rate—11 BPMs—came in the third debate in response to a query about an impending banking crisis. In contrast, George Bush exhibited more BPMs overall in the debates than the other two candidates; his average was 53 BPMs as opposed to Bill Clinton's 45 BPMs. (And Bush's average 56 BPM rate in the third debate equaled one of Saddam Hussein's in the Dan Rather interview, but Bush's rate never, ever approached Hussein's 120–128 BPM eyeblink storms.) Bush blinked more often during his closing statements in the second and third debates (79 and 67 BPMs, respectively), averaging out at 66 BPMs overall in the closings. Bush's BPMs reached 64 both in the first and in the second debates in response, respectively, to questions about his degree of concern (or lack thereof) about the ethnic cleansing in the Balkans, and about the degree of concern he had for the future of the so-called new world order. His third-highest BPM was in response to a question in the third debate about a 1990 tax hike. Although Governor Clinton's overall average BPM during the question-and-answer periods was only 45, his highest BPM, 78, in response to a question about his ability to send troops into combat when he himself had arranged not to go, was in fact the highest eyeblink rate of any candidate in reply to any question posed during all three debates. His second-highest blink rate, this one 67, came in response to a question in the first debate about the character issue. The third-highest, 44 BPMs, occurred in response to questions about the bad economy and his personal life, posed during the second debate.

The *hedonia hypothesis*, then, serves to indicate rather sensitively the varying degrees of stress experienced by individuals. And all this adds a new dimension to then Secretary of State Dean Rusk's statement to ABC newsman John Scali during the 1962 Cuban missile crisis: "Remember, when you report this, that, eyeball to eyeball, they blinked first." For more insights into the workings of the minds of world leaders, see *stylogram*; for insights into the ways by which such leaders often gain and maintain control of power agendas, see also *heresthetic*. And for an example of verbal tics in action, see *I think*.

holiday heart *noun*, a cardiac syndrome in which a patient experiences arrhythmias, hot sweats, dizziness, and sometimes chest pain during or after heavy intake of alcohol, especially during stressful holiday seasons: "*Holiday heart* usually appears in chronic drinkers who go on a binge or people with underlying heart problems who drink too much" (*Boston Globe*, December 15, 1986).

THE STORY: According to the *Globe* citations, *holiday heart* was first used in 1978 by physicians at a New Jersey medical school. However, a 1977 citation for it in the *Washington Post* of December 31 antedates the New Jersey reference, causing one to believe the term was in use long before the seventies: "Doctors in heart and emergency hospital wards have begun to see a new problem associated with holiday drinking—*Holiday Heart Syndrome*."

In the *Washington Post* piece, Dr. Ernest K. Noble, director of the National Institute of Alcohol Abuse and Alcoholism, said that *holiday heart* is one of the problems to be expected by physicians over long weekend holidays, for example. Although physicians say that *holiday heart* usually does not end in a heart attack or death, patients exhibiting its symptoms nevertheless should seek medical care promptly.

Holiday heart can cause the pulse to race at 150–220 beats per minute, according to Gerald Pohost, the chair of the American Heart Association's Council on Clinical Cardiology. "It gives people this very frightening sensation of impending doom," said Dr. Pohost, who is also the director of cardiology at the University of Alabama in Birmingham, in an Associated Press interview published on December 21, 1992.

Only 1 to 5 percent of people experiencing atrial fibrillation die, and of this percentage, only a fraction would be victims of *holiday heart.* So said Milford Maloney, a past president of the American Society of Internal Medicine, quoted in the same Associated Press story. (A related term is *Passover effect,* discussed at *Lake Wobegon effect.*) See also *casino feet, pizza-cutter's palsy.*

horrenderoma also **horrendeoma** *noun, slang,* a mass, such as a tumor, that is especially large or difficult or impossible to treat: "She arranged a stat CT scan that showed a golf-ball-sized mass in his frontal lobe, most probably a lymphoma but possibly some other terrible *horrenderoma*" (Robert Marion, M.D., *The Intern Blues,* 1990).

THE STORY: Medical slang has always been especially colorful and descriptive: the terms *gork, flat-line* (verb), *sickler* (one affected with sickle-cell anemia), and *AMA* (*a*gainst *m*edical *a*dvice) are but four examples. The word *horrenderoma*—also, according to physician readers of "Word Watch," spelled *horrendeoma*—illustrates the merger of *horrendous* with the suffix *-oma* (from the Greek *oma*), a suffix forming nouns to mean a tumor, or neoplasm, of the body part indicated by the stem to which the suffix is attached. Yet another such term, also appearing in Dr. Marion's book, is *fascinoma,* defined there as "an interesting case." See also *neomort.*

insurance technician *noun,* a member of a health-insurance company's utilization review team, such as a registered nurse reporting to a physician in the company's employ, who, under the managed-care system, reviews the ongoing treatment of hospitalized patients against established company treatment guidelines: "The insurance company was on the phone again. 'It was a physician,' [Dr. Joseph] Nelson said. 'He identified himself and seemed very short with me. He made a point to say that I had hung up on his *insurance technician* and that he thought I was rude in doing so'" (*Roanoke* [Va.] *Times & World-News,* March 22, 1992).

THE STORY: Here's a scary job title to add to the already alarming list of concerns that patients in ICUs and CCUs, and, indeed, the entire populace, have about matters of health care. By linguistic structure, *insurance technician* is formed in the manner of the familiar *dental technician* and *x-ray technician,* and the perhaps less familiar *nail technician* (now the preferred term for what used to be called a *manicurist*) and *legal technician* (an independent paralegal who is basically a preparer of legal documents not requiring the attention of an attorney). As might be expected, when I called numerous health-insurance providers, my calls were not returned after the respondents had learned that I wanted to see job descriptions for *insurance technicians*. Doctors commonly refer to managed health care as "the *hassle factor*," said the *Times & World-News*. This *hassle factor*—heavy paperwork and justification of treatment plans—focuses sharply on cost savings while, it is alleged, often imperiling the quality of patient care.

In the single citation to date for the utilization-review sense of *insurance technician* (other senses denote actuaries, adjusters, and underwriters), a story is told—a story that will have to substitute for the formal job description sought in vain from the insurance providers. Several years ago, a woman in her early sixties appeared at an emergency room complaining of shortness of breath and chest pains. Lab test results and a chest x-ray looked fine. The doctor did, however, admit her because she was clearly in intense chest discomfort. Three days later, while the patient was still in the CCU, the doctor was interrupted during examinations of other patients by a phone call from an *insurance technician* who wished to know why the patient was in the CCU three days after admission, with no firm diagnosis. While discussing the case with the *insurance technician*, the doctor was stat-paged. The cause of the stat page was the lady with the inexplicable chest pains. She had died—from a heart attack.

Let me end this story with the doctor's final words to the *insurance technician*'s physician-supervisor as he related them to the *Times & World-News*: "He [the insurance-company doctor] went on to say, 'Now we have a problem with Mrs. So and So. We have a problem with her admission.' And I said, 'You have no further problem. You no longer have a problem. She has just died.' And there was a pause on the other end and he said, 'Well, I'm sorry.' And he hung up."

isopraxism *noun*, a nonlearned neurobehavior in which members of the same species behave or perform in a like manner: "Dressing like your colleagues and neighbors dress 'reflects a deep reptilian behavior principle called "*isopraxism*,"' says [research anthropologist David B.] Givens. '*Isopraxism* involves . . . doing the same thing as,' he says. 'You're allies. You look alike, think alike. It's easier to be accepted if you look like others. "Same" is safe'" (*Washington Post*, May 10, 1993).

THE STORY: As you read the word *isopraxism*, you are watching a preexisting word, *isopraxis*, undergo initial transformation into a variant spelling. The longevity of the new variant cannot yet be predicted. David B. Givens, director of academic relations at the American Anthropological Association, used the *-m*; this variant spelling first appeared in the nontechnical media in a United Press International story dated March 24, 1981. In an interview with me, Dr. Givens remarked that the *-m* spelling, commonly seen in the literature of anthropology, is "more for the ordinary reader, as opposed to *isopraxis*, which is better understood by science types. . . . With the *-m* spelling, ordinary people might be inclined to use the word more." With the *-m* spelling, though, ordinary people may perceive the word as just another *ism*, which it is not.

Isopraxis is the coinage of neuroanatomist Paul D. MacLean, M.D., the retired chief, Laboratory of Brain Evolution and Behavior, National Institute of Mental Health, now a senior scientist there. His word first appeared in print in 1975 in his piece "The Imitative-Creative Interplay of Our Three Mentalities," in *Astride the Two Cultures. Arthur Koestler at 70* (H. Harris, ed.). In that piece, the coiner explained his word-creative rationale: "Because 'imitation' is such a 'loaded' word in the social and behavioural sciences, commonly implying 'conscious' learning or mimicking, I shall avoid it in the context of the experimental work, referring instead to *isopraxis*, or *isopraxic* behaviour, meaning performance of the same kind of behaviour." His word, modeled after the preexisting medical term *echopraxia*, is a linkage of two words of Greek origin; the prefix *iso-*, one sense of which is "equal; uniform," coming from *isos*, "equal"; and *praxis*, one sense of which is "habitual or established practice; custom," coming via medieval Latin from the Greek *praxis*, itself from *prassein*, "to do."

In his book *The Triune Brain in Evolution: Role in Paleocerebral Functions* (1990), MacLean elaborated on the coinage: "The word *isopraxic* may seem a little forbidding the first time it is encountered. . . . I found myself resorting to the use of the term when I needed a word that was purely descriptive and had no causal overtones. There are no dictionary words that do the work of *isopraxis*."

For many years, Dr. MacLean has studied animal behaviors ranging from those of reptiles to those of primates, behaviors that cannot be explained solely on the basis of some forms of learned imitation. The genesis and controller of these behaviors, such as the simultaneous, acceptive nodding of female and juvenile lizards in response to the "display" made by a territorial male lizard (likened by MacLean to the group gobbling response of tom turkeys or the hand-clapping response of a theater audience), lies in what he calls the *R-complex* of the brain. (The human forebrain has evolved in a hierarchical way into three basic patterns, also seen in the brains of turtles, pigeons, rats, and monkeys, for instance. The patterns in humans are characterized by MacLean as reptilian, paleomammalian, and neomammalian. "In mammals," MacLean has written, "the major counterpart of the reptilian forebrain is represented by a group of massive ganglia including the corpus striatum, globus pallidus, and satellite grey matter." This is the *R-complex.*)

Although the mammal-like reptiles that were the forerunners of modern mammals have long since disappeared, neurovestiges of them reside within us in the *R-complex*, evidenced by the "mentality" it stimulates and controls. More than twenty behaviors, most centering on self-preservation and survival of the species, can be traced to this complex. In terms of human beings en masse and *mass isopraxis*, this phenomenon can be seen in some mass migrations of people in the past, mass rallies (often associated with militant nationalism), mass violence and hysteria, and the sudden mass adoption of fashions and fads.

jogger's paw *noun*, a painful burn on the pads of dogs that accompany their owners while jogging, caused by hot running surfaces and preventable by keeping the dogs off asphalt and concrete in hot weather: "In addition to their ankle sprains and shinsplints, joggers have a new affliction they can commiserate about: the heartbreak of *jogger's paw*. . . . As more runners take Fido along to relieve the boredom of long jaunts through the city, veterinarians report a surge in painful burns on the foot pads of jogging dogs" (*Wall Street Journal*, July 21, 1986).

THE STORY: The term *jogger's paw* is an interesting example of a relatively small subclass of English compounds made up of a possessive noun (the one experiencing the condition, often but not exclusively a malady) and another noun (the condition itself, expressed in terms of its physiological site or in terms of a characteristic sign or symptom). Taken together, the two nouns name the condition.

This rather productive compounding process is evident especially in the language of medicine, sports, and performance medicine: *smoker's tongue*, *pitcher's arm*, *swimmer's ear*, *athlete's foot*, *guitarist's nipple*, *diver's palsy*, *runner's high*, and *harpist's cramp* are instances, not to mention *gin-drinker's liver* (alcoholic cirrhosis), *smoker's cough*, *writer's cramp*, *housemaid's knee*, *toper's nose* (rhinophyma), and the rather alarming *obstetrician's hand*, also called *accoucheur's hand*. This last condition is defined in the twenty-seventh edition of *Dorland's Illustrated Medical Dictionary* thus: "the contraction of the hand in tetany; the hand is flexed at the wrist, the fingers at the metacarpophalangeal joints but extended at the interphalangeal joints, the thumb being strongly flexed into the palm; so called because of a dubious resemblance to the position assumed by the hand of the obstetrician when examining the vagina." See also *casino feet, holiday heart, pizza-cutter's palsy*.

kangaroo care *noun*, a supplement to traditional incubator-centered neonatal intensive care in which prolonged skin-to-skin contact between mothers and infants occurs along with attachment of respirators, monitors, and feeding tubes as well as continuance of all essential life-sustaining medical care, such as suctioning, in an effort to stabilize infant body temperature, avoid apnea, achieve steady weight gain, and curtail irritability: "'*Kangaroo care*'— mothers holding their premature infants all or part of each day instead of the babies being isolated in incubators—appears to be good for both parent and child" (*International Herald Tribune*, June 13, 1992).

THE STORY: *Kangaroo care* was developed around 1982 in Colombia as a result of an incubator shortage; this, according to the June 10, 1992, issue of the *New York Times. Kangaroo care* is still used chiefly in Third World countries. When mother and baby *kangaroo*, the baby joins its mother on a recliner for as short a period as twenty minutes to as long as six hours.

Although this method of care still requires detailed medical study, the *Times* reported that in a randomized trial at the University of Florida, it was found that babies who *kangarooed* in the delivery room for prolonged periods stayed in the ICU only 3.7 days as opposed to their counterparts who received traditional isolated care and remained in the ICU for 10 days or more.

lovemap *noun*, a complex of indelible brain traces ultimately playing a role in determining the types of stimuli that will sexually arouse one and enable one to fall in love or adopt certain patterns of sexual behavior: "People's *lovemaps* are pretty much set by the age of 8" (*Psychology Today*, May 1988).

THE STORY: Citations indicate that this word was coined by Dr. John Money of Johns Hopkins University, a researcher who is credited with coining the term *gender identity*. A *lovemap* "depicts an idealized lover, love scene and a program of erotic activities" (*New York Times*, January 23, 1990). Dr. Money, who discussed the subject in a 1990 book entitled *Vandalized*

Lovemaps, coauthored by Dr. Margaret Lamacz, pointed out that if a young child is subjected to neglect, physical abuse, or incest, his or her *lovemap* may be "permanently distorted, with the result that [the child] develops sexual perversions, or, as they are known in today's clinical language, 'paraphilias'" (*Washington Times*, January 25, 1990).

Though some paraphilias are harmless enough, others can involve sadism, exhibitionism, or the desire to commit murder. Therefore, it may be concluded that the sexuality of people such as child molesters, exhibitionists, rapists, and serial killers, as well as those having less deviant sexual orientations, has its genesis in very early childhood, during which the initial associations between sex and love are established.

mouse terrorism *noun*, the engendering in the public mind, through scientific studies involving laboratory mice as subjects of experimentation, of an unwarranted fear of potential health hazards: "The mouse-vs.-man analogy is essential to those who seek to terrify us about food additives, pesticides and other trace-element chemicals. . . . The time has come for us to recognize that '*mouse terrorism*' poses a serious problem in terms of maintaining our high standard of living and our good health" (Elizabeth M. Whelen, M.D., Springfield, Mass., *Sunday Republican*, June 3, 1990).

THE STORY: Widespread scares involving substances such as cyclamates, nitrates, hair dyes, and saccharine, said Dr. Whelen, president of the American Council on Science and Health, a consumer-education group, "have two things in common: rodents, and a federal regulation declaring that any chemical causing cancer in a laboratory, in any dose, is a cancer risk to humans and must be purged at any cost." Dr. Whelen regards as specious the assumption, based on factlets drawn from scientific studies, that a mouse is "a miniature man."

A related term is *mouse unit*, used in the literature to mean "the smallest amount of a substance that will produce a specified change in a laboratory mouse," evidenced by this citation from the December 1988 issue of *Discover*: "Only very minute amounts of the toxin, on the order of 5 to 20 *mouse units* . . . are injected into a patient's vocal cords." This *mouse unit* is unrelated to the term denoting the handheld device that controls the movement of a computer cursor.

myc *noun*, a gene known to be frequently disturbed in cancer tissue, and one that in its normal state, bears an enormous number of the characteristics critical to the maintenance and life of all body cells: "Among the most dangerous and widespread mutations [that scientists] have found is one that disrupts a gene with the deceptively folksy name of *myc*. . . . The gene is so frequently disturbed in cancer tissue, and in its normal guise it bears so many trademarks of being critical to the life . . . of all . . . cells, that researchers . . . call it *McGene*: everywhere they look, there it is, the *myc*" (*New York Times*, May 5, 1992).

THE STORY: Pronounced [mick], *myc* is a respelling of the element Mc in *McGene*, itself a slang term created by association with the trade name *McDonald's*, the fast-food chain. *McGene* is formed in the manner of thousands of takeoffs on this trade name, three being *McJob* (a low-paying, easily obtainable, no-future job, often in the service sector) and *McPaper* (a term paper churned out at the last possible minute with little or no substantive research and thought), and *McDoctor*—another term for *urgicenter*.

Another term of recent development in the lexicon of genetics is *chromosome walking*, which prompts images of fingers perambulating through the Yellow Pages. One big problem in the field is pinpointing genes in an effort to find their exact locations and determine how mutations within them cause disease. Once a gene's general locale on a chromosome has been pinpointed, scientists start at a so-called marker, a known locale, and move in one direction or another down the chromosome strand under scrutiny, searching for the exact site of the gene. That's *chromosome walking*.

A third term is *suicide gene*. Designated *ced-3*, this is the genetic material responsible for what is called *programmed cell death*, that is to say, the process by which individual cells in the body self-destruct, or "commit cellular suicide," in order to assist other tissues that are undergoing new development. As an instance, when activated at exactly the right time, *suicide genes* can and do assist in the formation of an amorphous *mitten* of fetal tissue into a human hand having all five fingers. Identification of the *suicide gene*, as related in the journal *Cell* in late 1993, has implications for people with Alzheimer's, rheumatoid arthritis, and some cancers. It is also relevant to stroke and traumatic brain injuries.

neomort *noun*, a brain-dead patient, kept alive for an indefinite period by life-support systems while his or her organs await transplantation. Also called *biomort; respirated cadaver; the undead*: "*Neomort* and *neomortia* . . . relate to the state of brain-death, more specifically the proposal . . . that the 'usable organs of newly dead people be kept in their owners' bodies' as a form of storage. . . . The *neomorts* would be kept on life support systems in a state of *neomortia* until the parts were needed" (*New York Times*, December 26, 1985).

THE STORY: *The Second Barnhart Dictionary of New English* says that American psychiatrist Willard Gaylin coined *neomort* in 1974, as attested by this citation from his article "Harvesting the Dead," which appeared in the September 1974 issue of *Harper's*: "Uneasy medical students could practice routine physical examinations . . . everything except neurological examinations, since the *neomort* by definition has no functioning central nervous system." According to the *Times* citation, it has been suggested that about 150,000 *neomorts* could be available for organ and blood procurement over a ten-year period.

In his 1989 book *We Have a Donor*, Mark Dowie explained that *biomort*, in lexical parlance an allonym of *neomort*, was coined to denote "a third form of being (sort of living, sort of dead)." *Biomort* is said to have first appeared in print in a 1979 legal opinion published in the *Utah Law Review*.

Neither *neomort* nor *biomort* has gained wide currency; in fact, Dowie has pointed out that primary-care physicians consider them too offensive to be used in public. The same holds with *gork*, a medical slang word for a person who has lost brain function as a result of stroke, senility, or another cause. Although the origin of *gork* has long been an etymological mystery, Robert L. Chapman in his *New Dictionary of American Slang* said that it is an acronym formed from the phrase God only really knows, commonly used to refer to a patient's mysterious ailment, and lexicographer J. E. Lighter, in the *Random House Historical Dictionary of American Slang*, postulated GOK (God only knows), which can be traced to 1915, as a possible etymology. See also *horrenderoma*.

off the grid *idiom*, away from populous urban and suburban areas and into desolate areas, living off the land and safe from the coming Apocalypse: "[James (Bo)] Gritz, who was briefly on the ticket with David Duke in '88 and ran for President himself in '92, is, at 55, a leader of the radical right-wing survivalist movement. He quotes Scripture, prophesying end times in the next few years, times when we shall all have to accept the mark of the beast. . . . 'We are going to live our lives according to our ways,' Gritz is saying now. . . . 'personally I'm going to go *off the grid*, because every time I've lived *off the grid*, like Vietnam, I've been very happy'" (*New York Times Magazine*, January 8, 1995).

THE STORY: Hillel Schwartz, the author of a scholarly examination titled *Century's End*, has studied the varied ways that human beings behaved during the past 1,000 years on the eves of new centuries. Based on his studies, Schwartz forecasts the emergence, from 1995 through 1999, of widespread paranoia associated with portents of natural disasters and actually occurring disasters, warnings of the coming extinction of planet Earth, and an obsession with the occult in general.

Schwartz was quoted thus by *Washington Post Magazine* writer Peter Carlson on January 1, 1995: "There has always been something essentially woo-woo about the year 2000." Schwartz then characterized *woo-woo* as "a kind of cheerful zaniness, . . . which is also a little dangerous, a little off the beaten track."

Acute woo-woo might be the degree of unease about the coming millennium and what certain individuals believe will be total societal collapse, evidenced by the vocabulary in use by some of the more than 10,000 people "living *off the grid*, both literally and philosophically, in the hills of eastern Washington, northern Idaho and western Montana" (*New York Times Magazine*). Those people who have moved *off the grid* have gone far beyond the imperatives of the *moral panic* discussed elsewhere in this book, and they have needs unfulfillable even by the *intentional communities* and *gated* communities equipped with *hydraulic bollards* discussed in other chapters, too. They're just gone, period. Gone from the IRS, even. Living in tepees. Living in their hand-built cabins, eating *T.V.P.* (textured vegetable protein), a kind of dried food with the shelf life of a petrified forest. Other terms in their vocabulary are *mark of the beast*, the bar code that will be implanted in every person's forehead or on the right hand, signaling the advent of a cashless, all-seeing, all-surveilling slave society; *end times*, the Apocalypse, Armageddon, or the total collapse of (un)civilized society, with the various meanings dependent upon one's viewpoint; *Anti-Christ Banksters*, a compound exhibiting an interesting use of the perjorative suffix *-ster* (e.g., *gangster*) and meaning the shrewd moneylenders whose mission it is to bankrupt America and hoard the proceeds for their own use in the *New World Order*; *New World Order*, an enslaving new global society with a world government; and ZOG, Zionist-Occupied Government.

Off the grid, formed in the manner of *off the wall* or *off the beam*, is interesting because it is a military term now denoting the survivalists' psychosocial behavior. The Joint Chiefs of Staff's *Dictionary of Military Terms* defines *grid* as "two sets of parallel lines intersecting at right angles and forming squares; the grid is superimposed on maps . . . to permit identification of ground locations." When you're *off the grid*, you're off the map.

Paris Lip *noun*, 1. a nonsurgical, collagen-insertion procedure to define and enhance the Cupid's bow of the top lip. Also called technically *lip augmentation*. 2. the pouty appearance so achieved. Also called *killer-bee-sting pout*: "Call it the *Paris Lip*. The newest pucker in fashion was introduced . . . with a roundup of movie-famous lips from 1920–1990—including Madonna's" (*USA Today*, October 24, 1990). "A slice of the fashion world that flocked to the Ritz last night had been curious all week about '*Paris Lip*.' Lauren Bacall, still looking and sounding suave, proved with a slide show that women in the past 50 years have never been afraid to show off their lips" (*San Francisco Chronicle*, October 22, 1990).

THE STORY: The *Paris Lip*, popular not only among models and actresses but also among teenagers and middle-agers seeking a sexy look, was developed by a French plastic surgeon. The procedure became available in the United States in 1992. The *Los Angeles Times* said in a September 21, 1990, story that "plastic surgeons . . . are reporting two and three times the requests for '*lip service*' (the new slang for what doctors call *lip augmentation*)" than they did in 1988. At least sixteen injections of collagen—a purified protein derived from cowhide—may be required to achieve the desired results. Patients willing to pay the $700–$1,000 fees should remember that the procedure is painful and the results merely temporary.

pharming *noun*, a genetic engineering technique by which the embryos of livestock, such as pigs and cattle, are injected with human genetic material encoded to produce chemicals normally generated only by the human body, so that blood, proteins, and transplantable organs from the new generation of fully grown animals so bred can be used in medicines and in cross-species organ transplants. Also called *barnyard biotechnology*; *gene pharming*; *molecular pharming*; *transgenics*: "This marriage of high-tech biology and low-tech agriculture, known as '*pharming*,' has long intrigued the biotechnology industry. And while most products are still more than five years away, proponents predict that *pharming* will transform the rural landscape in the next century" (*San Francisco Chronicle*, July 6, 1993). "*Pharm* cows, *pharm* pigs, *pharm* goats and *pharm* sheep could help end the organ-transplant crisis and provide new, protein-based drugs. . . . But *pharming*, critics contend, also could change the genetic character of the animal kingdom forever" (*Orlando Sentinel Tribune*, April 11, 1993).

THE STORY: *Pharming*, a double pun of sorts, was voted the most interesting new word of 1992, according to the Canadian press. It may prove to be one of the most controversial techniques of our century. In fulfilling their roles as *pharm* animals, the *transgenic animals*, as they are called, will serve as so-called *bioreactors*, or pharmaceutical factories on the hoof. It is impressive that *pharming* involves such things as attempts to produce in the blood of *transgenic rabbits* alpha-1 antitrypsin and erythropoietin, two rare human proteins of use in treating emphysema and cancer-caused bone-marrow damage, respectively. It is equally impressive that genetically engineered pig organs could save the lives of thousands awaiting transplants (30,000 Americans were awaiting transplants in 1993, with fewer than 15,000 expected to receive them).

Critics, nonetheless, are disturbed about the possible patenting by corporations of human genetic material and the ethical difficulty of making vast sums from what is really the "signature strand," or essence, in the creation of life. Many scientists, on the other hand, view *pharming* as the next best thing to the introduction of antibiotics in the 1940s.

Certainly the field has brought into the language an entirely new vocabulary: fifteen years ago, for instance, the word *transgenic* simply did not exist, at least not in the general parlance. See also *neomort, Xenomouse.*

pizza-cutter's palsy *noun*, a weakness of the muscles in the hand caused by pressing the handle of a roller-blade pizza cutter into the palm during repeated slicing: "sprout-picker's thumb, telegraphist's cramp and *pizza-cutter's palsy*—popular names for occupational afflictions that span the centuries and take in ways of living from the rustic to the cosmopolitan" (*Financial Times* [London], March 27, 1990).

THE STORY: This term can be seen as far back as 1988, when H. Royden Jones, M.D., used it in a letter to the *New England Journal of Medicine* to describe a case of work-related motor dysfunction resulting from undue pressure on the ulnar nerve. He had seen it in a patient whose hand had become so weakened that the man had difficulty inserting his car key into the ignition lock. (The cure is simple: use another type of cutting instrument.) According to the London *Financial Times*, the term *repetitive strain injury* (*RSI*) or *work-related upper limb disorder* would be the preferred technical nomenclature for such a malady.

Pizza-cutter's palsy joins others in the set of *possessive* + *malady* that abound in the medical literature. A few more examples are *tanner's ulcer* (technically more often called *chrome ulcer*, which is produced by chromium or its salts and is seen in tanners or others who work with chromium), *sponge-*

diver's disease (burning, itching, erythema, necrosis, and ulceration seen in sponge divers who come into contact with the stinging tentacles of certain Mediterranean sea anemones), and *ragpicker's disease* (inhalational anthrax). See also *holiday heart, jogger's paw.*

'roid rage also **roid rage** *noun, slang,* a severe behavioral disturbance characterized by mood swings, mania, delusions, unreasonable irritability, accentuated aggression, and combativeness, seen in athletes and others who have taken anabolic steroids. Also called *'roid mania; steroid rage:* "[The] young athlete should know that there are dozens of . . . steroid reactions, and that some, such as acne and uncontrollable *'roid rages* . . . might cause immediate difficulties" (*FDA Consumer,* November 1987). "Normally easygoing, he recalls bouts of *roid rage,* an urge to destroy that often strikes steroid users" (*Los Angeles Times,* October 8, 1989).

THE STORY: The term *'roid,* a clipped form like *'lude* from *Quaalude,* occurs in various other combinations such as *roid boy* (a user of steroids) and *roid slip* (the medical chart of a steroid user). A derivative noun *roider* also means "user."

A very early citation for *roid,* dated December 21, 1980, comes from a letter to the editor of the *New York Times Magazine* written by Barr H. Forman, M.D., an associate clinical professor of medicine at the Yale University School of Medicine: "Please be advised that no one uses *'oids,'* but rather *'roids,'* instead of steroids. Who should know better than I—a 'gland man' (endocrinologist)?"

Other words in this specialized lexicon include *juice, gorilla juice,* and *sauce* (steroids in general); *D-ball* (Danabol); *Bol* (Bolosterone); and *test* (testosterone). *Joy rider,* perhaps influenced by *joy popper,* refers to a nonathlete who uses steroids solely for the purpose of improving physique. To be *buffed* is to have achieved the desired bodybuilder look. *Buff,* a slang adjective now in the general parlance, means "well-built," as in "He's so *buff.*" To *stack* is to take a mix of steroids all at once. A *dork* is an uninformed, indiscriminate user of steroids; it also means "a jerk."

softgel *noun,* a one-piece, hermetically sealed soft gelatin shell containing medication in a liquid or semisolid state, which has been formed, filled, and sealed in one operation: "Many persons have a hard time differentiating between one-piece *softgels* and two-piece hard-shell capsule dosage forms. . . . I hope that the use of this new name will help serve to make that differentiation" (Frank E. Young, M.D., then-commissioner of food and drugs, FDA, August 28, 1986).

THE STORY: Here's an example of how events can shape a word. Soft-gelatin capsules were widely used prior to the notorious incidents of tampering with two-piece medicine capsules that occurred from 1983 into the late 1980s, when this term—then new in 1988—appeared in "Word Watch." But in the aftermath of the poisonings, consumers frequently shied away from the tamperproof soft-gelatin capsules, pharmaceutical industry analysts found, because the very word *capsule* on the label led people wrongly to believe that the bottle must contain tamper-prone two-piece capsules.

Several substitute terms for *soft-gelatin capsule* were suggested in an effort to eradicate the troublesome *capsule*. One suggestion was *pearl*, because that is what the dosage resembles. In the end, however, the collapsed form *softgel* won group approval. *Softgel* is a fixture in the lexicon these days thanks to the poisonings and tamperings of the eighties.

Thucydides syndrome *noun*, a symptom complex characterized by acquisition of influenza followed by development of staphylococcal tracheitis, pneumonia, or toxic shock syndrome, often resulting in death: "MacDonald et al and Sperber and Francis report the emergence (or reemergence) of *Thucydides syndrome*. . . . It now behooves physicians to be aware of this new entity and to consider quickly the diagnosis of TSS in a patient with influenza whose condition suddenly worsens" (*Journal of the American Medical Association*, February 27, 1987).

THE STORY: In October of 1985, Alexander Langmuir, M.D., formerly the chief epidemiologist at the Centers for Disease Control, postulated in the *New England Journal of Medicine* that the catastrophic plague of Athens (430–427 B.C.), heretofore a medical mystery and described in detail by Thucydides (himself a survivor of the epidemic), was actually influenza complicated by a "toxin-producing strain of staphylococcus." Dr. Langmuir, the coiner of this medical eponym, also predicted that the disease might strike again, perhaps as an adjunct of a major flu epidemic.

Shortly after his article had been published, patients exhibiting similar symptoms were seen in a Minnesota epidemic. The symptoms noted by Thucydides included high fever, hoarseness, coughing, sneezing, thirst, nausea and vomiting, blisters, amnesia, and peripheral gangrene. It is believed that the Athenians, having been debilitated by the influenza, succumbed to staphylococcal superinfections through small cuts or irritated nasal passages. (The bacterial strain associated with *Thucydides syndrome*, as noted in the current medical literature, is *Staphylococcus aureus*.) Langmuir did not maintain in his piece that the plague reported by Thucydides was identical to toxic shock syndrome as we know it today, however. He merely noted that the "same basic pathogenetic mechanisms were involved."

universal reactor *noun*, a person who is sensitive to a majority of the components of the environment—for example, air, water, food, housing, and drugs: "Known medically as a *universal reactor*, [she] is allergic to practically everything. Her doctor prescribed living on the beach as the best thing for her health" (*Los Angeles Times*, December 15, 1986).

THE STORY: It is said that *universal reactors* undergo a great deal of distress from the "chemicalized" products and environment of industrial America, according to a piece in the April 22, 1987, *Boston Globe*. William Rhea, M.D., the director of the Environmental Health Center in Dallas, has said that terms related to *universal reactor* are these, all of which reflect to some degree the distress alluded to by the *Globe*: *environmentally ill* (often abbreviated *EI*), *total-allergy syndrome*, *20th-century disease*, and the slang *chemmie* (a word formed like *foodie*, but which denotes a person who is especially sensitive to human-made chemical products).

Universal reactor has been extant for sixteen years. And the branch of the health-care profession concerned with such matters is called *clinical ecology*, also known as *environmental medicine*. Some specialists subscribe to the controversial theory that "man-made pollution is the cause of systemic allergic illness" (*American Journal of Medicine*).

urgicenter *noun*, a for-profit medical clinic, typically located in a business district or shopping mall, that offers same-day treatment without appointments or referrals for relatively minor medical complaints such as flu and sprains, but that does not provide the ongoing, comprehensive, specialized care for severely ill patients that hospitals do: "The chains are buying into another phenomenon: the *urgicenters* . . . that have sprung up in business districts and shopping centers. There are 2,500 such mini-clinics . . . today, 1,400 more than there were a year ago" (*Washington Post*, April 3, 1985). "If you don't have a private doctor, check out the *urgicenters*. . . . These storefront clinics ... are essentially group practices that are open early, late, and on weekends" (*New York*, September 8, 1986).

THE STORY: The word *urgicenter* is formed by junction of the element *urg-* (as in *urgent*), the connective *-i-*, and the noun *center*. The term, which first appeared in general print sources around 1984, is synonymous with a slightly older term, *doc-in-a-box*, which can be traced to at least 1983. Other synonyms are: *immediate-care facility* (the technical designator), *surgicenter*, and the irreverent *McDoctor*.

wallet biopsy *noun*, *slang*, a speedy but close examination of a patient's financial status and health-insurance coverage before admittance to a hospital. Also called *green screen*: "Helicopter operators ... do *wallet biopsies* ... before transporting [patients] to hospitals" (United Press International, October 4, 1987). "At Pittsburgh's Presbyterian University Hospital, patients who lack insurance coverage are required to make a down payment of $130,000 before undergoing a liver transplant, a hospital spokesman said. Such requirements, common at transplant centers, are sometimes pejoratively referred to as '*wallet biopsies*' or '*green screens*'" (*Washington Post*, November 29, 1988).

THE STORY: W. Gifford-Jones, M.D., wrote in *The Doctor Game*, "There is no such thing as minor surgery, but there are a lot of minor surgeons." Similarly, there is no such thing as cheap surgery in this country, as *wallet biopsy* proves.

Though used chiefly with respect to pretransplant evaluations, *wallet biopsy* is also used in connection with emergency-room care, or denial thereof. Bernard S. Bloom, Ph.D., a research associate professor at the University of Pennsylvania, remarked thus in a letter to the editor of *The Atlantic Monthly*, dated May 22, 1989: "The 1989 edition of *Current Concepts in Surgical Procedures of Dubious Value* recommends *wallet biopsy* be performed immediately preceding acute remunerative surgery."

If and when a comprehensive health-care reform bill passes Congress, the *wallet biopsy* will go the way of other procedures now deemed generally inappropriate, such as the lobotomy.

white coat hypertension *noun*, transitory elevation in a patient's blood pressure caused perhaps by some form of anxiety in the presence of a physician or other health-care professional. Also called *cuff hypertension*; *office hyper-*

tension: "You're probably experiencing something called *white coat hypertension*. . . . Some people have these momentary increases in blood pressure" (*Washington Post*, May 1, 1990). "Twenty-one percent of 292 patients with untreated borderline hypertension . . . were found to have normal daytime ambulatory pressures. . . . These patients were defined as having '*white coat*' *hypertension*" (Thomas G. Pickering, M.D., et al., *Journal of the American Medical Association*, January 8, 1988).

THE STORY: A review of the citations accrued for this term from the medical literature suggests that *white coat hypertensives* may be affected by the gender, status, and ethnicity of the attending health-care professional. The article by Dr. Pickering and his colleagues also indicates that *white coat hypertension* is more commonly seen in patients who are "female and younger, . . . weigh less, and [were] more recently diagnosed than patients whose pressure was elevated both in the clinic and in ambulatory monitoring."

Finally, some physicians disagree as to the very choice of terminology: for instance, E. C. Abbott, M.D., of Halifax, Nova Scotia, pointed out in the May 20, 1988, issue of the *Journal of the American Medical Association* that the modifier *white coat* is really a misnomer, since many caregivers do not wear white coats. Dr. Abbott prefers *clinic hypertension* or *office hypertension*, terms that focus on "the effects of interaction in a medical environment rather than on the apparel of the health worker who is measuring the blood pressure."

Xenomouse *trademark*, used for a genetically engineered laboratory rodent: "The bioengineered rodent debuted last week in the journal *Nature*, joined by a similar creature, Cell Genesy's *Xenomouse*, in this month's *Nature Genetics*" (*U.S. News & World Report*, May 9, 1994).

THE STORY: *Xenomouse* and its compatriot *HuMab-Mouse*, of GenPharm International, are noteworthy because their immune systems are partly mouse and partly human.

"Both mouse strains carry a key piece of the human immune system: the machinery for making . . . antibodies that help the body fight off foreign invaders such as bacteria," said *U.S. News*.

When a *Xenomouse* is injected with a certain chemical, it will produce human antibodies designed specifically to attack that very chemical substance. It is hoped that in the future, vast amounts of mouse-generated antibodies can be harvested to fight cancer, for instance.

The *Xeno-* prefix comes from the Greek *xenos*, "stranger," and meaning here "strange, foreign, or different." *Xeno-* has sustained long and rather prolific use in the language of science, with *xenobiotic*, *xenoblast*, and *xenocyst* being examples. And *xenogenetic* means "derived or obtained from an organism of a different species." *Xenomouse* surely is that. See also *pharming*.

Business Speak:
An Economy of Words

address hygiene	incent
amnesty consumer	intrapreneur
anticipointment	ISO-9000
anxious class	Just Say No defense
B+ category	karoshi widow
bright-collar	kata tataki
category killer	keh
constant whitewater	keiretsu
corporate concierge	Krone
decession	mahosker
delta-hedging	office (*verb*)
diversities	offsetting behavior
festival marketplace	open-collar worker
fiver	private bank
flanker	quant jock
garmento	sug
Generation E	tree hugger
gold-collar worker	vested termination
grapho-therapy	viatical settlement
greentapping	washing emporium
hi-pot	wolf ticket

When we reach for words to describe the business of life and
the world of business, we tend to invade the Seven Liberal
Arts, and sometimes call upon the Seven Deadly Sins.
—Robert Warren Kent, *Money Talks*

Kent's is an apt thought, given that the marketplace of today is but a microcosm of the high-velocity, conflicting, often confusing changes in play globally. In the words of Jean de Grandpré, a president of Bell Canada, "It's a
misconception that business is somehow separate from the man in the
street." To that extent, the words of business and economics and finance and
advertising and all the rest reflect what's happening in society as a whole. For
instance, take a look at *restructure, reinvent, reengineer,* and *rightsize/downsize.*
All of them are nineties words so generally familiar that they are not discussed as lexical items in this chapter. But all of them are "perestroika
words," ones that denote the disintegration of America's top-heavy corporate structures. Just as the ponderous bureaucracies of the former Warsaw
Pact countries have self-destructed, so too have many of the rigid, perk- and
paper-laden, traditional "command structures" of America's corporations. In
short, good-bye bureaucracy; hello, ad-hocracy. *Hi-pots,* often assigned to
work teams, are charged with interdisciplinary, interdepartmental tactical
and strategic planning and the inception and implementation of projects to
be brought to closure on time, within budget.

All the types of tensions and opposing forces of private life are present in
the workplace. After all, workers spend more time *officing* than they do re-

laxing, and, with the advent of the *virtual office* discussed in chapter 9, "Word Perfect in the Nineties: Hi-Tech, Hi-Sci," the beepered, modemed generation of *mobiles* will work outside the office setting. In terms of pressures, conflicts, and tensions, many companies are trying to make the workplace more employee-friendly; hence, the advent of the *corporate concierge*. But in point of contrast, workers are under tremendous pressure to perform in the *constant whitewater* of "reinvention," and the language of human resources is still characterized by bureaucratic impersonality, illustrated best by *vested termination* and use of *diversities* to mean people of various gender, ethnic, and racial groups. Another pair of terms pointing up the positive and the negative polarities in today's business sector is *keiretsu/karoshi widow*. While *keiretsu*, a Japanese borrowing, denotes imaginative use of partnering to get jobs done, *karoshi widow*, another borrowing from the same language with no known counterpart in English, denotes the survivor of a partner deceased from overwork.

Another disturbing crossover into business from private life is violence in the workplace. The workplace, now the setting of the so-called postal worker syndrome, can be as violent and abusive as the most violent and abusive marital or familial setting: the Society for Human Resource Management reported in a late 1993 survey of 500 professionals in the field that 75 percent of violent incidents in the workplace were fistfights. Of the others, 17 percent were shootings, 7.5 percent were stabbings, 6 percent were sexual assaults including rapes, and less than 1 percent were explosions. The results? Lowered productivity, lower-quality products, lowered esprit de corps, mental health problems among workers affected by the incidents, legal problems, higher turnover, and most recently, use of the idiom *going postal* (formed like *going ballistic* or *going bonkers*), to denote sudden, explosive workplace violence. All this in contrast to *ISO-9000*, which is supposed to work to ensure quality control.

Just as the language of commerce reflects global and private life, so does it reach out into many other sectors. The effect is double-edged, as *karoshi widow* proves. Another example is to be seen in the next chapter, "Wordpower: Manpower, Womanpower, Peoplepower," where *glass ceiling*, *rug-ranking*, and *sticky floor* represent negative, downright regressive attitude patterns in the office of the nineties. The business practices customized to their needs by underworld figures are discussed at *narcokleptocracy* and *cocaine industrial park* in chapter 5. Politics, now as big a business as Big Business, utilizes many of the marketing techniques and strategies found to be effective in industry. One is *inoculation*—addressing a potentially bad media problem before it is aired and making it benign. And advertising, very much a part of business per se, must, by necessity, have its own chapter because it is now inextricably tied in with politics. Hence, words like *hot button* and *infomercial* have migrated to chapter 8.

Generational contrasts constitute the central thesis of this chapter. This means the eighties versus the nineties. The legacy of the eighties transformed into the realities of the nineties. A few more key, recurring, commonly understood expressions illustrate the point: *change, competition, lean and responsive, core business, transitional employment, joblessness.* The condition in which these expressions first began to take hold to a highly repetitive degree is a *decession*—the central coinage discussed in this chapter. It is undoubtedly *the* language symbol of the first half of the nineties, just as the coiner's other invention, *cocooning,* characterized the private life of the affluent in the eighties.

Points of contrast between the last two business generations are to be seen more sharply in the following two lists of entries from this chapter, the first one representing the Zeitgeist of the eighties, and the second one, that of the nineties: (1) *bright-collar, gold-collar worker, intrapreneur, quant jock;* (2) *B+ category, Generation E, ISO-9000, open-collar worker, kata tataki.* The first group denotes a bullish attitude, an era full of *intrapreneurial* opportunities far beyond the most aggressive entrepreneurship, and the risks and antics to be seen on Wall Street. The second, opening appropriately enough with "B+"—this in reference to a new kind of hotel of appeal to those with very slim T&E budgets—denotes the pared-downness, the new demands, the insecurities, and the lowered expectations in the last decade of the century. *Generation E*—the antithesis of the so-called *slackers,* or *Xers,* in *Generation X*—and the *open-collar workers* are the upside. They are the nineties equivalents of the *intrapreneurs* and *gold-collar workers* of the eighties.

The language of business, whether of the eighties or the nineties, sometimes incorporates euphemism in the same manner as the military-industrial complex. Corporate mergers and takeovers are occurring in this decade just as they did in the eighties, but the language used to refer to them has become intentionally opaque in a concerted, conscious effort not to alarm shareholders. Therefore, we see "comfort terminology" such as "new corporate structure" and "strategic combination" instead. A prime example of soothing euphemism discussed in this chapter is *delta-hedging,* a swept-wing substitution for *portfolio insurance,* the older, and less comforting, synonym.

"It is an immutable law in business that words are words, explanations are explanations, promises are promises—but only performance is reality." So spoke Harold S. Geneen, emeritus CEO of ITT. Geneen speaks to the reality, not the virtuality, of doing business in an increasingly complex world. Let's hope that *Generation E* is up to the job.

address hygiene *noun*, the legible, accurate, and complete addressing of mail so that it is machine- and human-readable for fast and accurate sorting and prompt delivery to the correct addressees: "When this intricate [U.S. Postal Service mail-sorting] system works well, it flies. . . . When it works badly— for example, when letter-writers confound the computers by failing to practice what postal workers call *'address hygiene'*—it makes news" (*Washington Post*, July 22, 1994).

THE STORY: With the recent hike in the price of first-class stamps, mailers wanting a return on their investment but not returned mail will, no doubt, pay close attention to their *address hygiene*. Good *address hygiene*, says the Postal Service, is not exemplified by such wordings as "President Bill, Washington, D.C.," or by handwritten material in which 3s look like 8s and 1s resemble 7s. Acronyms, too, can be problematic for the optical scanners in sorting operations, which can decipher about 30 percent of the handwritten material.

Address hygiene, an example of government jargon at its best, is derived by association with the preexisting compounds *dental hygiene* and *personal hygiene*. The same process is in play with the new idiom *going postal*, derived by association with *going ballistic, going bonkers, going crazy, going nuts,* and *going belly-up*. Defined as the sudden attacking or murdering of coworkers or others in a workplace setting, the idiom appeared in the *Wall Street Journal* on October 13, 1994: "The fear [is] that a co-worker could suddenly *'go postal.'*" This expression takes its cues from Patrick Henry Sherrill's attack on an Edmund, Oklahoma, post office in 1986, in which fourteen people were killed and six wounded, followed in subsequent years by several other such incidents. From these, the expression *postal worker syndrome* emerged.

amnesty consumer *noun*, a former illegal alien who has resided in the United States five years or longer, has been granted legal status, and has accumulated enough capital through continuous work to obtain the credit needed to purchase durable goods and real estate: "One group of Hispanics that should be watched closely . . . are *amnesty consumers*" (*American Demographics*, September 1987).

THE STORY: "Word Watch" contained an entry for this term back in September of 1987, when it had been in use for only three months. It was coined by Carlos Arce, at this writing still the president of NuStats, Inc., an Austin, Texas, market research firm. In an interview in 1987, Arce pointed out that 2.5 million people would become *amnesty consumers* during the period beginning May 1, 1987, and ending May 1, 1988. (Approximately 3 to 4 million illegal immigrants are now living in the United States, according to 1994 statistics.) Arce said that these "underground Americans," who make up 1 million households, are "ready to buy," now that they are free to lay the paper trails that heretofore could have resulted in their detection and deportation. Arce characterized *amnesty consumers* as determined, industrious, conservative, and clever.

anticipointment *noun*, a state of mind, especially of a consumer, characterized by great anticipation of the advent of a new product, for example, and followed by equally great disappointment in the quality of the expected product or outcome: "Mike Mischler, CBS vice president of advertising promotion, described the show's promotional campaign as . . . low-key to avoid what he calls '*anticipointment*'—or unrealistic viewer expectations" (*Los Angeles Times*, January 2, 1989).

THE STORY: Advertising and broadcasting—fecund fields for the development of trendy blends—gave us yet another one, *anticipointment* (never spelled with two *p*'s). When this word appeared in my February 1990 "Word Watch" column, I had no firm idea who the real coiner was, so in an act of edgy etymologizing, I named three possibilities, dictated by information in the citations then at hand, but I didn't commit myself. *Business Insurance* indicated that the coiner was a senior European brokerage executive. *Advertising Age* said it was CBS television executive George Schweitzer (a theory picked up by Sid Lerner and Gary S. Belkin in their 1993 book *Trash Cash, Fizzbos, and Flatliners: A Dictionary of Today's Words*). *Electronic Media* indicated that the creator of this word was the vice-president for research at Frank N. Magid Associates, an Iowa-based media consulting firm.

Well, they were all wrong. The greatly *anticipointed* coiner surfaced in the summer of 1990. His name is Ray Jacobs, at that time a principal with the Los Angeles–based advertising agency Jacobs and Gerber, Inc. Here's what he said in a letter to the editor of *The Atlantic Monthly*, published in the June 1990 issue:

> It started in a holiday greeting card sent out by our . . . agency . . . in 1978 [that is, almost ten years before citations for the word had begun to appear in the media with any regularity]. The card read, "There's only one word that truly describes the warmth and spirit of the Holiday season . . . *Anticipointment*." When the card was seen on a wall at WNAC-TV in Boston, in 1980, the word was quoted in the *Boston Globe* in an article describing the current condition of the station. The station, now WHDH-TV and still one of our clients, has much improved, to our delight. Another client, Mick Mischler, the vice-president of advertising and promotion at CBS, quoted the word in an article that ended up in the *Los Angeles Times* recently and was noted in your Word Watch. The word has apparently surfaced elsewhere in print, and I can only say I hope that what started out as a quirky, contracted, multi-syllabic word will become a commonly used word to describe what I am currently feeling.

anxious class *noun*, U.S. workers at all levels of competence and rank who are affected by the prospect of joblessness, who are overworked in their presently held positions, whose wages have failed to increase or keep up with inflation, and whose worth in the workplace is no longer valued over the long term, as was once the case: "A class consciousness may be emerging from . . . shared anxiety—an awareness among millions of Americans that they occupy the same unsteady boat, even if they are doing well in high-paying jobs. Labor Secretary Robert B. Reich, giving the phenomenon a name, describes 'the *anxious class*' as 'consisting of millions of Americans who no longer can count on having their jobs next year, or next month, and whose wages have stagnated or lost ground to inflation'" (*New York Times*, November 20, 1994).

THE STORY: The *anxious class* is just one more item in the proliferating lexicon of an unstable era marked by lowered, or *B+*, expectations, an era in which corporate management battles *constant whitewater*, and, ever ready to glom onto the latest recommendations of the latest generation of maharishi-consultants, engages in endless "reenvisioning" and "reengineering" sessions, while exhausted *cross-functionals* try to *time-stuff* their way through myriad tasks once assigned to other colleagues now in the category of *vested* (or unvested) *terminations*. Thus the new *anxious class* has risen from the fog of "managing change," a euphemism for, among other things, *managing self-created chaos*, itself, in this writer's opinion, the direct result of a broad-scale failure to foresee, forecast, and "premanage" global economic change, given the existence at least ten years ago of clear early warning signals.

Not since World War II has the constituency of a *class* in the socioeconomic sense been so broad; just as people of all backgrounds and education levels once fought totalitarianism together, so do today's managers, support staff, technicians, and line workers experience the same angst in the workplace. But unlike, for example, Marx's *working class* and others of that ilk, the *anxious class* is leaderless. It has no linguistically identifiable rhetoric or vocabulary setting it off, and no designated enemy—no Mahogany Row running dog—against which it rails and fights. "Instead," the *New York Times* said, "business is seen as also a victim, caught in a global competition that forces cost-cutting and layoffs."

Though the *anxious class* has generally adopted an understanding attitude toward top management and its efforts to forge the corporate canoe ahead in the *whitewater* of the marketplace, this is where the cohesiveness of the group ends. Mirroring a fragmented society, members of the *anxious class* are each out for themselves in their highly individualized attempts to survive. These attempts involve everything from keeping one's own counsel about one's self-recognized professional weaknesses and deficits to working well beyond normal hours and taking work home without notifying a superior in order to create the impression of high performance. The tactics are indicative of the high levels to which competition has soared: workers are, in effect, competing with three other contenders—the (global) marketplace, their peers, and the limits of their own physical and emotional stamina.

Just within the span of the nineteenth and twentieth centuries, humankind has been introduced to the Marxist dialectic and the capitalist dialectic tailored to the Industrial Age; now, in the post-Industrial Age, the dialectic of lowered expectations and perpetual insecurity reminiscent of Britain after World War II is upon us. The *New York Times* headline writer of the piece cited earlier caught the spirit of the phenomenon: "The Rise of the *Losing Class*." See also *constant whitewater*. For insights into various manifestations of fear in society as a whole, see also *drive-by hatred, moral panic*.

B+ category *noun*, used in the hotel industry to denote a new, moderately priced, typically refurbished small hotel that is short on glitzy opulence, such as a richly appointed lobby and multiple dining facilities, but long on old-fashioned comfort, and featuring a single dining room offering the highest quality of cuisine: "He [William Kimpton, the CEO of Kimco Hotel and Restaurant Management Company] recognized that hotel prices are raised, and profits cut, by such extras as big banquet facilities, expensive lobbies and other entertainment that most guests rarely use. He set out to create a new kind of hotel class that some experts call the *B+ category*" (*New York Times*, February 16, 1994).

   THE STORY: For those surfeited with the sameness of the decor and the exorbitant costs associated with what might be called *l'hôtel d'opula*, where the food is beautiful and pricey yet tasteless, *vive la différence*. Affordable elegance and terrific food characterize the *B+* hotels, ones that reflect the taste and ambiance of their European counterparts, and at a fraction of the price of the five-stars. Targeted to the upscale American business, professional, and leisure travel markets, *B+* hotels are usually on the smallish side, having about 100 rooms, with the older buildings and the interior appointments refurbished in exquisite, understated taste. For instance, the small lobby might have a gas fire and furnishings reminiscent of a nice personal study or living room. In the comfortably furnished guest rooms, coffee and tea are always available. The general manager serves wine in the lobby at 5:00 P.M. every day. It's quiet: no Tailhook (or other) conventions would ever dream of booking at one of these hotels. A chef with world-class credentials presides over the kitchen, making the hotel attractive not merely for breakfast (as is typical with the big five-stars) but for dinner as well.

   The emergence of this niche market is no surprise, especially in a business travel world where T&E budgets are heavily scrutinized, when travelers are exhausted with the pace and increased frustrations of the business day, and when many business travelers end up doing much of their work from their hotel rooms. A *B+ category* hotel is just the thing for the *mobile* working in a *virtual office*. See also *virtual office*.

bright-collar *adjective*, of, relating to, or being a well-educated, fiscally conservative but socially liberal, professionally successful knowledge worker born after 1945 who has a preference for independent work, risk-taking, and individualistic decision-making: "*Bright-collar* workers may need new ways of organizing work—greater autonomy and flexibility, more unstructured time for communicating ideas and new social arrangements and interpersonal ties that foster it" (*Psychology Today*, January 1989).

THE STORY: *Bright-collar*, which joins *blue-collar*, *pink-collar*, *steel-collar*, and *gold-collar* in the lexicon of the workplace, was coined by Ralph Whitehead, a professor of journalism at the University of Massachusetts. Professor Whitehead is also the coiner of *new-collar*, a term he created in 1985 to denote a younger member of the baby-boom generation; for example, a car rental agent or a driver for a package-express company, whose job does not fit into the professional stratum or involve physical labor. He conceived *bright-collar* as far back as the late sixties while working as a newspaper reporter in Chicago. At that time, the *Chicago Sun Times*, with which he was affiliated, seemed to be attracting younger readers, unlike some other papers. Delivery trucks for the *Sun Times* were decorated with the slogan "The Bright One," which referred not just to the paper but to its young, upwardly mobile readers, many of whom were managers. Though some people in the industry felt that all members of the younger generation were and would remain "hippies," Whitehead felt that this group would eventually evolve into a definitely structured stratum of the workforce. In thinking about the situation, Whitehead was influenced by *bright* in the newspaper slogan and by *collar* in *blue-collar*. Therefore, his coinage *bright-collar* reflected continuity with the past and a sense of the future.

It was not until twenty or twenty-five years later, however, that his coinage achieved currency in the print and electronic media. Today it is used with various nouns, such as *worker* and *voter*, to denote the 20 million knowledge workers born since 1945, who constitute 25 percent of the workforce. According to Whitehead, the word first appeared in print in a January 17, 1988, *Boston Globe* story, four weeks before the New Hampshire presidential primary. Peter Jennings then did a long video essay on *bright-collars*, thereby bringing the word to instant national attention. During the 1990 Massachusetts gubernatorial elections, the *bright-collars*, not classifiable into a voting bloc easily accessed by political party leaders, did play a decisive role in the outcome of the race, a tight one between Democrat John Silber (an articulate university president with a firm philosophical background) and Republican William Weld (an articulate, entrepreneurial attorney), both of whom were in many ways attractive to the *bright-collars*. Though the competition for votes was acute, Whitehead says, "It's pretty clear that *bright-collar* women gave Weld his narrow margin of victory (no more than 5 percent of the electorate)." See also *gold-collar worker, green collar fraud, open-collar worker.*

category killer *noun,* a very large retail store that specializes in a single broad line of merchandise stocked in enormous quantities and in many varieties, and that sells the merchandise at deep-discount prices, thereby dominating the market: "Perhaps the best example of a *category killer* is Ikea, a Swedish company that opened its first U.S. store a year ago. . . . Ikea . . . stocks more than 15,000 items—all home furnishings and housewares. . . . The store's own restaurant and nursery accommodate hungry customers and weary parents. But best of all, Ikea has low prices" (*Wall Street Journal,* June 17, 1986).

THE STORY: *Category killers* have been around since the 1950s, when Toys "R" Us Inc. emerged. However, the widespread adoption of this merchandising strategy by other retailers and subsequent use of the term outside the world of merchandising, marketing, and advertising were new in the mid-1980s. The term itself is an example of a compound deemed "non-self-explanatory" by dictionary editors: at first glance, it brings to mind serial killing rather than merely the strangulation of smaller retail competition.

constant whitewater *noun,* the unremitting turmoil that characterizes today's corporate life—demanding quick decision-making, great flexibility and creativity, crisis management, and physical stamina—caused by increased global competition, a resurgence of mergers and acquisitions, and many restructurings and downsizings: "*Constant whitewater*[,] adapted from river rafting, . . . refers to management in an age of mergers, cutbacks, and re-engineerings. 'It's as if you're constantly managing amid turbulence,' says management consultant Mitchell Marks. 'Some *whitewater* is fun, but it takes a lot out of you'" (*Wall Street Journal,* October 18, 1994).

THE STORY: Hal Lancaster, who reported on *constant whitewater* in the piece cited here, called it in an interview with me "one of the ten deadly euphemisms of today's business," and Delta Consulting Group director Mitchell Marks added in a separate interview that managers need—but don't get—a moment or two of *still water* in which to collect their thoughts, gather their strength, and reflect deeply and meaningfully on business problems and their solutions outside a perpetual crisis environment. Both men remarked that *constant whitewater,* a term that bears absolutely no relation to the Clintons' Whitewater real estate problems, is a business condition showing no signs of receding—at least in the foreseeable future.

Marks remarked that *constant whitewater* may have evolved in 1992 as an antonymous expression to the preexisting expression "We're not in *still water*," heard at "total quality management" seminars that addressed the need for new "(en)visioning" by CEOs. In terms of (en)visioning, yet another expression has emerged: *thinking out of the box* (also called *thinking outside the nine dots*). This idiom, regardless of its wording, means to create new processes, as opposed to refining or expanding upon old formulas and methods. The expressions derive from tests given by management consultants to participants in training seminars, the first of which involves a diagram containing what looks like sixteen boxes forming a single, larger box. Those tested are asked to indicate, in thirty seconds, how many boxes are in the diagram. At least seven more can be found by the person who is resourceful and clever enough to think outside the clearly visible sixteen boxes. The expression *thinking outside the nine dots* derives from a diagram of nine dots arranged horizontally by threes, with equal space intervening and each row of the three aligned vertically with the other rows. Persons tested are asked to join all the dots with only four straight lines, without lifting their pencils. This feat can be accomplished at any starting point. To do so, the person's lines must go outside the nine dots, but most people automatically think that they have to stay within the nine dots. Said Development Dimensions International spokesperson Nancy Hrynkiw on November 14, 1994, to me, "*Thinking outside the nine dots* involves thinking about a problem without the constraints that 'how things are now' sometimes impose."

The necessity to think fast and resourcefully, not to say originally, has trickled down throughout downsized corporate structures to the beleaguered *cross-functional*. Yet another new buzzword of the nineties, a *cross-functional* is a manager or worker who, in a short-staffed company, must now perform an array of tasks once assigned to others who have been let go: "The overworked *cross-functional* . . . [has] been given additional, different duties— and thus must work 'cross functionally'—because other workers have been fired as companies slash staff" (*Washington Post*, March 7, 1994). *Cross-functionals*, the *Post*'s Business extra informs us, are under intense internal and outside pressure to perform at high levels for long hours (one of the characteristics of *constant whitewater*); they fear that they will be the next to be *outplaced*, to use yet another term of art.

An associated trend—one seen in personal and corporate life—is what the February 25, 1993, issue of the *New York Times* has called *time stuffing*; that is, the performing of multiple, usually clerical tasks at the same time. You've probably seen it, heard it going on over the phone, and done it, but never had a term for it. Consider the person who talks on the phone while opening and reading mail and signing documents. That's a *time stuffer.*

corporate concierge *noun*, an employee in a firm who assists other employees with the personal business they no longer have time to do, such as purchasing theater tickets, hiring nannies, making restaurant reservations, taking care of car maintenance, and arranging home repairs: "He is a concierge, apparently the first *corporate concierge* in America, the head porter of a big company that has decided it is a good idea to have somebody on the payroll minding other workers' personal business so they can keep their minds on their work" (*Wall Street Journal*, April 1, 1993).

THE STORY: Here's an evolving new sense of *concierge*, a word going back to a Latin term meaning "fellow slave." The *corporate concierge* at the Purchase, New York, corporate headquarters of PepsiCo has plenty to do for his fellow workers, because he has been tasked with the chores once done by housewives before the advent of the two-career family and by secretaries, "when," in the *Journal's* words, "there still were secretaries." The *corporate concierge*—"this ultimate employee-benefit frill"—was hired after a PepsiCo employee survey revealed that the workers were stressed out and had no free time during which to handle necessary errands. Employee response to the new service became so strong that the *corporate concierge* ended up with very little free time of his own and had to start taking work home at night.

decession *noun*, a period of recessionary spending coupled with depressed thinking by consumers: "America has entered a phase we're calling 'Decession'" (Faith Popcorn, *The Popcorn Report*, 1991).

THE STORY: Faith Popcorn, head of the New York City trend-analysis firm BrainReserve, identified *cocooning*. Now comes another coinage, this one a blend coined in 1990 and melding *depression* (the emotional kind) with *recession*. Popcorn said that *decessionary* thinking is fueled by guilt, regret, and bitterness about events of the eighties (impulse spending, overextension of credit, major encumbrances like the purchase of a second home, and health risks). Other contributing factors are job dissatisfaction, anxiety over the drug culture and pervasive violence, fear of a rudderless society (symptoms being the S&L debacle, the deficit, environmental apathy, and the instability of corporations), and economic worries on a grand scale. All these combine to generate a *"decession* consumer pathology" marked by hypernegation, downscaling of all personal spending, a distrust of the business and government sectors, a return to the use of cash rather than plastic, and a profound lack of confidence in the quality of essential goods and services like food, medicine, water, and cars.

This pathology in turn has created the angry "vigilante consumer," a species capable of bringing down established corporations. *Decession* erodes traditional brand loyalties, Popcorn said, to the extent that the few survivors will be the so-called entrepreneurial brands, small-company brands, "Euro/Pacific brands," and a few traditional ones that have been positioned using these psychological handles: humor and wit, relief from stress, a feeling of security, elements of nostalgia and fantasy, the possibility of body/mind improvement, and authenticity.

delta-hedging *noun*, a continuing options trading strategy intended to produce returns exactly offsetting a dealer's potential losses; a stop-loss strategy. Also formerly called *portfolio insurance*: "Whatever you call it, . . . [d]elta-hedging can break down in volatile markets, just when it is needed most" (*Wall Street Journal*, March 17, 1994).

THE STORY: A generalized linguistic trend of the nineties is to change unpalatable language to something more acceptable, while carrying on as usual the business denoted by the unpleasantries. This might accurately be called "the new aliasing of unpleasantries." Examples abound. Here are two: A U.S. senator accused of marital infidelities calls it "socializing," not "womanizing." The CEO of a telecommunications corporation involved in a merger consciously eschews use of *merger* in press interviews; the word harkens to the wild-and-woolly takeover days of the eighties and might be alarming to investors. Instead, he suggests, use something else, like *strategic combination* or *new corporate structure*. And so it is with *delta-hedging*, which now replaces the eighties term *portfolio insurance* in Wall Street parlance. The latter term got a bad name, or so says the *Journal*, when, in 1987, it "backfired on investors. . . . It goes by an alias these days—the sexier, Star Trek moniker . . . '*delta-hedging*.'"

Options are financial deals that give purchasers, or customers, the right to buy or sell securities or other such assets at prearranged prices over some future time period. An option's value can yo-yo wildly even with very minor alterations in the underlying security's price. In the term under discussion, the element *delta* is used because the relationship between the option's price and the value of the underlying asset is called the option's *delta.*

diversities *plural noun*, employees of all genders, races, and ethnic groups: "Managing diversity . . . defines the responsibility of managers and human re-source personnel to create a climate in which all employees—regardless of gender, race or ethnic background, to name a few of the *'diversities'*—are al-lowed to flourish. It also includes making sure no anti-discrimination laws are broken" (*Washington Post*, May 8, 1994).

THE STORY: *Diversity*, and the management of it, are *the* buzzwords of the nineties workplace. The whole concept of *multiculturalism*, from which the meaning of *diversity* derives, has been institutionalized in American English. From academia and the public schools, it passed into the workplace, where we now have *managers of diversity* as full-fledged job titles and positions.

It is predicted that by the turn of the century, the workplace will be pop-ulated by *diversities* to the extent that white males will constitute merely 15 percent of newly hired employees. But since current facts and figures indicate that 91.3 percent of human resource executives responsible for managing di-versity are white, and only 5 percent are African-American, not to mention the 1.7 percent and 1.6 percent who are Hispanic and Asian, respectively, there is some measure of skepticism as to whether the demographics of gen-der, race, and ethnicity will appreciably change by the year 2000. The upside is that the smaller companies, which in toto constitute the bedrock of Amer-ican industry, seem to be much more innovative and creative in their hiring and promotion policies.

In terms of language, *diversity*, an abstract noun usually used in the singu-lar, has, like *ethnicity*, come to be used in the plural, particularly in the litera-ture of HR, or human resources. For information on yet another abstraction that HR people have granted "human" status, turn to *vested termination.*

festival marketplace *noun*, a lighthearted, tastefully designed complex of businesses, such as ethnic food markets, small restaurants, taverns, specialty retail shops, food courts, flower vendors, and offices, often in a group of ren-ovated buildings or along a waterfront, intended to encourage patrons to dine, shop, or simply browse for fun. Also called *festival mall*: "Unlike ordinary big shopping centers, . . . *festival marketplaces* have no department stores. Their staying power depends on an intricate blend of . . . good taste and . . .

canny design that makes visiting them fun" (*Fortune*, July 27, 1981). "The Japanese city will open that country's first *festival marketplace*—an inner-city waterfront mall popularized more than a decade ago by Faneuil Hall in Boston and Harborplace in Baltimore" (*Washington Post*, July 23, 1990).

THE STORY: Almost 700 citations for this term were at hand in 1990, the year that I wrote an entry for *festival marketplace* in "Word Watch." Such a large accumulation of printed evidence attested not only the popularity of this shopping-area design but also the staying power of the term denoting it. According to the May 13, 1990, edition of the *New York Times*, James W. Rouse, developer of Boston's Faneuil Hall Marketplace and Baltimore's Harborplace, is the "father" of the *festival marketplace*, now a fixture in most self-respecting cities. The term *festival workplace* has also evolved, referring to a complex of offices combined with food courts: "Catfish Town [in Baton Rouge] was redeveloped as a '*festival workplace*' . . . and is 90 percent leased" (*Governing*, August 1990).

fiver *noun*, a person who donates 5 percent of his or her income to charity and five hours a week to volunteer service: "The campaign will use public service advertising to draw attention to what it calls the *fivers*—the 20 million people who contribute 5 percent or more of their annual income, and the 23 million who volunteer five or more hours a week" (*American Demographics*, March 1987).

THE STORY: This meaning of *fiver*, a word that has enjoyed widespread use for over 140 years in the sense of a five-dollar bill and that also has the sense of a five-pound note in Britain, was used in the charitable-giving sense by Independent Sector, the country's biggest philanthropic coalition, during its attempt to reintroduce the old practice of tithing as a way through which charitable contributions could be doubled by a targeted year. Although there is no complete profile of a typical *fiver*, churchgoing seems to be a characteristic link to generosity. This is a far cry from yet another established sense of *fiver*, a five-year prison sentence.

Fiver brings to mind *dimie* (or *dimey*), perhaps originally a Boston word meaning a "small glass of beer costing ten cents": "I learned about history from sitting in Jim Cronin's bar drinking *dimies* and hearing tales about great-grandfathers of classmates who had fought in the Civil War" (*Boston Business*, Fall 1986). Current prices of beer notwithstanding, this is a sort of "relic word" for which little or no printed evidence exists, except for an entry in linguist Richard A. Spears's valuable *Slang and Jargon of Drugs and Drink*, where it is labeled "U.S.," and an entry for the *-ey* spelling in the *Random House Historical Dictionary of American Slang*, taking it to 1961. The quotation from *Boston Business* comes from an essay in that magazine written by Bostonian John Spooner entitled "Night Music," reflections on his Harvard days during the mid-1950s. Even the writer never saw *dimie* in print during those days; he told me in an interview that his spelling was based simply on intuition and recollection. Readers familiar with the word from days of yore are invited to *drop a dime*, as the current idiom goes, and get in touch via this publisher.

flanker *noun*, a new product similar to and having the same brand name as another established product in a line, that is created to address market segmentation, to support sales of the main product, and to gain new sales: "This is the so-called *flanker* . . . which, bearing the same name as a maturing item, benefits from all the advertising that may have preceded its introduction, as well as transferred customer loyalty (the famous 'halo effect')" (*DM News*, August 1, 1986). "Definitions are often disputed, but in the marketing world these new-products-that-are-really-just-variations-on-old-products are known as 'line extensions'—basically, the same product in a different form—or '*flankers*'—generally a similar product in the same brand line. Often, they are priced at a lower level than the originals" (*New York Times*, December 13, 1984).

THE STORY: This specialized sense of *flanker*, long used in advertising and marketing circles, has never enjoyed wide use in general, non-business-related publications. Other examples of *flankers*, aside from, say, a shampoo that is added to a well-known, successful detergent and bar-soap brand-name line, might be pocket diaries sold as accessories to a line of desk calendars and office diaries, and diet versions of established soft drinks and foods.

Flanker is an example of a class of words ending with the suffix *-er*, which convey meanings such as "one that does X," as in *driver*; "one that has X," as in *eighteen-wheeler*; "an inhabitant of X," as in *Berliner*; and "one that manufactures X," as in *armorer*. *Flanker* falls into the first category of this class, called "*-er* agent nouns."

garmento *noun*, *slang*, a fabric buyer or jobber, or a clothing designer or manufacturer: "'They're all real-estate people and *garmentos*,' said one long-term Southamptonite after surveying the [party] tent, with pointed reference to the Grand *Garmento*, himself, Calvin Klein" (*New York Newsday*, August 1, 1989).

THE STORY: Not a new word at all, *garmento* is, according to the August 1985 issue of *Smithsonian*, "a term of derision used by Seventh Avenue's more up-to-date folk" for "a lineal descendant of the street peddler who wheels and deals and wheedles his way to a precarious livelihood." *Garmento* is just another example of the English language's prolific use of the suffix *-o*, which, when attached to a noun or an adjective, creates an often derogatory noun, the meaning of which denotes persons or things associated with what is specified by the base form. Words so formed include, for instance, *bucko, cheapo, sicko, pinko, freako, wino,* and *weirdo*. Other terms formed in this manner that lack pejorative denotations and connotations are *kiddo* and *daddy-o*. See also *blendo*.

Generation E *noun*, entrepreneurs under forty years of age who are the founders, cofounders, owners, or controlling shareholders of companies with revenues of $1 million or more: "Bravo! As a typical 'Generation E' entrepreneur, I . . . cannot overstress our computer savvy, which we learned in grade school and have a deep desire to exploit" (Brian K. Roemmele, CEO, Avalon America Corporation, Temecula, Calif., letter to the editor, *Success*, February 1994).

THE STORY: With every extreme, there is an opposite. Here, *Generation E* is the obverse of *Generation X* (see *Xer*), a group of twentysomethings who have been characterized by some critics as having surrendered to a kind of psychic bathos, the central notion of which holds that success in a world tainted by the self-absorption and greed of the baby boomers is not only futile but unsavory.

According to Doug Mellinger, the CEO of PRT Corporation of America, a software consulting firm to Fortune 500 companies, and himself a member of *Generation E*, the *Eers*, or the *Gen E's*, as I choose to call them, are engaged not merely in earning a salary or creating wealth for greedy motives; rather, they are interested in creating new jobs through the creation of new wealth. He, along with the editors of *Success*, came up with the term *Generation E* in March 1993 during a meeting about a proposed article in *Success* about these new, young, highly motivated, computer-literate entrepreneurs. They sound like just the right clients for the emerging American sense of *private bank*.

gold-collar worker *noun*, an employee in a brain-intensive business who regards his or her intellect, experience, talent, expertise, and inventiveness as monetary assets to be leveraged with respect to relationships with current or potential employers: "*Gold-collar workers* view themselves as their own best investment" (Robert E. Kelley, Ph.D., telephone interview, April 1986). "Experts estimate that *gold-collar workers* represent more than 25 percent of today's work force, a percentage that continues to grow. . . . Although *gold-collar workers* spend considerable time in teams, individual quiet time remains crucial. . . . Studies show that when someone is interrupted, it takes up to 20 minutes to get back up to speed" (*Chicago Tribune*, August 7, 1994).

THE STORY: Here's a gilt-edged word that in retrospect is a gilt-edged emblem of the gilt-edged ethos of the eighties. Robert Kelley, an adjunct professor at the Carnegie-Mellon University Graduate School of Industrial Administration and a senior management consultant at the Stanford Research Institute (SRI International), coined *gold-collar worker* in 1984. The term forms part of the title of his 1985 book *The Gold-Collar Worker: Harnessing the Brainpower of the New Workforce. Gold collars* were described as "a new breed of worker." The coiner-author went on: "They deal with unique, complex problems requiring specialized expertise and experience, often involving long completion cycles and delayed feedback."

I had found the term in a citation from an article, "The Battle of the B-Schools Is Getting Bloodier," by John A. Byrne in the March 24, 1986, issue of *Business Week*: "'The *Gold-Collar Worker*,' a class [at Carnegie-Mellon] that advises students on how best to motivate the growing ranks of 'knowledge workers' in service businesses. . . ." The author of that piece and the coiner of the term agreed in separate interviews that creative people at ad agencies, consultants at think tanks, and others so highly skilled qualified as *gold-collar workers*.

Gold-collar falls into the same set as *white-collar*, which goes back to the 1920s; *blue-collar*, which dates to the mid-1940s; and *pink-collar*, which appeared in the late 1970s. See also *bright-collar, green collar fraud, open-collar worker*.

grapho-therapy *noun*, a program designed to alter a person's behavior or operating style, especially in the workplace, through transformation of his or her handwriting characteristics: "Some job seekers have gone so far as to submit to *grapho-therapy* in their quest for success" (*Business Month*, September 1988).

THE STORY: Richard Cohen, the critic at large for the *Washington Post Magazine*, related an alarming tale in the November 7, 1993, issue:

In France, a certain Michel Malat, 40 years old and out of work, . . . sent out about 250 applications for employment and . . . got . . . back about 250 letters of rejection. In each and every case, he enclosed a handwritten letter, which is the custom in France. It is also the custom to have these letters analyzed by a graphologist . . . When Malat had this done himself, he was told he is intelligent and rational, but lacks "flexibility and inventiveness."

Would that the unfortunate M. Malat had known about graphology's counterfoil, *grapho-therapy*.

According to Richard J. Klimoski, a professor of industrial psychology at Ohio State University, the term *grapho-therapy*, whose coiner is unknown, surfaced in the media in October 1988. This type of counseling is typically offered by consultants to individuals anxious to enhance their success ratio within the corporate sector through an emphasis on style as opposed to substance. The concept and the theory are regarded with high skepticism among professional psychologists, said Klimoski and others, given the difficulty in changing established behavioral patterns under the best of conditions and with the use of carefully thought out interventions.

The very existence of *grapho-therapy* can be interpreted as a response to the banning in the United States of lie-detector tests in the screening of potential employees: after the lie detectors were banned, some 3,000 American firms retained graphologists as personal consultants.

In the *Journal of Applied Psychology*, Klimoski and Anat Rafaeli wrote this about the use of graphology: "In Europe, where it was developed, graphology [generally considered a valid diagnostic tool by psychologists] is routinely used by an estimated 85% of all companies" to evaluate character. But in a study in which twenty graphologists evaluated the handwriting of eighty real estate executives to determine if there was a correlation between their handwriting styles and their success in terms of sales, Klimoski and Rafaeli found no such correlation. (Typical characteristics examined by graphologists include size, slant, width, zones, regularity, margin, pressure, stroke, lines, connection, and word and line spacing.) The inferences that graphologists try to draw from examination of handwriting typically relate to projected degrees or measures of a subject's social confidence, social activity, ego drive (as expressed in sales, for instance), interpersonal communication, work management skills, decision-making, health and vitality, economic maturity, empathy, and sympathy.

While *grapho-therapy* is relatively new, *graphology* is not: Suetonius, the Roman biographer of A.D. 80, found peculiarities in the handwriting of the emperor Augustus, and he recorded them. Camillo Baldi, who flourished in seventeenth-century Italy, initiated handwriting analysis based on study of its components. And Goethe promulgated the idea that one's character is revealed and projected in the way one writes. The word *graphology* also has a known coiner: Michon, a French churchman who studied handwriting for over thirty years, created the word in the year 1871.

greentapping *noun*, a method of automatically allocating money to any of a prechosen group of worthy causes during the course of commercial, especially credit-card, transactions: "*Greentapping* is the act of tapping the economic system for money to improve the world. . . . Is *greentapping* a word that will make the next edition of Webster's Dictionary?" (*Card Courier: The Newsletter for Practical Idealists*, Working Assets Funding Service, January 1990).

THE STORY: Well, it didn't make entry in *The American Heritage Dictionary of the English Language, Third Edition*, published in 1992, because at the time of editing we did not have a substantial accrual of citations over a period long enough to attest the longevity of the word. Here's the story behind the coinage: According to Peter Barnes, a founder of Working Assets, he and his colleagues searched "for several years" for a word describing cardholders' allocation of monies for worthy causes, such as the environment, human rights, peace, eradication of hunger, and economic justice. So they "invented" *greentapping* to denote the process that the November 23, 1989, issue of the *Boston Globe* said "goes against a flattening trend in corporate giving, which declined in real dollars last year to $4.75 billion, or 1.55 percent of pretax profits, its lowest level since 1982." A customer using a telephone credit card, might, for instance, allocate 1 percent of the money owed on a bill to a number of worthy causes by signing up for Working Assets Long Distance, which uses the US Sprint System.

Though *greentapping* is not often seen in print, the practice continues, and the success of the founding group is not debatable: according to a November 7, 1993, citation from the *New York Times*, Working Assets made $2.5 million in donations to worthy causes since its inception. Such causes are selected by vote from subscribers.

Reasons for the success of Working Assets, and therefore *greentapping*, are several: the group recognized early on the trend toward judging a company not so much by its product but by its reputation; the ethos of greed began to subside, with baby boomers now wanting to put something back into the quality of life rather than merely take; and, with changes in communications regulations, the group has become a telephone-time reseller rather than an agent for Sprint. In the reselling deal, Working Assets buys time and resells it at deep-discounted, competitive prices to its subscribers. Working Assets directly controls the billing. In a typical transaction, a subscriber would pay, say, $40.00 on a $37.56 bill, and the difference would go into a charitable pot for disbursement at year's end. The subscriber's total *greentapped* contributions are, of course, tax deductible.

hi-pot or **Hi-Pot** *noun, slang,* a young executive with high potential for rapid corporate advancement: "The *Hi-Pots*, as they are known, are shifted often into ever more demanding jobs, and their performance is reviewed by top management" (*Fortune*, September 8, 1980).

THE STORY: *Hi-pot* has been a part of corporate inside language for at least three decades, but it made international news in 1992 in stories about an outside directors' coup at General Motors. At that point, *hi-pot* was associated in the public mind with GM; however, it has also been used at companies such as Ford: "Ford defines *hi-pots* as those persons having the ability to progress a certain number of job levels over a certain period of time" (*Automotive News*, June 27, 1988). In fact, the *Fortune* citation relates to Amoco.

incent *verb,* to stimulate to action; provide incentive for or to: "The government felt that we needed to *incent* activity which is highly risky" (Edmund Pratt, CEO, Pfizer Inc., transcript, *The MacNeil/Lehrer NewsHour*, September 25, 1986). "It [the agreement] *incents* us to reduce our leverage and makes the bank more comfortable as well" (Leon Level, vice-president and treasurer, Burroughs Corporation, *American Banker*, May 13, 1986).

THE STORY: *Incent,* a back-formation from *incentive,* is sure to incense certain readers. A back-formation is a new word created by removing from an existing word a true affix or an element mistakenly thought to be an affix. This process, which reverses the more usual trend of word formation by deleting, rather than adding, elements, is frowned on by many linguistic conservatives. It has been suggested that people object to back-formations particularly when the new words thus formed are easily recognizable as such. But, as Roy Copperud has said in his *Usage and Style: The Consensus,* "Usefulness is what wins back-formation acceptance" over time.

Whether or not the vast majority of English speakers will find *incent* useful enough to accept is an open question. Printed evidence for it to date generally restricts it to the corporate and financial communities. Examples of other back-formations that have gained wide acceptance are *edit*, formed from *editor; peddle*, from *peddler; sedate*, from *sedative; televise*, from *television; diagnose*, from *diagnosis; donate*, from *donation;* and *laze*, from *lazy.*

Strangely enough, *incentive* has spawned yet another verb, *incentivize*, also objectionable to many: "I think the President's fiscal policy is a big part of this problem, and this bill will help *incentivize* everybody to solve . . . the problem" (Richard Gephardt, transcript, *The MacNeil/Lehrer NewsHour*, July 17, 1985). The word has also been used by people like Orville Freeman, Senator Frank Lautenberg, an executive vice-president of NCR, and an accounting professor at Northwestern University.

Overuse of the very productive suffix *-ize* to create coinages such as *accessorize, concretize, envisionize, decimalize, rubble-ize, sprinklerize, finalize, privatize, prioritize, reprivatize,* and *audibilize* may offend eye and ear, creating what I have called the "ization" of English. Nevertheless, critics—this one included—would not turn a whisker or a hair at *criticize, symbolize, formalize, hospitalize, publicize, nationalize, popularize, modernize, epitomize,* or *rationalize,* ten words that, taken together, have been extant for a total of over 2,505 years. Not to mention a returnee: *Balkanize.*

intrapreneur *noun,* an employee of a large corporation who takes direct responsibility for turning an idea into a profitable finished product or new business by courageous, often unorthodox risk-taking, great inventiveness, and sustained follow-through: "The *intrapreneur* may be the creator or inventor but is always the dreamer who figures out how to turn an idea into a profitable reality" (Gifford Pinchot III, *Intrapreneuring,* 1985).

THE STORY: Scratch a word's history deep enough and often you'll find a controversy. Such is the case with *intrapreneur,* the intracorporate opposite number of *entrepreneur,* which has been in our language for over 150 years. Having made three transatlantic phone calls to *The Economist* about the word (all in a dull day's work for harmless drudges), I am now satisfied that Gifford Pinchot III really is the coiner of *intrapreneur,* contrary to Ralph Landau's assertion in the August 22, 1983, issue of *Business Week* that Norman Macrae, then the deputy editor of *The Economist,* not Pinchot, had coined it. "It wasn't me; it was Gifford Pinchot," Macrae told me.

To some readers, the issue of coinage may be as trivial as such British controversies as the rights-of-way at toad crossings; it isn't. One of the lexicographer's responsibilities is to unearth the true origins of words. In his book *Intrapreneuring*, Pinchot mentioned that he coined the term in the fall of 1978. He also pointed out that *intrapreneur* was his "shorthand for intracorporate entrepreneur"—a fact refuting previous speculation that the word is a compound formed of the prefix *intra-* and (*entre*)*preneur*. *Intrapreneur* has generated a number of derivational forms—*intrapreneuring*, of course, and *intrapreneurial*, *intrapreneurially*, *intrapreneurialism*, and *intrapreneurship* as well—just one indicator of its potential staying power in English. The word made it into *The American Heritage Dictionary of the English Language, Third Edition* in 1992.

ISO-9000 *noun*, a set of worldwide quality standards, originally based on those used in Britain and Canada, requiring companies to create a paper trail to track and eliminate product defects, thereby assuring customers of the quality and safety of the products they buy: "A skeleton-faced Star Trek ghoulie beckoned ominously from a sign posted at [a Virginia company's headquarters]. 'ISO-9000,' the sign read. 'Resistance is futile; you will be assimilated'" (Lynchburg, Va., *News & Advance*, January 2, 1994).

THE STORY: *ISO* is the abbreviation for the Geneva, Switzerland–based International Organization for Standardization, which created its corpus of international quality-control standards between 1979 and 1987, using input from representatives of twenty nations, including the United States. The *9000* is a "nonce number," just appended for no special reason. The standards were adopted in 1988.

An entire new industry of consultants and independent auditors involved in certifying complying companies has sprung up. Seventy-three countries, including ours, have accepted the standards, thereby enhancing the growth of this new consultancy industry. The toy and construction products industries were the first to gain certification. Everyone in a company participates in showing on paper exactly how he or she contributes to the product development and manufacturing processes, among other things. Audits are made every six months to ensure compliance. The result? Better quality products but lots more paperwork, initially.

Just Say No defense *noun*, an antitakeover, antimerger strategy by which a corporation simply refuses to entertain the advances of a suitor and makes that fact well known before any such advances are contemplated or made:

"The *Just Say No defense* still survives for CEOs who steer clear of initiating any merger activity at all, or who pursue only 'friendly' deals where control wouldn't pass to a dominant shareholder" (*Wall Street Journal*, December 3, 1993).

THE STORY: Derived by association with Nancy Reagan's antidrug slogan of the eighties coupled with the final element in eighties Wall Street lingo, such as *Pac Man defense* (defined by David L. Scott in *Wall Street Words* as "a defensive antitakeover tactic in which the target firm attempts to take over the acquiring firm"), *Just Say No defense* is symbolic of the return, in the nineties, of the specter of the *corporate raider*, the Man in Black who stalked Wall Street in the eighties.

Significant to the flurry of corporate mergers particularly at the start of 1994 was the euphemization of the *raider* and words associated directly with him. For instance, when references were made to events such as the QVC/Viacom-Paramount situation, *hostile takeover* was often eschewed in favor of the more benign *strategic combination, strategic merger, combination, new corporate structure,* and *corporate marriage.* See also *delta-hedging.*

karoshi widow *noun,* in Japan, the wife of a man who has died of overwork: "In a nation that has been accused of encouraging chronic workaholics, officials . . . are only beginning to recognize the injurious effects of the abnormally long hours workers put in. . . . Both women are among Japan's growing number of *karoshi widows*" (*Chicago Tribune*, April 22, 1990).

THE STORY: The word *karoshi* comes from *karō,* a verbal noun in Japanese meaning "overwork," itself from the Chinese *ka-,* "exceed," and *ro-,* "labor," and the Chinese morpheme *-shi,* "death." The condition *karoshi,* a fatal complex of apoplexy, high blood pressure, and stress that physicians associate directly with excessive working hours, affects thousands of Japanese workers, typically supervisors and middle managers aged forty-five to fifty who have otherwise been deemed fit, albeit characterized as *moretsu sha-in,* "fanatical workers," or *yoi kigyo senshi,* "good corporate soldiers."

Japanese workers were, in 1990, putting in thirteen- and fourteen-hour days routinely, and were averaging 2,250 hours a year at their jobs. In 1988 and 1989, two *karoshi widows* received financial restitution ($19,500 in one case) based on Labor Ministry requirements stating that payment could be made if it could be proved that the victim had worked for an abnormally long number of hours within a week of death. In 1990, such cases of *karoshi* were still being classed by the Labor Ministry as "industrial accidents." If *karoshi widow* ever sustains enough widespread currency in English to warrant inclusion as a borrowing in dictionaries, it will join other Japanese borrowings such as *banzai* attack, *geisha* girl, *kabuki* dancer, *kamikaze* pilot, *karate* chop, *samurai* sword, *sumo* wrestler, and *tatami* mat, not to mention that permanent solution to a temporary problem, *hara-kiri*.

kata tataki *noun phrase*, used to denote the practice of singling out redundant employees in Japanese firms who are targeted for changes in their employment status: "Some layoffs have been disguised by the practices of *kata tataki*. . . . A boss tells an employee, We have no work for you so you'll have to go—and by the way, this is voluntary, right?" (*Time*, April 19, 1993).

THE STORY: If *karoshi* doesn't get Japanese workers, *kata tataki* will—at least in this period of economic downturn. At this writing, Japan's lifetime employment system is undergoing seismic shocks because of a sharp downturn in profits, a dip in productivity, and a generally unstable economy. But "major Japanese firms—unlike their U.S. counterparts—are cutting their work forces by every means short of layoffs: slashing recruitment; encouraging early retirement; terminating part-time workers . . . ; and transferring employees to affiliated firms and suppliers," said the March 3, 1993, *Washington Post*.

What is more, the corporate culture in Japan is loath even to use Japanese terminology equivalent to our words *fire*, *terminate*, *layoff*, and the bald *termination*, an abstract noun that has now come to mean, in American personnel parlance, "an employee who has been terminated." For example, in Japanese, to *fire* an employee would be expressed by the verb phrase *kubi ni naru*, translated literally "to become a decapitated head," according to William E. Nass, a professor of Japanese in the Department of Asian Languages and Literatures at the University of Massachusetts. In lieu of such brutal language, the term of choice is the superficially more benign *kata tataki*, which conjures the image of a light tapping on a person's shoulder. In an interview Nass pointed out that *kata* means "shoulder" and *tataki* means "a tap," it being derived from the verb *tataku*, "to strike or beat." (Workers tapped for departure who refuse to go voluntarily may be assigned demeaning, menial tasks, such as cutting trees and writing mandatory daily compositions at remote rural facilities, or they may be resituated in ergonomically inhospitable areas such as dimly lit basements and assigned no tasks whatsoever.) Nass went on to say that *kata tataki* is "a kinder, gentler way of indicating the obvious, but in any case you're equally dead." And the Japanese word for the practice of forcing a voluntary quit by imposition of insulting work or no work at all is *iygarase*, "annoyance." See also *vested termination*.

keh *noun*, a Korean-American financial pool, adapted from a traditional Korean institution, in which members of a group who implicitly trust one another contribute a fixed sum of money to a monthly pot, taking turns as recipients of the month's collection, often in cash, with the organizer getting the first accrual and the subsequent order of payouts determined by negotiation or by drawing lots: "The *keh* goes a long way to explaining the [Washington, D.C., Korean] community's remarkable success. Nobody knows for sure how much money is tied up in *kehs*, but estimates of $100 million at any one time in the Washington area are conservative, say businessmen and academics who have studied the phenomenon" (*Washington Post*, November 3, 1991).

THE STORY: The *keh*, being interest-free, tax-free, and paper-free, is an ideal investment technique for people who want to start up businesses but who have little or no credit history, no capital to speak of, no knowledge of the American banking system, and limited understanding of English. The Korean Association of Greater Washington has reported that about 80 percent of Korean households participate in at least one *keh*.

An understanding of the *keh* debunks widespread speculation that the phenomenal growth of Korean-American businesses in this country is generated by secret Korean government funds, special U.S. government loans, or grants from groups like the Unification Church. Mutual trust is key to the success of a *keh*. It is the kind of trust almost unheard of in Western culture. Default would bring great shame not just to the defaulter but to that person's whole family. Such conduct most certainly would result in ostracism to a degree that marriage or future employment in the community would be impossible. "The incentive to save and to not let down the group is so strong that for some, 'living is terrible—no good food, good clothes, good car—to pay into the *keh*,' [Ki Duck] Choi said" (*Washington Post*).

The *keh* was traditionally regarded in Korea as the province of women because the so-called dirty work of household finance was left to the women. Only in the United States has the *keh* evolved into a critical capital-generating technique involving men. In high-level business *kehs*, payouts involving sums as high as $1 million are not that uncommon, though in some *kehs*, ceilings, as of $100,000, are set.

keiretsu *noun*, intercompany cooperation: "An important Japanese business structure—'*keiretsu*' . . . is making deep inroads here. . . . This is . . . an unintended byproduct of computer technology" (*New York Times*, February 6, 1994).

THE STORY: The writer in the citation, none other than Jim Manzi, the chairman and CEO of the Lotus Development Corporation, was speaking of the Japanese word that means "linkage." In business in Japan, it is a group of companies linked by interlocking directorates, presidents' clubs, cross-shareholding, customer-supplier agreements, and sociohistoric ties. The result is an extended intercorporate family, a powerful one. Mitsubishi, Sumitomo, and Mitsui are examples. Member companies use intercorporate team play to pool skills, labor, expertise, technology, and capital. The result? A razor-sharp leading edge in many markets.

Some American managers have taken the idea of *keiretsu* and translated it into a cloned form that best fits our business climate and its regulations. Ours is an electronic *keiretsu* by which companies and their subsidiaries, for instance, use groupware (software enabling multiple workers to work on a project simultaneously from multiple sites) to share information and coordinate operations. The so-called enabling technologies—things like mobile computing and E-mail—were, ironically enough, in Manzi's view, developed not for external corporate linkups but for internal communications. As Manzi has said, "Technology, though, has a way of taking unexpected turns." See also *virtual office*.

Krone *verb*, to teach (subjects in an organizational setting) to be more acutely aware of the ways in which they think through problems in an effort to alleviate, if not stop, the decline in American competitiveness. Subjects are asked to bear in mind constantly the six essential factors influencing organizational health—expansion, freedom, identity, concentration, order, and interaction—factors that the subjects must relate to the demands of the workplace. At the same time, the subjects must consider whether their behavioral patterns result from outside stimuli, forces within the self, or a purpose beyond the self (with the latter conclusion preferred, of course): "At Pacific Bell—until the state's Public Utility Commission called a . . . halt to the practice—employees have been *Kroned*, indoctrinated in a mode of comprehending the world that owes its soul to the [late wandering Russian] mystic [George Ivanovich] Gurdjieff. . . . As one *Krone* memo puts it, . . . the aim is 'to generate in the minds of resources the ability to use their own progressive, systematic intelligence in a way that they can manage their process of continuously going beyond the limitations of their own and others' typically reductive, analytic intelligence so that they can lead their own and others' thinking toward sustained competitive effectiveness and meaningful development of people'" (*Harvard Business Review*, January 1988).

THE STORY: Officially called *Leadership Development*, the informal eponym *Krone* or *Kroning* comes from the name of Charles Krone, a Carmel, California, management consultant who helped develop the principles for a series of ten two-day mental exercise sessions, costing Pacific Bell a controversial $40 million to implement. Other terms in the *Krone* lexicon are to be found in a glossary excerpted from the May 4, 1987, issue of *Newsweek*: *end-state vision* ("a goal"), *internal resource* ("an employee"), and *metanoic* ("acquisition of a clear vision"). Reactions to the program were decidedly mixed. The *Harvard Business Review* noted at the time that an Oakland, California, auto dealer said he "got the best results by kicking butts and taking names."

The verb *Krone* in and of itself is of interest because it joins a relatively small class of surnominal verbs, the most recently famous being, of course, *Bork*. Here are citations illustrating two others: "Veteran HEW . . . staffers are in shock after getting a look at the fiscal 1979 budget figures. . . . In the words of one battle-scarred old hand, 'They almost out-*Nixoned* Nixon'" in terms of cutbacks below the HEW request" (*Washington Report on Health and Medicine*, December 12, 1977); and "Once not long ago in a place not far away people of a prosperous land were unhappy. They were afflicted with a malaise. No one was quite sure whence the malaise had come, but it was thought to have been *Cartered* in with inflation" (*Business Week*, October 7, 1985). See also *Rembrandt*.

mahosker *noun*, *slang*, money, especially in the form of a paycheck: "'The *mahosker* isn't here. It don't come until later.' 'The what?' 'The checks. The company don't bring them here until after two'" (Jimmy Breslin, *Table Money*, 1986).

THE STORY: Had Jimmy Breslin not so cleverly glossed the word *mahosker* in this piece of fictional dialogue set in New York City during the time the subway tunnels were being dug by the *sandhogs*, or underground laborers (many of whom were of Irish ancestry), some of his readers would have been mystified. As it was, Breslin led several scholars on a merry chase through English, Irish, Yiddish, and Hebrew tomes in an attempt to unearth the origin of *mahosker*. This painstaking etymological quest, which Breslin found very amusing when I told him about it during an early-morning telephone interview in 1987, resulted in the conclusion that *mahosker*, in a manner similar to *kibosh*, just may be of Irish or Yiddish origin or of both.

At the outset I was impeded by a lack of evidence for the term in those primary sources lexicographers always turn to—sources such as the *Oxford English Dictionary*, Craigie's *Dictionary of American English*, Wright's *English Dialect Dictionary*, Mathews's *Dictionary of Americanisms*, Dinneen's *Irish-English Dictionary*, and the Royal Irish Academy's *Dictionary of the Irish Language*. An examination of the works of H. L. Mencken, Eric Partridge, Harold Wentworth, and Stuart Berg Flexner, as well as scholarly journals specializing in American dialect, yielded nothing. Even Frederic G. Cassidy, Ph.D., the chief editor of the *Dictionary of American Regional English*, was unfamiliar with *mahosker*, though he felt it must be closely related to the word *mahoska* (or *hoska*), which I had found in David W. Maurer's *Language of the Underworld* (1981), defined there as "any kind of narcotics, especially heroin (East Coast, particularly New York City)."

Still at square one, I placed that call to Breslin, who said that the word means essentially "anything heavy—power, money, even a badge—or anything conferring power. . . . If a cop goes into a bar and holds up a badge, saying 'This is the real *mahosker*,' he might mean 'Here's the power, the badge: Now where's the drink?'" He also suggested a Hebrew or a Yiddish origin rather than an Irish one.

Not willing to concede the matter with the etymologist's rather limp "origin unknown," I sought the opinions of two scholars—a well-known authority on New York dialects, Joseph Malone, Ph.D., of the Department of Linguistics, Barnard College; and the preeminent authority on Yiddish, Marvin I. Herzog, Ph.D., the Atran Professor of Yiddish, Columbia University, and also the editor in chief of the *Great Dictionary of the Yiddish Language*.

Professor Malone, also a specialist in Gaelic, had originally suspected that *mahosker*, with a silent *r* (exhibiting the New Yorkers' *r*-dropping pronunciation), "might reflect the Irish *mo thosca*, literally 'my business' (with connotations not far from the way the Italian [*la*] *cosa nostra*, 'our thing,' has developed)." Malone added that "the slang-based semantic fit is plausible [in view of the various examples given by Dinneen's *Dictionary* at the entry *toisic*] . . . and the phonetics, despite disguising by both English and Irish orthography, is quite close indeed. Assuming an *r*-less pronunciation of *mahosker* . . . the English in phonetic transcription would be approximately [məhäskə], while the Irish would be [məhŭskə] or [məhôskə]." All that hav-ing been said, Malone later encountered, quite by accident, the word *makhózke* in *Harkavy's Pocket Dictionary*, a lexicon of New York Yiddish terms published in 1900. This word means "business; dealings," and, according to Professor Herzog, is pronounced [məKHzōkə]. (Nothing being simple, the origin of the Yiddish word is itself a mystery: it may come from Hebrew or from northern German.) Given the similar pronunciations and the not too divergent meanings of these two words, the separate Irish and Yiddish ety-mologies seem to converge in the English form *mahosker*. Malone made the point that "a convergence like this is not at all far out. Given the kick-off co-incidence of sufficient semantic-phonetic similarity in the two donor lan-guages (that much *would* be coincidence, because the Irish and Yiddish . . . roots have nothing whatever to do with one another), all that'd be needed would be social mingling among members of both groups—not at *all* unlikely, given the nature of street life in old New York City of the day—and one or more individuals with imagination and a flair for language." Furthermore, the *mahoska* (or *hoska*) in the book of underworld slang appears to be a variant English spelling of *mahosker*. The form *hoska* could be an English-internal aphaeresis (that is, the loss of a short, unstressed vowel from the beginning of a word, as is the case with *squire* from *esquire*), or it could be the result of a speaker's having dropped the Irish *mo* ("my"), also failing to readjust the stem initial from THosca [hôskə] to Tosca [tôskə].

Malone, obviously a betting man, said the odds in this complex etymo-logical horse race are "around 85 percent that either the Irish or the Yiddish etymology is right on the nose (or at least glancing off one nostril)" and that the odds for a dual Irish-Yiddish etymology are "better than 15 percent but worse than 85 percent," a theory that Professor Herzog found "ingenious." And that's the whole megillah.

office *verb,* **1.** to work in or have as an office: "[She] has accepted the posi-tion of . . . Supervisor. . . . She will be *officing* at 1005 17th St., Room 850" (organizational announcement, US WEST Communications, undated). **2.** to provide (one) with an office: "You wouldn't expect to find someone like Ken Norton in the William Morris office, or even to find him *officed* in Bev-erly Hills" (*Los Angeles Times*, June 11, 1985). **3.** to provide an environment appropriate for performing work and communicating ideas, especially in an automated setting: "[Japan] has launched a national debate on how to reap the benefits of *officing*" (*High Technology Business*, October 1988).

THE STORY: The *Oxford English Dictionary* contains this citation from the July 1936 issue of *The Atlantic Monthly*: "A local newspaper has just carried two want ads containing this wording:— 'Chance for public accountant to *office* with lawyer.' 'Chance for high grade realtor to *office* with lawyer.'" Obviously, the writer found these usages worthy of note at that time. Readers who love to hate such instances of functional shift from noun to verb may be surprised to learn that *office* in this sense has been extant at least since 1892: "An attorney *officing* in the same building" (*The Nation*). At least 115 instances of the verb's occurrence in print turned up in recent years, including evidence of the use of the *-ing* form as a modifier: "new *officing* and manufacturing facilities" (*Oil & Gas Journal*, September 20, 1982).

The third sense is relatively new. According to the story in *High Technology Business*, Duncan Sutherland, who in 1981 started the Advanced Systems Laboratory at Wang, "coined the verb '*officing*.'" Of course, he did nothing of the sort; rather, he attached a new, highly specific meaning to a verb that first appeared in English as early as 1440, in the now obsolete sense "to perform divine services; officiate." See also *snide*.

offsetting behavior *noun*, the tendency in people to engage in an activity more frequently when the expense, risk or danger associated with the act is reduced: "'*Offsetting behavior*' . . . is simple. . . . If the cost, or danger, of doing something goes down, people will do it more. . . . *Offsetting behavior* . . . is a force business and government should consider" (*New York Times*, April 10, 1994).

THE STORY: If you delay meeting a publishing deadline until the very last minute because you rely on E-mail and the fax machine for delivery, you're engaging in *offsetting behavior*. If you key in a document without concern for spelling errors, typos, and poor syntax because you have software that checks spelling and grammar, you're engaging in *offsetting behavior*. If you drive very aggressively in all types of weather and take crazy chances because your vehicle is equipped with antilock brakes and air bags, you're an *offsetter*, all right.

One of these days, insurance companies are going to realize that lower premiums for drivers with antilock brakes and air bags on their vehicles are not necessarily called for: the number of near misses and outright crashes increases in proportion to the number of these so-called safer cars, according to the *Times*.

In terms of written communications, reliance on technology to do everything but think out a document can result in inferior writing. When one considers that from middle school on up, students are relying on assists from spelling- and grammar-correction software in their writing, one has to be concerned, lest the new *digerati* become the new illiterati.

open-collar worker *noun*, a long-distance telecommuter. Also called *lone eagle*: "Homes and communities . . . need to change to accommodate *open-collar workers*, said Telluride, Colo., architect and developer John Lifton. He hopes to break ground in 1996 on a 500-home community called Skyfield to cater to these workers. Besides the scenery, world-class skiing, and golf, Lifton believes other things will help draw *open-collar workers* to his community. For example, . . . he is planning to build a number of small offices as part of the rental core" (*Washington Post*, March 26, 1994). "The Federal Home Loan Mortgage Corp. (Freddie Mac) gave its blessing for . . . the director of home mortgage standards . . . to join the growing ranks of . . . '*lone eagles*'" (*Washington Post*, March 26, 1994).

THE STORY: *Open-collar workers* are knowledge professionals such as manufacturers' representatives, entrepreneurs, and self-employed people like writers, software designers, bankers, lawyers, analysts, and accountants, who have reached the conclusion that they'd rather not live on the urban treadmill anymore and that, thanks to high-tech communications, they don't have to tie the location of the home to the vicinity of the office. Undoubtedly, some *open-collars* can also be classed as *bright-collar workers* and *gold-collar workers* who have been able to leverage their knowledge professionalism into a new lifestyle of the nineties, one that will fit in nicely with the *villaging* perceived by some planners as a piece of the culture to be created by the Information Superhighway.

There are already approximately 10 million *open-collars* in the marketplace, with the number expected to soar by 50 percent in the next five years. John Hemschoot, the Freddie Mac *lone eagle* mentioned in the second *Post* citation, has called the phenomenon "the most important social movement since the rise of the two-wage-earner family." Of course it is: the *open-collar* phenomenon is sure to affect the demographics and dynamics of rural and city life, not to mention housing choices. And the migration, like others in other times, is running east to west. People are returning to places once visited on vacations. They're trying to find peace and quiet and public safety. And they're looking to reduce the general hassle factor. See also *bright-collar worker, gold-collar worker, virtual office*.

private bank *noun*, **1.** chiefly in Europe but also in the United States, a bank, or a bank-within-a-bank, that is engaged in wealth management and preservation strategies, including asset protection and investment enhancement, serving the needs of the already wealthy in order to maintain that wealth: "Of all the *private banks*, Morgan's [Morgan Guaranty Trust's] membership requirements are the highest: $5 million in net worth is needed to open a new account" (Susan Harrigan, *New York Newsday*, January 22, 1989). **2.** In the United States, a usually small bank-within-a-bank that is engaged in wealth creation by providing capital to clients having a net worth of at least $250,000 and a minimal annual individual cash flow of at least $100,000, basing the loan repayments on individual cash flow from the venture for which the loan was made, as opposed to basing the repayment on the degree of success achieved by the venture. Typical loan requests from the about-to-be-affluent individual client might be money for a startup surgical practice, including funds for the purchase or renovation of a building to house that practice: "Understanding wealth-creation *private bank*[*ing*] is . . . difficult. It requires enlightened bank management capable of understanding subtleties. . . . There is a world of difference between making loans to highly affluent people who have large trust assets to offer as sources of loan repayment and collateral, and making a large loan to a cardiovascular surgeon, out of school for only two years, who has little or no net worth, but who earns $500,000 a year for starters. . . . The surgeon . . . wants to borrow as an individual for business purposes" (Marilyn MacGruder Barnewall, *American Banker*, June 10, 1992).

THE STORY: The term *private bank* might be aptly described as a basket containing apples and oranges, for its two senses involve entirely different activities, and neither seems to be well understood by the general media or the nonspecialist public. Marilyn MacGruder Barnewall, called by *Forbes* "the Dean" of American *private banking*, has said, "There are two kinds of *private banks*. One centers on wealth management [sense 1] . . . which the Europeans have developed and at which the Swiss appear to lead the way; and there is *private banking* based on philosophies of wealth creation . . . at which the Americans appear to lead the way [sense 2]." According to Barnewall, *private banks* engaged in wealth management and preservation evolved in Europe "probably [as] a result of that continent's history of wars and the need of affluent people to preserve their wealth under difficult and changing economic conditions . . . as well as political rulers." Because of the bank confidentiality laws in place in Switzerland, Swiss banks have led and continue to lead the pack in the provision of wealth management and preservation strategies; however, other nations, such as Luxembourg, have now modified their bank secrecy statutes, and so have begun to compete with the Swiss in this marketplace.

In the United States, *private banks* focusing on wealth management and preservation are prevented by federal regulations from offering the level of services required by the very rich, and thus are not in a position to compete effectively on a level playing field with the Swiss. (As an example, investment advisory by banks is still prohibited in the United States.) In this country, wealth-managing *private banks* cross the normal organizational structure lines by combining the usual services offered by their trust and retail banking divisions, thereby enabling the client to access the services of both divisions from one banker rather than from several—one-stop shopping, so to speak. This sense of *private bank* made the news (and hence, the citation files) in the late eighties in stories centering on the specialized, adjunct services offered to clients, such as income tax preparation, bill paying, making travel arrangements, giving advice on the purchase of art for collections, buying theater tickets, and even the referral of clients' children to exclusive nursery schools. These stories were published at a time (1989) when the millionaire population in the United States was growing at an average rate of 20 percent annually. (Thomas Stanley, the chairman of the Affluent Market Institute at Georgia State University, was quoted by *New York Newsday* to the effect that in 1989 the household with an annual income of $1 million or more spent $100,000 a year just on personal loans. And in that year, the millionaire population here numbered 1.4 million.)

All but lost to the general reader is the second sense, the wealth-generating sense of the term. Barnewall has said in *American Banker* that "the strongest loan-repayment asset that a wealth-creation client [not just surgeons but also accountants, attorneys, airline pilots, and real estate developers] brings to the table is personal cash flow, not declared income. . . . The typical wealth creator who qualifies for *private banking* has a full-time occupation outside of the deals he or she invests in. The borrower's personal cash flow should be sufficiently strong to repay the loan within five to seven years. . . . The average term for these loans, by the way, is one year."

All this differs substantially from the way by which commercial banks write business-purpose loans to wealth creators, for in them the success of the venture funded is the primary source of loan repayment. And these business-purpose loans are written for *businesses*, not for individuals. Business lending to individuals is, therefore, the mission of *private banks* in the second sense. It is still a highly specialized banking skill unavailable in traditional banking divisions—retail, trust, and commercial—according to Barnewall, who went on to say, "Rather than just combining already existing bank services already available to affluent clients through various bankers or numerous bank locations, the wealth-creation, credit-driven *private banks* provide a new and unique service that could be made available at most traditional banks, regardless of size."

quant jock *noun, slang,* an expert in mathematics and related fields who is employed at a stockbrokerage firm, an investment bank, or other such institution. Also called *rocket scientist:* "But Harvard MBAs are trained in a mode of decision-making based on manipulating data. Quality, customer satisfaction, and employee loyalty tend to get lost. The students, for the most part, like the power of numbers. *'Quant jocks'* (quantitative kids) who 'nail' (master) the numbers courses are the epitome of B-school success" (*Business Week,* March 24, 1986). "That rare breed of *rocket scientists* . . . academics highly trained in mathematics who apply their quantitative skills to Wall Street deals" (*Business Week,* July 21, 1986).

THE STORY: At one time in the eighties, *quant jock,* or just *quant,* denoted a B-school whiz kid, as evidenced by the context of the March 24 citation. Soon thereafter, the term came to mean such a B-school graduate in the corporate setting. *Quant jock* and *rocket scientist,* not to mention *numbers cruncher, arb, white knight,* and *raider,* became lexical symbols of the merger-takeover era of Wall Street during the 1980s. In the mid-1990s, "The *Quants* Are Back," as a recent national headline ran. There's nothing really new under the sun when it comes to making money.

sug *verb, chiefly British slang,* to attempt to sell (products) in person or by telephone, for example, while pretending to be engaged only in market research: "It would be surprising if at some time or other you had not been *sugged.* It can happen in the street, even in your own home. It is the action of unscrupulous salesmen, or worse, capturing your attention by posing as market research interviewers" (*Financial Times* [London], March 13, 1986).

THE STORY: The story is short and sweet: *sug,* unlike *dis, suss,* and *igg,* is an acronym formed from the phrase "to *s*ell *u*nder the *g*uise of market research."

Advice for the recipient of such a pitch—you, the unfortunate *sugees* of the marketplace: Tell 'em to *sug off*. See also *push-polling*.

tree hugger *noun*, **1.** *slang*, a job seeker who has been employed by one company for his or her entire career and who is now regarded as disadvantaged because prospective employers prefer candidates with multifaceted experience at a number of firms in a number of positions: "This poor bloke is a *tree hugger*. In another time, of course, what the *tree hugger* represented was known—and valued—as loyalty" (*Sales & Marketing Management*, January 1988). **2.** *offensive slang*, an environmentalist, often one regarded as radical or extremist: "Yet Senator Usdane concedes that [Bruce] Babbitt is no . . . 'tree hugger,' in his words—on environmental policy" (*Christian Science Monitor*, October 16, 1987).

THE STORY: Both these senses connote zealous loyalty to an institution or a cause, but the first one suggests an insecurity not inherent in the second. The first sense is the newest, for it reflects a changed view in the employment marketplace, seen as early as the eighties and applicable to an acute degree in the nineties, the Era of Change. Job-hopping, once considered highly detrimental to serious career advancement, began to be encouraged by headhunters: "A . . . *tree hugger* . . . is increasingly seen as narrow in experience and someone who's fearful of the unknown," said Jacques Lapointe, the president of Retail Recruiters International, Inc., in the January 4, 1988, issue of the *Monitor*. The tension in the nineties involves employee fear of leaving one job for another that might be discontinued; yet employers demand a varied menu of experience in hires.

A number of citations for the second sense have turned up, among them this one: "Few of these rivalries compare to the neighborly strife [*sic*] between California and Oregon. Californians sometimes sneer at Oregonians as being '*tree huggers*' and 'hicks,' while many Oregonians retaliate with disdain for 'hippies' and for refugees from the high cost of living in California" (*New York Times*, October 20, 1986).

Tree hugger, which was used off and on during the 1992 presidential election campaign, is a non-self-explanatory compound similar in its formation to *wall creeper*, a person, not a vine, indigenous to the Washington, D.C., power-party circuit. Consider this citation from the June 15, 1987, issue of *Newsweek*, where the subject is Alan Greenspan during his term as chairman of the Council of Economic Advisers: "He became known as one of Washington's *wall creepers*, arriving at a reception, working his way around the wall of the room, and leaving when he got back to the entrance. He seemed always in a hurry."

vested termination *noun*, a vested employee who has been let go by a company: "TO: All *Vested Terminations*   FROM: —— ——, Vice President, Human Resources   SUBJECT: Summary Annual Reports . . . We have attached a summary of each of the reports filed with the Internal Revenue Service for [our] benefit plans. . . . Federal Law requires this information be shared with you . . ." (memorandum from a multinational publishing company to those concerned, September 15, 1993).

THE STORY: All right. I know what you're thinking: 101 Things to Do with a *Vested Termination*. Things like these: Move into a Roach Motel. (If you can afford it, that is.) Call the Orkin Man. Become an Orkin Man. Become a Dominatrix and go after the Terminatrix. Encase yourself in a costume representing something in the class Insecta and picket the terminating company.

But wait! *Vested termination* in and of itself isn't such a howler after all. It is merely one of the latest in a long line of dehumanizing terms used chiefly by careerists in business, particularly those in a field they prefer to call *human resources*. Consider the lingo in these interoffice communiqués:

TO: All *Desks*, All *Locations*
[When will we see "TO: All *Screens*"?]

This *position* creates, writes, and oversees all capital campaign literature for the University, and reports to the Vice President, Public Affairs.

The Managing Editor is now ineligible for inclusion in the Executive Bonus Plan because all but one of her *reports* [that is, the people formerly reporting to her] have been reassigned to someone else.

In the second quarter the Division took on five new *hires*.
[So far, we haven't seen new *fires*, a use that hasn't caught on.]

The stated mission of the Corporation is the intelligent management of intellectual and artistic *properties*.
[You've arrived when you become a *property*, but don't forget that The Great Gray They will now *manage* you.]

Certainly the business world of the nineties is a study in contradictions. Just how sharp these contradictions are becomes apparent when one contrasts the examples cited earlier with their opposites, terms like *corporate concierge*, *flexiplace*, *parental leave*, and *teamer*, which connote corporate commitment to various aspects of the People Principle, with the goal being to increase productivity in a more caring environment.

Still other contradictions are to be seen in these opposing pairs chosen from many others in the set: *hi-pot* versus *sticky floor*, *corpocracy* versus *adhocracy*, *affirmative action* versus *appearance discrimination*, *core business* versus *corporate bloat*, *work teams* versus *hierarchy* and *empire*. Here, we see the business world exposed as simply a microcosm of the contradictory, increasingly destabilized global society in which it operates.

But returning to the term at issue, wouldn't you agree that its user has gone Stalin one better, if that be possible? After all, those not liked by that tyrant were called *nonpersons*, a word still considered an animate noun, notwithstanding the negative prefix. In truth, *vested termination* is a metaphor for the jobless, don't you think? It's been said that when you lose your job, you might as well be dead. But as a *vested* (or unvested) *termination*, you're not quite alive and you're not quite dead, either, and you're not even a nonbeing. Put simply, you're a resident of a netherworld, the world inhabited by abstract nouns, this one ending in *-ion*. This *-ion* suffix is entered and defined, without benefit of definite or indefinite articles, as is the wont of lexical style, this way in *The American Heritage Dictionary of the English Language, Third Edition*: "result of an action or process" and "state or condition."

George Orwell was right when he wrote that "if you want a picture of the future, imagine a boot stamping on a human face—for ever." In this instance, the future is now, but in the corporate culture that spawned the first memorandum cited in this entry, the face is no longer human.

viatical settlement *noun*, an insurance settlement by which a company purchases life policies from terminally ill patients, provides them with immediate, usually much-needed cash, and then profits from the assigned policy when the insured dies. Also called *death futures*: "Since 1988, when the first company began, about 60 '*viatical settlement*' companies have sprouted across the country. . . . Last year [1993], viatical companies bought about $200 million worth of policies, . . . more than 90 percent of them from patients with AIDS" (*Seattle Times*, March 4, 1994). "There's a dryly technical term for such transactions: *viatical settlements*. . . . Cynics call them '*death futures*'" (*Newsweek*, March 21, 1994).

THE STORY: The insurance industry has revived the rare word *viatical*, which goes back at least to 1847. It is derived from the noun *viaticum*, first recorded in English in the year 1562, meaning the last Communion given a dying person, and coming, of course, from Latin. (To the ancient Romans, *viaticum* meant variously "traveling money," "provisions for a journey," and "money made by a soldier in wars; prize-money.") In English, the noun *viaticals* came to mean articles for a journey, and, in botany, plants growing along frequented places, such as roadsides and garbage heaps. This plural form, labeled "rare," was defined in *Webster's New International Dictionary* (the 1934 unabridged edition) as "baggage; impedimenta." Now, because of its revival, *viatical* may enjoy reentry in dictionaries—a rather unusual phenomenon. The situation is a small signature example of the effects of the AIDS epidemic on the English language.

washing emporium *noun*, a Laundromat featuring arcade games and other forms of entertainment, food, and alcoholic beverages. Also called *slosh and wash*: "It was more or less a normal Monday night at Washbucklers, a '*washing emporium.*' . . . With two tanning booths, a pool table, video games, a large overhead television screen, a comfortable lounge with romantic lighting and a wine-and-beer bar, all open until 11 nightly, it's a popular spot to hang out in. . . . Some sailors call [A Bar of Soap] '*slosh and wash*'" (*Boston Globe*, March 15, 1990).

THE STORY: The coin-operated laundry may prove to be "the new social center of the '90s," much like the general store of earlier times, according to Washbucklers owner David Catero of Rutland, Vermont. These advanced Laundromats—many featuring ice-cream parlors, stores, fax machines, mailboxes, photocopiers, snack bars, dining rooms, and study areas—sometimes even offer matchmaking services. Dee Dee Mandino, the operator of a chain of Connecticut Laundromats, has held "Love at First Rinse" parties for "the squeaky clean singles," featuring a deejay, line dancing, and relay races. According to the *Globe*, Mandino has suggested the Laundromat as "a safe, less pressured alternative [for singles] where social barriers and facades are down." And it has been pointed out that one can observe a great deal about another person's character, personality, and habits by watching the person's behavior while doing clothes: "Does he sort? Does she separate? But . . . you have to watch out for the bleachers," said Millie Trykowski, who manages a Laundromat in Connecticut.

The thing may be very nineties, but it goes back at least to 1982, according to a letter to me from a Word Watcher who wrote that one of the original *washing emporiums* was Suds and Duds of Ames, Iowa. It featured reading tables and beer.

wolf ticket also **wolf's ticket** *noun, slang,* a bad conduct report or a poor efficiency rating filed by management against a worker: "It also threatens blue-collar workers like those at the Lenin shipyard in Gdansk, about 50 of whom were fired after an attempted strike. . . . Many . . . workers have also received *wolf tickets* . . . making it hard for them to get new jobs" (*Time,* November 8, 1982).

THE STORY: *Wolf ticket* as used in the Eastern European context goes back to czarist times in Russia. *Wolf ticket,* as in the sports idiom *sell wolf tickets,* may derive from the argot of the American underworld. The story behind the dual ports of entry of this term into English is tangled and complex, with many obscurities remaining. In Russian the term *volchiy bilet,* where *volchiy* is an adjective literally translated "wolfish" (itself derived from the noun *volk,* "wolf") and *bilet* is "ticket," has long been used to denote a document depriving a person expelled from an institution of the right to be accepted by any other institution on Russian territory. Russian and Polish informants have attested use of the term as far back as 1863, for some of their ancestors were known to have received *wolf tickets.* Other informants have attested its continued use in the Soviet Union, especially during the 1920s and 1930s when so-called undesirables were blacklisted from university studies or jobs because of their political views or class origins. And the Jewish refuseniks of more recent years suffered similar punishment. Such people could work only in the most undesirable climes—Siberia, for instance—where the wolf population abounds. (Wolves have long been a source of terror among people in certain parts of the former Soviet Union; a famous story about how the Red Army had to be called out to kill the animals by the thousands after they had, in packs, broken down cottage doors and killed scores of rural residents is an example.)

It is suspected that the predatory and scavenging nature of the wolf, as perceived by the people in Russia, plus the wolf-inhabited regions to which *wolf-ticketed* individuals were driven, contributed to the creation of the compound *wolf ticket,* certainly not a *ticket to the stars* or to *paradise,* as in the well-established, parallel, English-language idioms. Smirnitsky's *Russian-English Dictionary*, published thirty years before the collapse of the former Soviet Union, does not enter *wolf ticket*, but it does enter the expression *poluchit' volchiy pasport*, translated literally into English "to receive a wolfish passport" and defined in that lexicon as "to get on the blacklist; be blacklisted." But Doroszewski's *Dictionary of the Polish Language* does enter the *bilet* form of the compound. This meaning of the term, and the term itself, have therefore remained extant by virtue of sustained governmental and/or state oppression, regardless of whether the rulers were royal or red. It is possible that émigrés from Russia in 1905, 1918, 1945, and most recently 1970–80 brought the expression to the United States, where it then worked its way into the sports idiom, but that has not yet been proved.

To sell wolf tickets means to boast or brag, and it may derive from the story about the boy who cried wolf. Informants have pointed to an early meaning of the idiom, which was to sell tickets to a game or other event that the seller knew would never be staged. Maurice H. Weseen, in his *Dictionary of American Slang* (1934), defined the verb *wolf* as "to deceive; to betray." And *American Tramp and Underworld Slang* defines the noun *wolf* as "a 'rambler' . . . riding fast trains by virtue of nerve and main force, and despite the train crew's opposition." These strands may have influenced the established Black English idiom *sell a wolf ticket* or *sell wolf tickets*, meaning variously "to boast or brag; talk big but be unable to back one's claims; lie or deceive; try to psych (someone) out; spoil for a fight." (Another idiom in that same lexicon, *wolf it*, means "to talk big but fail to follow through.")

A typical contextual example of the idiom in the sports context is this one, taken from an Associated Press story dated December 20, 1985, in which the person speaking is a basketball player: "Most guys in the league push and shove and it's all a facade. Most guys are *selling wolf tickets*." The sports idiom has also begun to undergo a reversal of elements and a resultant functional shift from verb idiom to adjective or modifier, evidenced by this citation from the November 20, 1985, issue of *Sports Illustrated*: "And oh yes, she has . . . threatened a staff member of the USC *Daily Trojan*. . . . In short, nothing that any self-respecting, competitive, turf-guarding, *wolf-ticket selling*, media-understanding guy wouldn't do."

In bringing the story to closure, if not to a definitive etymological conclusion, we should take note of the prolific proverbial and idiomatic expressions in both Russian and English in which the word *wolf* figures prominently. Consider first these Russian proverbs, which I have translated into English:

"If you're going to live with the *wolves*, you've got to howl like the *wolves*"; "The *wolves* will be sated but the sheep will live unharmed"; "Give the *wolf* the best food and still he will want to control the forest"; "The *wolf* is not beaten for being gray, but for devouring sheep in August and May"; "The *wolf* was sorry for the mare and ate her up with loving care"; "The *wolf* is near!" (used by a person who is afraid to speak frankly for fear of eavesdroppers); "A *wolf* lives by its legs"; "The *wolf* that trots finds the meat"; "Think only of the *wolves* and you'll never enter the forest"; and "Work is not a *wolf*; it won't go anywhere."

While Russian contains more proverbial usages of *wolf* than it does straight idiomatic expressions like *wolf down a meal*, English abounds in such idioms. Early ones are, for example, *a wolf in the stomach* ("a monstrous or canine appetite," so defined in Captain Francis Grose's *Classical Dictionary of the Vulgar Tongue*) and *a wolf in the breast* ("a gnawing pain in the breast," attributed by Eric Partridge and Paul Beale in their *Dictionary of Slang and Unconventional English* to use by "beggar women" in the mid-eighteenth to early nineteenth centuries). And *Wolf of Tuscany* meant "an Italian soldier," so used by British troops in the North African campaign of World War II. Finally, there are these old standards: *big bad wolf, wolf whistle, wolf pack, pack of wolves, cry wolf, wolf at the door, lone wolf, wolf in sheep's clothing*, and *throw to the wolves*. Lest the Wolf Lobby think that I am down on wolves, let me conclude by revealing my favorite Russian proverb: "Invite a pig to dine and he'll put his feet on the table." See also *dance with (the) wolves*.

4

Wordpower: Manpower, Womanpower, Peoplepower

action figure
appearance discrimination
boy toy
bumbo
dozens
dress correctness
gaydar
glass ceiling
laughism

lobola
LUG
reasonable woman standard
rug-ranking
sticky floor
TLB
trailing spouse
wife (*verb*)

In the modern workplace, men are the drones,
and women are queen bees.
—Camille Paglia, *Vamps & Tramps*

I am the greatest.
—Muhammad Ali

The most favourable laws can do very little
towards the happiness of people when the disposition
of the ruling power is adverse to them.
—Edmund Burke

Burke also wrote that "there is nothing which will not yield to perseverance and method." In terms of the perseverance and method of feminism, especially in the last thirty years or so, one of its signal accomplishments has been the realization, in American English, at least, of *the* most important shift in usage in the last four-hundred years—a marked trend in edited and unedited prose toward freedom from irrelevant gender-tagging and sexist stereotyping. Yet, in spite of society's heightened awareness of social justice, a certain segment of the populace, in the manner of the "ruling power" identified by Burke, remains "adverse" to change. Herein lies the impetus for many of the hard words passed among various individuals and groups in the country—the hard words shouted on some campuses, the hard words whispered in some of the less enlightened boardrooms, the hard words mouthed or hinted in some tenure committees.

This same mean-spiritedness in the world of advertising has been exposed by social critic John Leo. But the Attitude he identified in an article titled "Madison Avenue's Gender War," which appeared in the October 25, 1993, issue of *U.S. News & World Report*, attempts to capitalize on existing tensions between males and females of all ages, by portraying women and girls in ads for the trade as strictly in-your-face. Here's an example: "One [ad], for Bodyslimmers by Nancy Ganz, shows a woman from the neck down, wearing a sexy one-piece undergarment. The text says: 'While you don't necessarily dress for men, it doesn't hurt, on occasion, to see one drool like the pathetic dog that he is.'" Add to that one an advertisement for *Working Woman*, also intended for trade, not public, consumption, which features a successful-looking woman with her finger on the trigger of a handgun. Her tag line reads, according to Leo, "I didn't get to where I am today by reading *Good Housekeeping*."

Getting beyond the rhetoric of Attitude, the sensitive student of English knows full well that this language, with its penchant for foreign borrowing and adoption of the new, is by definition multicultural and highly elastic. Its elasticity to change is exemplified by the many gender-free coinages it has accepted in recent years. And the English language is multicultural, not in sociopolitical terms, but strictly in historical and etymological terms: after all, it can trace its roots back thousands of years to Indo-European. In bringing together into one lexicon diverse linguistic elements from diverse peoples, nations, and cultures, the English language—*the* prime exponent, in fact, of multiculturalism—has been much more accepting of and tolerant to change and new ideas than some of its own speakers and writers have been.

The short list of words in this chapter attests to the issues behind the sportive debates going on in this country about the roles and rights of its inhabitants—female and male, gay and straight, married and unmarried, "minority" and "majority." From *action figure*, which is about much more than toys, to *trailing spouse* and the verb *wife*, which reflect the tensions and imperatives affecting marital roles in times of change; from *gaydar* and *LUG*, which signify matters of interest to gays and straights alike, to *bumbo* and *TLB*—the first, derogatory, and the second, a reverse-term of respect (hard-earned? grudging?)—the chapter exposes issues meriting more than passing thoughts.

The debates show no signs of immediate resolution, and it is not the mission of the chapter to resolve them. It is, however, the intent of the chapter to expose the trend of shrill animosity that seems to be increasing between the sexes. The rhetoric of hatred is abroad in the land. Emergence of the word *laughism*—a scary word, regardless of one's viewpoint—is central proof of the situation. *Laughism* carries with it the issues of human respect and disrespect, political correctness and censorship. Into the same category fall *dress correctness* and *appearance discrimination*, the existence of which proves yet another of Burke's observations that "the march of the human mind is slow."

It is in the workplace that women, after the long march of feminism, are still considered less than even "separate but equal." Strong language that is, I know. But the perpetuity of the limiting term *glass ceiling* and the existence of *rug-ranking*, denoting the umbilical tie between an administrative assistant's job and salary and those of the immediate supervisor, validate the assertion. What is more, the nineties workplace has contributed the ultimate limiting term to the lexicon—*sticky floor*, denoting the dead-ending of the careers of many women *and* minority men, not merely the ones employed in service-industry jobs but now the ones seeking tenure in academia.

The Canadian actress Margot Kidder once remarked that "being a career woman is harder than being a career man. You've got to look like a lady, act like a man, and work like a dog." The majority of the words in this chapter bear her out. But now that *sticky floor*, affecting both men and women, has been added to the lexicon, we will, no doubt, hear more from both sexes, who, in the words of Myrna Kostash, will tell us, "We are tired of being janitors in the corridors of power."

From *lobola*, or bride-price, a custom still extant in some African nations, to *wifing* in the United States, to *gaydar* as it must be used in some workplace settings, the words here alert you to What Is, as opposed to What Appears to Be. Indeed, as we have seen in previous chapters, we live in a looking-glass world in which the reality is often virtual. But words, the marks of those who have gone before, do not lie: the ones here are, in fact, disturbing artifacts of an unfinished social progression—called by many critics "progressive" or even "liberal"—that is, in fact, a regression. That regression—in the workplace, crossing over into virtually all professions—is likely to accelerate, given the agenda of some ultraconservatives elected in 1994 to state and federal office.

In "The Blue Meridian," Jean Toomer penned these lines:

> Men,
> Men and women—
> Liberate!
> Each new American—
> To be taken as a golden grain
> And lifted, as the wheat of our bodies,
> To matter superbly human.

Is it an impossible idea? Read on and then decide.

action figure *noun*, a toy configured as a male or female human being, an alien being, or a robot, for example, whose appendages and other parts move readily during play: "That old boy toy, G.I. Joe, will never die. A touchstone for a generation of American men who wasted hours in suburban basements playing with the foot-high plastic *action figure*, G.I. Joe . . . even disappeared for a few years" (*New York Times Magazine*, September 11, 1994). "And if G.I. Joe has a female counterpart—a G.I. Jill to represent all the women serving on active duty in the Persian Gulf—she is nowhere to be found on these shelves. Among all the '*action figures*' lining a long wall . . . only the proverbial token woman exists—a Robocop named Anne Lewis, an 'ultra police S.W.A.T. specialist'" (*Christian Science Monitor*, December 11, 1990). "Girls' *action figures*, such as . . . She-Ra, are also becoming popular" (Reuters, February 12, 1986).

THE STORY: The term *action figure*, for which over 900 citations were generated electronically, goes back at least to 1977 if not before. It has been called a euphemism for "a unisex doll," that is, a doll appropriate to be played with by boys as well as girls. In fact, William Lutz, author of *Doublespeak: From Revenue Enhancement to Terminal Living—How Governments, Business, and Advertisers Use Language to Deceive You*, considers *action figure* to be on a par with other terms such as *vegetarian leather*, meaning "vinyl."

Action figures as such go back to 1964, when G.I. Joe was first introduced. Since that year, the figures have evolved into designs closely reflecting characters in the movies and on television, a phenomenon called *media crossover*. Most of these characters are superheroic: "Girls are playing with frilly dolls that have man-luring names and awesome wardrobes, and boys are playing with armed *action figures* that stand ready to battle for control of the universe" (*New York Times*, June 15, 1989). This citation is indicative of a situation causing some measure of controversy among parents and child psychologists who disagree as to whether or not *action figures* are really just dolls and whether or not boys should be playing with "dolls." Others are concerned about a possible regressive trend in which dolls designed especially for girls simply reinforce stereotypical roles, particularly between the ages of two and five, the period of life during which children learn and internalize such stereotypes.

appearance discrimination *noun*, treatment or consideration based on a judgmental attitude about another's physiognomy or physique rather than on personal merit, as on the job: "A number of *appearance discrimination* lawsuits, especially by overweight people, have been won recently" (*Washington Post*, March 25, 1994).

THE STORY: Beauty may lie in the eye of the beholder, but in the workplace the bottom line is performance judged on an objective look at an employee's merits. Given this reality, it is indeed stunning to learn that in a society hypersensitive to litigation, workplace discrimination rooted in matters of personal appearance has actually become an increasingly high-profile legal issue. And studies have shown, the *Washington Post* reports, that people who are deemed "unattractive" by "society's standards" can and do end up earning less money than their colleagues and more fortunate peers, and they suffer in other ways as well in the work environment.

Freada Klein, a consultant on employment discrimination and bias issues who is based in Boston, said to the *Washington Post* that "the latitude for a woman's appearance is generally narrower than for men. It all overlaps with ingrained societal stereotypes and bias about what is acceptable appearance for women."

The citation for *appearance discrimination* given at the outset refers to a recent case in which a young woman charged that she had been fired from her position as an audiovisual technician at a major-market northern Virginia hotel, allegedly because of being hirsute (she had a mustache). Experts interviewed during the course of the case and its attendant publicity pointed out that though many men have made and pursued discrimination complaints based on the issue of having beards, sideburns, and mustaches, few if any had ever heard of such a case involving a woman.

The employee in question was later reinstated by the vendor employing her on a contract to the hotel. See also *dress correctness, staring* at *mad-dog, thighism* at *laughism.*

boy toy *noun, slang,* a man or a woman when regarded as a sex object: "Paul Newman no longer wants to be seen as a sex symbol. He's 69 now and thinks being the *boy toy* of yet another generation of women is 'undignified'" (*New York Times,* May 22, 1994).

THE STORY: *Boy toy,* an example of intentional rhyming, in which process two freestanding and rhyming words are juxtaposed to form a compound, with one word in the set used in an exaggerated or figurative way, takes its cues from the Lower East Side graffiti artists who used the word liberally with spray paint in the early eighties.

The pop star Madonna mainlined *boy toy* into mass culture in the year 1985, when the term appeared prominently on her belt buckle, pictured on the *Like a Virgin* album cover. So says Liz Rosenberg, a vice-president at Warner Brothers and the spokesperson for Madonna. *Boy toy,* also the name of one of Madonna's companies (it's even on the checks written by that organization), was Madonna's in-your-face-with-Attitude tag name, says Rosenberg. She took the negative connotations and flip-flopped them into what she regarded as the very positive.

In a quantum act of gender cross-dressing, *boy toy* in the nineties is fast becoming a fixture in the prose of what I like to call *Menglish,* the language used by, to, of, and about men, especially in mainstream, general-interest magazines like *Spin, Details,* and *GQ,* which are targeted to men. The crossover is seeping into the general print media as well.

What is more, *Menglish* is characterized by a pervasive use of *boy*—alone and in combinations like these: *poster boy, party-boy, homeboy, skidge boy, good boy, bad boy, couture boy, boyfriend, frat boy, b-boy, desk cowboy, political cowboy, boychik,* and a host of others including *toy boy* (a young gigolo).

Skidge boy, a male urban activist whose appearance is marked by grunge attire and pierced body parts, has its roots in the San Francisco and Los Angeles gay communities. While the origin of *skidge* is unknown, one of the characteristics of the person's attire—a leather jacket—echoes the origin of *boy,* which goes back to a Latin word meaning "a leather collar; a fetter," used long ago to control and restrict a servant or slave. And one of the early meanings of *boy* in English was "a male servant." The meaning of *boy,* "a young man," didn't become current until the fourteenth century.

Does the pervasive use of *boy* in *Menglish* signal an infantilization of the American male to the point of the baby peas of nouvelle cuisine? Not! So say the editors of the magazines in interviews with me, though their explanations of the phenomenon differ with age groups targeted by their publications. The twentysomethings said the use simply reflects uses in the entertainment and rap world, and signifies a free-and-easy prose reflecting a young man's new self-assurance, tolerance, and independence, which they link to, yes, the Beastie *Boys*. Older editors of magazines targeted to the thirty- and fortysomethings (and over) said variously that *boy* usages are mere fads, driven by TV and films, and that these usages of *boy* say to womanists who object to *girl*, "What's the matter? *We* call ourselves *boys*. Why are you so uptight about *girl?*"

Sassy, a magazine targeted to teen girls, has a column guest-edited each month by a celebrity. The title of that column is "dear *boy*." *Dirt*, the brother publication, has a column titled "dear *girl*."

All this says that while the elders in the profession of gender bashing rant and rave over things like "word-rape," *Menglish* is, all by itself, and with little fanfare, thriving. And more important, the kids of the next generation are getting—linguistically, at least—onto greater parity. Now *that's* hope.

bumbo *noun, offensive slang*, a feminist who regards beautiful women as bimbos and thinks that intelligent women must be unattractive: "I simply do not believe that smart women must necessarily be ugly. If a few feminists want to look like female bums, that's their privilege. But a '*bumbo*' label fits them better than the '*bimbo*' tag they try to pin on beautiful females" (Al Neuharth, *USA Today*, September 14, 1989).

THE STORY: Fightin' words, these. Al Neuharth, the founder of *USA Today* and the coiner of *bumbo* (*bum* plus the *-bo* from *bimbo*), posited in a controversial editorial that certain strident feminists who believe beauty contests like the Miss America Pageant denigrate women pressured the print media so much that as a result the media markedly decreased coverage of the pageants, especially in the late eighties. Receiving Neuharth's biggest *bumbo* editing award in 1989 was the *New York Times* because of its skimpy coverage of the Miss America events: "No story Sunday. A brief, three-paragraph piece on page 3, Monday," he complained. The coiner goes on to call this phenomenon *bumboism*, and concludes that "*bumbos* are our biggest threat to both feminism and fairness in the media."

Denotational controversy aside, Neuharth's coinage is interesting because he's added one more *bumbo* to a trio of preexisting *bumbos*. All four *bumbos* are called "homographs" in dictionaryese, meaning two or more words that are spelled alike but have different meanings and origins and sometimes different pronunciations. (Homographs are typically signaled in dictionaries by way of superscript numerals, so I'm using that style here.) *Bumbo*[1], also spelled *bombo*, denotes a colonial beverage of rum, sugar, nutmeg, and water. Though its exact origin is unknown, this *bumbo* may derive from imitative baby talk: "George Washington ran for the Virginia House of Burgesses in 1758. Washington . . . made sure the voters, many of them planters, received '160 gallons of rum, beer and cider on Election Day.' The practice . . . was called 'swilling the planters with *bumbo*'" (*New York Times*, April 3, 1984). *Bumbo*[2], also spelled *bombo*, *bumboo*, and *bungo*, is a word of West African origin. It denotes a tree of Sierra Leone that yields a fragrant resin. *Bumbo*[3], also spelled *bombo*, is of unknown origin but was influenced in its formation by *bum*—both terms having the meaning "the buttocks or the rectum."

dozens *noun*, a ribald game of oral wit and strategy, in which contestants trade personal insults, many of them gender slurs, in front of an audience, which, by its degree of laughter, determines the winner. Usually used in the phrase *playing the dozens*. Also called *snaps*: "Wait, it's only a *game*—a mock battle of tongues known as playing the *dozens*" (*Dartmouth Alumni Magazine*, November 1994).

THE STORY: Your grandmother's so old, she remembers when the Book of Genesis first made the best-seller list. Your mother's so ugly that when she died and went to Hell, the Devil turned and ran.

These "I-don't-*give*-no-respect" one-liners, made up by this writer, are examples of the types of gender-specific slams issued by contestants when *playing the dozens*, also called *bagging, capping, cracking, dissing* (another, newer, sense of the word *dis*, discussed elsewhere in this book), *hiking, joning, ranking, ribbing, serving, signifying, slipping, sounding*, and, of course, *snapping*.

The game is a way of venting one's frustrations harmlessly in a kind of oral *paintball*, spraying, as it were, one's opponent with a stream of choice invective, thought out on one's feet and delivered without missing a single beat. Though traditionally a male game, say James Percelay, Monteria Ivey, and Stephan Dweck, the authors of *Snaps* (1994), women are now engaging in it too. But, the authors add, "Fortunately for men, most battles remain within the sexes."

Called by one critic "the blues of comedy," the *dozens* (a plural noun used with a singular verb) is rooted deep in African-American culture. In a rather grim, puritanical decade fixated on political correctness, reading examples of the *dozens* can be rather a jolt, for many are downright dirty. On the other hand, word battles are a lot more fun than, say, legal or physical battles; this game, and the cultural etymologies behind it, really say to us, "Lighten up and chill out, for God's sake."

The game *dozens* takes it cues from the work of the *griots*, the oral historians of Africa, who traveled about, learned about the villagers' various indiscretions, converted amusing tales of these into verse and song, and then proceeded to regale audiences with them. This was a very early form of *signifying*.

The word *dozens* is of disputed origin. Probably the most plausible derivation is from the slave auctioneers' practice of selling healthy slaves individually but grouping the sick, infirm, and the elderly ones into lots of twelve, called then the *dozens* or the *dirty dozens*. Another theory holds that American field slaves played this game, with the objects of their verbal barbs the house slaves who had more status and privileges. The house slaves' mothers were alleged to be just ones among *dozens* of women sexually available to the white landowners. Still other possible etymologies associate the usage *dozens* with the unlucky throw of twelve in craps; with a sense of the verb to *dozen* meaning "to daze or stupefy"; and with the usage of *dozens* in the 1930s to refer to a Kansas City red-light district centered on 12th Street.

dress correctness *noun*, varying ideas about the appropriate style of clothing that should be adopted by women who wish to rise to positions of power and responsibility in the workplace: "*Dress correctness* thrives wherever large numbers of women are competing for positions of power, money and prestige that were previously held only by men" (*Washington Post*, January 5, 1992).

THE STORY: In a world fraught with controversy about PC, or *political correctness*, is it any surprise that *dress correctness* should surface as a new term of art in the arena of *sticky floors* and the *glass ceiling*? Concern about the nature of women's attire in the workplace first became a national issue upon publication of John Molloy's 1977 best-seller *Dress for Success*. In that book, he recommended a corporate uniform that became standard issue in subsequent years: a dark suit typically accompanied by a white tailored blouse, often accented with a black or multicolored neck scarf that was tied in a bow.

The correctness of *dress correctness* is, however, in the eye of the beholder:

in 1983 a woman executive at a major accounting firm, who had acquired more new clients than any other candidate for partner, was denied a partnership. According to news reports, her supervisor remarked at the time that the male partners "might like her better if she would 'dress more femininely, wear makeup, have her hair styled, wear jewelry,'" and so on. In the nineties some women have thumbed their noses at all such dicta and have adopted shorter-skirted dresses with high heels, but not many: statistics show that even in the poor economy, women's suit sales rose by 24 percent while sales of short skirts decreased by 17 percent.

gaydar also **gay-dar** *noun, slang,* the intuitive aptitude among gay people to identify one another, no matter how invisible, well concealed, or outwardly straight they may appear or wish to appear, in terms of sexuality: "*Gaydar* doesn't only apply to stereotypical things, which just about anyone can pick up on" (*Out*, October/November 1993). "For years, gays in the federal government feared that any overt sign of their sexual orientation would lose them their jobs and came to rely on . . . 'gay-dar' as it is known—to detect their compatriots amid the legions of federal workers" (*Washington Post*, August 8, 1992).

THE STORY: The last syllable in the noun *radar,* itself historically an acronym like *sonar* and *snafu,* took on a new function as the second constituent element in *gaydar,* a word that most probably began its linguistic life in the sixties as *gay radar.* Informants of both genders spanning three generations in the gay community attest usage to the sixties, if not before, and have pointed out that though the word infrequently appears in the mainstream press, it is a fixture on the electronic nets.

As Michael Musto, the author of "*Gaydar:* Using That Intuitive Sixth Sense," explained in the October/November 1993 issue of *Out,* "*Gaydar* is an intuitive aptitude that surpasses anything in nature. . . . There's something . . . that tips us off with great certainty, even when they're holding a live grenade or sporting a wedding ring." He discounted all the *signifiers* purposely used by those wanting to be spotted, and then gave a sampling of almost-indescribables, such as a certain campy sense of humor, perhaps incessant talk about one's mother, or a man's desire to try on a number of outfits before purchasing one—any of which, combined with other intangibles, can be a tip-off. And, he said, *gaydar* "pierces . . . the physical and emotional language of the closet cases."

One informant pointed out to me that to him, *gaydar* is operative when he and a man he has never met before pass and their eyes lock together just for one split second too long. Perhaps that's the best defining statement yet.

glass ceiling *noun*, the unofficial yet nearly impenetrable barrier impeding advancement of women and minorities aspiring to rise from middle to senior corporate management positions or from entry-level academic positions to tenured professorships: "[In the spring of 1990] Labor Secretary Elizabeth Dole [planned] to launch an initiative to combat the *'glass ceiling'* that seems to limit or discourage women from reaching top management positions in the corporate world" (*USA Today*, August 10, 1990). "Of course in this age of salary gaps and *glass ceilings* paycheck problems do remain" (*Working Woman*, November 1987). "While the *'glass ceiling'* keeps a select group of women from . . . top jobs, more than half of all women employed by state and local governments work on the *'sticky floor'* of low-paying, low-mobility jobs" (Catherine White Berheide, *Women in Public Service, A Bulletin of the Center for Women in Government*, SUNY-Albany, Fall 1992).

THE STORY: Looking through the glass darkly, one can define *glass ceiling* as "what the men in the boardroom are standing on." These are the words of a woman participant at a March 1988 University of Southern California conference entitled "Women, Men, and the Media: Breakthroughs and Backlash." The term itself was first introduced in the mid-1980s by none other than the venerable *Wall Street Journal*. Interest in the term increased in the early 1990s because of the Labor Department's intended *glass ceiling reviews* of U.S. corporations.

When I defined this term in 1991, I said, "Whether or not *glass ceiling* sustains long-term currency is dependent upon the behavior of the corporations and other employing institutions in this country." Today *glass ceiling* is not only in wide use, it has become a fixture in the language. It now appears regularly without "shudder" quotes: "Women, while still less than 10 percent of the work force here [in a Lynn, Massachusetts, General Electric plant], are changing the culture. Catherine Lyons, 35, has broken a *glass ceiling*, having become a plant manager overseeing nearly 100 workers in a multiskilled shop" (*New York Times*, September 5, 1993).

Be that as it may, Ann M. Morrison, Randall P. White, and Ellen Van Velsor of The Center for Creative Leadership in Greensboro, North Carolina, made a bleak assessment of the situation for women in the workplace in their 1987 book *Breaking the Glass Ceiling: Can Women Reach the Top of America's*

Largest Corporations? The authors, who examined this ceiling and the concrete wall that lies beyond it, concluded that once women do succeed in breaking through the first barrier, "they unexpectedly encounter another barrier—a wall of tradition and stereotype that separates them from . . . the inner sanctum of senior management, the core of business leaders who wield the greatest power." The authors then went on to predict that only a handful of the seventy-six women executives they studied will ever reach general management level, thereby debunking the myth that the passage of time and infusion of newer, younger managers will ease the transition of women from the middle to the top corporate strata.

This assessment is borne out in a January 23, 1994, letter to the editor of the Business section of the Sunday *New York Times* by Joyce D. Miller of Washington, D.C.: "It is premature to declare that the phrase '*glass ceiling*' be given a decent burial," because "it concerns minorities [now] as well as women, and those at all levels of the work force . . . who find their career growth limited by policies and practices that hamper their productive energies." The position held by the writer of this letter is executive director, *Glass Ceiling* Commission, United States Department of Labor. See also *sticky floor.*

laughism *noun*, inappropriately directed laughter, such as ethnic taunts: "Brace yourselves: '*Laughism* . . . has just been banned at the University of Connecticut. The proper response, says George Will, is 'derisive laughter,' but Will goes on to make the serious point. 'At bottom, none of this is funny. It flows from the tyrant's impulse to extinguish privacy'" (*National Review*, July 29, 1991). "Laughter continues to be directed at the University of Connecticut more than a year after the school lifted a prohibition on 'inappropriately directed laughter'" (*Hartford Courant*, August 8, 1991).

THE STORY: The word *laughism* is now passé, at least in the context of the University of Connecticut. It was driven off the linguistic stage to the boos, hisses, catcalls, and, yes, derisive laughter of those concerned about preservation of free speech. At the same time, the very existence of *laughism* signaled a serious people problem on campuses and in the general society, a problem that continues. *Laughism* went out of currency within about five years, after references to inappropriate laughter had first appeared in the University of Connecticut's 1988 presidential policy on harassment. (A high-profile incident in which Asian-American students had been taunted and spat on by their white peers had prompted the policy.) In 1989 this policy banned other things, such as the use of offensive names, inconsiderate jokes, and "conspicuous exclusion from conversations" (also called *conversational exclusionism*). But in 1990, well before the *National Review* piece cited earlier appeared, the U.S. Supreme Court's *fighting words* standard had replaced the prior wording in the presidential policy statement. (This standard curbs offensive speech only in face-to-face confrontations that are deemed likely to result in immediate violence.)

Meanwhile, back in the newsrooms, a derisive coining frenzy was in progress: words like *thighism, crabgrassism, hairism,* and *richism*—spun off of *laughism*—proliferated and then died out in a linguistic life cycle reminiscent of mayflies. Thank God, one critic has said, that Americans can never take themselves too seriously for too long. That, he said, has kept the impulses of the tyrants in check. See also *non-ism.*

lobola also **loboler** or **lobolo** *noun,* among black families in southern Africa, a traditional series of payments made by a bridegroom to the family of his bride. Also called *bride-price:* "Originally, parents charged *lobola* to compensate for the loss of the daughter's labor in their household. In return, the groom was entitled to the wife's labor and all children born to the couple. The amount of the *lobola* is arranged by the couple's relatives" (*Inter Press Service Report,* July 7, 1986).

THE STORY: Use of this word in English goes back to the year 1825. According to Clement Doke's *Zulu-English Dictionary,* the word *lobola* is a verb stem meaning "to supplement a marriage by handing over cattle, etc., to [the] guardian of the bride to ensure the right of the bridegroom to any issue of the marriage." A noun associated with the verb means the goods used in the bride-price transaction. Evidence indicates that the word occurs both in the Zulu and in the Xhosa languages, which are closely related members of the Bantu language group.

A 1982 citation from *Drum,* a leading black magazine in Africa, indicated that "*lobola* has gone commercial"; that is, money in escalating amounts began to replace livestock in this transaction. Young people and their families in South Africa, for instance, expressed some measure of frustration and disillusion in the mid-1980's because the amounts could vary from as low as $350 to as high as $5,000, depending on the educational background of the bride and her family's economic status.

Recurrence of the word in American and British publications in the eighties is just another small indicator of how news events in southern Africa and local customs there elicit world interest. Because of the frequency of occurrence in a broad array of English sources over time, *lobola* gained entry in the third edition of *The American Heritage Dictionary of the English Language* (1992).

LUG also **lug** *acronym, slang,* lesbian until graduation. Also called *four-year lesbian:* "The *LUG* . . . phenomenon . . . has alienated many people—not only straight alumni but lesbians, who suggest that it trivializes their long and difficult journey" (*Newsweek,* June 21, 1993).

THE STORY: The *Newsweek* citation affords a glimpse of one side of the controversy surrounding the choices made by *LUGs*. Interviews in 1994 with various people of both genders and all ages in the gay community and media revealed yet another view, this one that the *LUG* phenomenon is an instance of youthful experimentation with sexual choice in an atmosphere more tolerant and supportive of diversity than what is often the case in the workplace, for example. It was also pointed out that with the convergence of the feminist and gay movements in recent years, young women feel freer to *out* themselves earlier than before. Whether they choose to remain lesbian or to *straighten up* at a particular juncture is a matter of personal choice.

The term *LUG* itself is on the verge of transforming into a noun, an indicator of possible lexical perpetuity. Telltale signs of nouning are its occasional occurrence in lowercase; its use in the plural, especially in oral citations; and its unitary pronunciation. See also *gaydar.*

reasonable woman standard *noun,* the standard, or benchmark, used in some jurisdictions in sexual harassment cases to determine whether a hostile work environment exists: "In determining whether conduct or statements are sufficiently severe to rise to the level of unlawful sexual harassment, some state courts have relied upon a *'reasonable woman'* standard. Under federal law, however, an objective standard, the 'reasonable person' standard, as well as the victim's subjective perception are applied to determine whether a hostile or abusive work environment exists" (N. Elizabeth Fried, *Sex, Laws and Stereotypes,* 1994).

THE STORY: The often unreasonably dense language of the bar is shot through with *reasonable* compounds, to which *reasonable woman standard* may be added as a response to incidents of alleged sexual harassment occurring in the workplace: *reasonable belief, reasonable care, reasonable cause, reasonable charge, reasonable compensation, reasonable diligence, reasonable excuse, reasonable probability, reasonable provocation, reasonable rate, reasonable regula-*

tion, reasonable time, and, of course, the one familiar to all former jurors—
reasonable doubt.

Also in that short and incomplete list is the *reasonable man rule,* which
holds that in the review of an administrative determination, the court will
not substitute its own judgment or discretion for that of the agency, but will
consider the evidence in support of the order sufficient where it is of such
character that a reasonable man considering it would make the same determination.

The idea behind the *reasonable woman standard* is similar, as is the use of
the gender-neutral *reasonable person.* The evolution of these compounds
from *man* to *person* to *woman* signifies a changing and narrowing of legal denotations to reflect actions and actionable behavior in the workplace.

rug-ranking *noun,* compensation policies that assign secretarial grades and
salaries strictly on the basis of the reporting relationship and not on skills, ac-
countabilities, and job content: "*Rug-ranking* bothers many advocates for
women in the workplace . . . ; they find it altogether too reminiscent of the
days when women were legally chattels and socially dependent" (*New York
Times,* March 17, 1994). "Oh, heavens. I thought we'd done the whole secretary argument. I thought all those tedious quarrels about *rug-ranking* and
who makes the coffee were lost in the mists of time" (Michele Landsberg,
Toronto Star, August 7, 1990).

THE STORY: The story is twofold: It's about a term that, having most probably originated in Canada, made its way across the border into U.S. English
several years later. And it's about "The secretary/she," at the beginning of the
turn of a century when over 90 percent of the secretaries in the United States
are still women. In terms of its national origin, *rug-ranking* can be traced
as far back as a March 1990 origin citation from *Canadian Datasystems:*
"*Rug-ranking* often assigns the poorest chairs to the workers expected to
sit in one place and type the longest," a usage attested and antedated by a
Word Watcher from Ontario who had heard it in this sense as far back
as 1980.

N. Elizabeth Fried, Ph.D., a Dublin, Ohio, compensation consultant, assigned *rug-ranking* to the practice defined here in 1993, after a conversation
with a Canadian during a several-year study of secretarial compensation
practices. Fried then used the term in print on March 16, 1993, in a press release headed thus: "Survey Reveals '*Rug-Ranking* Method' of Secretarial Pay
Loses Ground."

In March of the next year, *rug-ranking*, hyphenated, gained national attention in connection with a lawsuit filed by a former executive secretary at a television sports network, who had been demoted—later fired—after her boss had been demoted in a corporate restructuring.

Fried has found that most forward-looking companies are departing from *rug-ranking* now: the movement toward more progressive, content-based practices began to make some headway in 1988, jumped significantly in 1990, and showed continued growth through 1992.

Rug-ranking joins two other terms in this chapter denoting limitations to career advancement—imposed obstacles that take their linguistic cues from the language of physical property: the *glass ceiling* and the lowly *sticky floor*, the latter not worthy of a rug.

sticky floor also **sticky floors** *noun*, a condition in which women and minority men in entry-level or low-wage positions find themselves unable to rise to higher positions in a particular career path or workplace setting: "While the 'glass ceiling' keeps a select group of women from government's top jobs, more than half of all women employed by state and local governments work on the '*sticky floor*' of low-paying, low-mobility jobs" (Catherine White Berheide, *Women in Public Service, A Bulletin of the Center for Women in Government*, SUNY-Albany, Fall 1992). "'Separate sisters'—women in minority groups; women in 'traditional' women's jobs; women who stay at home . . . ; elderly, rural, some poor and younger women . . . charge that the feminist movement . . . [has] not adequately addressed . . . the *sticky floor*" (*U.S. News & World Report*, March 28, 1994).

THE STORY: The 1992 citation was the first print occurrence of a new term coined by Berheide, guest editor of the *Bulletin* and an associate professor of sociology at Skidmore College. In creating the new term during her research on the immobility and occupational segregation of certain groups especially in the government workplace—groups that include paraprofessionals like library assistants, administrative support people like clerks, and service/maintenance workers like groundskeepers—Berheide sought a term that would be analogous to and yet the obverse of *glass ceiling*. Hence, she initially chose *floor*. *Sticky*, which, when combined with *floor*, evokes the unmistakable imagery of "women's work," was chosen over other possibilities to capture the essence of the difficulty many people experience when moving up, even a short way up, from dead-end positions typically paying less than $20,000 a year.

After *sticky floor* appeared in 1992, it not only took on an *-s* plural form as a variant, but it also moved into use in academe to denote the plight of those women and minority men unable to obtain tenure as faculty members in some U.S. colleges and universities: "The Luncheon Speaker, Sharon Leder [an English professor], said there was a new term in Academia for those seeking tenure: '*sticky floors.*' Without making that first step of tenure, they [newly hired and untenured faculty] cannot begin to reach the 'Glass Ceiling'" (Report on the Virginia State Convention, American Association of University Women, April 30, 1993). See also *glass ceiling.*

TLB *abbreviation, slang,* tough little broad: "Well, they finally nailed Tonya Harding, my favorite tough little broad. . . . I can't control my fascination with *TLBs,* and the phrase is one I learned from a self-described tough little broad of my teenage days. She used it in the context of a warning about what was going to become of my private parts if I didn't stop messing with hers" (Hank Burchard, *Washington Post,* April 3, 1994).

THE STORY: Here's the nineties version of what was once called "a tough little cookie." Interestingly enough, Burchard's usage made its national media debut at roughly the same time as Naomi Wolfe's *babe* in *Culture Babes.* Adieu, *bimbos;* bonjour, *broads* and *babes.*

The definitive criteria of a true *TLB* are these, according to Burchard, who has known and admired many of them, his grandmother and MD mother included: to the manner not born, a rough childhood, underdoggishness, shortness of physical stature, and nonmembership in a so-called prestige religious denomination or ethnic group. A *TLB* also does not center her life on men; she can take them or leave them—as the case may be. In so being, a *TLB* exudes a certain powerful aura by virtue of her own "apartness." Positive traits? Determination, grit, warmth, wit. Motto? Don't tread on me. A prime-time example? Carla in the television series *Cheers.*

The downside? We witnessed it.

trailing spouse *noun,* a spouse in a two-career marriage who relinquishes employment in order to follow his or her mate to a new locale where the mate has obtained employment: "More and more couples are looking at relocations carefully, and the *trailing spouse* is saying, 'I am not going to give up my career, willy-nilly'" (Springfield, Mass., *Sunday Republican,* June 8, 1986).

THE STORY: This term, which appeared in one of my first "Word Watch" columns, is still extant. The real story is, however, that to date no one has come up with a more colorful synonym for it. An example of a high-profile *trailing spouse?* Hillary Rodham Clinton.

wife *verb*, to be relegated to a life of housewifely tasks and concerns: "Liddy Dole's closest aides and supporters were afraid that this ambitious and visible woman would be *wifed*, a mysterious process by which candidates' wives are often turned into adoring Nancys. They were concerned that her identity and résumé would be undercut by a term as helpmeet" (Ellen Goodman, *Boston Globe*, April 5, 1988).

THE STORY: The verb *wife*, meaning "to take a wife," has been in the English language since the year 1387; however, it has long been labeled by dictionaries *obsolete* or *rare*. At last, we have a new, viable sense for this old verb. The gerund *wifing*, used in the same way as *parenting* and *mothering*, but also considered rare by most dictionaries, has come back into favor, as an accumulation of a half-dozen citations attests. A sample: "As our institutions begin to ease the pressure, perhaps husbands will be less wearied and be able to do some extra *wifing*" (Virginia Hyde, *Los Angeles Times*, April 13, 1987).

5

You Have the Right to
Remain Silent . . . and
That Is the Word of the Law

aggravated traffic disruption
bazuko
beeper boy
beeper gun
carjacking
Chip Smith charge
Club Fed
cocaine industrial park
creep defense
death qualify
Dirty Harriet Syndrome
drive-by hatred
electric mule
floral bondage
garage hopping
ghost rider
glading

go-fast
grease-trap theory
green collar fraud
home invasion
hubba
hydraulic bollard
Lerach (*verb*)
mushroom
narcokleptocracy
New York barricade
Paula Jones Disease
Rembrandt (*verb*)
Schindler defense
shoulder surfing
stranger homicide
token sucker
24/7

We can judge of the intent of the parties only by their words.
—Sir John Powell, *Idle v. Cooke* (1704), 2 Raym. 1149

Violence . . . is as American as cherry pie.
—Rap Brown, remark, ca. 1966

"Words after all are symbols, and the significance of the symbols varies with the knowledge and experience of the mind receiving them," wrote Benjamin N. Cardozo (*Cooper v. Dasher*, 290 U.S. 106, 54 S.Ct. 6, 78 L.Ed. 203 [1933]). Taken singly, as small clusters, or as a whole, the colorful, mostly raw vocabulary in this, a chapter focusing on the language of the law, its enforcers, its breakers, and the victims of its breakers, is symbolic of at least seven frightening trends reflecting the intent of the lawless and the failure of society to effectively deal with it. May it please the court of public opinion to list these trends below:

- Societal and urban terrorism, following, in great measure, the models established earlier in our time by state-sponsored international terrorism, to be seen at *carjacking, home invasion, grease-trap theory,* and *stranger homicide.*
- The formation of modern fortified communities, these gated ones reminiscent of the isolated, often besieged forts of the Old West, constructed in response to the new terrorism or fear of it, to be seen

at *hydraulic bollard*; and similar fortifications created by criminals to fend off the attentions of police and rival criminals, to be seen at *New York barricade*;

- The criminalization of children, resulting in a new class of highly dangerous, unpredictable inmates, feared even by old-time, hardcore, long-term prisoners, to be seen at *stranger homicide* and at *Fagin*, *takeover robbery*, *G-ride*, and *deep-end kids* at *grease-trap theory*;
- The apex in the development of the celebrity-criminal class in the United States, to be seen at *Club Fed*, where *postconviction expert* appears, at *creep defense*, where the *tough bitch defense* stands before the bar, and at *stranger homicide*, where a new reference book, the *Penal Michelin*, is launched and publicized;
- Inventive use of electronic communications devices to market drugs, issue threats, and commit other crimes, seen at *beeper boy*, *24/7*, and *shoulder surfing*, not to mention *garage hopping* and *drive-by hatred*;
- Firearms as the artillery pieces of choice in this, the Beirutization of American cities, seen in discussions of many of the words already listed here but particularly apparent at *beeper gun* and at *24/7*, where *streetsweeper*, *burner*, and *9* are also discussed;
- Drugs and drug money as the fulcrum of the lawlessness of twentieth-century local, state, national, and international life, to be seen at *bazuko*, *cocaine industrial park*, *glading*, *go-fast*, *green collar fraud*, *hubba*, and *narco-tunnel* at *narcokleptocracy*.

It is the result of the work of the busy, resourceful *narcokleptocrats* that a new kind of societal "collateral damage," to use the terminology of warfare, has emerged. This, in the thugs' own wording, is the *mushroom*—in military parlance, an *IC*, or innocent civilian. Oliver Wendell Holmes wrote that "the question in every case is whether the words are used in such circumstances and are of such a nature as to create a clear and present danger" (*Schenck v. United States*, 249 U.S. 47, 52, 63 L.Ed. 470, 39 S.Ct. 247 [1919]). In this case, it is the single word *narcokleptocracy* and all that derives from it that presents the clear and present danger to society. To governance. To the governed. To those victimized. To all of us. You are the jury. Deliberate at length and with objectivity. Then render your verdict.

In terms of linguistic process, if not due process, some of the words are of special interest if only because of the murk that surrounds their origins, and the twists and turns they involve. Examples are *hubba* and *bazuko*. And when you get past the *token sucker*—a term well on its way to obsolescence before ever fighting its way into dictionaries, you'll board the E train and end up not in Queens or Brooklyn, but in South Africa. The bray of the *electric mule* leads to rail yards and coal mines—a long semantic leap from the sound of European police sirens.

Samuel Johnson said this in *The Rambler* (May 28, 1751): "It is one of the maxims of the civil law, that definitions are hazardous." One can hazard to say that in terms of spurious civil litigation, the whiners are engaged in a full-court press. The results are captured in Steven Brill's new coinage, the eponym *Paula Jones Disease*. Whining, which sank to its nadir or rose to its apex (whichever, whatever) in the eighties and nineties, is exemplified in the criminal and the civil courts by the *creep defense*, where the (*tough*) *bitch defense* and the *Guyland defense* are brought to the bar. But by far the most cynical in this new codex of defenses is the *Schindler defense* used by a French war criminal in 1994. None of these words pass what Mortimer Zuckerman has called the "smell test." And *Paula Jones Disease* exudes, more than many others, the malodors in U.S. courtrooms today. Just reading through the entire list of words in chapter 5 evokes the smells, sights, and sounds of fury in the trial and litigation process.

Just as every legal issue has at least two sides, so does the language of the law and law enforcement. Just as the key vocabulary in this chapter is serious indeed, so does it have its own light side. In fact, the chapter opens with *aggravated traffic disruption*, a charge suggested by an angry, gridlocked Virginia motorist last year. That entry begins in the vicinity of the Fourteenth Street Bridge but ends with you sitting on a bus on I-95, where you'll learn about *bums* and *bombs*, and what a difference a regional pronunciation can make. Finally, the entry for the verb *Rembrandt* brings together a motley crew of linguistic dinner guests to the artist's table: four former U.S. presidents, one former vice-president, one former first lady, one U.S. senator, several judges, a television anchorwoman, a dress designer, the victim of a Cold War assassin armed with a sharpened, poisoned umbrella, and none other than Bernhard Goetz, another New York subway rider of some note.

If "the lawyer's vacation is the space between the question put to a witness and his answer" (Rufus Choate, 1799–1859), the language of this field can present with just as many unexpected retorts when cross-examined and studied. That's American English for you, according to the very letter of the law.

aggravated traffic disruption *noun*, an action, such as an unauthorized demonstration, an attempted suicide, or a terrorist act or hoax, that serves to obstruct, congest, or otherwise impede the ingress and egress of motor vehicles on a street, bridge, or other right-of-way, especially in peak drive time in an urban area: "As one of the 100,000 people who was delayed for over two hours because of Mr. Sadiq-I-Abubakar's alleged antics on Feb. 28, I think an *'aggravated traffic disruption'* statute is a wonderful idea" (Alex W. Thrower, an Alexandria, Va., resident, in a letter to "Dr. Gridlock," *Washington Post*, March 31, 1994).

THE STORY: The writer suggesting addition of this new statute to the code was galvanized to action as a result of an incident that brought traffic on the Fourteenth Street Bridge to a virtual standstill for seven or eight hours, while, in the words of Ron Shaffer, the writer of the "Dr. Gridlock" column, the alleged perpetrator "alternately demanded to see his daughter (living with his estranged wife) and threatened to blow up his car." (The "bomb" in his Mercedes later turned out to have been a hoax.) The District of Columbia, like many other cities, has had to deal with different types of gridlock-inducing incidents, some being unauthorized demonstrations pro and con abortion, protests about the Rodney King verdict, and so on.

Not only has Thrower suggested a new class of traffic violation, but he has also created an easy calculus for judges to refer to during the sentencing process:

$$T = \frac{(PH)}{24} + A$$

where, in Thrower's words, "'T' equals time to be served (in days), 'P' equals the number of persons inconvenienced, and 'H' equals the number of hours that traffic was delayed. Using the above formula, an approximate sentence for the crime committed on Feb. 28 would be approximately 22.8 years." The "A," he says, equals "the asininity of the offense," and he leaves that factor open as an n (for "unknown") to allow for judicial flexibility.

Such cases would have to be handled with care, of course. Recall the textbook case of *aggravated traffic disruption* that occurred some years ago on I-95 between Washington, D.C., and New York City—one that evolved into a contortion because of the pronunciation and misunderstanding of the pronunciation of a consonant-vowel-consonant monosyllable. In brief, people sitting in the back of a bus were being disturbed by a "bum" who was in and out of the bathroom. They decided to alert the driver to the problem by passing the word up to the front, "There's a *bum* on the bus." By the time this message had reached the driver, *bum* had morphed into *bomb*, an easy transformation, given that many residents of the Middle and South Atlantic States pronounce *bomb* as [bum], especially older ones and those from rural areas. As a result of the shift from /ŏ/ to /ə/ (this symbol, the schwa, represents an /uh/ sound), the bus was stopped, the police were called, the road was closed for hours until the matter was sorted out, and the entire area crawled with sniff dogs, robots, a SWAT team, bomb disposal squads, helicopters, and state troopers. And so it was not just a case of *aggravated traffic disruption*; it was a first-degree phonological misunderstanding. The moral of the story is that there *are* a few matters more pressing than Jimmy Carter's contested pronunciation of the word *nuclear*, as in [nyo͞o'kyuh-luh] [bum].

bazuko or **bazuco** also **basuco** *noun*, a highly addictive powder containing cocaine, kerosene, ether, and sulfates that is made from coca-leaf paste and that can be rolled into cigarettes for smoking: "While American drug users are discovering the cheap and toxic thrill of crack, Colombian youths are being sold its even less expensive and more dangerously addictive sister product, known here as *bazuko*, Suzuki, 'little devil,' or 'the thing'" (*Boston Globe*, September 11, 1986).

THE STORY: What do cocaine, music, and bazookas have in common? Nothing. According to an erroneous theory in the August 10, 1986, issue of the *Manchester Guardian Weekly*, *bazuko* "[got] its name from the bazooka: its effect is instant and violent." The now accepted etymology traces the word to the Colombian Spanish word *bazuco*.

Charles M. Lane of *The New Republic*, however, has seen the word spelled *basuco* more often than not. He believes the word to be slang for *básico* or *básica*, the masculine and feminine forms of the Spanish word for *basic*, as used in the phrase "basic cocaine paste." Said Lane in a letter to *The Atlantic Monthly* published in April 1987:

> In general it is common in Spanish to add short suffixes to ordinary words as a way of adjusting their meaning. Often these suffixes apply to size. For example, *-azo* makes *grande* ("big") *grandazo* ("enormous"). In the slang of certain Andean countries the suffix *-uco* can be attached to words to add an implication of power, large size, or other dread characteristics. The best example I know is *terruco*, the word Peruvian highland peasants and lowland slum-dwellers alike have come to apply to terrorists (*terroristas*). Since in Peru the *terru-*

cos come from the fanatical Maoist group Shining Path, it's no wonder that people have added such a suffix in describing them. Hence *básica* may have become *basuco* in a similar way—the *-uco* added just the right air of sinister, yet alluring, power.

Regarding the substance as opposed to the word denoting it, the *Globe* reported that *bazuko* was introduced on Colombian streets in 1981 when the drug dealers realized that their domestic coca did not refine well into export-grade cocaine. In a feat of waste-not, want-not marketing, they dumped *bazuko*, the semirefined paste, onto local markets. It took three years for the earliest example of the word's use in a general English-language publication to appear: the August 27, 1984, issue of *Business Week* is one of the earliest sources. *Bazuko* joins an ever-increasing list of terms for cocaine and its derivatives used recreationally: for example, linguist Richard Spears gives at least 168 in his book *The Slang and Jargon of Drugs and Drink*. See also *hubba*.

beeper boy *noun, slang*, a drug dealer who uses electronic telecommunications equipment in selling to customers: "Big profits in the drug trade do not come until one reaches a mid-level sales position. This includes the '*beeper boys*'" (*California Prevention Network Journal*, Fall 1990).

THE STORY: *Beeper boys* are typically street drug dealers who, through advances in telecommunications technology, have been able to retire from direct street selling, rather like call girls who once were streetwalkers. Customers call them for appointments to buy their wares. Nearly all drug dealers now use cellular phones or two-way radios, and more than 90 percent of them rely on beepers, especially the silent ones worn under the clothes that vibrate when a call comes through.

According to an April 24, 1989, story in the *Washington Post*, the *beeper boys* also use police scanners to learn of impending raids—a development that has forced many police departments to communicate on restricted channels and use numerical codes. Some narcotics officers have reported that the dealers' lookouts are using headsets similar to those worn by air-traffic controllers in spotting police movements and operations.

Incidentally, *beepers* became a $2.8 billion industry in 1993, according to the Yankee Group, a market research firm, and consumers (of whom the *beeper boys* are a subset) represent the fastest-growing users. See also *beeper gun, squeegee kid*.

beeper gun *noun*, used to refer to a .22-caliber, five-shot, stainless steel minirevolver fitted with a fold-up holster grip and that, when folded and inserted into a pocket, appears to resemble a beeper. Also called *pager gun*: "'Officers on the streets are constantly at risk, and they never know what they're going to face.' . . . *Beeper guns* are 'very dangerous and are an easily concealable threat to our officers'" (*Washington Post*, June 10, 1993). "On why there's no such thing as a '*pager gun*': 'What they are talking about is our little .22 five-shot stainless steel revolver, with an accessory called the holster grip. . . . The beepers I have seen are considerably smaller'" (Joel Achenbach's interview of Ken Friel, general manager of North American Arms, *Washington Post*, June 11, 1993).

THE STORY: *Beeper gun*, a.k.a. *pager gun*, is a term coined and popularized by the media, according to a public affairs spokeswoman for the District of Columbia Police Department, in a telephone interview with me during the summer of 1993, and Ken Friel, in a similar interview. This is the only point on which the two concurred. *Beeper gun*, which is just another metaphor for the escalating violence in our society, generated a stir during the weekend of June 5, 1993, when District police confiscated from a subject (who claimed he had thrown two beepers into the bushes during an arrest) a .22 fold-up weapon that appeared to look like a beeper. According to the District police's public affairs officer, this resemblance is especially marked when one fourth of the holster grip protrudes from a subject's pocket.

Although Police Chief Fred Thomas's concerns about the gun were explicit and clear, Ken Friel noted that the weapon is being used by some police officers as third backups in the event their service revolvers and second backups (usually ankle-holstered) are seized by an opponent.

The *beeper gun* is officially designated the ".22 LR Mini-Revolver w/ NAA Holster Grip" in the catalogs. Without the holster grip, the weapon lists for $162.50; with the grip, $195.50. It weighs 4½ ounces, has a 1⅛-inch barrel, is 4½ inches in overall length, is 2⅜ inches in height, and is ¹³⁄₁₈ inch in overall width, according to the 1993 edition of *Shooter's Bible*.

Friel added in an interview with me that with the holster-grip accessory, the gun increases in length and width by ¼ inch each, and weighs slightly more too. About 5,000 such guns were sold in 1992, said Friel, plus another 5,000 holster grips. Asked if the District police still regard the gun as a threat, since only the one had been confiscated by August of 1993, the spokeswoman replied, "We just don't know yet." See also *beeper boy*.

carjacking *noun*, armed vehicular theft in which a motor vehicle, often but not always a luxury model, is seized and then used as a means of escape or in the perpetration of subsequent crimes: "*'Carjackings'* are an emerging crime in the Washington area" (*Washington Post*, January 19, 1992). "*Carjackings* . . . have increased in the past few years until they are as common as fatal car accidents, a Justice Department study released yesterday shows" (*Washington Post*, April 2, 1994).

THE STORY: *Hijacking. Skyjacking. Shipjacking.* Then came *carjacking*, followed in November of 1993 by *taxijacking*. This lexical progression chronicles the permutations and variations of armed vehicular seizure over the years. In terms of the word at issue, the two *Washington Post* citations—the first dated 1992 and showing the word in "shudder" quotes, the second dated 1994 and using the word as a standard English form—prove the point that language reflects life.

"It's hard to tell whether *carjacking* is something new or whether it just has a new name," said a Justice Department statistician to the *Washington Post* in April 1994. "I suspect it's both," he added. In any event, from 1987 to 1992, a total of 177,500 attempted or successful *carjackings* had occurred in the United States. At the end of 1992, 25,000 had occurred for that twelve-month period alone. In the first half of 1992, *carjackers* had seized 245 vehicles in the Washington area, killing five people in the process. National attention was focused on this type of crime when, in September of 1992, a suburban Maryland woman was dragged to her death by *carjackers* as she tried to rescue her infant daughter and became entangled in a seat-belt harness. As a result of that incident, *carjacking* was classed as a federal felony, bringing with it a sentence of at least fifteen years in prison or a life sentence should a victim be killed.

The following characteristics define *carjacking* in terms of law enforcement and personal protection: time of theft is usually late at night, sometimes early in the morning at the beginning of commuter drive time; weapons of choice are firearms (at least 60 percent involve handguns); locales tend to be shopping tracts along suburban highways and urban high-crime areas, but during drive time, a victim's own driveway or the road to work; motive is often quick escape from another crime scene, joyriding, acquisition of a vehicle for use in the commission of future crimes, or money from resale of the vehicle; models commonly targeted include Nissan luxury models, Mercedes-Benz, Lexus, BMW, Audi, Cadillac, Jaguar, Lincoln, and Buick, as well as some inexpensive models. And the general characteristic common to all *carjackings*: it is a crime of opportunity. Cities having high *carjacking* rates as of 1992 were these, in order of frequency: Los Angeles (7,187), San Juan (6,838), Dallas (2,304), New York (2,112), Detroit (1,848), Chicago (1,200), and Baltimore-Washington (1,096).

Though FBI statistics indicate that *carjacking* may be on the decline because of increased motorist awareness, an increase in the use of car alarms and cellular in-car phones, heightened police vigilance and interdiction efforts, and stronger sentencing guidelines, such is not the case in, for example, Nairobi, Kenya, which, according to the December 19, 1993, issue of the *New York Times*, is also called *Nairobbery*. *Carjackings* in that city numbered an average of ten per day, typically while car-alarm-equipped vehicles were in moving or temporarily stopped traffic. High unemployment and civilian displacement because of tribal wars in central Kenya are believed to be the causes of desperation to survive through begging and various forms of armed theft. Crowds have been known to chase down and attack and burn *carjackers* in that city; in December of 1993, at least 489 suspects had been killed by Nairobi vigilante mobs.

Chip Smith charge *noun*, a centuries-old charge read to deadlocked juries in Connecticut, asking the jurors to examine with due regard and deference the opinions of their fellow members in an effort to persuade minority members to consider reasonably the majority opinion in order to reach a verdict. Also called *Allen supplementary instruction; Chip Smith:* "By then the deliberations had surpassed the previous Connecticut record of fifty-six hours, and the corridors heard talk of *Chip Smith*. . . . [Judge] Shaller read . . . the *Chip Smith charge*, and the jury reconvened" (Arthur Herzog, *The Wood-Chipper Murder*, 1990).

THE STORY: This citation relates to the celebrated murder trial of a former airline pilot accused of killing his flight-attendant wife and disposing of the corpse with a wood-chipper. The occurrence of the *Chip* in the *Chip Smith charge* read in the pilot's trial and the *chip* in *wood-chipper* is nothing more than one of those purely coincidental, ironic puns having special appeal to lawyers.

Of greater interest is the history of the term *Chip Smith charge*, for it reveals that in 1851, a Massachusetts court helped to make Connecticut procedural law. *State v. James "Chip" Smith* 49 Conn. 376, 386 (1881) is the case from which *Chip Smith charge* is derived, but *Commonwealth v. Tuey* 62 Mass. (8 Cush.) 1 (1851) is the case that inspired the *State v. Smith* judge to invoke the charge. In *Commonwealth* v. *Tuey*, the Massachusetts Supreme Judicial Court ruled in favor of a trial court judge's instructions to a deadlocked jury. These instructions read in part:

> Although the verdict to which a juror agrees must of course be his own verdict, the result of his own convictions, and not a mere acquiescence in the conclusion of his fellows, yet, in order to bring twelve minds to a unanimous result, you must examine the questions submitted to you with candor and with proper regard and deference to the opinions of each other. . . . In conferring together, you ought to . . . listen, with a disposition to be convinced, to each other's arguments. . . . If much the larger number of your panel are for a conviction, a dissenting juror should consider whether a doubt in his own mind is a reasonable one, which makes no impression upon the minds of so many men, . . . who have heard the same evidence. . . . If a majority are for acquittal, the minority ought seriously to ask themselves [the same questions].

The *Smith* case, tried in the Superior Court for New Haven County, involved the first-degree gunshot murder by James "Chip" Smith of Daniel I. Hayes, the chief of police of Ansonia. The jury, which had been deadlocked earlier until invocation of the controversial charge, handed down a guilty verdict, which was then appealed by the defense in a sixteen-ground brief requesting a new trial. In the eleventh point of that brief, the prisoner complained that the judge did not charge each member of the jury to be "governed by his own judgment, founded upon the law and the evidence, and not . . . by the judgment or opinions of others in agreeing to a verdict." The appeals court denied it, using *Commonwealth* v. *Tuey* as the prime logical basis for denial.

Fifteen years later, the validity of the *Chip Smith charge* was affirmed by the United States Supreme Court in *Allen* v. *United States*, 164 U.S. 492, 17 S.Ct. 154, 41 L.Ed. 528 [1896]. In *Connecticut Jury Instructions, Third Edition,* by Superior Court judges Douglass B. Wright and John J. Daly, published 130 years after the Massachusetts ruling, the wording of the *Chip Smith charge* in volume 1 (pp. 26–27) is almost identical to that of the Massachusetts court.

Club Fed *noun, slang,* a minimum-security federal prison, essentially a work camp, having dormitories instead of cells, recreational facilities such as tennis courts, and no fences, guard towers, walls, or searchlights: "The very best thing that a federal judge can do to help your client get into *Club Fed* is to pick up the telephone and call the director of the [Bureau of Prisons] . . . and then follow up that call with a detailed personal letter" (Attorneys Alan Ellis and Alan J. Chaset Jr. in *Champion*, a journal for defense attorneys, December 1991).

THE STORY: The Greed Generation of the eighties spawned not only a culture of consummate self-absorption and acute acquisitiveness but also an obsession with getting one's kids into The Right School—The Right Nursery School, The Right Kindergarten, The Right Prep School, The Right College. Letters were written. Connections were tapped. Prepayments, sometimes even before the birth of a child, were made. And now some people are having to use similar tactics to get themselves into The Right Prison, for God help the VIP criminal who ends up in a place like the Atlanta Federal Penitentiary. With federal prison populations at record highs, well-heeled clients are increasingly turning to *postconviction experts*—attorneys whose duties, among other things, include encouraging judges to do the paperwork necessary to get their clients into what one observer has dubbed the system's "top bunk."

Club Fed, coined by association with the trademark *Club Med*, goes back at least to a June 13, 1985, *Chicago Tribune* story (and probably earlier): of over 138 citations for it, most relate to celebrity inmates ranging from the likes of Leona Helmsley to Billie Sol Estes. *Club Fed* joins a fat list of other words for *jail*, *prison*, *penitentiary*, and *house of correction*: *cross-bar hotel*, *big house*, *bastille*, *bridewell*, *boob*, *bucket*, *brig*, *calaboose*, *chokey*, *cooler*, *coop*, *freezer*, *glasshouse*, *hoosegow*, *Joe Gurr*, *jug*, *joint*, *keep*, *lagging station*, *pen*, *pokey*, *quod*, *rock pile*, *skookum-house*, *squeezer*, *slammer*, *stockade*, *stir*, *tank*, *Texas steel*, and *up the river*.

But only in a *Club Fed* can inmates enjoy *Cuisine Prisonnière*, the nouvelle cuisine of the cell blocks, as described in *Prison Life* magazine, published on the outside for the 1.5 million on the inside. An example? Liver Day Special.

cocaine industrial park *noun*, *slang*, a large, state-of-the-art illegal drug manufacturing and distribution complex: "In 1984, U.S. and Colombian efforts smashed a '*cocaine industrial park*' in the jungle" (George F. Will, *Washington Post*, September 6, 1989).

THE STORY: *Cocaine industrial park*, like *narcokleptocracy* and *bazuko*, not to mention *beeper boy* and *24/7*, represents in the most precise and explicit way the deep inroads that the drug-smuggling problem has made in the infrastructure of our society. Consider the nature of a garden-variety *cocaine industrial park:* "14 laboratories, 7 airplanes, barracks for hundreds of workers, 11,000 drums of chemicals, 14 tons of cocaine."

creep defense *noun*, a legal defense strategy based on the premise that a defendant who has been accused of sexual assault is widely known to be sexually aggressive, and therefore that one who dates him assumes certain risks knowingly: "That [Mike] Tyson had a bad reputation is well known. Tabloids called him a 'serial buttocks fondler,' and his own attorneys employed what has become known as the '*creep defense*': Tyson was so crude that his dates had to expect he would want sex" (*Washington Post,* February 13, 1992).

THE STORY: Defense attorneys in several celebrity trials in recent years have attempted to turn their clients' notoriety to advantage. The *creep defense* failed, of course, to persuade a jury in 1992 that the former world heavyweight boxing champion Mike Tyson should be exonerated of charges of rape and deviate conduct.

Jurors were similarly unmoved by the *tough bitch defense,* or the *bitch defense,* offered in the 1989 trial of Leona Helmsley for tax evasion. It might be defined as a defense strategy predicated on the argument that a defendant is so hated by employees and business associates that they would be motivated to create a criminal case against her: "Like a student of some eastern arts of self-defense, [Helmsley's lawyer] creatively took one of his opponent's strengths—his client's reputation for being imperious and nasty—and tried to turn it to his advantage. He surprised prosecutors with a '*tough bitch*' *defense,* telling the jury that Helmsley employees falsified records so they could pay bills without having to deal with their mean-tempered boss" (*New York Newsday,* August 31, 1989).

Add to this short list of imaginative defenses the so-called *Guyland Defense,* discussed by Ron Rosenbaum in an article entitled "Long Island Babylon," which appeared in the August 22, 1993, issue of the *New York Times Magazine:* "The classic Guyland twist to this story [about a Long Island physician accused of spousal murder] is that when the doctor's alibi began to crumble, he confessed—and switched to what might be called the *Guyland Defense,* which, as I recall from watching the trial on the Court TV channel, amounted to asking the jury to decide that *living on Long Island itself* was enough to engender a homicidal depression severe enough to be exculpatory. (The jury declined to accept this novel courtroom strategem.)" Rosenbaum, the coiner of *Guyland Defense,* explained early on in his piece that "the *Guy-*

land" is a derivative retranscription of the outsider's condescending repronunciation of *Long Island* to *Lawn Guyland*. Irrespective of these linguistic details, it is clearly time to call a *postconviction expert*. See also *Twinkie defense* at *Twinkie*.

death qualify or **death-qualify** *verb*, to exclude, during jury selection, opponents of the death penalty from impanelment, in cases involving capital offenses: "[He] was convicted of capital murder, robbery, sodomy and kidnapping. He claimed that the trial court erred in allowing the state to *death qualify* the jury panel" (*National Law Journal*, September 16, 1985). "We are constrained to point out what we believe to be several serious flaws in the evidence upon which the courts below reached the conclusion that 'death qualification' produces conviction-prone juries. . . . We hold, nonetheless, that the Constitution does not prohibit the states from *death-qualifying* juries in capital cases" (U.S. Supreme Court Chief Justice William H. Rehnquist, Associated Press, May 5, 1986).

THE STORY: The term *death qualify* is an example of a verb compound that is not self-explanatory; that is, its unitary meaning cannot be deduced from the meanings of each of its constituent elements, in this case, *death* and *qualify*. Out of context, the term might be taken to mean "to qualify (someone) for the punishment of death."

This compound is one in a class of verbs formed by juxtaposing an initial noun element with a base-form verb. Examples are *plea-bargain, bargain-hunt, bargain-shop, judge-shop, board-certify, mind-boggle, profit-take, profit-share, coupon-clip, income-switch, channel-switch, union-bust,* and *brain-damage*. An attorney who reads "Word Watch" submitted a similar verb compound, *arm-rob*, for consideration. That one, however, is differently formed: the *-ed* in *armed robbery is clipped*, and the verb is formed of a noun compound.

Dirty Harriet Syndrome *noun*, a tendency in some women police officers, especially rookies, to overreact in stressful situations and to use excessive force, the counterpoint of the Dirty Harry Syndrome or the John Wayne Syndrome in men. Also called *Jane Wayne Syndrome*: "Women are not immune from using excessive force. . . . 'The cops call it the *Dirty Harriet* or *Jane Wayne Syndrome*,' she [Loyola University journalism professor Connie Fletcher] said" (*New York Times*, April 25, 1991).

THE STORY: We live in a world of syndromes, the proliferation of which might be a benchmark of our dysfunctionality. Two others that turned up in

1991 are *Beirut syndrome* and *first-in, first-out syndrome. Beirut syndrome* refers to the 1983 bombing of the U.S. Marine headquarters barracks housing troops sent to an embattled country without a specific mission: "But a *Beirut syndrome* emerges to replace the *Vietnam syndrome* President Bush says America has kicked. The military's reluctance to live in and work with uncertainty inhibits U.S. policy . . . in a crucial moment of change" (*Washington Post*, April 14, 1991). *First-in, first-out syndrome*, derived from standard accounting terminology, refers to political candidates' finances, or lack thereof: "Those with the fewest assets must make a fast start to escape the *first-in, first-out syndrome* that often erases little known and underfinanced candidates" (*Time*, April 8, 1991).

In the case of *Dirty Harriet Syndrome*, the term refers specifically to the tendency of some rookie officers to try to live up to preconceived tough-guy images. Such images have their antecedents often in cinematic stereotypes. Professor Fletcher said that "most brutality cases are with rookies." The same *Times* piece noted that "women are less likely to go along with the so-called *Blue Wall*, the code of silence that keeps officers from testifying against one another in cases of wrongdoing." See also *Colombian syndrome*.

drive-by hatred *noun*, random, senseless, seemingly motiveless acts of loathing typically directed at a victim not personally known to the perpetrator and taking the form of raging telephone calls, death threats, frightening faxes or mail, and even physical violence: "Some of the behavior associated with the Vietnam War protests or the civil rights movement may have been extreme . . . , but the hatred today is more frightening. 'It's more a random hatred,' he [Michael G. Gartner] says. 'It's . . . *drive-by hatred*'" (*Washington Post*, November 7, 1994).

THE STORY: Gartner, a former president of NBC News, coined this term in direct association with *drive-by shooting*, and he did so during an interview with a *Washington Post* reporter in late October 1994—at a time when many critics were deploring what they called "the coarsening of American discourse," especially during the bitterly fought midterm congressional and state elections. The quotation cited here is derived from that very newspaper story, in which the reporter explored the underlying reasons for "the hate . . . drifting through the air like smoke from autumn bonfires."

Though impossible to quantify, the hatred may be rooted chiefly in a pervasive fear in segments of the populace—fear of change they cannot control, fear of losing their jobs, fear of spreading crime, fear for their children's future. Manipulating that fear are some religious leaders, politicians, and talk-show hosts who indicate that violence, or at least violent expression, is sometimes an appropriate means to an end. And the accessibility afforded by electronic technology only makes hate attacks faster and easier. Consider the phone message, "Get off TV or I'll kill your family," received by two Nebraska teachers who had appeared in a commercial for a Republican congressional candidate. Recall the shriek, "Kill the bitch!" directed to First Lady Hillary Rodham Clinton in Seattle when she appeared there in 1994 to promote health-care reform. Remember the booth at the Virginia Republican Convention that sold shirts with the logo, "Where's Lee Harvey Oswald When America Really Needs Him?" Or take the salutation and the complimentary close in two letters by one writer to a (now reelected) Democratic congressman, written in October 1994: "Dear Slimeball Traitor," and "Have a rotten day and die of AIDS." See also *anxious class, moral panic.*

electric mule *noun, slang,* a European police siren: "They all heard the ululating claxon, that strident bray of an *electric mule.* . . . It was in the alleyway outside" (Hartshorne, *Whisper of Treason,* 1981).

THE STORY: The real name of the user of *electric mule* in this citation is Richard H. Blum, who also writes under the pseudonym of Thomas Adams. The term in the sense of a siren, obviously created by association with the sound made by the animal whose name forms its second element, is probably unfamiliar to most Americans.

Coal miners, however, will know *electric mule,* but in a far different sense, this one derived by association with the work capacity of the animal. A citation from the December 1989 issue of *Coal* refers to the Pettito Mine Equipment Company's "*electric Mule* that, with its short boom, is designed to pull . . . [coal] shields out of line and turn them." The *Oxford English Dictionary,* which traces the industrial sense of *mule* to 1903, indicates that this equipment can be used to tow canal boats, relocate dollies, or move trailers. The dictionary's earliest citation for *electric mule* in the general industrial sense is dated 1924.

Electric has, of course, joined with other nouns denoting animals to yield more compounds—*electric eel* and *electric ray,* for instance. But it has also combined with some less expected nouns to form compounds that, like the siren sense of *electric mule,* relate to crime and law enforcement: *electric teeth* (underworld slang for police traffic radar), *electric cure* (execution in an *electric chair*), and *electric dice* (dice loaded with metal slugs, controlled by the cheater with a magnet that is hidden under the playing surface).

floral bondage *noun*, the use of security devices and other measures to protect plants, especially in public places, from theft: "Gardeners and landscapers believe there are professional [shrub] rustlers out there, fully equipped for large shrubs and small trees. The result has been the new science of *floral bondage*, which is still in the freewheeling experimental stage" (*New York Times*, May 24, 1990).

THE STORY: In the summer of 1993, a Washington, D.C., metropolitan area resident lost all her potted plants on the back deck to *plantnappers* a.k.a. *shrub rustlers* a.k.a. *flower pirates*. If she had only engaged in *floral bondage*, she might have saved her plants. Most *flower-snatchers* operate in the summer months; peak time is around Mother's Day.

The phenomenon seems to have started in New York City, but by 1993 it had moved into other areas across the nation. Measures being taken to foil these botanical thieves include the use of barbed wire, cables, chains, and duckbill anchors that snap open after being buried five feet under the ground to secure the plants; alarms and beepers are sometimes attached to the plants, and surveillance cameras are also deployed.

Experts are now suggesting that one avoid planting flowers in popular colors like red and yellow. Choose instead "wheat-colored" ones, especially when planting mums; thieves don't care for that hue. Since peonies are especially popular among thieves, don't plant them. Instead, plant the "self-protectives" that have thorns or spines. According to the *Times*, in 1988 "more than 100 shrubs and plants were taken from the fenced Conservatory Garden," one of them being a five-foot-tall ornamental with a thirty-pound root ball.

As might be expected, we now have a law-enforcement term for the theft of plants, metal, benches, and other fixtures from public places or buildings. It's called *acquisitive vandalism*.

garage hopping *noun*, *slang*, burglaries perpetrated by teenagers who rove from neighborhood to neighborhood, stealing from suburban garages whatever is readily portable and marketable: "Authorities . . . fear . . . there will be even more 'garage hopping,' as the burglaries are called" (*Washington Post*, June 25, 1992).

THE STORY: Add this term to others in the *hopping* set: *car hopping, table hopping, bar hopping,* and *job hopping. Garage hopping* usually goes into an upswing in the late spring and continues throughout the vacation months—the silly season for teenage mischief—in the same seasonal pattern as *plant-napping.*

Garage hoppers work in several ways, according to northern Virginia police. Groups of teenagers scope neighborhoods, looking for unlocked cars in driveways, from which they steal the remote-control garage-door openers to gain entry. Or they may choose an even more efficient and even more alarming method: they cruise neighborhoods with their own remote-control opener and try to open as many garage doors as possible, using the same frequency—not a task for a *quant jock*, since most of the doors built prior to 1974 will open on one of twelve frequencies.

Popular theft items for the garage bopper-hoppers are garden tools, expensive sunglasses, car radios, bicycles, beer, and even stray cash. The items are loaded into a waiting vehicle or are stored for later pickup and sales distribution. Some groups can hit as many as four garages a day. The relatively light penalties for first burglary offenders (often as little as a year's probation) are one reason for the popularity of *garage hopping.* Spare the rod, spoil the garage.

ghost rider *noun*, a person who pretends to have been a passenger aboard a mass transit vehicle that has been involved in an accident and who subsequently claims personal injury in the accident: "For some time, mass transit operators have worried about a growing phenomenon: '*ghost riders,*' people . . . [who] often race on board and claim they were victims" (*New York Times,* August 18, 1993). "These '*ghost riders*' have been reported in New York, Chicago, Cleveland, Los Angeles, Philadelphia, Dallas and Broward County, Fla., among other places" (Associated Press, August 18, 1993).

THE STORY: *Ghost riders*—and they haven't made it into the sky yet—are of two kinds: the *jump-ons*, who, after boarding the vehicle post-accident, have their names recorded as bona fide passengers on a vehicle at the time of an accident; and the *add-ons*, who never were at the scene of an accident in the first place but later claim to have been so injured. This kind of urban transport fraud, difficult to prove without surveillance and stings, can result in as much as hundreds of millions of dollars in payments. Some dishonest attorneys and physicians have bought in and cashed in: they hire *runners* to recruit *ghost riders;* the *runners,* the more sophisticated of whom respond quickly to police-scanner accident reports, board a wrecked vehicle, distribute brochures with designated phone numbers, and encourage passengers to report neck or back injuries. Given any delay in police arrival at the scene, some *runners* are prepared to switch roles and become *ghost riders* as well.

The *Times* story gave a typical *ghost-rider* recruitment scenario, recorded by hidden video cameras. It went like this: "One tape made inside a bus crash in September 1992 shows a man jumping onto the bus three minutes after the accident and declaring to the passengers on board: 'All you people who want to get paid you stay right there. . . . Wait for the ambulance. . . . Your neck hurts, your legs hurt. . . . You'll get some money. . . . They pay.'"

Add to this the *wreck script,* a prop used by staged-auto-crash freeway gangs, who hire poor immigrants for as little as $100 each to ride in their *crash cars:* "Searches of suspects' apartments and glove compartments have found '*wreck scripts*' detailing roles and actions for accidents, authorities said. In one case . . . the rear of a station wagon used in a [staged] crash had been filled with tires to absorb impact" (*Washington Post,* July 14, 1992). The object of the *wreck-script* scam? The same as *ghost riding:* insurance money.

Though criminal *ghost riders* aren't in the skies yet, and it is hoped that they never will be, another kind has long been there, possibly sitting beside you on commercial aircraft: these *ghost riders* are airline employees, often flight-attendant supervisors (active or retired) who travel incognito to assess the real quality of crew performance and service to passengers. See? There's a silver lining to every black cloud.

glading *noun, slang,* inhalation of easily obtainable household and industrial products, such as air fresheners, especially by young teens and adolescents, to get high. Also called *bagging, huffing:* "Huffing, glading, bagging. . . . The street names are obscure, but the products aren't. There's . . . Glade and . . . about 1,400 other household items. . . . [S]ubstance-abuse professionals say inhaling household products for a buzz is frighteningly common, especially among younger kids" (*Roanoke* [Va.] *Times & World-News,* October 16, 1994).

THE STORY: Inhalation of products like gasoline, glue, and the nitrous oxide in whipped-cream dispensers (called *whippets* by the *huffers*) is not at all new. What is new—and alarming—is the very early age, sometimes as young as eight, at which youngsters avail themselves of these *gateway drugs*-under-the-kitchen-counter that can and do lead to the abuse of other substances later on. Favored by *huffers* are Freon (one child and friends sucked the parents' air conditioner dry several times before they were caught), butane, propane, paint thinner, hair spray, dusting spray, nail polish remover, wart remover, typewriter correction fluid, felt-tip markers, fabric protectors, and cooking-oil spray.

Glading, huffing, or *bagging* is easy because it is done with cheap products, most of them readily obtainable. It is also virtually undetectable once the mental and behavioral alterations it induces (which include euphoria, giggling, hallucinations, and a falling-down-drunk demeanor) have passed— unless, that is, the youngster starts to develop a rash or sores around the mouth and nose. After a very short (sometimes only a three-minute) high, a *huffer* may want to do it again. The substances so inhaled can lead to *sudden sniffing death*, a term patterned on *sudden infant death syndrome* and caused by respiratory failure or cardiac arrest.

go-fast *noun*, an aerodynamically styled, high-performance runabout capable of speeds up to eighty miles per hour, equipped with muffled, typically underwater exhausts, night optics, and state-of-the-art radios, that is used by smugglers to transport cocaine and other drugs from offshore islands such as Bimini in the Bahamas into Florida waters: "*Go-fasts* are just the logical heirs to the motorboats [that] rumrunners used during Prohibition" (*Newsweek*, October 27, 1986).

THE STORY: This noun, a compound made up of a verb plus an adverb, is also used as a modifier: "He attributes the sudden interest in tournament king mackerel fishing to the American love affair with gadget-filled, *go-fast* machines" (*Washington Post*, October 13, 1985); "High-speed Scarab *go fast* boats can hit 80 mph, outpacing even some law enforcement airplanes" (*Life*, December 1985). Other verb/adverb modifiers of the same class are *go-easy* and *go-slow*, but these two show no signs of becoming nouns.

grease-trap theory *noun*, a theory held by some Florida law officers that crime problems there are rooted in the in- and out-migrations of thousands of people, some of whom are criminals and others of whom become criminals: "Detectives across the state explain the [bizarre crime] phenomenon succinctly. They call it the '*grease-trap theory*.' When the weather up north starts turning cold, the scum start moving south" (*U.S. News & World Report*, October 11, 1993).

THE STORY: Florida has been called the last stop in the migratory pipeline from north to south, but it is also the first stop for those migrating from south to north. The dreams or schemes of the migrants notwithstanding, Florida—and especially parts of south Florida—is a place of constant flux, a place of transition. It is also a place of violence. But America is a place of increasing violence. Consider just three other locales, stories about which made their way into the citation files. Washington, D.C., called by some critics the crime capital of the nation, is so fraught with gun-related street violence that, according to a fall 1993 *Washington Post* article, very young children in the District are now writing their own wills, in which they stipulate the clothes in which they wish to be buried and set the forms for their funeral rites. An October 31, 1993, *New York Times* citation revives usage of the literary name *Fagin.* We are informed that "modern-day *Fagins* [in Los Angeles] . . . [are] training young boys not to pick pockets, . . . but to invade banks with automatic weapons [in *takeover robberies*], terrorize patrons and tellers and flee with money . . . in stolen cars [called *G-rides* for "gangster rides"]." Then there's Long Island, the setting of "a tabloid pandemonium of spouse-slayers, serial killers and demented dungeon-builders" (*New York Times Magazine*, August 22, 1993).

Florida's situation, made internationally visible in 1993 by the tourist slayings and earlier by the random freeway/interstate overpass attacks on motorists, is really nothing more than a hand-mirror reflection, however grotesque, of what is wrong with the national society and the national character. Gross fragmentation of the civil structure and the demise of civility itself are pathologies not specific to the Sunshine State. The transient nature of the population and Florida's geographic location simply make the calculus of crime more acute: Drugs. Guns. Vice. Yawning disparity between affluence and poverty. A public education system in decay and in overdrive, overloaded with too many students per teacher. Emotional illiteracy in much of the urban youth. A state of disconnect between the cultures of the elderly and the young. All these metastasizing strands are there, and more: one of the state's major problems is its juvenile justice system, which is confronted with a host of so-called *deep-end kids*, or *deep-enders*, the repeat offenders who constitute the majority of the 17,000 youngsters tried in Dade County alone each year. These kids are often responsible for some of the most appalling crimes. "'You get rich, you die or you go to jail,' says . . . a teenager who deals drugs [in Miami]" (*U.S. News & World Report*). See also *home invasion.*

green collar fraud *noun*, a false, deceptive claim by a manufacturer that its product is environmentally safe. Also called *eco-hypocrisy:* "'When a few companies deceptively exploit "green consumer" sentiment,' said [the then New York consumer affairs commissioner Mark] Green, 'it poisons the well for all environmentally conscious consumers. To advertise that these products are environmentally benign—and charge up to 15% more—is *green collar fraud*'" (news release, New York Consumer Affairs Office, March 13, 1991). "'There is too much *"green-collar" fraud* in the marketplace,' said Craig Merrilees of the National Toxics Campaign. 'There's too much undocumented, unsubstantiated, false and misleading advertising'" (Federal News Service, April 13, 1990).

THE STORY: In a letter to me dated March 18, 1991, a special assistant/advocate in the New York Consumer Affairs Office indicated that the office's use of *green collar fraud* was probably the first occurrence of the term in print. Not so: evidence for its prior use goes back at least to 1990. Examples of this type of fraud are disposable diapers touted as compostable, when, in some locales, specialized composting facilities are needed for their disposal; plastic garbage bags advertised as degradable into a "harmless organic powder" by way of their "photodegradable additives"; plastic garment bags supposedly made of recycled plastic that is itself biodegradable; and plastic-aluminum-paper drink boxes described as containing a degradable additive. Little if any portion of a plastic sheet or bag will actually degrade in a landfill because photodegradable additives do not constitute enough of the volume of the material to make degrading possible. And the plastic itself won't degrade because it is a synthetic petrochemical compound impervious to the action of all existing enzymes in a landfill environment.

Aside from the legalities attached to the meaning of *green collar fraud*, there is yet another interesting lexical point to be made: *green-collar* is a constituent element in yet another compound antedating the *fraud* term. This second compound, though botanical in denotation, bears its own legalities: "No one knows for certain just how much pot is being grown in the United States. But it is likely that billions of dollars worth of the stuff is produced (underground, naturally) by farmers known in the trade as *'green-collar workers'*" (*Washington Post*, April 4, 1984). *Green-collar workers* seem to be enjoying a thriving business more than ten years after this citation emerged: recent studies show a marked increase in the use of marijuana by U.S. youngsters on the high school and college levels. But they don't call it *pot*: now they call it *skunk* and *boom*. (Whether or not they realize that a well-known Dutch laxative in the sixties was called *Boom*, this writer knows not.) Other linguistic changes are in place within the subculture of *boomers*: *getting high* or *stoned* is passé. The idioms of choice in the nineties are *getting lifted*, *booted*, *red*, *smoked out*, and *choked out*. Popular kinds of marijuana are called *chronic*, *chocolate tide*, *indigo*, *Hawaiian*, and *Tropicana*. A water pipe similar to a bong is a *shotgun*. And *joint* has been replaced by *blunt*, a word that takes its derivation from Phillies *Blunts*, the cigars. Today's potheads cut the *Blunts* open, hollow them out, and refill them with weed. The more efficient agribusiness methods put into place by resourceful *green-collar workers*—specifically, new harvesting and processing methods—have created a smoking material twenty times as potent as what was sold on the street in the sixties and seventies. The marketplace is less averse to the risk factors inherent in pot smoking, a fact that drives the market and makes for a potentially alarming situation.

It's a long semantic leap from the corridors of the New York Consumer Affairs Office to the fields of illegal pot growing, but that's an example of the reach of the English language. See also *glading*.

home invasion *noun*, armed robbery of a private residence that occurs when the occupants are there and that involves violent entry: ". . . corruption including drug-related crimes and '*home invasions*,' a police term for robberies when residents are at home" (*Newsweek*, November 11, 1985).

THE STORY: Battering rams, sledgehammers, and, of course, firearms like sawed-off shotguns and automatic weapons are typically used in gaining forced, violent ingress to occupied dwellings. Once inside, the robbers may merely tie up the occupants, but more often than not, they will physically attack those in the dwelling, then loot the house.

Though the term *home invasion* appeared in quotation marks in the eighties, it has since become part of the mainstream lexicon of the nineties. Yet another term has joined this alarming lexicon: *takeover robbery*. The MO of the *takeover robbery* mimics that of the *home invasion*. Only the target is different: "The FBI reported 126 '*takeover*' robberies—in which bandits armed with high-powered weapons terrorize employees and customers—in the 1st 5 months of '92. The number is 3 times as many as were committed in the same period in '91 in the 7-county [Los Angeles] area" (*USA Today*, June 8, 1992).

And the story doesn't end with those statistics and one new term. An October 31, 1993, *New York Times* story reported the emergence of modern *Fagins*, who are presently engaged in coaching young boys to perpetrate these heists. Using boys as young as thirteen, many of whom are homeless or parentless or both, the *Fagins* in the Los Angeles area direct *takeover robberies* from a distance. Their *disposable henchmen* had carried out 448 of these supervised robberies in the L.A. area by the end of 1992, according to the FBI. The robber-children escape, if they are lucky, in getaway cars called *G-rides* (gangster rides)—vehicles that have been *carjacked* or otherwise purloined and that are usually ditched during high-speed getaways. See also *carjacking, grease-trap theory.*

hubba *noun, slang,* crack cocaine: "Jennifer, an 18-year-old transvestite, is smoking *hubbas,* or rocks of crack" (*Newsweek,* May 25, 1988).

THE STORY: The origin of this word, also used by some California grade-school children, along with *crack dealer,* to mean various school-yard games, is unknown, as is often the case with language of the streets and underworld. Most probably *hubba* in the crack sense is a clipped form of *hubble-bubble,* a term used for a hookah, or water pipe. A second possibility is that *hubba* is formed off *hub,* meaning "the enlarged base by which a needle can be attached to a syringe or other device." It is unlikely that *hubba* is a shortened form of the interjections *hubba-hubba* and *hubba-bubba.* See also *bazuko.*

hydraulic bollard *noun,* a perimeter protection device preventing illicit vehicular ingress and egress that shoots three-foot-long steel cylinders emplaced beneath the surface of the ground up into vehicles whose drivers attempt to defy it: "Hidden Valley, the private, residential development 35 miles north of downtown Los Angeles, became the world's first to purchase a $50,000 *hydraulic bollard.* . . . About 28 vehicles have been damaged since the bollard was installed last April. Its use sparked a local controversy and threatened lawsuits" (*Roanoke* [Va.] *Times & World-News,* February 2, 1993).

THE STORY: The vocabulary of counterterrorism denoting protective devices at embassies, power plants, airports, military installations, and nuclear sites has started to seep into the general American parlance as a result of barricade mentality and the *gating* of affluent neighborhoods. (This seepage began well before the bombing of the World Trade Center in New York City.)

The *Times & World-News* of February 2, 1993, indicated that "the Los Angeles Department of Public Works is struggling with a deluge of applications from neighborhoods that want to barricade public streets" in a resurgence of what the newspaper called "medieval strategies for protecting hearth and home." Communities engaged in such self-protection are called *fortified communities,* a compound that echoes the names of frontier towns like *Fort Collins* and *Fort Dodge.*

Use of such devices by these communities has raised questions. Are such *gated* areas by definition elitist and therefore socially divisive? Or is this sort of defensive tactic a God-given right? Whatever the answer, the *gating* (and even *moating*) of subdivisions has become routine in some parts of the country: an estimated 3 to 4 million Americans now so reside. (Nearly that number are U.S. prison inmates.) In the state of California alone, more than fifty such developments had been proposed by April of 1994, and 500,000 Californians were already living in the areas. See also *bomb blanket, gerbil tube, intentional community, New York barricade.*

Lerach *verb,* to be the object of a stockholders' class action suit alleging securities fraud: "When share prices of . . . stocks drop—particularly if company officers have recently exercised options to sell at much higher prices—a New York lawyer, William S. Lerach, is apt to file a class action alleging securities fraud. So ubiquitous have the suits become, . . . attorneys now refer to them as 'getting *Lerached*'" (*New York Times,* September 9, 1993).

THE STORY: In a corporate climate populated to some degree by vigilante shareholders and directors who make it their business to hold the grand panjandrums' feet to the fire, it is not surprising that a new eponymous verb, *Lerach*—pronounced [LEER-ack]—should appear and join the set characterized by *Bork* and *Souter.* This eponym is restricted in use generally to the legal community engaged in the representation of high-technology firms. The verb evolved because, in the words of *Times* writer Lawrence M. Fisher, "William S. Lerach is by most accounts the most prolific and successful practitioner of the class action that accuses companies of securities fraud"; in fact, says Fisher, Lerach is "the most hated man in high tech."

Attorneys and managers in the high-tech sector feel that their companies have been targeted for potential litigation because of the very volatility of the industry, a volatility that drives the yo-yoing of prices. Nevertheless, the surname *Lerach* on legal papers alleging fraud is so powerful that it does drive many firms to make out-of-court settlements.

Lerach has been involved in at least 400 securities class action suits during the years. And in the past twenty years, his firm has disbursed at least $4 billion in damages to client-investors. He hasn't restricted his attention to Silicon Valley, either. Others sued include the likes of Ivan Boesky, Charles

Keating, and Michael Milken, actions that seem to redefine, or at least add a new meaning to, the established term *white knight*.

How does this white knight, the champion of the shareholder, keep track of suspect goings-on? By computer databases and search programs. See also *Rembrandt*.

mushroom *noun, slang,* an innocent person on the scene of a gun battle, who is wounded or killed: "*Mushrooms*—that's the drug gunman's brutal slang for innocent bystanders who pop up unexpectedly in his line of fire" (*New York Times*, August 1, 1988). "The victims have been of all races, all classes, all ages. This summer, in one eight-day period, four children were killed by stray gunshots as they played on the sidewalks, toddled in their grandmothers' kitchens or slept soundly in their own beds. . . . So many have died that a . . . term has been coined to describe them: '*mushrooms*,' as vulnerable as tiny plants that spring up underfoot" (*Time*, September 17, 1990).

THE STORY: Most probably, the thugs got *mushroom* from the video-arcade game Centipede, popular in the eighties, in which the player attempts to shoot a crawling centipede or another creature such as a spider or scorpion that weaves its way through clumps of mushrooms. In this game, the player gets points, albeit only a few, for eliminating the mushrooms, whose only function is to be in the way. However, *mushroom* has a long history in its various slang usages derived from analogies to the fungus's growing patterns, its shape, and the environment it prefers. Therefore, these aspects have to be taken into account when looking at the latest, street-crime extension of the word.

Surely one of the earliest figurative extensions of *mushroom* was the meaning "a person or family suddenly raised to riches and eminence: an allusion to the fungus, which starts up at night" (*1811 Dictionary of the Vulgar Tongue of Buckish Slang, University Wit, and Pickpocket Eloquence*). Other such meanings are "a man" (going back to the late nineteenth and early twentieth centuries and attested by Eric Partridge in his *Dictionary of the Underworld* with a reference to a 1936 book by James Curtis entitled *The Gilt Kid*) and "a market-trader who appears only occasionally and spasmodically, viewed with suspicion by regular stall-holders" (a meaning attested to 1979 in the eighth edition of Partridge's *Dictionary of Slang and Unconventional English*).

Still other meanings, related to the shape of the fungus, go back to the mid-1850s, with development continuing to the present day, as evidenced by the familiar reference to a spreading cloud of debris after an explosion: "an umbrella" (1856) is one of the earliest, followed by "a hat often worn by demure ladies" (1850s and 1860s, attested in the 1859 edition of J. C. Hotten's *Slang Dictionary*), "the female pudenda" (nineteenth century), "the great clock seen in most taverns" (attested in 1909 and earlier), and "the spineless heads of the peyote," a drug-culture sense given by Eugene Landy in *The Underground Dictionary*, supplemented by the meaning "psilocybin," a hallucinogenic chemical causing hyperactivity, irritability, and anxiety, attested by Jay Robert Nash in his *Dictionary of Crime*. Still another meaning is directly related to the optimal growing environment of the fungus: "The Royal Fleet Auxiliary crew considered themselves '*mushrooms*'—they were kept in the dark about almost everything" (Gareth Parry in a report on the Falkland Islands War, *Guardian*, July 2, 1982). In the United States, workers have taken this growing-environment association a step further. Posted on many an office bulletin board is the following (anonymously written) message: "This company treats us like *mushrooms*: They keep us in the dark and feed us bullshit" (personal correspondence from Word Watcher Ron Schaumburg, Oradell, N.J., February 24, 1989).

Similar extensions have occurred with *crocus*, also to be found in the eighth edition of Partridge's dictionary: "a usually itinerant quack," "an herbalist," "a miracle worker," and "a fair-weather trader who appears for a while when winter is over." See also *IC*.

narcokleptocracy *noun*, the class of people (such as military officers, politicians, drug enforcement agents, police, lawyers, and customs officers) within a country that is engaged with drug dealers in large-scale illegal narcotics traffic, theft, corruption, and violence. Also called *drugocracy*: "The Suárez family [in Bolivia] was able to build its base with the help of Gen. Luis García Meza . . . establishing . . . a *narcokleptocracy*" (*Newsweek*, July 28, 1986). "Some Americans and Mexicans fear that drug corruption . . . might infect the national government [of Mexico], and turn the country into a *drugocracy* like Bolivia used to be, or a battleground like Colombia is" (*The New Republic*, February 23, 1987).

THE STORY: There is a measure of irony in the fact that *narcokleptocracy* is a lexical *mule* (in the drug-smuggling sense). It is a *portmanteau word*, that is, a carrier: it is formed by merging two or more words or parts of words. *Narcokleptocracy* is formed by merging the noun *narco*, "a narcotics agent," with *kleptocracy*, "a ruling body or order of thieves; government by thieves," itself formed by merging *klepto-*, "steal; stealing," from the Greek *kleptein*, "to steal," and *-cracy*, "government; class of citizens," ultimately derived from the Greek *kratos*, "strength; power."

Narcokleptocracy is at least twelve years old: an early indication of its existence is to be found in yet another *Newsweek* story, this one dated November 23, 1981, and also focusing on Bolivia. But by far the most informative context was a March 13, 1982, story in the *Washington Post*: "The Bolivian economy . . . virtually runs on *cocadollars*, with what one diplomat has called a '*narcokleptocracy*' of military, government and drug traffickers taking in a fortune from the sale of cocaine and other contraband."

A related new word, one that echoes the warning in *The New Republic* citation, is *narco-tunnel*, used in a June 4, 1993, Associated Press story, with reference to a sophisticated 1,452-foot underground passage equipped with air-conditioning, lights, and a track for carts, dug 65 feet below the U.S.-Mexican border in the Tijuana–San Ysidro, California, area. The *narco-tunnel*, which was 5 feet high and 3 to 4 feet wide, was 50 feet short of completion on the U.S. side when discovered. A completed *narco-tunnel* beneath the Arizona-Mexico border was discovered in 1990. U.S. authorities, who aren't sure how many other such tunnels are planned or are in operation, say that the situation is "really scary." See also *cocaine industrial park*, *Colombian syndrome*.

New York barricade *noun*, a two-by-four nailed across the door of a crack house to prevent entry by clients or law enforcement officers: "They were faced with raiding a barricaded apartment like the one . . . where [he] was shot as he took a sledgehammer to the door. The two troopers . . . learned through surveillance that the drug dealers had *New York barricades* . . . and sold drugs through a door slot" (*Boston Globe*, February 21, 1988).

THE STORY: State names have long been used in combination with other nouns to yield interesting compounds, especially in the fields of zoology and botany: *Virginia creeper*, *Oregon jay*, *Florida wax scale*, and *Alabama terrapin* are a handful of thousands of examples. City names have also been used this way in various fields: *New York minute* (a very short period of time), *full Cleveland* (white-belted, polyester attire), *Taos hum* (a mysterious low-frequency noise first associated with Taos, New Mexico, still of unknown scientific origin), *Chicago style* (a method of butchering animals), *Denver sandwich* (a western sandwich), and *Philadelphia lawyer* (a very shrewd attorney) readily come to mind.

New York barricade, which at first glance might suggest traffic control, de-tours, or meter maids in the manner of *Jersey barrier* and *Denver Boot*, falls in-stead into the lexicon of the drug culture, a lexicon that makes prolific use of such geonouns: *California cornflakes* (cocaine); *Texas tea* (marijuana); and the jocular *Manhattan white*, also called *New York City silver* and *subway sil-ver* (an imaginary, highly potent albino marijuana that grows from seeds flushed down the New York City sewer system), not to mention the familiar *Acapulco gold*.

See also *gerbil tube* and *hydraulic bollard*, used by law-abiding citizens who are frightened enough by the U.S. criminal element to insulate themselves from it, in much the same way as the criminal element must insulate itself from its clients and law enforcement personnel.

Paula Jones Disease *noun*, abuse of the U.S. court system for political, per-sonal, or financial purposes, as by filing a meritless lawsuit that only serves to consume the time of defendant and court alike, and concomitantly destroys the defendant's reputation: "As taxpayers we all see it when someone who slips on a sidewalk or falls in a playground or has some other bad luck sues the city or town, hoping to walk away with a payoff to avoid the cost of liti-gation. *Paula Jones Disease* is running wild" (Steven Brill, *Washington Post*, June 5, 1994).

THE STORY: Brill, the founder of Court TV and editor in chief of *American Lawyer*, is the coiner of this eponym. He referred specifically to the job dis-crimination suit brought in the spring of 1994 against President Clinton by Paula Corbin Jones, who, as an employee of the state of Arkansas at the time of the alleged incident, was allegedly pressured by the then-governor, Clin-ton, to engage in a sex act in a hotel room. The plaintiff did not complain at the time, nor did she file suit within the established deadline for such cases.

In what Brill has called *harassment litigatitus*, the defendant becomes en-meshed in a "world-class example" of a "lame duck . . . case" that, in effect, is "a crippling disease" in terms of his effective leadership of the country. Brill has proposed that the risk of the cost of litigation be placed squarely on the loser of the case. Such a procedure would preclude the efforts of those who, for instance, sue their former companies after having been terminated and under circumstances that can only be deemed risible (the companies often settle out of court in order to avoid the much higher costs of trying the cases and winning). The new procedure would also serve to control spurious med-ical malpractice suits, personal-injury suits, some libel actions, and many of the shareholder class-action suits against corporate executives accused of wrongdoing in the marketplace.

Rembrandt *verb, slang,* to frame (someone) for a crime: "But to her thousands of supporters, which include feminist groups, a bevy of lawyers, numerous Milwaukee cops, and, lately, the editorial board of Milwaukee's leading newspaper, [she] was . . . 'Rembrandted,' in the parlance of the street" (*Vanity Fair,* October 1991).

THE STORY: This eponymous verb came from an article by Bob Drury and Marnie Inskip entitled "Was Bambi Framed?" relating to the jailbreak and recapture of a woman accused of murdering her police-officer husband's first wife.

Surnames are often so used, suffixed or otherwise altered, especially in an era of pop enculturation: "With the flood of books on her parents and the decade they presided over, is there really room for another account? Isn't America *Reaganed* out?" (*Vanity Fair,* July 1991). This type of presidential surnominal verbing was seen in the late 1970s with *Nixon* and in the mid-1980s with *Carter.* It was seen in the Bush-Clinton campaign with reference to the *Trumanization* of the candidates' rhetoric.

But by far the most notorious case is, of course, the Great *Borking* of Judge Robert H. Bork, a situation stemming from the 1987 U.S. Supreme Court confirmation process, which ended in his defeat. This verb resurfaced, after a lull, in the fall of 1991, during the Clarence Thomas Supreme Court hearings. Instances of its use can be found in a diverse array of sources, including the *New York Law Journal, The New Republic, National Journal,* the *Chicago Tribune, Legal Times, Texas Lawyer, Manhattan Lawyer,* the *Washington Post, Washington Times, The Nation, Advertising Age,* and a host of others. Clearly, this verb arrived in the nineties: citations for it show fewer and fewer instances of parenthetical glosses (short definitions in parentheses to help mystified readers), and its occurrence in lowercase (like *lynch,* after Captain William Lynch, and *guillotine,* after Joseph Ignace Guillotin, M.D.) is on the rise—all signs of staying power.

It has been suggested that the very name *Bork,* "pronounced like a mildly suppressed burp," as Clarence Page of the *Chicago Tribune* put it in a July 10, 1991, piece, lends itself to this sort of shift, much more so than other names such as *Thomas* ("Appoint someone we like, or prepare to be *Borked* and *Thomased* once again," *Washington Post,* October 23, 1991), *Towerize* ("There was some concern . . . early on . . . that Judge Thomas would be *Borked.*

There's now concern that he could be *Towerized*," NBC's Jim Miklaszewski, quoted in *Hotline*, October 9, 1991), *Souter* ("What remains to be seen is whether Thomas is *Borked* or the Senate *Soutered*," *National Journal*, July 13, 1991), and *quayle* ("'to *quayle*' means to construct a rambling and totally meaningless sentence containing many large unrelated words," *Chicago Tribune*, January 1, 1989). The name *Bork* was even the subject of Contest #115 in *Advertising Age* during 1987. According to the November 23 issue, readers were asked to predict the next expression for "not working right." Almost all submitted things like these: *borked up, It's Borken, It Bork-fired, It's gone Bork-serk!,* and *Defective Borkmanship*—an obvious redundancy, at least to some.

Still other surnominal verbs have moved in and out of the language as fast as a flying *quayle*. *Norville* is an example of an ephemerum: "Last week I read in the newspaper that Deborah Norville was irked at the use of her name in the following manner: 'Jane Pauley was *norvilled* out of a job.' In other words, thrown over for a younger, blonder version" (Bella English, *Boston Globe*, August 13, 1990). Columnist English then went on to generate a whole menu of other choice morsels, among them the given-name verb *barbara*, from that of a former First Lady, defined in the *Globe* this way: "to achieve great popularity for no apparent reason. (A *recent Wellesley College graduate stated: 'Heavens, no. I don't plan to work. I plan to barbara.')*" This usage parallels that of *Ralph*: "It's a style with as many hometowns as George Bush. The Gap's out-*Ralphed* Ralph Lauren. . . . The company might be called the Japan of retailing" (*New York Times*, August 23, 1992).

First names can also function as nouns (common, as opposed to proper) with meanings derived from events associated with the bearers of those names. Consider *georgi*, for instance. A *georgi* is a lethal weapon by which poison is injected into a victim, typically via the sharpened point of an umbrella: "They had lured him to this flat and given him a *georgi*. A poison named for the unfortunate Bulgarian, Georgi Markov, who had been poisoned by a tiny pellet [of ricin] jabbed into his thigh by a man's umbrella" (J. C. Winters, *Berlin Fugue*, 1986). And surely *Bernie*, an eponymous derivative from *Bernhard Goetz*, must not be overlooked. It means "any victim who might be armed and prepared to use the weapon on an attacker." *Bernie* is one of many New York City gang terms contained in the text of and the glossary accompanying *Close Pursuit*, a 1988 novel by Canadian writer Carsten Stroud, who spent six months on the beat with members of the NYPD while writing the book. See also *imeldific, Krone, Lerach*.

Schindler defense *noun*, a strategy used by a defendant charged with crimes against humanity, in which it is asserted that, while the defendant stipulates he or she may have committed some crimes, such as wrongful arrests, those crimes were tokens to avoid commission of other crimes and to save a greater number of lives than otherwise would have been the case: "Caught after decades of hiding, [former French Milice officer Paul] Touvier presented a '*Schindler defense*'—that actually he was saving Jews" (Ted Morgan, *New York Times Magazine*, May 22, 1994).

THE STORY: *Eichmann booth. Gestapo tactics. Waldheimer's disease.* And then, in 1994, fifty years after the fact and a year after release of the Oscar-winning film *Schindler's List*, came the *Schindler defense*, yet another term associated with the Nazi perpetrators of the Holocaust, and one, which, like all the others, proves that the lights in Europe, once extinguished, have never been relit.

Derived, of course, from the surname of Oskar *Schindler* (the Sudeten German munitions industrialist and entrepreneur-profiteer who used his money and resourcefulness to save from the gas chambers the 1,100 Jewish slave laborers "employed" in his Krakow factories during World War II), *Schindler defense* was a baldly cynical, twisted, and opportunistic ploy. It would have played to both orchestra and gallery, or so thought the first Frenchman ever to have been tried for a crime against humanity after having been pardoned by the president of France on another set of such charges requiring the death penalty.

This Frenchman, Paul Touvier, an officer in the Lyons jurisdiction of the pro-Nazi political police of Vichy—a group that, for all practical purposes, was running the country by June 1944—arrested seven Jews and ordered them to be shot in a Milice reprisal for the murder by the Resistance of one Phillipe Henriot, a rabidly pro-Nazi Vichy cabinet member and propagandist. Touvier alleged, when finally brought to trial, that Werner Knab, then the chief of the Gestapo and the SS in Lyons, had demanded 100 Jews for execution in return for the attack. Touvier also claimed to have gotten his own superior, Victor de Bourmont, to bargain Knab down from 100 to 30 Jews. Then Touvier said he had suggested to de Bourmont that the victims be rounded up in stages, starting with 7, in a sort of let's-wait-and-see-how-this-plays-out policy.

"This was the so-called '*Schindler defense*,' in which Touvier said: 'Still, I saved 23 men,'" wrote Morgan in "The Hidden Henchman." The author added, "Touvier's '*Schindler defense*,' that he had arrested 7 Jews in order to save 23, was clearly invented after the fact," or maybe after the movie.

The evidence at trial clearly indicated that Touvier had, in fact, maintained his own clerkish "lists" of potential candidates for arrest in the area's Jewish population. There was no evidence at all that the German police chief (deceased, of course, so unable to testify) cared enough about the murder of a mere Vichy cat's-paw to "avenge" his death, especially when Gestapo prisons were full of Jewish victims readied and waiting for execution. And the Nazis were fully engaged in the complicated logistics of moving masses of troops from central France to the Normandy front.

Sitting in his glass cube, the *Eichmann booth*, this unregenerate anti-Semite, war criminal, and lister of names was asked by a judge: Who was responsible for the deaths of these seven Jews? To which Touvier replied, "London, because the order to kill Henriot came from Radio-London."

To make a long trial short, let's end by saying that the *Schindler defense* was a flop: the judges and jury found the defendant guilty as charged and sentenced him to life imprisonment. See also *Waldheimer's disease*.

shoulder surfing *noun, slang,* the theft of computer passwords or access codes, such as long-distance telephone access codes, by reading the numbers over the shoulders of authorized users: "How do outsiders discover a company's codes? By 'shoulder surfing,' 'dumpster diving' and stealing calling cards" (*Investor's Business Daily*, May 10, 1991).

THE STORY: According to the *Seattle Times* of August 11, 1991, "Long-distance toll fraud costs AT&T, Sprint, MCI Communications and other long-distance companies as much as $1.5 billion a year—up from an estimated $500 million in 1985." *Shoulder surfers* operating in the telephone marketplace are typically found in airports, train stations, and other crowded areas. In some instances, the *shoulder surfers*, who sell the numbers for $5 to $10 each to *call-sell operations* located in private residences, position themselves on balconies above phone booths and use binoculars to read the numbers off calling cards.

But *shoulder surfing* is also a workplace security problem. The November 1990 issue of *DEC User* noted that "[data pirates outside a system] can simply use a few proven hacker techniques such as a program called Demon Dialler, gaining access via a modem and the public networks. From inside the system it is even easier; 'shoulder surfing'—stealing a password simply by watching the user key it in—is a popular pastime." See also *channel surfer* at *trawler, elevator surfing*.

stranger homicide *noun*, the random killing of a victim by a person or persons unknown to the victim, usually an amateur or amateurs: "Although there are no statistics that chronicle senseless killings, the trend is reflected in the rise of '*stranger homicide*' statistics. About a third of all homicides are committed by strangers—three times the number compared to 20 years ago" (*Los Angeles Times*, December 26, 1993).

THE STORY: Curiouser and curiouser, stranger and stranger: more innocent victims are now being killed during street incidents, holdups, and other violent confrontations than is the case with domestic quarrels and neighborhood disputes. As a result, and put baldly, the body counts in terms of *mushrooms* are steadily escalating. More than that, however, the emerging term *stranger homicide* bespeaks of a sea change in the nature and the unwritten rules of the U.S. criminal subculture. "Robbery and burglary used to almost be a profession," said Marc Riedel, a professor of criminology at Southern Illinois University, to the *Los Angeles Times*. Now, though, "mostly amateurs" are perpetrating the *stranger homicides* and other violent crimes plaguing the nation. Riedel went on to say that the new perpetrators are "more clumsy, more impulsive and more likely to kill" than their predecessors. This change began to take ominous form in the late seventies with the arrival of crack cocaine on U.S. streets and the subsequent coalescence of the big-time, 24/7 drug gangs.

Not surprisingly, the situation has come to the attention of the senior-citizen prison inmates, old-timers who now have to confront and deal with an entirely new breed of cat in their cell blocks. Paul Allen, aged sixty-six and a bank robber who has resided a good portion of the last thirty years in various correctional institutions, is mystified, appalled, and alarmed by these new inmates, whom he characterized as "more . . . terrorist than . . . criminal." Allen now feels out of place in a criminal element so radically transformed. Said he to *Los Angeles Times* reporter Miles Corwin, "There was a distinction between a thief and a murderer in my time. . . . If you had to leave a lot of bodies behind, you just wouldn't do the job. These kids today are foreigners to me. I have no idea what they're thinking." Law officers concur. They offer some reasons for the decline in the quality of criminal behavior: many perpetrators are crack addicts with very short fuses and low comfort levels; many are juveniles with no understanding of or regard for the consequences of any of their actions; and many more are sociopaths than before. Convict Allen has found the situation so unnerving that he has done what no one had been able to get him to do before: he has decided to go straight after all these years, not necessarily because it's the right thing to do; rather, he can't bear the thought of having to serve one more minute of hard time with these killer youths.

Useful insights, all of them: for those newly convicted, first-time prisoners fighting through the ministrations of their *postconviction experts* to gain entrée into *Club Feds*, knowing one's neighbors on the (cell)block now seems essential in maintaining a high quality of life, if not life itself, within The System. Perhaps Frank Sweeney, the ex-con president of Frank A. Sweeney and Associates of Demarest, New Jersey, a newly formed consulting firm that advises first-timers in the federal correctional system on survival there, should add a chapter on coping with the new breed of killer in his proposed guidebook, "a kind of *Penal Michelin*." In an interview with *New York Times* reporter Charles Strum dated January 23, 1994, Sweeney said the book, intended "to annotate the Government's own 'Facilities' manual," would be a ready reference for the so-called *new fish*.

Reference-book editors, take note: Here is a burgeoning market, virtually untapped, that has great potential not just in print but in electronic and video licensing as well. If Sweeney got celeb criminals to write individual chapters reflective of their proven expertise, interested purchasers could look forward to disquisitions on practically every topic in virtually every profession or skill as they relate to life in the Can: prison medicine and how to make it work to your advantage; alternatives to prison cuisine; housekeeping and guest accommodations on the block; investing techniques from behind bars; establishment of a prisoners' savings-and-loan association; hacking your way into the freedom of cyberspace; obtaining a prep-school-quality education behind the red-brick wall; jailhouse law by a judge; plumbing, politics, and public affairs; playing God: how to run a cult; and ways to achieve a level playing field (or boxing ring or skating rink) through athleticism. *You* choose the chapter writers. See also *Club Fed, mushroom*.

token sucker *noun*, a subway-token thief who jams a turnstile token slot with paper or with cardboard tokens and then uses the mouth and teeth to retrieve real tokens subsequently embedded there by passengers: "Known in the parlance as trolls and *token suckers* . . . [the thieves] have continued to victimize the [New York] Transit Authority, its 2,897 turnstiles and its riders" (*New York Times*, August 8, 1989).

THE STORY: If technology is the mother of prevention, then the days of

New York City's *token suckers* have ended in the nineties, with the introduction of plastic fare cards. Now, lexicographers must be on the alert for a new hackers' term for similar, but more sophisticated, and, it is hoped, more hygienic, ploys. (Hackers have already succeeded in counterfeiting ATM cards, so why not these?)

Back in 1989 during a typical week (July 17 to July 23, to be precise), the New York Transit Authority was confronted by no fewer than 1,779 inoperative turnstiles, amounting to a 61 percent breakdown rate, with most of the turnstiles having been disabled by *token suckers*, some of whom are known to have resold the tokens for $1 apiece.

Token sucker is important even now, though, because it serves to introduce a whole class of people who either live their lives on subway trains or in subway tunnels, the latter group called, in New York, *mole people*. Another group, which engages in panhandling, is called the *skels*: "If you want to see the *skels*, ride the E," said a conductor to Nicholas Dawidoff, who wrote an article about subway panhandling in the April 24, 1994, issue of the *New York Times Magazine*. "The *skels* are . . . the really disgusting homeless," the conductor elaborated. *Skel*, more often than not spelled *skell*, has long been a fixture in the argot of the New York City police. Very possibly *skell* derives from the now obsolete English verb of obscure origin *skelder*, defined by the *Oxford English Dictionary* as "to beg; to live by begging, esp. by passing oneself off as a wounded or disabled soldier" (many New York subway panhandlers pass themselves off as disabled or ill in order to elicit sympathy and money). *Skelder* is first attested in print in 1601. It is also possible that *skell* is a clipped form of the noun *skellum*, meaning variously "a villain, scoundrel, or robber," attested in print to the year 1611, and having its roots in Dutch. The Dutch word *schelm* goes back to Middle Low German to a word that meant "scoundrel, corpse, carrion," akin to the Old High German word *skelmo*, glossed by *Webster's Third New International Dictionary* as "[a] person deserving death." Citational evidence indicates that *skellum*, now most often spelled *skelm* or *schelm*, enjoys almost exclusive use in South Africa. There, it is also used attributively to mean "sly; cunning."

When you get on the E (for Etymology) train, you never know where you'll end up.

24/7 or **24, 7** *adjective & adverb, slang*, available twenty-four hours a day, seven days a week. Used of illicit drugs, specifically crack cocaine: "On every block there are four or five different 'crews,' or gangs, each touting its own brand of the drug, known to aficionados as 'Scotty' (as in 'Beam me up'). Some blocks are 'hotter' than others, depending on the availability of the crack. On the hottest blocks Scotty is available '24/7'" (*New York Times Magazine*, October 1, 1989). "Stickup artists, girls, the Fury [the police]. You can't trust nobody, so keep your back to the wall and your eyes open—*24, 7, 365*" (Richard Price, *Clockers*, 1992).

THE STORY: This street term—a set of Arabic numerals functioning grammatically as two parts of speech—exemplifies an entire class of English words, usually informal or slang, that involve total or partial use of numerals. Others are *10-4* (the communications sign-off), *4 ×4* or *4 By* (the vehicle), *220* and *440* (the track-and-field events), *1040* (the tax form), *20-20* (of vision acuity), *86* (a verb meaning to eject a patron, as from a bar), *88* (used with *the* to mean "a piano"), *10* (a beautiful woman), *3D* (the film technology), and *212* (a New Yorker).

A single-numeral noun, *9*, has also surfaced. It is any semiautomatic weapon, usually a 9-millimeter handgun used by street criminals, especially relatively young offenders: "[He] has been shot four times in 10 years. He pulls up his pants leg and reveals his 'battle scars,' two gunshot wounds on the shin, five on the knee. [He], of course, always fired back; he preferred to use his 9 mm semiautomatic, the weapon he called his '9'" (*Washington Post*, February 2, 1992). (The form *9*, unlike its counterparts styled as .22, .32, and .45, respectively, does not convey by decimal point the idea of weaponry by caliber.) The *9* has, in fact, become a metaphor for the street criminal's gun as a business tool, a source of perceived power, and an expression of personal style. Nickel-plated *9s* compete with those having pearl handles in a deadly game of oneupmanship. These guns are also called generically *burners*. The top of the line seems to be the *streetsweeper*, a 12-gauge semiautomatic shotgun, described by the *Washington Post* as "a marriage of shotgun and revolver, producing high firepower. For example, a no. 5 magnum load shell contains about 210 pellets, meaning that without stopping to reload, a shooter could spray a city block with at least 2,500 pellets."

6

Going Ballistic:
The Fighting Words of
Warriors and Espiocrats

arruugah
atomic mafia
bodywash
bomb blanket
bubble
burn notice
Colombian syndrome
erk
frozen rope

hippo
IC
influence mine
Iraqi manicure
million-dollar wound
16th republic
smoodge
walk the cat back
withinwalls

The field of combat was a long, narrow, green-baize covered
table. The weapons were words.
—Admiral C. Turner Joy, USN
(on a year of truce negotiations in Korea, December 31, 1952)

Modern war needs modern lingo.
—William Safire

The avenger stole upon the citadel and destroyed it from
within. Yet both the avenger and the citadel were largely
creations of the same historical condition.
—John le Carré, Introduction, *The Philby Conspiracy*

The past two decades in particular have witnessed the intersection of the
overworld of global politics and military operations and the underworld of
terrorism, state-sanctioned criminality, and anarchy. The tangled skein of
words in this chapter is the lexical ensign of this, "an era of violent peace," to
quote former chief of naval operations Admiral James D. Watkins.

The borders of the Iron Curtain countries were destroyed in 1989, but in
their stead sprang up the turf of the new killing fields of our time, some of
them superintended by generals of genocide whose training had taken place
not in command and general staff colleges but in penitentiaries. Terrorism,

that systematic weapon of war that knows no borders and seldom has a face—to paraphrase French premier Jacques Chirac—forsook, for a moment in time, its countries of previous choice—Britain, Lebanon, and Israel—only to appear, unannounced and certainly uninvited, at the entrance to the basement garage of New York City's World Trade Center early in 1993. The World Trade Center bombing created, in the words of the state's governor, a new problem. This problem, new for New York and America, was only one of many worldwide. Anarchy was another: It has attended life in the Balkans, some of the former Soviet Union's former central Asian republics, and parts of Africa. It shows no signs of vanishing. Both Britain and the United States have engaged in wars with opponents that one critic has called "comic-opera countries," wars in which the new high technology of combat weapons systems enjoyed hands-on field-testing. And much of it was viewed in real time on American television screens. Grenada. The Falklands, Kuwait-Iraq. These are the geopolitical-military metaphors that validate Winston Churchill's remark that "when the war of the giants is over the wars of the pygmies will begin." Add to the list, then, these, among many: Chechnya. Haiti. Somalia. Rwanda. Liberia. Sierra Leone. Afghanistan. The Philippines. Panama. Mexico. Central America. Russia itself. North Korea, accused of building a nuclear arsenal just as South Africa has destroyed its. And Burma—"an anguished, hushed battlefield outside the focus of network video cameras and the concerns of the outside world," or so described by A Quick and Dirty Guide to War: Briefings on Present and Potential Wars by James F. Dunnigan and Austin Bay (1991).

The killing fields of Vietnam have long been silent. The stench of diesel and cordite has evanesced. But some of the words that gained currency in that other time and other place were still relevant to events of the eighties into the nineties, and they reside here: bodywash, million-dollar wound, and IC (innocent civilian), the latter of which came, in the war between Saddam Hussein and the Coalition, to be replaced by "collateral damage." It was also in the Persian Gulf that we came to learn about influence mines, the Iraqi manicure, and smoodge. Each war has its causes, its victors, its casualties, its language.

Crescents of armed conflict now center, we are told, on "cultural identity," which really means a form of modern tribalism disguised by nationalism and armed with sophisticated toys. In this, the New World Disorder, the lexicon remains fragmented, ever changing, seriously unfinished and untidy, and impossible to forecast. But some points can be made, especially with respect to the spillover of tribal nationalism into domestic life in various countries, including the United States. In terms of terrorism, signified in this chapter by *bomb blanket* and a host of related words having a deceptively domestic-sounding ring (*security research broom* being just one example), its reach is now not merely international; no, it has become urbanized and domesticated into the fabric of American life to such an extent that *hydraulic bollards*, the counterpart of British counterterrorism units' *Lazy Tongs*, have found their way onto the perimeters of America's growing number of gated communities. Domestic urban terror and violence operate with one of the forms of currency now driving the international geopolitical-military markets in some countries: drug money. The inroads made by the *narcokleptocrats* mentioned in the previous chapter have been so deeply significant that it was, in fact, a toss-up whether to enter *narcokleptocracy* there or here.

"Armed conflict will be waged by men on earth, not robots in space. It will have more in common with the struggles of primitive tribes than with large-scale conventional war," predicts Martin van Creveld, a military historian at Jerusalem's Hebrew University. Just two terms prove his point: *Colombian syndrome* and *atomic mafia*. Both represent cooperation of and operations by criminals in political vacuums, criminals whose appeal derives from tribal nationalism and panders to the same for market share. *Colombian syndrome*, which takes its cues from the narcokleptocracies in Central and South America, denotes the alleged fusion within a country like Serbia of the political leadership and high underworld figures (the overlords and the underlords) who, as warlords, together control trade, banking, real estate, law enforcement, and the agenda of the armed forces. You have seen the results on CNN. The second is *atomic mafia*, the newest of a cluster of more than a half-dozen *mafias*—a group of criminals who smuggle nuclear-weapons-grade materials from depots in the former Warsaw Pact countries to interested parties willing to pay the going price. Add to that *mafia* the *train mafia* from China that routinely attacks passengers on the Trans-Siberian Railroad, and it is easy to see the dynamics of criminality and tribal nationalism in fusion, approaching fission and critical mass.

Espiocrats are not immune to subornation, either, especially when they have champagne appetites, beer budgets, and a certain emptiness of soul. "[He was] not a Soviet apologist. [He] did not believe in anything at all. He is the type of modern man whose highest expression lies in his amorality," wrote U.S. district court judge John P. Vukasin, Jr., in August 1986, prior to his sentencing of U.S. naval officer Jerry A. Whitworth for espionage. He might have been writing of Aldrich Ames, the CIA counterintelligence officer convicted in May 1994 of spying in a Philby-like manner for the Soviet Union, later Russia.

"A secret service, in designating its intelligence targets, declares its own ignorance and thereby points to the areas in which it is most easily deceived. A penetrated secret service is not just a bad one; it is an appalling liability," John le Carré wrote in his introduction to *The Philby Conspiracy*. The citadel, which guides the sword that draws lines in the sand and vectors forces to strategic geopolitical targets, is therefore suborned from within. As was the case with the British secret service after Philby, the CIA must engage in *walking the cat back*—reconstructing, as best they can, the events in the espionage case, working back from end to inception. *Walking the cat back* is only one of several espionage terms in this chapter, others being *bubble*, *burn notice*, *frozen rope*, and *withinwalls*.

Vice Admiral Nils Thunman, USN, a former deputy chief of naval operations, observed in 1985 that "the oceans are becoming more opaque, not less." This observation is acute. The iron borders are down. But the bounds of civility and humanity, however fragile they ever were, are crumbling too. The citadel of statescraft has been breached. The waters in which the ships of state navigate are roiled and opaque. The last word in this lexicon is far from having been written, but the dangers of a coming pandemonium are writ large indeed.

arruugah also **arruuugaaahh** *interjection*, used as the official U.S. Marine Corps cheer: "The recruits, along with 4,000 base personnel, their families and friends, gave the Marine cheer, a grunting noise which one Marine Corps public relations official said is spelled *arruugah* while another said it is *arruuugaaahh*" (*Washington Post*, June 5, 1986).

THE STORY: Attention, a few good men: What more need be said, other than Semper Fi? Turn to the story behind *quux*.

atomic mafia *noun*, a group of criminals who smuggle nuclear-weapons-grade material from stockpiles and depots in countries formerly behind the Iron Curtain for sale to interested parties elsewhere: "German justice officials, worried that their country is becoming the headquarters of an '*atomic mafia*' specializing in buying and stealing sensitive materials from stocks in the former East Bloc, are moving to give investigators and prosecutors new tools against the burgeoning crime" (*Washington Post*, October 20, 1992).

THE STORY: This alarming new term joins others relating to the Atomic Age, such as *atomic veteran*, "a former member of the armed forces of the United States who was exposed to radioactivity during the testing or use of atom bombs in or after World War II."

Mafia, also a key element in various compounds, has three established senses as a base form, one denoting the nineteenth-century secret terrorist organization in Sicily; another meaning the international criminal organization active especially in Italy and the United States since the late nineteenth century; and last, one referring to a tightly knit group of trusted associates. Long-standing examples of this last meaning include the *Irish Mafia* of John F. Kennedy, the *Arizona Mafia* of Barry Goldwater, the *Southern Rim German Mafia* of Richard Nixon (so called because the members of this inner sanctum came from southern California and Florida, and many of them had Germanic-sounding surnames), the *Georgia Mafia*, or the *Magnolia Mafia*, of Jimmy Carter, and the *Brezhnev Mafia* of the late Soviet leader.

Three other *mafias*, these very recent and very sinister, have surfaced: the *Dixie Mafia* (narcotics and other criminal traffickers operating in the urban South), *organ mafia* (an illegal European kidney-brokering operation), and *train mafia* (gangs of mostly Chinese thugs who rob, terrorize, rape, and murder especially the Chinese passengers aboard the Beijing-to-Moscow trains of the Trans-Siberian Railroad—thugs supervised by Beijing taxi drivers and street-stall owners called *getihu*, who are taking advantage of the legal vacuum and the breakdown of civil law on both sides of the Russo-Chinese border in the wake of the fall of the Soviet state).

bodywash *verb*, to conceal the circumstances surrounding the death in combat of a member of the armed forces operating in an officially noncombatant country, by removing the corpse from the death site, secretly transporting it to another country or area, and then fabricating a fatal accident: "These roles created a problem when personnel were killed while on secret missions in noncombatant nations, said a former officer assigned to the CIA to plan such missions. The solution, said the former officer . . . was *bodywashing*. He explained, 'If a guy was killed on a mission, and if it was sensitive politically, we'd ship the body back home and have a Jeep roll over on him at Fort Huachuca'" (*Philadelphia Inquirer*, December 16, 1984).

THE STORY: Essentially, *bodywashing* is the laundering of embarrassing remains. The *Inquirer* citation is taken from a piece by Frank Greve, a national correspondent for Knight-Ridder, and Ellen Warren. The writers referred specifically to U.S. combat deaths that were alleged to have occurred in Nicaragua and El Salvador. These writers also pointed out that the word actually goes back as far as the sixties. Their sources indicate that *bodywashing* occurred during the Vietnam War, when it was felt necessary to remove the remains of American servicemen from politically sensitive countries such as Laos and Cambodia. The same source quoted in the citation here also mentioned that helicopter crashes were sometimes arranged as part of the *bodywashing* process: "We'd arrange a chopper crash, or wait until one happened and insert a body or two into the wreckage later. It's not that difficult."

bomb blanket *noun*, a relatively lightweight covering for an unexploded bomb, made of ballistic nylon or a combination of nylon and Kevlar, with a fire-resistant coating, used by bomb-disposal squads in conjunction with a safety circle (a wraparound device weighing fifteen pounds and measuring seventeen by seventy-two inches) to suppress and contain an explosion. In the case of an explosion of great magnitude, the blanket will rise to a parachute configuration, with drooping sides, thereby containing the blast. Also called *bomb suppression blanket:* "The Burlington Industrial Fabrics Co. has developed a *bomb blanket* . . . that . . . has effectively suppressed the explosive force of a pipe bomb" (Michael Dewar, *Weapons and Equipment of Counter-Terrorism,* 1987).

THE STORY: The deadly subculture of terrorism and counterterrorism has spawned an extensive lexicon, much of which remains unfamiliar to general readers. It is a word stock rich in euphemism overlaid with suggestions of domesticity. Some other terms are *appliqué armor, bomb curtain, security research broom,* and *Lazy Tongs.*

Appliqué armor is defined as "lightweight armor, often of fiberglass or high-impact plastic, fitted onto conventional, soft-skin vehicles as additional protection against blast, low-velocity small-arms fire, and acid bombs, first developed by the British Army in an attempt to protect Land Rover crews." The *bomb curtain,* defined as "a simple white mesh curtain weighted at the bottom to catch flying glass blown inward by the force of a bomb detonated outside a building," is to be found in government and military installations throughout the United Kingdom. The *security research broom,* reminiscent of *sweep* in the sense "to *sweep* a room for hidden microphones," is "a non-linear detector designed to locate concealed, active, passive, or remotely activated surveillance devices and time- or remote-controlled explosive devices." Shaped like a small handheld push broom and wired to a battery and earphones, this device markedly decreases the risk factors and the time required to search buildings, motor vehicles, and people. *Lazy Tongs* is a trade name for a portable roadblock configured in a lattice arrangement supporting 170 detachable, sharp, hollow-finned spikes that will puncture automotive tires. When fully deployed like a giant spiked Slinky across a road, *Lazy Tongs* resembles a long series of reversed Z's. See *hydraulic bollard* for information about the use of a similar vehicular obstacle in civilian communities in the United States.

bubble *noun*, a room with transparent walls, typically located within another room in an embassy, for example, designed to be secure against electronic eavesdropping, and used for carrying on sensitive conversations and transmitting or receiving secret communications: "There were fears that perhaps other listening devices were placed in a supersecure *bubble* . . . where secret conversations can be held" (Reuters, March 4, 1987).

THE STORY: In the sixties, a security *bubble* was available for use by secret agent Maxwell Smart; fans of the show *Get Smart* will recall that Max's *bubble* never seemed to work very well. This sense of the noun *bubble* gained attention in the eighties as a result of the security breaches at the U.S. Embassy in Moscow. The word in the security sense was also used in connection with the 1986 Reykjavík, Iceland, summit: "As soon as the party arrived at the U.S. Embassy, [Secretary of State George] Shultz said: 'Let's go to the *bubble*. . . .' The *bubble* was crammed so full of chairs that there was no room for a table" (*Newsweek*, October 20, 1986).

Bubble also has another specialized sense developed relatively recently, this being the designated protective airspace surrounding an aircraft while in flight: "We will draw a 500-foot *bubble* around an aircraft, and a near-midair collision will be defined as any time that *bubble* is penetrated or when either pilot feels that his aircraft is hazarded" (Donald Engen, an FAA administrator, on *The MacNeil/Lehrer NewsHour*, June 7, 1985).

burn notice *noun*, an official statement circulated by one intelligence-gathering agency to other such agencies, domestic or foreign, stating that a person or group is unreliable for any of various reasons: "A European intelligence agency had brought Ghorbanifar to the attention of the CIA in 1980, the year after the Shah fell, but the information he had supplied had proved to be so untrustworthy that the CIA had put out a *burn notice* on him in 1984" (*New York Review of Books*, October 22, 1987).

THE STORY: Figurative extensions of the verb *burn* abound in the lingo of the underworld and in the jargon of law enforcement, so it is no surprise to find variations on this theme in the lexicon of the secret services. *Burn*, meaning "to swindle; cheat; victimize; rob," was first used with some regularity during the 1800s, but it can be traced as far back as the mid-1600s. It also came to be used in the sense "to kill (someone) with a firearm." From the "swindle" sense evolved *burn artist*, defined as "a swindler" and later as "a drug dealer who swindles buyers." And a law enforcement idiom, *burn a mark*, means "to frighten a shoplifting suspect into dropping a pilfered object."

The definition of *burn notice* given here is based on one found in the *Dictionary of Military Terms* (1987), written by the Joint Chiefs of Staff Terminology Group. The *burn* in *burn notice* derives from the intelligence-related sense of the verb meaning "to expose deliberately the true status of a person operating under cover." The adjective *burned* is used in intelligence circles "to indicate that a clandestine operator has been exposed . . . (especially in a surveillance) or that reliability as a source of information has been compromised," wrote the Joint Chiefs' team of lexicographers. A *burn bag* is a receptacle for the transport and disposal of classified documents targeted for destruction as prescribed in regulations.

Colombian syndrome *noun*, a situation within a country that is marked by fusion of the political leadership with high underworld figures in a mutually advantageous and profitable relationship resulting in joint control of trade, law enforcement, property, the armed forces, and the banking system: "'The so-called *Colombian syndrome* is developing [in Serbia],' said Dejan Popovic, a professor at Belgrade University law school" (*Washington Post*, November 21, 1992).

THE STORY: The countries on the peninsula bounded by the Adriatic, Aegean, and Black Seas have, because of their long-standing internecine hostilities, spawned a number of English terms, the most notorious recent coinage in translation being *ethnic cleansing*—a term that joins others of greater longevity such as *Balkanic* (1915), *Balkanism* (1924), *Balkanoid* (1932), and of course *Balkanize* and *Balkanization* (1920).

Now comes *Colombian syndrome*, transplanted from the *narcokleptocracies* of South and Central America to Belgrade. The term refers specifically to the alleged link between the government of Serbia's president, Slobodan Milosevic, and various criminals, many of whom also played or are playing prominent roles in the ethnic wars in Croatia and Bosnia-Herzegovina. According to organized-crime reporter Vanja Bulic of the Belgrade magazine *Duga*, "'The biggest heroes of the war so far are criminals. . . . There are about 3,000 Belgrade criminals in Bosnia at the front'" (*Washington Post*). These criminals seem to be highly regarded by the government for their loyalty, courage, and imagination, and their activities in maintaining a lucrative black market in spite of UN-imposed sanctions. The black market, and the necessities purchased through it, are essential in preserving the social fabric and the relative tranquillity in Belgrade.

But from the front lines still other terms have emerged: the *Happy Bosnian* (also called a *beer bottle bomb*) and the *basement-to-penthouse missile*. The *Happy Bosnian*, a *Balkanic* surface-to-air Molotov cocktail, is made from a Sarajevsko beer bottle, paint thinner, and a glass-encased acid stick. This bottle, having been wrapped up in panty hose to preclude overly quick dispersion of the flames upon landing on its target, is taped to a handle and then mounted atop an AK-47 assault rifle. It is deployed by use of blank rifle cartridges to a range of 300 yards. According to John Pomfret of the Associated Press in a story dated September 4, 1992, the inventor of the *Happy Bosnian* was a thirty-six-year-old metal worker called "Ranko." The *basement-to-penthouse missile*, a term with a Beirutian ring to it, is another street-fighting weapon whose parts attest to the shortage of just about everything in the war zones. It is made of large, empty plastic thread spools. The spools are stuffed with flammable material and are detonated with Petard firecrackers. (Petards are a product of Austria.)

Yet another geopolitical malaise is *Iraq Syndrome*, an aggressive conviction, representing a change in public opinion toward U.S. policy in the Gulf War, that America is and should be militarily and geopolitically invincible: "In correcting the mistakes of the last war, military thinkers often set in motion the mistakes of the next one. And while the generals may have put the *Vietnam Syndrome* behind them, the *Iraq Syndrome* may be only just beginning" (*Los Angeles Times*, December 9, 1990). This citation, from an Op-Ed piece by George Black, the foreign editor of *The Nation*, is one of a number accrued since 1990. It joins others like *Beirut syndrome* (discussed in brief at *Dirty Harriet Syndrome*) and the familiar *Stockholm syndrome*, a phenomenon in which a hostage begins to identify with and grow sympathetic to his or her captors—so named after the city where a hostage in a 1973 bank robbery became romantically attached to one of her captors. In the case of *Iraq Syndrome*, one of its inherent, often unstated dangers was exposed by Ken

Kashiwahara on *Nightline* on March 8, 1991: "Americans [are] now believing that all future conflicts can be resolved quickly and decisively, with relatively few casualties." See also *Colombian necktie* and *Colombian roulette* at *Iraqi manicure*, and *narcokleptocracy*.

erk *noun*, *British slang*, an enlisted man of the lowest rank in the Royal Air Force, especially a member of a ground crew; an aircraftsman: "Most of the time we helped the *erks* keep the planes in good shape. Bloody basket cases they were, when we first took them up there from Kent" (Anton Emmerton, *Ghost Pilot*, 1987).

THE STORY: This word, which can be traced at least to 1925, is not to be found in most abridged dictionaries of American English, chiefly because its use is so narrowly particularized by subject matter and by geography. Also spelled *irk*, the word first meant "a naval rating," according to the *Oxford English Dictionary*. Early evidence attesting its use in terms of the air force is to be found in a 1928 letter by T. E. Lawrence in which he refers to Cranwell as "a home from home, for the *irks*." The origin of *erk* is obscure, like that of *crash and burn*. A 1940 *Reader's Digest* citation suggests that it is a corruption of A.C., the British abbreviation of *aircraftsman*. But Eric Partridge stated in a reference dated 1944 that "this odd word is, the writer believes, a shortened pronunciation of the italicised letters in *air* mechanic (perhaps in the form of 'air mech'). . . . Some airmen less convincingly maintain that it comes from 'lower-deck hand.'"

Another British slang word for a ground crewman happens to be *kiwi*, an extension in meaning of the term denoting the flightless New Zealand bird. And one American equivalent is *groundhog*. All these words fall into the same register as that of *gob, swab, leatherneck, jarhead, gyrene,* and *grunt*.

frozen rope *noun*, a highly significant intelligence intercept: "The senior technician . . . put on his headphones. The conversation was being taken down on high-speed tape. . . . 'Tell Meade that we finally caught a *frozen rope* down the left-field line.' A '*frozen rope*' was the current NSA [National Security Agency] nickname for a very important signal intercept" (Tom Clancy, *Clear and Present Danger*, 1990).

THE STORY: Baseball fans will immediately recognize *frozen rope*, a straight and sharply hit line drive, which has made the semantic leap from bull pen to the corridors of the Puzzle Palace. Yet another item in the jargon of the world of intelligence-gathering, *ISSA*, is harder to trace, and well it should be. This abbreviation refers, possibly, to a particularly sensitive security clearance. Spy headhunter Don Wallach placed this ad in a newspaper recently, according to a story in the Washington Business extra of the March 1, 1993, *Washington Post*: "If you have an active SBI or *ISSA* or NSA POLY, we want to talk to you immediately." (*SBI* means special background investigation and *NSA POLY* means National Security Agency polygraph.) In response to the reporter's question about the meaning of *ISSA*, Wallach replied, "I can't tell you what an *ISSA* is, but the person who's got one will know." See also *frozen smoke* at *aerogel*.

hippo *noun*, an armor-plated four-wheel-drive, all-terrain but nonamphibious anti–land mine personnel carrier capable of transporting eight to ten people, used by the South African police and army: "Two *hippos* recently sped to an open field in Soweto where a crowd was attempting to execute . . . a black teen-age girl. . . . As the *hippos* arrived, witnesses say, the crowd . . . fled and police opened fire" (*Wall Street Journal*, June 20, 1986).

THE STORY: Printed evidence for *hippo* in this context goes back at least to 1977, with spotty general use in the media until 1986. Many of the citations inaccurately described the *hippo* as an armored car. Its very name suggests amphibious capability, also a misconception. Had I not called the Embassy of South Africa in 1988, the definition of this word in the June 1988 issue of *The Atlantic Monthly* might have been incorrect. In response to questions regarding the origin of the designation *hippo*, a military attaché explained that all military transport vehicles in South Africa are named for animals indigenous to that country. He then offered several other examples: the *eland*, an armored car, and the *kudu*, a spotter plane—both named after antelopes—and the *ratel*, an armored personnel carrier named after a nocturnal carnivorous mammal similar to our badger, an animal he characterized as "very tough."

The unidentified speaker in this extract from the BBC *Summary of World Broadcasts* of October 9, 1985, provides another example of the zoology: "The question is, who is prepared to take things further? Is it the forces of the state, with their *Buffels* and *Hippos* . . . who sjambok [beat] grandmothers and pregnant women?" In South Africa, the word *buffel* means "buffalo," and the vehicle called that is, like the *hippo*, an anti–land mine personnel carrier. See also *birdcage*, *elephant*.

IC *abbreviation*, an innocent civilian: "It was standard Vietnam cover-up. Whenever a few *ICs*—innocent civilians—were killed by mistake—or in less blameless ways—you came up with a hair-raising story of a firefight. No one questioned you" (Nelson DeMille, *Word of Honor*, 1985).

THE STORY: Use of this very bloodless abbreviation in the context of human suffering and death brings to mind a statement attributed to Stalin: "A single death is a tragedy; a million deaths is a statistic."

Nelson DeMille glossed *IC*, whose precise origin is unknown, for the benefit of readers who were never *in-country*, and well he might have: the Vietnam War spawned an entirely new jargon, as is revealed in the number of glossaries at the ends of books on that conflict. Other terms in the jargon include *BC*, "body count"; *mighty mite*, a commercial air blower used for injecting tear gas or poison gas into enemy tunnels; *Kit Carson scout*, a former enemy soldier acting as a forward guide and interpreter for U.S. forces; *crispie critter*, a soldier who has been burned to death—usually used of enemy soldiers; *beehive*, an artillery round filled with hundreds of tiny darts; *Butcher Brigade*, a derogatory term for the Eleventh Infantry Brigade after the Mylai massacre; *MOOSE*, "move out of Saigon expeditiously," an acronym referring to troop displacement; and the idiom held over from the Korean War, *cut a choagie*, to move out quickly from a position.

In the case of this last expression, it most certainly derives from the Korean *katta chogi*, a rude way of saying "Get outta here!" In Korean, *chogi* means somewhere "over there," and *katta* is the rude, peremptory form of "go." According to information from a Word Watcher who had lived in Korea for at least ten years, the phrase is used by Koreans when speaking angrily to a child or during an argument with another adult. American soldiers picked up on the phrase as part of the regular conversation passing between young soldiers stationed there and the young women working in bars. For instance, one soldier or girl might say to another, "Hey, let's *katta chogi*," meaning "Let's split." It's but a short respelling leap from *katta* to *cutta* to *cut*, and from *chogi* to *choagie*. Such are the words of foreign deployment, occupation, and war. For more information about innocent civilians in the wrong place at the wrong time—on the mean streets, specifically—see also *mushroom*.

influence mine *noun*, an explosive mine activated by the effect that a target vessel produces in the vicinity of the mine or by the target vessel's effect on radiation emanating from the mine: "There have been alarming indications both that the Iranians are building new mines and that they may be acquiring new, so-called *influence mines* from Libya" (*Washington Post*, November 28, 1987).

THE STORY: One of the early meanings of *influence* was "an ethereal fluid thought to flow from the stars and to affect in some way the actions of human beings." In the compound *influence mine*, the word *influence*, a synonym of *induction*, has come to mean "the production of an electrical charge, magnetism, or electromotive force in an object by the proximity without contact of a similarly energized body or by the variation of a magnetic flux," a similar, if much more technologically precise, meaning.

Influence mines are designed to detonate without coming into physical contact with a vessel. They can be triggered by changes in water pressure as the target vessel passes nearby, by detection of the magnetic pull of the vessel's hull, or by sound waves produced by engines within a given distance. The word *influence* is integral to numerous related compounds; for instance, *influence field* ("the area affected by a ship's minesweeping equipment"), *influence release sinker* ("a sinker that holds a moored or rising mine at the seabed and releases it when activated by a subtle effect produced by a ship"), and *influence sweep* ("a technical surveillance operation designed to produce an effect similar to that produced by a ship and thus activate mines").

Iraqi manicure *noun*, *slang*, removal of a prisoner's fingernails and often toenails under torture by interrogators of the Mukhabarat, the security police of Iraq headed by Quasay Saddam Hussein, a son of the head of state: "An '*Iraqi manicure*' is customarily administered in the dungeons of mild-mannered Quasay's security forces" (*Vanity Fair*, August 1992).

THE STORY: Fear of the *Iraqi manicure*, or *pedicure*, is just one of the forces driving the smuggling market, especially the one alleged to exist between Iraq and Jordan, according to an article in *Vanity Fair* by Leslie and Andrew Cockburn, which delved into the story behind the powerful, profiteering elite that arose in Iraq after imposition of post–Gulf War economic sanctions. This "sanctions-era free market" operates to the benefit of everyone: the smugglers get rich and stay safe, the merchants who sell to them get rich, the government functionaries who are bribed get rich, and the people get 1,300 calories of food from the government a day, individually. Procured with U.S. currency, the staples in demand in the smuggling trade are rice, sugar, and meat. Telex machines update all mercantile participants as to fluctuating black-market exchange rates.

Iraqi manicure joins other sinister geoeponymous terms in English, some being these: *Chinese water torture*, *Russian roulette*, *Colombian roulette* (the smugglers' practice of ingesting small bags of cocaine before transit from the country of origin to a target country and then excreting them at the destination, a life-threatening tactic, should the bags break within the body cavity), *Colombian necktie* (the slitting of a victim's throat and then the pulling of the person's tongue out through the neck, a grisly procedure often seen after internal battles among drug dealers in U.S. cities and abroad), *Italian football* (a thrown bomb), *French connection*, and *Spanish windlass* (a straitjacket for restraining a prisoner). See also *Iraq Syndrome* at *Colombian syndrome*.

million-dollar wound *noun*, a combat-caused or self-inflicted wound that does not disfigure, permanently disable, or kill a combatant but is serious enough to warrant permanent removal from a theater of operations: "Some found their private routes out of the [Vietnam] war. You could shoot yourself in the foot, the *million-dollar wound* that could put you back in The World with only a bit of a limp; one grunt . . . tried it, aiming for his toe, but he hit his arch instead, and his foot had to be amputated" (*Newsweek*, December 14, 1981).

THE STORY: This term, which goes back at least to World War II and was described as "a passport out of the war, a ticket home," in the July 3, 1980, issue of the *New York Times*, was given renewed currency in the Gulf War. It has been around long enough, however, to pick up an extended, more generalized sense, "any convenient excuse for exiting an unpleasant situation," as evidenced in this September 21, 1981, citation from *Time*: "[Burnout] is like a declaration of bankruptcy—necessary sometimes, but also somewhat irresponsible and undignified. It is a *million-dollar wound*, an excuse, a ticket out. The era of 'grace under pressure' vanished in the early '60s."

Million-dollar wound was joined during the Vietnam War by another numerative compound, *thousand-yard stare*, a battle-hardened look characteristic of U.S. combatants in Southeast Asia. In terms of the Gulf War, it was joined by *golden BB*, the Soviet-inspired doctrine holding that if enough projectiles—bullets, shells, warheads, and missiles—are launched into the sky, incoming enemy aircraft and missiles will fall.

16th republic *noun*, the military-industrial complex of the former Soviet Union, regarded as a political, economic, and potentially threatening entity:

"At a recent press conference in Moscow, a Russian legislator called the Soviet Army 'the *16th republic*'" (*Washington Post*, January 22, 1992).

THE STORY: This allusion to the army as the newest of the fifteen republics once forming the USSR was made because the coiner felt that the army, and indeed the entire defense complex, share certain key characteristics with the geographic republics: it is "hungry and unsettled but well armed and trained." Ever since the emergence of the Soviet Union as a world power, its army has been "perceived in the West as a symbol of Soviet communism—solid, powerful and threatening." The *Washington Post* Op-Ed writer, Alexei Izyumov, an economist and political analyst with the Russian Academy of Sciences and a fellow of the Freedom Forum Media Studies Center at Columbia University, went on to say that "the collapse of communism and the breakdown of the Soviet state have brought the armed forces and the military industry to the brink of disintegration: soldiers sleeping in tents in freezing temperatures, officers having no idea about their future, military engineers desperately trying to get enough food for their families."

This military-industrial complex is still one of the largest in the world, cutbacks notwithstanding: it still employs 11 million people. Counting dependents, the number soars to 40 million, thereby making the *16th republic* the third-largest, ranking only after Russia and Ukraine in size and might. And the *16th republicans*, unlike their fellow citizens, are the most threatened by joblessness, food shortages, housing shortages, and inflation. They cannot moonlight to make ends meet or stage strikes and protests in the same manner as civilians. All this puts Boris Yeltsin's concerns about army loyalty during the crackdown on a mutinous parliament in October 1993 into stark perspective.

Whether or not the term *16th republic* sustains longevity of use in English depends directly on events in the former USSR, specifically, the degree of success sustained by the demilitarization program, which must involve well-planned, immediate conversion of people and plants from the profession of arms to the pursuit of peace. Otherwise, another coup may make *16th republic* a household word in the manner of *10 Downing Street, 1600 Pennsylvania Avenue, Fourth Estate,* and *sixteenth arrondissement.*

smoodge or **sploodge** *noun, slang,* the extrusion of smoke and other particles from an underground target, indicating to an attacking aircraft pilot that the target has sustained a hit and has been destroyed from within; the matter so extruded: "On instructions from intelligence targeteers, the F-117 pilots carried GBU-10s, which could be dropped from a higher altitude than GBU-27s but also lacked some of the penetrating punch. More than a dozen planes dropped two bombs each. When pilots later looked at their gun camera videotapes, they saw tremendous explosions but no 'smoodge'" (Rick Atkinson, *Crusade: The Untold Story of the Persian Gulf War*, 1993).

THE STORY: It isn't often that a lexicographer gets a chance to speak directly with a top gun pilot about the etymology of a word, and so my conversation in the spring of 1994 with Major Gregg Verser, USAF, an F-117 pilot who served in combat during Desert Storm, was a special treat, as was a later interview with Rick Atkinson, at that time the Berlin bureau chief of the *Washington Post*. Major Verser, who at the time of our interview was a professor of French at the United States Air Force Academy, told me that he and his colleagues were more familiar with the variant *sploodge* (pronounced [sploodzh]) than with Atkinson's spelling *smoodge*. Verser also pointed out that *sploodge* can be used as a verb, as in this typical sentence: "Look at that stuff *sploodge* outta there."

Atkinson, who got his spelling from oral evidence given him three years ago at Nellis Air Force Base by three other F-117 pilots, told me in a telephone interview that the visual effects of the extruded material resemble, in the pilots' view, "squeezed-out peanut butter."

Major Verser said that *sploodge* "forms a mind-picture of an ugly sound, representing ugly stuff," and his metaphor was river mud when disturbed by a heavy object impacting it underwater.

Though the etymologies of the two words are uncertain, it is possible that *smoodge* is a blend of elements from *smoke*, *smut*, *sludge*, and *ooze*. Such might also be the case with *sploodge*, though its derivation from the rude sound made by disapproving troops, as in a base movie theater, cannot be ruled out. And if that is the case, then the two words are not spelling variants; rather, they are two separate words denoting the same thing.

walk the cat back also **walk back the cat** *idiom*, to attempt to understand (the true nature of a situation and the reasons it happened) by reconstructing events chronologically from present time to the past: "Since the arrest of Aldrich H. Ames, the Central Intelligence Agency official accused of being a Soviet *mole* (a spy within the C.I.A.), agency officials have been reported to be *walking the cat back*" (*New York Times Magazine*, April 10, 1994).

THE STORY: For some time before the arrest of Ames, counterintelligence officers here were engaged in a *cat-and-mouse game*, attempting to root out a mole. They did so because they smelled a *dead cat on the line*, not a decomposing feline still holding a receiver to its ear.

The word *cat*, as you may have gathered, is the centerpiece of many a good idiom, the second expression in the foregoing paragraph being a fixture in southern dialect, referring to a dead catfish on a trotline, signaling, in this particular instance, something rotten in Langley. (The intelligence-community idiom, traceable to U.S. foreign service usage going back to at least 1977 and meaning "to back down from a negotiating position," is attested to 1986.)

Having *belled the cat*, those accomplishing this feat proceeded to *let the cat out of the bag* to the national and international media. But Ames wouldn't talk at first: *the cat had got his tongue.* His wife, an alleged *copy-cat* spy, could have been described as *the cat that had swallowed the canary.* On a day when it *rained cats and dogs*, these two were arraigned in Alexandria, Virginia, proving that *there's more than one way to skin a cat.* Meanwhile, an internal investigation at Langley is still trying to put the toothpaste back in the tube. All it's turned up so far is proof that *when the cat's away, the mice will play.*

No doubt the KGB-controllers of this *cat's-paw* had been following the order of battle set down by the proverbial Russian peasant, the same one who, in this book, has given advice at *I think* and *wolf ticket:*

RULE 1: *The cat knows precisely whose meat it eats.* (Especially when a Swiss bank account is opened up in its name.)

RULE 2: *Only the cat covers up its own mess.* (True, but you've got to erase those incriminating disks.)

RULE 3: *The cat's cheers are the mouse's tears.* (For a while, that is, until someone smells a rat. Then every dog has its day. In court.)

RULE 4: *The cat that bags the mouse will itself be bagged.* (That's the zero-sum game of counterintelligence.)

We can be sure that while the CIA *walks this cat back*, intelligence officers will be *fighting like a sack of cats* to contain the damage and protect their assets. Who knows who else has been compromised? For *in the darkness* of the world of espionage, *all the cats are gray* (Rule 5).

withinwalls *adjective*, privy to or involved in covert operations, especially eavesdropping: "The current piece of chat among Washington's *withinwalls* personnel was the discovery by a congressional investigation committee of fifteen illegal taps on its telephone lines" (William H. Hallahan, *Foxcatcher*, 1987).

THE STORY: This bit of governmental jargon rarely appears in print. *Stonewalling* and *wall creeper* aside, *withinwalls* reflects the same sort of usage seen in other terms such as *backstairs* political gossip, *behind-the-scenes* maneuvering, decision-making in the *corridors of power*, *under-the-table* deals, *closed-door* hearings, an *open-door* executive policy, a diplomat with *drawing-room* manners, *cloakroom* negotiations, advice from a *kitchen cabinet*, and *back-channel* communications with the embassy of a potentially hostile nation. It is possible that *withinwalls* derives from the in-wall placement of electronic surveillance devices or that it comes from the idea that sensitive information must be contained within the walls of highly secure, surveillanceproof sites.

7

The Politics of Meaning...
in So Many Words

chicken run
civil religion
grassy knollism
heresthetic
inoculation
I think
jingo-jangle
Kojak Liberal
moral panic
push-polling
red-diaper baby
smoking bed

Sovok
Stephanopouli
stylogram
there
toyi-toyi
tsotsie
Velcroid
Waldheimer's disease
Wall in the Head
White Iraqi
Xerocracy

Politics are too serious a matter to be left to the politicians.
—Charles de Gaulle

He was right, the president of France. The nature of the terms in this chapter are the proof.

By words men are ruled, said Disraeli, who knew something about it. The lexicographer might add that the changing language of politics is a history of the utterances, reactions, and deeds of the governors and the governed in the course of pursuing international and national goals. This small slice of the English lexicon is a mirror image of the conflicts and tensions attending a dynamic national and international life just since 1986.

Domestically, we moved from the *jingo-jangle* of the Reagan years into the political gridlock of the Bush presidency, and in the process we held three presidential elections in which the spin doctors and other handlers engaged, when necessary, in *inoculation*—a word that takes its immediate cues from commerce but has deep roots in medicine and psychology. Surely the eighties and nineties can be dubbed "Years of the Spinners," in that they successfully blurred the boundaries between the spheres of politics and communication to such a degree that it was difficult for me to decide where the language of politics ended and the language of advertising and public relations began. (Thus, it is no accident that the language of the media follows in chapter 8.) When the spin doctors were not at work using words to rule, the candidates and incumbents were proving themselves expert in the arcane field of *heresthetics*, or the politics of manipulation, on a grandly subtle scale. And a frustrated public sometimes turned its attention to the *stylogram* as a way of "getting inside the heads" of candidates and incumbents alike.

The *Velcroids*, or photo-opportunists, crowded into pictures with world leaders, only to be upstaged by the *Stephanopouli* who exclaimed, in response to hard questions about the Clintons' involvement in the Whitewater scandal, "There's no *there* there!"—a usage that in effect created a new meaning of the word, Gertrude Stein's prior use notwithstanding, and in truth, characterized the very profession of spinning.

If the Reagan presidency was "Teflon," and the Bush administration was "kinder and gentler," then the Clinton administration, with its prodigious use of the phrase *I think*, must be characterized as the "thinking presidency." At the entry for *I think*, you will read transcripts from the Office of the Press Secretary that attest to the existence of this verbal tic.

"Politics makes strange bedfellows," wrote Charles Dudley Warner 125 years ago. No doubt he would not have been surprised at the noxious fumes emanating from the *smoking beds* of some politicians in our day. In terms of the up close and personal, at least one U.S. senator–attorney, he very well versed in the art of oral argumentation, has learned with his own *smoking bed* that Groucho Marx was right in saying that "politics is the art of looking for trouble."

Certainly on the global front, some leaders—the "Wrecking Ball Babies of the Nineties," such as the ones in Haiti and Serbia—have been exceptionally busy proving that the very idea of a New World Order was a fanciful misconception of the real thing—the New World Disorder. Is it any wonder, then, that some members of the domestic populace have been affected with *moral panic?* Confused violence often attends rapid change, especially when that change occurs in a political vacuum, transmitted worldwide by television satellite. What is more, fear of the unknown, and superstitions attached thereto, have always accompanied the turns and twists of new ages and new centuries. This was the case almost 500 years ago in the time of Dürer, and it is the case today in the time of the Information Superhighway. In Dürer's 1498 *Apocalypse* woodcuts, the significant forces and fears of the times are starkly apparent, and eerily apropos to the nineties: the genesis of a new order (the Reformation), conflicts between societies (the worlds of North and South), a recurring epidemic (black plague), and an increased feeling of impending doom as the year 1500 drew nigh.

In 1995 the Four Horsemen depicted by Dürer in the fourth woodcut of the *Apocalypse* series—War, Famine, Pestilence, and Death—are silhouetted on the landscape of the globe, grinning, while the screaming heads scream, the diplomats deplore, the *Stephanopouli* explain, the administration thinks, and some citizens become morally panicked.

The evolvement of *chicken run* in terms of white flight in South Africa is an example of the continuance of the social unrest that went on in that nation. *Toyi-toyi* points up the tensions inherent in South Africa's momentous transition from white-dominated racism to its own form of democracy. The legacy of the "Evil Empire" whose Wall came tumbling down in 1989 is evidenced by *Wall in the Head*, a term denoting the psychosocial barrier that still serves to disunite an officially reunited Germany. And *Waldheimer's disease*, whose very etiology lies in the modern Dark Ages of Nazi-dominated Europe, not only represents a cause of the erection of the Berlin Wall in the first place, but also resonates with the Zeitgeist of Dürer's times when "Death's bony nag [trod] upon a bishop falling into the gaping jaws of the Dragon of Hell" (Francis Russell, *The World of Dürer*). The eponymous blend *Waldheimer's disease* will not allow you to touch that dial, or click that channel selector from the C-SPAN of your mind. This term forces us to recognize and confront the facts of genocide and the subsequent amnesia of its perpetrators, its abettors, its sympathizers. In the process, we confront and uncover the agenda of Holocaust deniers, apologizers, and revisers. This is a useful exercise as the world surveys the results of "ethnic cleansing" in the Balkans.

Akin to *moral panic* is *grassy knollism*, the latter a form of career conspiracy theorism to a degree that might have caused it to gain hospitable reception in the dark mental reaches of those living in Dürer's time. But offsetting *grassy knollism* and the rest of the political detritus of our day is *civil religion*, not a national religion, and not Christianity, but instead an awareness held by the Founders that the United States is grounded in the belief in a higher judgment, one to which the country and its leaders remain accountable. *Civil religion* denotes and connotes the very principles that, in the past at least, have set this country apart from other nations, particularly those that are still stalked by the shadow of the *Sovok*, those that labor to communicate by *Xerocracy*, and those that still produce generals of genocide, who, it may be predicted, will, in the future, conveniently succumb to *Waldheimer's disease*.

The meaning of this short list of political lexical significa is clear. What is unclear is when and if the language will be changed by the reappearance of statesmen and stateswomen, as opposed to politicians enamored of *push-*

polling. That question speaks to the meaning of politics, if not to the politics of meaning . . . in a very few words.

chicken run also **chicken-run** *noun,* emigration of large numbers of people from a country or an area in it that is undergoing violent political, especially racial, upheaval: "In spite of the attempts of the South African government to minimize what has become known as the *chicken run,* the exodus of English-speaking South Africans is clearly accelerating" (*Maclean's,* February 3, 1986). "'To whites, we say we want you to stay, we need your skills,' African National Congress leader Nelson Mandela said last week, when reports of a new *chicken run* surfaced in the local media. . . . A real estate broker . . . says the current *chicken run* is mild compared [with] those of 1961 and 1976" (*Washington Post,* April 30, 1993).

THE STORY: Here's a term whose frequency of occurrence in print is dictated by fluctuating events in the sub-Saharan area of Africa. It is a lexical indicator of the varying degrees of fear among whites in South Africa. In one of the small ironies of history, *chicken run* once referred not to the flight of whites out of South Africa but to the flight of white refugees *into* South Africa from Zimbabwe (then called Rhodesia): "This situation . . . has resulted in an equally earnest *chicken-run* of the garrison town's racist settler population fleeing to the remaining of the Salisbury regime's strongholds— Salisbury and Bulawayo—but mostly for temporary refuge before proceeding south to fascist-ruled South Africa" (transcript from the *BBC World Broadcasts,* October 27, 1979); "A growing number of white farmers are said to be abandoning their homesteads and taking the *chicken run* to South Africa" (*Washington Post,* April 28, 1978). It had always been assumed that when blacks eventually got power, the whites would have to get out, or try to. With apartheid a thing of the past, it was predicated in early 1994 that a mass emigration of whites would occur, despite the strict financial disincentives then in place. To date such a mass exodus has not occurred, however.

Chicken run, used derisively in South Africa, is a compound most probably formed of the adjective *chicken,* meaning "cowardly," and the noun *run,* meaning "a route or course traveled." Furthermore, it is probably a pun based on the farmers' meaning of *chicken run,* "a fenced-in area where poultry may roam, eat, and exercise." In its South African context, *chicken run* is unrelated to the well-known game of *chicken,* in which drivers go head-on at each other, with the first one to swerve away being the *chicken.*

civil religion *noun*, **1.** a general understanding of a universal, transcendent religious reality apparent in the American experience, characterized by an awareness that the nation was founded on the belief in a higher judgment, to which it is still accountable; the set of beliefs, symbols, and rituals constituting and reflecting a public religious dimension to American life: "While some have argued that Christianity is the national faith, and others that church and synagogue celebrate only the generalized religion of 'the American Way of Life,' few have realized that there actually exists alongside of and rather clearly differentiated from the churches an elaborate and well-institutionalized *civil religion* in America" (Robert N. Bellah, *Daedalus*, Winter 1967). "America may have a (sometimes creative) *civil religion*, but it has also gotten by as a civil society. Alongside its public religion, its schools have been productive on the basis of a public philosophy" (Martin E. Marty, *New York Times*, July 22, 1981). **2.** *slang*, an activity, an interest, or a set of principles to which scrupulous devotion is accorded by a large group, such as the people of a country: "The game of baseball is our national pastime, the making of money our *civil religion*, and the watching of television our communal opiate" (Laurence Shames, *New York Times*, July 23, 1989).

THE STORY: Many of the symbols and rituals of *civil religion* as defined in the first sense are fixtures in our national life. These include the content of the presidential oath of office, especially its ending; the wording of our national motto; the content of the Pledge of Allegiance; the existence of national cemeteries such as the ones at Arlington and Gettysburg; the Tomb of the Unknown Soldier; and important days on our "ritual calendar" such as Memorial Day, Thanksgiving Day, and Veterans Day. It is therefore surprising that *civil religion* remains unentered in most dictionaries, given also its wide use in academic discourse, the controversy surrounding it, its recent extension in meaning as exhibited in the second sense, and the continued use of words reflecting its existence, especially in inaugural addresses.

Evidence of a *civil religion*, unique to America and certainly influenced by the ethos of eighteenth-century Europe, is particularly strong in the inaugural addresses of all U.S. presidents (except Washington's second and the remarks made by Lyndon B. Johnson upon taking the oath of office aboard Air Force One after the John F. Kennedy assassination). These selections make the point: "the Invisible Hand which conducts the affairs of man" (Washington's first); "that Being in whose hands we are, who led our fathers, as Israel of old" (Jefferson's second); "the belief that the rights of man come not from the generosity of the state but from the hand of God" (Kennedy);

"But there is a higher power, by whatever name we honor him, who ordains not only righteousness but love, not only justice but mercy" (Ford); "We are a nation under God, and I believe God intended for us to be free" (Reagan's first); and finally, "We have heard the trumpets. We have changed the guard. And now, each in our way, and with God's help, we must answer the call" (Clinton).

Contrary to assumptions, Robert Bellah, quoted first here, is not the coiner of *civil religion*. In his *Daedalus* article, he stated that "the phrase *civil religion* is, of course, Rousseau's." It is taken from chapter 8, book 4, of *Du Contrat social* (*The Social Contract*), April 1762.

grassy knollism *noun*, persistent conspiracy theorism, substantiated by few, if any, hard facts: "Harry Hopkins would have been at home in the land of *grassy knollism*" (*Boston Globe*, August 17, 1990).

THE STORY: Ever since the November 22, 1963, assassination of President John F. Kennedy, persistent rumors of another shooter—this one on the *grassy knoll* before which the presidential motorcade passed in Dallas that day—have surfaced. *Grassy knollism* was an extension waiting to be coined, for its antecedent, that *grassy knoll* in the Texas city, has been referred to thousands of times in subsequent years by the media and investigative writers. An early reference to the knoll appeared in the testimony of one William Newman, a Korean War veteran who "stood in front of the *grassy knoll* and saw the President shot" (*Washington Post Book World*, October 31, 1993), and who told the Warren Commission that he had felt a shot passing over his head and had pushed his wife to the ground to protect her. (Newman and his family can be seen in pictures of the incident, lying on the ground.) In "The Ghosts of November," an investigative report in the November 1994 issue of *Vanity Fair*, Anthony and Robbyn Summers stated that "two policemen encountered men behaving suspiciously on the infamous '*grassy knoll*.'" Moving from Dallas to Los Angeles, the September 16, 1994, issue of the *Washington Post* quoted John Gregory Dunne with reference to the national spectacle of the O. J. Simpson murder trial, to the effect that the bloody murders of the athlete's wife and her friend and the half-truths, allegations, leaks, and smears associated with the case were "a nirvana for conspiracy theorists, halcyon days, not since JFK and the *grassy knoll*," in which usage it was presumed that all readers would know exactly what he meant.

Other relatively recent references to the knoll are to be found in headlines and book titles. Consider this headline from the November 22, 1992,

Washington Post: "THE CROWD ON THE GRASSY KNOLL: The JFK Assassination: Rising Stakes in the Contest of Confessions and Conspiracy." And consider the title of a book by John R. Craig and Phil A. Rogers, *The Man on the Grassy Knoll,* where the denotation and connotations are so explicit as to need no further explanation. And, as might be expected, the term has, of late, come to be used in jokes and spoofs. An example is an excerpt from an April 1, 1992, Capitol Hill publication—a fake promo of a fake movie titled *"Russ:* The story that won't go away"—where the topic is the congressional check-kiting scandal in particular: "Starring Bruce Willis as Jack Russ . . . A bank out of control, a Congress in anguish, a Speaker under fire, a diversion of funds to the Contras, a downed Korean airliner, and a moonless night on a Capitol Hill *grassy knoll.* Only he knows what really happened. Based on the chilling report by the General Accounting Office. Directed by Oliver Stone."

In the thirty years since the event, no fewer than 2,000 books about the Kennedy assassination have appeared, many of them promoting the theory of a conspiracy involving organized crime, the intelligence community, the military-industrial complex, even the executive branch, if all allegations are to be listed. *Grassy knollism,* a derivative of all these prior usages and the thoughts behind them, is therefore an item of historical, reportorial, political, and social literacy: the term in and of itself is meaningless without an understanding of its connotations as reflectors of certain aspects inherent in the American psyche, the aspects that demand a Meaningful Answer to the senseless.

Grassy knollism connotes the often conflicting emotions associated with an inexplicable tragedy of global implications, one perpetrated, if we are to believe the Warren Commission, by a nonentity or perhaps a group of nonentities. And by its own linguistic constructs, *grassy knollism* and its antecedent are vague, generic, vacant-lottish, and low-rent. *Grassy knollism* thereby becomes the perfect metaphor for the unanswered: contrast its grayness with the specificity and color of, say, *Ipatiev House, Ford's Theater,* and other topographic names and addresses associated with governments, their actions, and their defeats—*Beirut, Berlin Wall, Waterloo, Watergate, 10 Downing Street, 1600 Pennsylvania Avenue, Foggy Bottom, Bay of Pigs, Whitehall,* and *Golan Heights.* In looking at that short list alone, one might have predicted the emergence of something like *Dallasism,* but that didn't happen. And, of course, the name *Texas School Book Depository Building,* which denoted the site where Lee Harvey Oswald was alleged to have fired the killing shots, was never a contender: In *The Torch Is Passed* . . . , an account of the assassination compiled from Associated Press stories and photographs, published by the *Washington Star*, the team of writers characterized the term as "a rather wooden name that would dismay writers for years." *Grassy knoll*, though dowdy and generic, was less unremarkable and less unwieldy and, at the same time, more heavily loaded with connotations of mystery than the Depository. *Grassy knoll* has also come to be used as an open attributive compound, attested by this citation from the October 2, 1994, issue of the *Richmond Times-Dispatch*. In it Dr. William Maples, a forensic anthropologist at the University of Florida who was one of a group that had examined corpses in Russia purported to be the bodies of the slain Romanovs, said this: "The *grassy knoll* type of people are always going to point out the lack of absolute certainty" [of the accuracy of DNA studies performed on tissues from the corpses, judged to have been 98.5 percent accurate]. Surely no other term in the American lexicon is so weighted with mystery and so flexible in its contextual usages.

But to return to the headword: *Grassy knollism* appeared in print again in 1992, this time in a column by Robert A. Jones in the January 12 *Los Angeles Times*, in which he discussed the controversial Oliver Stone film *JFK*: "*Grassy knollism* is as old as the assassination itself. On its own, *grassy knollism* generates as much editorial heat as a plugged drain . . . [but] Stone took *grassy knollism* and made it into a $40-million movie. And that changed the rules of the assassination trade. . . . The former owners of the Kennedy debate, our friends along the Eastern seaboard, found themselves displaced. Outgunned." He added: "Hollywood, operating with its usual disregard for historical honesty, had snatched away a piece of intellectual turf from the ink-stained wretches back east. Said wretches, accustomed to fine-sifting the nuances of the Kennedy legacy, knew they had lost control." Indeed, a word to watch. In June 1992, it was at the top of my "Watch List." It remains there.

heresthetic *noun*, strategic political maneuvering, management, and manipulation, the ultimate goal of which is to structure a situation so that one wins, regardless of whether the other participants are persuaded to accept one's views. Common tactics include agenda control, strategic voting, and reformulation of issues: "*Heresthetic* is a word I have coined to refer to a political strategy. . . . It is true that people win politically because they have induced other people to join them in alliances and coalitions. . . . Typically they win because they have set up the situation in such a way that other people will want to join them—or will feel forced by circumstances to join them. . . . And this is what *heresthetic* is all about: structuring the world so you can win" (William H. Riker, *The Art of Political Manipulation*, 1986).

THE STORY: Riker, a professor of political science at the University of Rochester, and a game theorist, told me that he derived *heresthetics* (whence *heresthetic*) from the Greek word transliterated into English as *haireisthetoi*, a word that has to do with the act of choosing or selecting. In a chapter entitled "Political Theory and the Art of *Heresthetics*," which appeared in *Political Science: The State of the Discipline* (1983), Riker explained that the Greek root seemed particularly appropriate, for *heresthetics* is a branch of knowledge "that should have been, but was not, invented by Athenian philosophers and sophists."

An early example of *heresthetic* in action was Abraham Lincoln's methodology of outmaneuvering Stephen A. Douglas in their debates. (Lincoln split the Democratic party by asking Douglas a question about slavery, forcing him to take a stand that, no matter what his answer, would alienate half his support.)

I was alerted to the existence of *heresthetic* by an August 25, 1986, citation in the *Wall Street Journal*, in which the writer noted that "*heresthetic* is largely an American art. . . . And it is still an open question whether the American experiment in representative government, led hither and yon by skilled manipulators, can resist the challenge of a determined totalitarianism." Derivative forms of the word include *heresthetician*, *heresthetical*, and *heresthetically*. Perhaps someday there will appear *heresthete*, a megamanipulator of history's agenda. One can only hope not. See also *inoculation*.

inoculation *noun*, a preemptive political-advertising tactic in which a candidate attempts to foresee and neutralize in advance potentially damaging criticism from an opponent by being the first to confront troublesome issues, specifically in electronic media advertisements: "The surge in negative advertising has even given rise to the countertactic known as *inoculation*: ads designed to answer potential negative ads even before the attacks air" (*The New Republic*, November 3, 1986). "Campaign strategists are far from unanimous on the power of *inoculation* to save potentially vulnerable incumbents" (*Congressional Quarterly*, December 7, 1985).

THE STORY: This highly specialized sense of *inoculation* was spun off from the established meanings "introduction of a disease virus or other antigenic material into an organism in order to immunize, cure, or experiment," and "the act or an instance of familiarizing another with something new, as an idea."

In the year 1961, William J. McGuire, a social psychologist, first took *inoculation* from the annals of medicine and applied it to the study of persuasion and attitude changes ("The Relative Efficacy of Various Types of Prior Belief-defense in Producing Immunity against Persuasion," *Journal of Abnormal and Social Psychology*, 1961). He and his colleagues demonstrated, in a famous experiment, that a subject exposed to weak argumentation running counter to his or her attitude together with strong refutation of that argumentation will be much less susceptible to future attacks against his or her attitude. Such *inoculation* works because it gives the subject a chance to rehearse cognitively the arguments supporting the attitude already held. Therefore, in order to set up a really strong defense against future attacks, a political candidate should offer a weakened version of the criticism that is to be expected, along with a very intense refutation of that criticism.

An example of *inoculation* in a large dosage concocted by spin doctors might be kickoff TV ads in which a candidate expecting criticism for insensitivity to the plight of American farmers after the Great Flood of 1993 is pictured on a tractor (or in a boat) with a farmer, listening to the farmer's views and offering assistance. Candidates vulnerable to ageist attacks might open their media campaigns with ads picturing them jogging, walking briskly, or playing tennis. Those having careerist, rather than family-oriented, public images might be pictured with their own and others' children. And a candidate who worries about a *smoking bed* might set up a TV interview in which he and his wife open the issue themselves and then strongly refute alleged sexual dalliances or in some other way turn the issue aside. See also *heresthetic, smoking bed.*

I think, used as a filler by a speaker in an attempt to buy time or collect thoughts prior to or during delivery of the substance of an answer; used as a qualifier in a remark or an answer: "*I think* that there will be a lot of work done in Congress on this. *I think* the President talked with members of the leadership today about it some. There were meetings, as you know, at a staff level that started yesterday. These will be ongoing. *I think* that we're going to work very aggressively with members of Congress. We're going to do a number of events over the course of the next couple of months to support

NAFTA. *I* don't *think* there should be any question about the level of the President's support for this" (Dee Dee Myers, press secretary to the president, White House press briefing, transcript, September 8, 1993, 2:20 P.M. EDT). "*I think* it depends upon, obviously, what happens in the next couple of days. *I think* if we carry the Senate—the House, *I think* we'll carry in the Senate. *I* don't *think* the Senate will let this plan go down. *I* don't *think* they will do that to the country" (William J. Clinton, press availability, Capitol Hill Press Pool, transcript, August 4, 1993, 10:07 A.M. EDT).

THE STORY: "Think before thou speakest," wrote Cervantes in *Don Quixote*. "I think, therefore I am," penned Descartes in the *Discours de la méthode*. "*DOOmal, DOOmal, DOOmal, inDYŪK—i poDOKH* (The turkey thought, thought, thought—and died from the effort)," says the old Russian peasants' proverb.

Certainly the predecessors of today's young meritocrats gave considerable thought to the meaning of thinking, if not to the politics of meaning. And certainly one who expects to survive encounters with the Washington media has to think on one's feet, as Cervantes advised. The Clinton White House, populated as it is with Rhodes Scholars, Aspen Strategy Groupers, and Renaissance Weekenders, has defined itself by thinking. But the Russian proverb about the turkey cuts right to the heart of the matter, indicating that the exertion, if not the politics, of thinking can be seriously stressful. Conversely, the effects of nervousness, pressure, and chronic fatigue can manifest themselves in the speech patterns and mannerisms of those affected. And mannerisms by definition are habit-forming. Such is the case with *I think*, which has taken on a new meaning, or should I say, nonmeaning, in the Clinton administration. What we're looking at in the first two citations and the ones to follow is an unexceptionable expression turned into a *verbal tic*, in the parlance of linguists and lexicographers.

In the Clinton White House, characterized by a *Washington Post* reporter as a spaghetti of reporting structures and entangled, byzantine loops of power and influence where meetings are indeed "ongoing" and often endless, and where, in the words of many commentators, "kids" and "children" wield the power, *I think* has clearly become symbolic. The usage probably passed by osmosis from the top down, usually the case in organizational settings. It now stands out as the single most obtrusive linguistic characteristic of the administration. It occurs hundreds if not thousands of times in present-tense, past-tense, positive, and negative constructions, most particularly in the president's extemporaneous remarks, and especially in those given at the outset of a question-and-answer session and in reply to "hard" questions from reporters. The expression is also to be heard over and again in the remarks of Dee Dee Myers, the former White House press secretary. All of this comes from a close reading of randomly selected White House Communications Office transcripts, in which I found, to my surprise, the term *Capitol Hill* spelled *Capital Hill*, for wont, it seems, of spell-checking software on this, the first rest stop of the Information Superhighway.

Here are some more citations quoting Myers and Clinton that prove the point. The citations begin with White House transcripts of Myers, who used the expression *I think* a full 79 times in 102 replies to reporters' questions during the September 8 briefing, or about 1.3 times per answer:

> *I think* some of it was—there were some oversights, which have largely been taken care of. But *I think* the most important issue is that Congress gives the White House broad authority in dealing with personnel issues. There was nothing in there that was illegal. Nobody is accusing us of doing anything illegal. *I think* the discrepancies that were outlined were minimal and have been largely corrected.
>
> But, for example, *I think* the Justice Department said with reference to the Vince Foster letter. . . .
>
> *I think*, obviously, it's tragic—violence against foreigners as well as violence against Americans.
>
> Well, *I think* that's what—the comprehensive crime bill, and *I think* certainly the Brady bill, which would help take guns out of the hands of criminals by creating a waiting period. *I think* that's critically important. . . . The President's going to continue to fight for it, and *I think* we'll get it done.
>
> *I think* it's not just the health care overhaul, although that's certainly important. *I think* it's government in general. *I think* over the period of the past couple of decades, in particular, there has been an erosion in people's confidence in government.

In every instance, *I think* is unnecessary to the discourse. At best, it smacks of a fight to get one's foot in the door during a brainstorming session at a corporate retreat or in a law school study group. At worst, it signals a scary mix of arrogance and unease in the pressroom.

But let's not stop with the press secretary. Let's take it from the top—from the mouth of a Yale-educated attorney-president, whose use of the language, from *bull* to *wazoo*, has been dissected in the press from every angle except this one. It says something about the man, when you realize that he uses *I think* in quantity chiefly in his extemporaneous remarks not to the voting public, as during televised "town meetings," but to the press, most especially after those initial, "hard," questions. Could this be a signal that the perpetual campaigner is more at home on the perpetual sales call than in confrontation with, say, a Brit Hume, at a press call?

In the press availability of August 4, within a thirteen-minute period—from 10:07 A.M. to 10:20 A.M. EDT—Clinton uttered *I think* an amazing fifteen times, once in his opening remarks, and fourteen times thereafter in answers to seven questions (an average of two *I thinks* per answer). And on September 7, 1993, in remarks made after Vice-President Gore had presented the National Performance Review, Clinton used eight *I thinks* in two answers to the two questions that he took, with all of the *I thinks* occurring in his seventeen-sentence answer to the first question, a provocative, or "hard," one inquiring why the newly devised plan for reinventing government stood a chance of success when all past attempts by others had failed. Under the circumstances, the question could not have been unexpected.

In the Q&A following formal remarks by the president in an East Garden meeting with the New York and New Jersey media on July 22, 1993, which lasted sixty-four minutes and involved seventeen questions and answers, Clinton said *I think* 34 times—two per answer, or, put another way, 1.8 times a minute. Example:

> *I think* they will take the surcharge off capital gains, which I hope will be done. *I think* they will do more on the research and development tax credit and more to revitalize the real estate markets than the Senate bill does. *I think* all these changes will come in, and *I think* that will give more of a pro-growth, pro-investment, pro-business and pro-jobs shape to the final bill.

On October 4, 1993, the president responded thus at the San Francisco Hilton to a reporter's question, Does this (Yeltsin's use of force in Moscow) taint the move toward democracy in Russia?

No. I *think*, first of all, as I said today in my remarks, clearly, he bent over backwards to avoid doing this. And I *think* he may even wonder whether he let it go too far. But I *think* as long as his commitment is clear, to get a new constitution, to have new legislative elections and have a new election for the presidency so he puts himself on the election block again, I don't *think* it does taint it.

Even if one does not have access to White House transcripts, one can hear these usages in televised speeches and read them in the national print media. As an instance, on August 9, 1993, *U.S. News & World Report* published seven questions and seven answers by Clinton relating to issues such as Bosnia, taxes, NAFTA, and the apparent suicide of Vince Foster. Here, the president used nine I *thinks*, clustering most of them (four) in his answer regarding the Foster death.

Critic Michiko Kakutani wrote in January of 1994 that the expression I *feel* was beginning to supplant I *think* in Washington talk-show discourse. Such may be the case with the talking and screaming heads, but we can take comfort in the fact that our president is continuing to *think*. Said he, in the famous March 24, 1994, prime-time news conference devoted almost in its entirety to the Whitewater matter, "But I *think* he [White House associate counsel William Kennedy, reassigned after disclosure of his nonpayment of Social Security taxes for his nanny] should not have done what he did, and I *think* he should fully pay."

If it's the thought that counts, isn't it great that at last we have a president who can think?

jingo-jangle *noun*, *slang*, jingoistic rhetoric and theatrics: "America was ready for such a fantasy [the film *Rocky IV*]. . . . It is what one scholar calls the conquistador spirit that people come to see, a kind of Grenada in a prize ring at similarly low cost with similarly satisfying results. The *jingo-jangle* Stallone admits is at the heart of the work is, in his eyes, not a bad thing—not after the shoving around America took in the world of the '70s" (*Newsweek*, November 23, 1985).

THE STORY: This word is a compound formed with the noun *jingo*, "a blatant, often belligerent patriot," and *jangle*, a noun meaning "a loud, harsh sound." *Jingo* comes from the phrase *by jingo!*, used in the refrain of a bellicose nineteenth-century English music-hall song, and is itself an alteration of *Jesus*:

We don't want to fight, yet by Jingo! if we do,
We've got the ships, we've got the men, and got the money too.
— G. W. Hunt, *Song*, 1878

Jangle comes from the Middle English verb *janglen*, "to chatter," itself from the Old French *jangler*, probably of Germanic origin. *Jingo-jangle* is, for sure, a word with a certain ring to it, even if it isn't music to Ivan Drago's ears.

Kojak Liberal *noun*, a new, tough-minded liberal who believes that violent crime has become a basic issue of civil rights for law-abiding citizens in the inner cities, because such crime prevents them from bettering their lives, and who therefore thinks that enhanced law enforcement is a key means of alleviating the problem: "What the cities need are '*Kojak Liberals*.' . . . *Kojak Liberals* . . . argue that for now, the biggest problems confronted by the inner city poor are created by rising violence and lawlessness" (E. J. Dionne Jr., *Washington Post*, June 15, 1993).

THE STORY: *Kojak Liberals* follow the logic that poverty causes crime, but they also believe the obverse: Crime causes poverty and perpetuates it. Crime stunts economic development in inner cities, they say, and militates against the creation of new jobs. *Kojak Liberals*, therefore, set law enforcement as a top priority in working to cure these ills. Dionne named Lee Brown, the Clinton administration's drug czar, and Willie Williams, the Los Angeles chief of police, as practitioners of *Kojak Liberalism*. The term derives, of course, by association with the police officer Kojak, the protagonist of the television series of the same name, a character played by actor Telly Savalas. This character practiced tough urban love: he was a tough cop with a warm heart.

Kojak Liberal and the attendant *ism* are examples of a growing pop cultural trend that associates real-life situations and people with screen titles and characters, and, in effect, assigns to those cinematic titles and characters new meanings. Recent examples are *Murphy Brown*, the single mother who needs no further introduction; *Home Alone*, used as an adjective in 1992 and 1993 news stories to modify *kids*, *children*, and *parents* in reference to youngsters left at home by parents who vacationed in Acapulco over a Christmas holiday; and *Fatal Attraction*, used, for example, by the *Washington Post* of December 1, 1991, thus: "a *Fatal Attraction* psychotic who screamed rape."

moral panic *noun*, mass anxiety about crime and juvenile violence in the United States, fueled by instant and repetitive media coverage of high-profile, often sensational criminal incidents: "The surge of hysteria over crime and juvenile violence . . . resonates a kind of *'moral panic'* that is not unlike earlier panics in our history over such things as witchcraft, communists, chlorine and crack cocaine" (Ted Chiricos, *Tallahassee* [Fla.] *Democrat*, March 25, 1994).

THE STORY: Chiricos, a professor of criminology at Florida State University, used facts and figures to assert that *moral panic* "distorts as much as it exaggerates. It treats a profound and enduring problem as if it were a sudden firestorm. It promotes responses that will have political more than substantive relevance." Factors contributory to *moral panic*, Chiricos said, are a media feeding frenzy, focusing the nation's listeners, viewers, and readers on high-profile crimes and high-profile crime locales; and the occurrence of highly publicized and quite brutal incidents, such as the Reginald Denny beating in Los Angeles, the south Florida tourist murders, and the Long Island Rail Road commuter slayings, that, in and of themselves, seem to "define, for many, the essence of the crime problem."

Defining the essence of a situation or even an idea and reinforcing an often oversimplified view by way of the electronic and print media has become de rigueur in this sound- and view-bitten society, one in which intellectual operations now involve pictures and sound much more than text. If *moral panic*, the next step on the seismic scale above moral outrage, is a result of such media coverage, then conversely, media coverage of domestic events noncriminal in nature can be viewed as seismic indicators of a national Zeitgeist espousing the idea of morality, sometimes undefined and amorphous, as it is seen to inform political and international life and the personal behaviors of the national leadership. Is it any accident that, in the nineties, one encounters more and more often compounds in which the word *moral* and its derivatives appear? *Values*, another word with as many meanings as there are those who espouse them, seemed to be the code word of choice during twelve years of Republican leadership. Now *moral* and its derivatives speckle the texts of critics, pundits, and politicians in the time of the Clinton presidency, harkening to Jimmy Carter's use of the phrase *the moral equivalent of war* and its subsequent offshoots. (Defined by William Safire in his 1993 *New Political Dictionary* as "fervor without destructiveness," the phrase goes back, he said, to a 1910 usage by William James in an essay entitled that, appearing in *International Concilium*.)

In this, a nation that is at once decidedly lawless and at the same time grounded in a not evanescent puritanism, is it surprising, in a Democratic presidency, to read again and again usages like the following? *Moral ambiguity* and *morally ambiguous*, used variously to characterize a writer's analysis of the behavior of a key American general in the conduct of the Gulf War; a palliative, lawyerly letter written by a U.S. senator to defuse allegations of extramarital "socializing"; and the real character of a Nazi industrialist depicted in a major film about the Holocaust. *Moral authority*, used by a reporter at a White House press conference in March 1994 with reference to Hillary Rodham Clinton and the possible erosion of it after the Whitewater allegations had surfaced. *Moral vanity*, used by the conservative columnist George Will in respect to the Clintons. *Moral example*, used by the press in regard to the role of the president of the United States. *Moral education of the nation*, used by critics in reference to the film *Schindler's List* as a useful teaching tool to that end. *Wilsonian moralism* and *American moral exceptionalism*, used by Henry Kissinger in his 1994 book *Diplomacy* in discussions of the legacy of Woodrow Wilson, which, he believes, partially drives the intellect and intent of U.S. foreign policy. *Moral power*, used in regard to slogans such as "Remember Clarence Thomas!" uttered by Republican opponents of the Clinton administration during the Whitewater affair. *Moral Rorschach test*, used by Sally Quinn in the October 19, 1994, issue of the *Washington Post* with respect to the Rosario Ames espionage case (and to the Bobbitts, Tonya Harding, the Menendez brothers, and the O. J. Simpson case). *Moral justification*, *moral assault*, *moral leper*, *moral respect*, and *moral pragmatism*—all used by *Washington Post* columnist E. J. Dionne Jr. in the April 19, 1994, issue in a piece titled "The Politics of *Moral Annihilation*."

E. J. Dionne Jr. defined *moral annihilation* as the total destruction of an opponent's *moral standing*, rendering the opponent into the *moral equivalent* of a Hitler, a Stalin, an Al Capone, or a de Sade. He asserted that Clinton "is a victim of *moral annihilation*."

Dionne's use of *moral annihilation* brings to mind the not-so-private language of the New Puritans, more commonly called the Religious Rightists, or Religious Right Extremists. Certain expressions are used again and again in the pronouncements of the Religious Right, and many of them include the word *moral*, in addition to *Christian, values, family, strong stand, control, order, traditional*, and so on. Frederick Clarkson and Skipp Porteous, in their *Challenging the Christian Right: The Activist's Handbook* (1993), listed these: *moral absolutes, moral decency, moral rebirth, morals and ethics in school, strong stand on family and moral issues*, and *traditional morality*. See also *anxious class*, *drive-by hatred*, *off the grid*.

push-polling *noun*, a last-minute political telemarketing tactic used in a campaign on behalf of a candidate, in which the voters called are asked general survey questions with potentially damaging assertions about an opponent interspersed within the survey: "The question, in the midst of a telephone poll, was as shocking as it was designed to be: Would you still favor . . . a . . . candidate for the . . . state assembly, if you knew he voted to give guns back to juveniles who had used them in crimes? . . . It's known as '*push-polling*,' and it has increasingly become a weapon of choice to finish off a nasty election season" (*Wall Street Journal*, November 9, 1994).

THE STORY: The *Journal* indicated that pro-Democratic labor unions originated this tactic, which is more subtle than electronic and print media advertising and more effective at the end of a campaign when the airwaves have become saturated with political advertising, thus jading and dulling voters' sensibilities. Trouble arises when state statutes forbidding anonymous campaigning are abridged, for unlike the regulations controlling print and broadcast ads, federal regulations do not yet require congressional campaigns to identify who pays for these calls, said the *Journal*. This general lack of accountability, coupled with the effective force of direct, personal communication with voters who may be flattered by being asked what they think at a time when they may feel disenfranchised from decision-making, has become an issue of great concern to many lawmakers who remember well the *Willie Hortonization* of Michael Dukakis in his presidential bid against George Bush. Reform bills requiring *push-pollsters* to identify themselves up front and/or to file their telephone scripts well in advance of calling voters are certain to be debated in the near future.

red-diaper baby *noun*, a child of leftists active in the United States from about 1905 to the 1950s, who was born here in the period beginning about 1913 and ending in the 1960s: "He was an archetypal '*red-diaper baby*,' whose Polish-born parents were active in left-wing causes" (*St. Louis Post-Dispatch*, March 8, 1990).

THE STORY: Hundreds of thousands of people passed in and out of leftist circles from 1905 to the 1950s in this country, I was told by two *red-diaper babies* whom I interviewed for background when writing this word up in "Word Watch." Perhaps 50,000 to 100,000 *red-diaper babies*, now aged thirty-five to eighty, are alive. During the 1950s *red-diaper babies* tended to be moved around a great deal, from school to school and from locale to locale, if their parents had gained wide notoriety or had been jailed. These children observed or experienced varying degrees of persecution because of their parents' beliefs. Those who felt detached from the mainstream culture bonded with one another, and the bonds among them were strengthened by their contact at the same progressive schools and summer camps. A significant number of *red-diaper babies* who were of college age during the 1960s were active in groups such as Students for a Democratic Society (SDS).

If the exact number of *red-diaper babies* cannot be computed, neither can the origin of the term be pinpointed. Several theories—all unproven—suggest an etymology. The most commonly held and obvious one is that the word *red* is a reference to *Communist*. Another traces the term to members of the Communist party in California during the 1920s. These party members supposedly used the term to refer to others in the organization who seemed to regard their position as a birthright not requiring a high degree of hard work or commitment to party activism. A third theory—not only the most colorful, but the least probable—holds that Communist parents of the 1920s were so poor that they had to use the red flags they had been given in return for party dues as diapers for their babies. See also *White Iraqi*.

smoking bed *noun, slang*, sexual misconduct, alleged or actual, by a public figure, public knowledge of which is extremely detrimental to the figure's reputation and career: "'We thought all along a *smoking bed* would turn up,' [Mike] Salster [a former Virginia Republican party operative] said yesterday. 'He's going to develop a bad cough and be gone by 1994'" (Lynchburg, Va., *News & Daily Advance*, April 28, 1991).

THE STORY: *Smoking* in its use as a modifier has come a long way, baby, since its first appearance in the year 1648. What is more, *smoking bed* is a distinct variation on the theme of the *smoking gun*, a term meaning "a crucial piece of evidence used in convicting an accused person," used in print in 1974 to describe the cover-up instructions in the infamous White House tape of June 22, 1972—the evidence that caused Richard M. Nixon to resign the presidency.

Three springs after Republican operative Salster's use of *smoking bed* in reference to news reports in 1991 alleging that U.S. senator Charles S. Robb (D-Va.) had had an affair with a former Miss Virginia-USA, Tai Collins, Robb was confronting not a bad cough but a reelection campaign replete with what Michael Lewis of *The New Republic* called "the *smoking memos*." These referred to a series of memos written between the years 1987 and 1991 by the senator and his staff, in which they explored the issue of his personal conduct while "socializing" alone at Virginia Beach. In these materials, Robb wrote, "I've always drawn the line on certain conduct. . . . I haven't done anything that I regard as unfaithful to my wife, and she is the only woman I've loved, slept with or had coital relations with in the 20 years we've been married—and I'm still crazy about her."

When confronted by a reporter who had obtained copies of the memos, Robb, who did win the hard-fought election over two tough competitors, went a bit further in his lawyerly mode, saying this: "I chose my words with care. . . . I previously said I hadn't slept with anyone, hadn't had an affair. I clearly did not limit anything more than that. I drew a line and stuck by that line." Lewis called that line "sexual gerrymandering."

Clearly, a point of order is called for. It might be provided by another term in the set, the *Hart Rule*, used in the April 28, 1991, issue of the *Roanoke Times & World-News* in a story about the Robb case: "Intense scrutiny of candidates' private lives is an unpleasant fact of life in politics today. [Republican John Buckley] propounded a *Hart Rule*, which goes like this: 'Anything any politician did with a woman other than his wife prior to May 5, 1987, ought to be allowed to go unrevealed. After Gary Hart's exposure, politicians were on notice that their behavior had to change.'"

Sovok *noun, slang,* an embittered, cynical, irresponsible, lazy, and amoral person, a product of the former Soviet system, regarded as an impediment to societal reconstruction in Russia and other parts of the former Soviet Union: "A *Sovok* is 'Soviet Man'—not as the ideologists conceived him, but as he actually turned out. A *Sovok* is . . . the passive receptacle of decades of Soviet propaganda. Outwardly respectful of authority, a *Sovok* will think nothing of stealing from the state or cheating his neighbor. A *Sovok* is everything Russians despise about themselves" (*Washington Post*, September 8, 1993).

THE STORY: *Sovok*, pronounced [suh-VOK], comes from a common noun of the same spelling that means "dustpan." It is used, especially by members of the so-called Lost Generation, those born in 1945, in derisive reference to a regime they had been taught to revere, and which they later learned was fraudulent.

In looking at some of the important Russian-language borrowings into English during the last forty years, one is struck by their symbology. In them one can view clearly major passages in Soviet society, with *Sovok* being the epitaph. *Sputnik*, which burst onto the English-speaking landscape in 1957, symbolized the beginning of the U.S.-Soviet space race and the start of a major U.S. education reform movement that stressed mathematics, the sciences, and the need to speak foreign languages deemed important to the national interest. In the 1960s and mid-1970s came *zek* (a labor-camp inmate) and *gulag*, words conveyed into the English lexicon by the works of Aleksandr Solzhenitsyn, specifically *One Day in the Life of Ivan Denisovich* and *The Gulag Archipelago*—novels that exposed the brutality of the Soviet penal system. Next, in the late 1970s and early 1980s, came *nomenklatura*, a reborrowing, actually, for it had jumped the Iron Curtain from English into Russian. This word denoted the system of high-level Soviet pork-barreling and the class of Soviet citizenry enjoying the perks of the pork. Last, of course, in the mid- to late 1980s, came *perestroika* and *glasnost*, along with short-lived coinages in English such as *Gorbymania* and *Gorbasm*. See also *Wall in the Head*.

Stephanopouli *plural noun*, the young, relatively inexperienced advisers and staffers in the Clinton administration: "Clinton's young aides have the nervous manner of children who expect their father to blow up at any moment. It is disconcerting when the President dresses down his rosy-cheeked aides in public, and when he sends the *Stephanopouli* out to defend his messy past, about which they know little" (Maureen Dowd, *New York Times Magazine*, April 17, 1994).

THE STORY: Maureen Dowd—always a lexicographer's delight for her apt turns and twists of phrase (see *Velcroid*)—has taken the surname of presidential aide-of-all-trades George *Stephanopoulos* and turned it into a plural eponym worthy of note. It resonates on the same scale with *Lilliputians*, Swift's people in *Gulliver's Travels*.

In a *New York Times Magazine* piece titled "The Little-People Problems," Dowd commented on the Clintons' seeming inability to manage either "the help" or the staff in the White House in an effective, consistent, and, yes, kindly manner. The word *Stephanopouli* joins others of similar ilk, used repeatedly by the press corps: *children*, *kids*, and *young people*. In all these usages, the connotations are inexperience, nervousness, and the self-importance of being earnest.

It is highly unlikely that *Stephanopouli* will survive as a word, once there is a change in administrations. But its very coinage speaks to this president's assumption that he can rely upon factotums (*factoti?*) to "clean up after him," as Dowd stated. She concluded that this "is a question of grace," not of issues political or cultural. See also *I think*.

stylogram *noun*, a six-sided computer graphic, configured to relect the percentages of certain parts of speech used by a head of state in speeches and other utterances over the long term, intended to serve as an indication of underlying interests and as a predictor of policy: "To . . . Luis Sanchez, a Mexican opposition pollster . . . President Miguel de la Madrid Hurtado is an adjective. . . . Mr. Sanchez makes . . . *stylograms*, based on presidential percentages of nouns, verbs, adjectives and adverbs. Although Mr. de la Madrid and Mr. López Portillo have different speaking styles, their true selves come out . . . in *stylograms* that both lean toward adjectives" (*Wall Street Journal*, September 5, 1986).

THE STORY: The *Journal* citation was particularly helpful because it also contained an illustration of six *stylograms*. The *stylograms* are configured as circles, over which are superimposed three axes for parts of speech: adjectives-nouns, verbs-adverbs, and prepositions-pronouns. The circles are thereby divided into six sectors of equal measure. Superimposed onto these sectors are computer-generated graphs showing the preponderance of use of a particular part of speech, determined by parsing. The citation also suggests that words by subject category are traced: "This year's count shows the president favors economics (4,947 words) over domestic politics (1,209) words. [Sanchez] says the president's favorite word is 'no.'" See also *hedonia hypothesis*, *heresthetic*.

there *noun*, substantive political or legal implications; hidden evidence of possible wrongdoing; information withheld for a reason: "There's no *there* there!" (Paul Begala, *Crossfire*, CNN, March 28, 1994).

THE STORY: In the words of the Bard,

> *To be or not to be, that is the question:*
> *Whether 'tis nobler in the mind to suffer*
> *The slings and arrows of outrageous fortune,*
> *Or to take arms against a sea of troubles,*
> *And by opposing, end them?*
> . . . .
> *. . . ay,* there's *the rub.*

In March 1994, the Clinton administration was awash in a sea of troubles whose font lay in some real estate on the Whitewater River down in Arkansas. The *Crossfire* citation, taken from one of many sportive on-screen discussions of what had become known as Whitewatergate, is an example not just of an *oral citation*, but a *screaming citation*, uttered by a *screaming head* (for more on that term, see *schmooseoisie*). Paul Begala, one of the administration's most quick-witted wordsmiths and a Democratic party operative in the White House, took his text from Gertrude Stein's "classic slander of the city of Oakland, Calif." (William Safire, "On Language," *New York Times Magazine*, May 19, 1985). In so doing, Begala used *there* as a noun when replying to the repeated query "What's there to hide? What's *in* there?" posed with reference to information alleged to have been retained and not yet released by the Clinton administration and pertinent to the Whitewater investigation. And in so answering, Begala inadvertently (or advertently) created a new noun sense of the word.

Of course, some people called me after the broadcast. They worried that *there*—traditionally and variously an adverb (*Sit over there and answer all of Special Prosecutor Fiske's questions*), an adjective (*Those Rose Law Firm couriers there ought to know which documents may have been shredded*), a pronoun used to open a clause or sentence (*There's no end in sight to this scandal*), and an interjection (*Hello, there, Josh. This is George from the White House. I need to blow off some steam*)—could not possibly be a licit noun. If so used, they worried, this could constitute syntactic obstruction of justice to the mother tongue—a false functional shift, to be exact.

How wrong they were. *There* has long been analyzed as a noun with the meaning "that place or point," used thus in a sample sentence: *Pat Buchanan, nonplussed, dropped his line of questioning and went on from there.*

The rub is that I'm still not sure exactly what Begala really meant in there. The definition you see is merely an educated guess, based on a rummage through opacity delivered with concision. There you go. There may be something there, after all. Isn't there? Or is there? See also *snide*.

toyi-toyi *noun*, a dance characterized by hopping on one leg and then the other, with arm or fist raised high, and performed in groups in South Africa, chiefly by blacks as a symbol of their commitment to freedom and racial equality: "No image sums up the joy, relief and hope felt by millions of South Africans better than that of 75-year-old Nelson Mandela dancing at the African National Congress's victory party last week. . . . South Africa saw its new president-elect as a funky father of the nation, a beaming septuagenarian doing his own, stiff-armed version of the *toyi-toyi*, a warlike stomp that is synonymous with black protest against apartheid" (*U.S. News & World Report*, May 16, 1994). "But thousands and thousands did arrive: in groups of 100, piling out of 40-seat buses; and in long columns to the jog/dance/march known as *toyi-toyi*, most wearing the T-shirts of the time: Viva Mandela, Welcome Home Our Leader and Don't Worry, Be Happy" (*Manchester Guardian Weekly*, March 4, 1990). —*verb*, to perform this dance: "[He] . . . derides the pathetic attempts of whites to join the struggle, trying to *toyi-toyi* with black marchers because he knows that in the end they are not struggling for the same thing" (*The Independent* [London], May 5, 1990). "Protesters, holding aloft banners from local organizations as well as COSATU, Nactu [National Council of Trade Unions], the ANC [African National Congress] and similar bodies, sang, chanted and '*toyi-toyied*' as they were monitored by police in several vehicles and hippos" (BBC Summary of World Broadcasts, October 3, 1989).

THE STORY: The story of South Africa's freedom ride is writ large in these few citations for the noun and verb *toyi-toyi*. The long journey that was this ride began with a dance step, and ended with it. And now, in 1994, a new beginning was celebrated after the ANC's victory in the first all-race elections with the new president performing the dance. In a word, two words can be thought of as the lexicopolitical symbols of the evolvement of South Africa in our time: *apartheid*, now consigned to the history books, and *toyi-toyi*, a vital, living symbol of past struggle and future challenges.

The noun and the verb, pronounced [toy-toy], according to African languages scholar George N. Clements, Ph.D., of l'Institut de Phonétique in Paris, is really a term of unknown origin. In on-the-scene research done in 1993, Clements was unable to determine the etymology of *toyi-toyi*: His sources were informant interviews and consultations with other scholars of African languages and of Afrikaans. They could find no viable roots of the word in any members of the known African language groups.

Also of import are the various contextual glosses, or characterizations, used over the last decade by journalists from the West in describing *toyi-toyi*. These characterizations are diverse, and they differ markedly according to changing circumstances on the spot, changing times, and changing viewpoints. Based on journalistic citational evidence, *toyi-toyi* can be termed variously as militaristic, threatening, aggressive, and fearsome, as these excerpted lines indicate:

a *soldiers'* dance of the *Spear* of the Nation, the *military* wing of the
  ANC
martial dance
aggressive dance
stamping martial dance
dance of *defiance*
war dance
warlike dance
revolutionary dance
dance of the *revolution*
military-style dance

where the italicized matter is critical to the lexicographer's analysis of meaning.

    Other contexts, however, cast the dance as political:

foot-stamping, rousing *political* dance
vigorous *protest* dance
liberation dance
symbol of *resistance* to *apartheid*
the *controversial* dance popular with young blacks
the choreography of black *nationalism*

Still others veer from the politicization of meaning to more neutral description:

a *jogging, chanting* dance of the *townships*
rhythmical swaying and *waving* of the *arms*
hopping on one foot
jogging dance

Two other citations treat the term anthropologically:

tribal dance
a *trance-like* dance

But two others use the language clearly reflective of neocolonial condescension:

a *gyrating* dance

a rather *shambolic* . . . dance

In all, only one of these citations, which date into the early 1980s and end in 1990, is positive; it describes the *toyi-toyi* as "a *celebratory* dance."

A common thread, though unstated as such, is the attempt by Those Looking In to understand Those Looking Out. The attempt fails, at least in the early citations, because of a cultural apartheid. Even in 1994, postelection, a major Western newsmagazine employs "a *warlike stomp*" in its contextual gloss.

Analysis of the citations, taken from sources such as Reuters, the *New York Times*, the *Washington Post*, Inter Press Service, *The Times* (London), *Financial Times* (London), *Maclean's*, the *Los Angeles Times*, and the *Washington Times*, exposes the need for care by lexicographers in developing definitions based on printed citational evidence. For instance, if a dictionary editor had read only the citations in the first cluster and had constructed a definition based solely on them, the denotations and connotations carried by that definition would have been narrowly particularized to the violent, the martial, the aggressive, and only that. The same can be said for analysis restricted to any one of the other clusters. The fact is, the *toyi-toyi* can be performed fast or slow, in celebration or in despair, in joy or in anger, in resistance or in unity—depending on the impetus, the circumstances, and the time. It can also represent another emotion—hope.

Professor Clements added a very pertinent thought during a spring 1994 telephone interview: whites regularly join with blacks in doing this dance. All this, almost exactly four years after the quotation in *The Independent* was written. Yes, the *toyi-toyi* is more than choreography, more than a dance. It's a word that mirrors history in the making in the times of our lives. See also *hippo, tsotsie*.

tsotsie *noun,* a black thug in South Africa who preys on residents of the townships and those going there: "Four young black men leaped out of the car, hauled us out of ours, and demanded our keys and money. . . . The *tsotsie* who yanked me from the passenger side seemed reasonable enough, so before I handed him my money, I began the formality of showing him my press card. . . . But I never finished the transaction. On the other side of the car, a much rougher set of *tsotsies* had hauled out the driver. . . . One clubbed him over the head. . . . One shouted: 'Get out of the townships, you white [expletive].' Then he shot [the driver] in the head" (Paul Taylor, *Washington Post*, August 10, 1992).

THE STORY: Here's a word, used almost entirely in South Africa and nowhere else, that gained broad national and international currency in 1992, when the aforementioned attack occurred. While *toyi-toyi* represents the long, legitimate struggle for freedom from racism in South Africa, and *apartheid* is the symbol of past repression, *tsotsie* and the verb *necklace* (to set a victim on fire by dousing a tire that is around the victim's neck with gasoline and lighting it) are linguistic symbols of a society without humanity, driven by a government without humanity.

Tsotsie, like *toyi-toyi*, has no known roots in any African language group, according to African languages scholar George N. Clements, Ph.D. The *Oxford English Dictionary*, however, points out that *tsotsie* may be a corruption of *zoot suit*, since the characteristic attire of a *tsotsie* is, or was, narrow trousers or garments having an exaggerated cut: "The '*Tsotsi*' may be distinguished by his exceedingly narrow trousers which hardly reach his shoes, or else by his 'zoot suit'" (Cape *Times*, September 10, 1949). *Tsotsie*, like *Kaffir* (from the Arabic word for an infidel) and *Hottentot* (Afrikaans, derived from a Dutch word of the same and variant *O*-spellings meaning "a stutterer" and later meaning "an uncivilized, ignorant person"), is considered a term of disparagement to blacks. Here is a citation that illustrates the derogatory denotation: "As for Absalom—he is a 'skellum,' a '*tsotsi*'—the kind of Kaffir who ought to be sjambokked [beaten] every day: it would teach him some sense" (E.U.T. Huddleston, *Naught for your Comfort*, 1956).

Cold comfort, that. Sometimes the history of violence on all sides of an issue is to be read in dictionary citational evidence. See also *skel* at *token sucker*.

Velcroid or **velcroid** *noun*, *slang*, a person who makes a point of staying in close proximity to an important leader, such as a prime minister or president, in order to gain media visibility and maintain continued access to that leader: "Ever notice the people who chum up to the Prime Minister in pictures? Call them *velcroids*" (*Toronto Star*, March 14, 1992).

THE STORY: Just as *Teflon* presidents seem to deflect criticism, so do *Velcroids* "stick to their prey," in the words of the *Toronto Star*. In 1991 a list of Bush administration *Velcroids* was drawn up by the *New York Times*. Maureen Dowd of that paper listed John Sununu as a leading member of the group, especially during photo opportunities at the time of Desert Storm. Dowd named the malady that *Velcroids* suffer: it's *Velcrosis*.

The spin-offs from *Velcro* don't just stop there, however. Consider one of the crazes of the early 1990s: *Velcro jumping*. In this activity, people clad in Velcro-covered suits leap onto a trampoline called "The Flytrap," against which a Velcro-covered wall rises at a ninety-degree angle. The object is to bounce off the trampoline, hit the wall as high as possible, and stick to it for as long as possible: "From midnight until 5 A.M. after the prom, the [school] cafeteria was turned into an amusement center, complete with all the trimmings, including casino and carnival games, dancing, an auction, prizes, food and the big event, *Velcro jumping*" (*Fauquier* [Va.] *Times-Democrat*, June 9, 1993).

Waldheimer's disease *noun*, the selective forgetfulness of those who feel they must defy, revise, or expunge a record that will not stand up to critical scrutiny: "No one wants to talk to Austria, where the despicable president suffers from *Waldheimer's disease* (40 years later you forget you were a Nazi)" (*Maclean's*, April 11, 1988). "Our interview partners finally challenge a third myth—the myth of oblivion, sometimes described as '*Waldheimer's disease*.' . . . German history neither began nor ended in 1945" (*Los Angeles Times*, June 4, 1989).

THE STORY: When Alan Orich of the North American Jewish Students Union was quoted on July 6, 1987, by *U.S. News & World Report* to the effect that "the Vatican has shown the first symptom of *Waldheimer's disease*," he was using a double eponymous blend (*Waldheim* plus Alzheimer's) in which the strands of medical, moral, and historical issues are commingled.

With the recently observed trend in some circles toward revisionist history of the Holocaust, *Waldheimer's disease* was a term waiting to be coined, no matter how distasteful the thought of according Kurt Waldheim a place in lexical perpetuity. Some eighteen citations for it go back to 1986, when the details of the then Austrian president's military service in the Waffen-SS during World War II and allegations that the units with which he served had engaged in war crimes surfaced.

A more recent citation, this one taken from an article by Malcolm Bradbury in the *New York Times Book Review* of February 24, 1991, uses the term with reference to the late deconstructionist Paul de Man, who taught at Yale: "At several key moments when modern history has turned—Western Europe in 1945, Eastern Europe now—we have seen how moral crisis comes to those who have served a cause that history has, fortunately for humanity, repudiated. Often this develops into what Mr. [David] Lehman [in *Signs of the*

Times: Deconstruction and the Fall of Paul de Man] calls 'Waldheimer's disease,' the amnesia of those who must defy or erase the record." This term, which may have been coined by someone in the Chicago bureau of *Time*, seems to have a secure future in the English lexicon.

Wall in the Head *noun idiom*, the psychosocial barriers that serve to disunify Germans from East and West after legal unification: "Three years after German unification, every trace of the old wall has fallen. . . . But a '*Wall in the Head*' still runs through the town [of Klein Machnow, where the Berlin Wall used to block every northbound street], separating Easterner from Westerner and neighbor from neighbor. Its persistence testifies to the difficulties of remaking any of Eastern Europe's societies, even under ideal circumstances" (George Rodrigue, *Dallas Morning News*, October 10, 1993).

THE STORY: Anthony Bailey, the writer, toured the entire length of the fortified border that once separated East and West Germany. He walked along it, touched it, crossed it, and flew over it. In his 1983 account of the experience, *Along the Edge of the Forest*, he called the wall "one of the wonders of the modern world" in its own perverse way. Running 870 miles in length, it was guarded by 1,000 dogs and teams of special border police. It looked like a long scar from the air: It was equipped with plowed death strips maintained on a daily basis to expose footprints. It was fitted with watchtowers, lights, minefields, and barbed wire. Bricks, mortar, and special gates that were ramproof completed the installation. The edifice is estimated to have cost the former East German government $6 billion to construct and maintain since it went up on August 13, 1961.

Now comes *Wall in the Head*, an expression evocative of the societal scar caused by the physical scar. It is a direct translation, or "loan-translation," into English of the German *die Mauer in den Köpfen*, an expression coined by the German print media about a year after the wall came down in November of 1989. George Rodrigue, the Berlin bureau chief of the *Dallas Morning News*, told me in a November 1993 telephone interview that divisiveness in German society is most evident in the results of polled issues. For example, when asked in September of 1992, "Do you feel more unified now?" 30 percent of the Westerners said they did; only 11 percent of the Easterners said yes. Easterners, once passively dependent on and subservient to the state, are now confronted with high unemployment, a high crime rate, and the possibility of losing their property to returning Westerners. Westerners resent the huge outlays of money being transfused, via borrowings, into the East, and they expect from their Eastern cousins more assertiveness, entrepreneurship, and self-reliance. But one of the most divisive issues, according to Rodrigue, is the matter of foreign deployment of the German armed forces, now officered almost exclusively by Westerners but with a homogenized enlisted cadre: the Easterners, taking a passivistic line, oppose deployment to NATO, for instance; Westerners are generally for it. Bringing down this *Wall in the Head* is a worthy goal; after all, in its 1,000-year history, Germany has been united for little more than 75 years. See also *Sovok*.

White Iraqi *noun*, a monarchist who fled Iraq after the 1958 revolution in Baghdad: "But if we joke today about being *White Iraqis*, the sadness will not go away. It has been a long time to watch a good country die" (Nameer Ali Jawdat, *Washington Post*, August 2, 1992).

THE STORY: "A young woman whose father had been minister of finance in the monarchy called us '*White Iraqis*,'" said Nameer Ali Jawdat in the same article. The term was coined by association with *White Russian*, denoting the exiles of czarist Russia after the 1917 revolution—people connected in the public mind with driving taxis, running elevators, and selling champagne, especially in Paris during the twenties and thirties. The adjective *White* was also used, as in *White Guardist*, to refer to a member of a force fighting for the Finnish government against leftist insurgents during the civil war of 1918, and, in the case of *White Army*, to refer to a member of a counterrevolutionary force in Russia during its civil war of 1918–1921/22. See also *red-diaper baby*.

Xerocracy *noun*, a country or society in which government censorship is so pervasive that independent thought can be expressed only by way of clandestinely written, photocopied, and distributed newsletters and other tracts; the system of publishing and distributing such material: "The Shah's censorship turned Iran into a *Xerocracy* of underground broadsheets, which set the tone for the press after the revolution that removed the Shah in 1979" (*The Economist*, October 15, 1988).

THE STORY: *Xerocracy* surfaced about twenty-one years after *samizdat*, a Russian word meaning "the secret publication and distribution of government-banned literature in the USSR; the literature and other documentation so produced; a clandestine press." The first constituent element of *Xerocracy* points up the advances in technology available to the Iranians as opposed to that which had been available to Soviet dissidents early on. The word joins others spun off from -*cracy* in recent years: *telecracy*, the television business as it works to influence, form, and dominate public perception and opinion; *corpocracy*, a top-heavy corporate structure before the nineties trend of restructuring and delayering began; and *narcokleptocracy*, government of, for, and by drug lords and government personnel, being examples.

The story behind *Xerocracy* is a bit ironic. The late Shah's censorship, exercised through what many editors called his "Ministry of All the Truth," eventually resulted in what *The Economist* described as a "less monolithic" truth in Iran: "[After the revolution, the press] was free to the point of chaos: no rumour, no slander was too dubious to publish, and every faction had its mouthpiece. But when president Abolhassan Bani-Sadr fell in 1981 after a battle in the press, the mullahs consolidated their power by banning other peoples' publications and running their own." Today, Iranian newspapers debate and criticize governmental policy and draw pleasure from exposing scandals; however, the government system itself is never questioned.

8

And Now a Word from Our Sponsor: Sound Bites on the Ads, the Media, and the Spin Docs

advertising cinema
cascade (*verb*)
CNN effect
conversate
dual-channel person
edgy advertising
flyover people
hot button
infomercial
informate
lunch lid
media availability

mersh
muffin-choker
newszak
numeronym
paper curtain
pipe a quote
schmooseoisie
Spinnish
trawler
Twinkie
warmedy

Thanks to television, for the first time the young are seeing
history made before it is censored by their elders.
—Margaret Mead

When Margaret Mead made that statement, she might have been forecasting the real-time, living-room coverage of the Gulf War transmitted by CNN,
generating what has since become known as the *CNN effect*. This term is
central not just to chapter 8 but to the life and times of the broadcast industry and American viewing-audience demands.

When Archibald MacLeish said of CBS radio correspondent Edward R.
Murrow's coverage of the World War II blitz, "You burned the city of London
in our house and we felt the flames," he introduced the most important trend
in broadcast news presentation of this century. It might be called the *Murrow
effect*. Some fifty years after London burned, Iraqi convoys burned and Saddam Hussein retaliated with Scud attacks on the state of Israel—and the
fires burned in our living rooms. Owing to this *CNN effect*, the travel industry took a nose dive: people simply stopped and Velcroed themselves to
their screens as though they too were in a high-tech CIC, a combat information center. Not a single briefing was to be missed. Not a single piece of gun-
camera videotape was to be missed by America's modem pilots. Not a single
Scud was to be missed.

CNN effect will go down in the history of broadcast journalism as the single most important term in that industry's twentieth-century lexicon. After

the *Murrow effect* occurred, on-site reportage over the airwaves progressed with the televised debates in the 1960 presidential election between Kennedy and Nixon. It is felt by many analysts that television—and the degree of telegenicity of the winning candidate—decided the course of that election to a significant extent. Next came the first living-room war, Vietnam; and the ensuing protests, fueled to a high pitch by what was then considered "immediate" coverage from the battle zone. Finally came Watergate and the live hearings, which brought down a president of the United States. But the apex was reached in the years 1990 and 1991, when a line was drawn in the sand of the Middle East.

From the standpoint of language alone, the term *CNN effect* is significant, for it joins one other, *MTV Generation*, also a network derivation, in representing the pervasive power of the message delivered by the medium to the *flyover people* whose *hot buttons* must be activated by advertisers, marketers, newspeople, entertainment executives, candidates, and *tubers* (television's bicoastal whiz kids) in their pursuit of success.

In terms of success, the second most important word in the chapter is *trawler*, a.k.a. *channel surfer*, the most feared phenomenon in the television industry. That's you—the one sitting there in the couch commander's chair, holding your weapon of choice, the electronic channel selector, or zapper. It is ironic that the very same innovations in electronic communications technology that gave the industry the *CNN effect* have now empowered the couch commanders to swat unwanted commercials and programs like flies. This is very bad news to industry strategists. With an ever-increasing array of instant choices on the menu, couch commanders' attention spans have shrunk to the nanosecond level. And from the standpoint of national life, the situation is troubling too: abbreviated attention spans require clipped, compressed, often oversimplified presentations of important issues. Analysis, reflection, and informed public decision-making all suffer in the process.

The third newsworthy term is the blended borrowing *schmooseoisie*, the coinage of a Boston College English professor who is concerned about the emergence of a new national class of talkers. *Schmooseoisie* hints at the new Tower of Babble created by the radio and television broadcast industries in their talk and call-in shows. This new class is composed of those who talk as a career, and those who make a career of calling in and talking to the host-talkers. The blah-blah on the airwaves finds its written counterpart in some of the messages transmitted over the on-line computer nets. The whole phenomenon, though, echoes the exuberance displayed by the talking American public when telephones were first introduced and the party lines were constantly busy, and the CB craze in the seventies when an entire new sublanguage emerged. But what is even more important at this point is the use being made of the Tower of Babble by the politicians and high-level government appointees who, in effect, have become presenters of themselves as commercial products—all this, in the manner of the *infomercial* presenters, about whom we will speak shortly.

The spinning of politicians, the porkers in their barrels, and the *Stephanopouli* bring us to *Spinnish*, the lingua franca of the spin docs. Appropriately enough, this word first appeared in a cartoon. The fourth most important in the chapter, *Spinnish* essentially redefines managed news. The word reminds every one of us that in the nineties, more than ever before, things are often not what they seem. More often than not, the fix is in and the spin on the ball might better be called "Virtual English."

In watching words one can sometimes see a market in all the stages of its evolution. Such is the case with *infomercial*, alluded to earlier. It's now a fixture in the parlance. Why? Simply because the word denotes a huge, steadily growing, as of yet immature market that, in 1992 alone, grossed $750 million. Signs of perpetuity are lexical spin-offs from the word, the existence of a trade association, and an annual industry awards ceremony reminiscent of the Oscars.

The language of communications, the practitioners of which field must slavishly follow *The Associated Press Stylebook and Libel Manual*, is an unruly little language. It's offbeat, slangy, and shirt-sleevy—as might be expected by anyone who's been in a green room or a newsroom. The words *newszak*, *warmedy*, *mersh*, *muffin-choker*, and *lunch lid*—by their very linguistic structure and their meanings—capture the atmosphere of reportage and public communicative commerce. Well, the lid is off and Pandora's box is open. It's now up to you to delve in and find out who's *piping a quote* in there behind the *paper curtain*.

advertising cinema *noun*, a television advertising genre featuring often serialized slice-of-life minidramas, the endings of which involve a product pitch. Also called *present-tense drama*: "'*Advertising cinema* is not cinema. Involving the viewer is critical, but it's not an end in itself. You've got to be closer to selling your product, service, message or image at the end of a commercial than you were at the beginning,' says Bob Garfield of *Advertising Age*" (*Boston Globe*, March 9, 1989).

THE STORY: This genre uses personal relationships and values in such a way as to appear to transcend commercial intent. An example of *advertising cinema* was a famous serial run by a telephone company in which a generational conflict (this one, between father and daughter) was central to the advertisement, with a more or less happy ending achieved by use of the phone. Still another is a coffee commercial in which the pitch is cleverly woven into the strands of a man-woman romantic relationship, complicated by the arrival and departure of a mysterious other man, and most recently by the arrival and departure of the woman's son. Employment of this genre, which Bill Monahan, art director at Cabot Advertising, called *present-tense drama*, is still considered somewhat risky by experts. As the *Globe* reports, "The impact the genre has had on its viewers is extraordinary, ranging from admiration to loathing." See also *infomercial*.

cascade *verb*, to circulate (information, for example) widely and quickly, throughout the various ranks of an organization; distribute (material) through channels: "The handouts for today's meeting have been designed to make it easier for you to *cascade* the meeting's key messages to your people" (a photocopied cover document for a corporate seminar entitled *Management Focus '88*).

THE STORY: This new sense of *cascade* is an example of the corporatespeak of the late 1980s, and, as one critic recently put it, "a preview of the lingua franca of the far future when the state has indeed withered away." It is possible that this sense of *cascade* is related to a noun sense of the word hitherto restricted to electricity: "an arrangement of devices, each of which feeds into the next one in succession." If this neat theory holds, and it is only one theory, then *cascade* joins other terms borrowed from the lexicon of physical science and mathematics, such as the noun *dynamic*, the adjectives *centered* and *focused*, the noun *space* in the emotional-psychological sense, and the ubiquitous noun *facilitator*, words that serve to depersonalize and redefine people and their activities in terms of mass, energy, and process, as opposed to the biology of life.

But another, less intellectualized, and perhaps more likely theory has it that the verb *cascade* in the sense at issue derives from the trade name *Cascade*, used for a brand of mimeograph and spirit duplicating paper, once preferred and used in mountainous quantities by publishers of *fanzines*, especially the science-fiction ones, before the era of desktop publishing. Given that the citation for *cascade* derives from a management meeting of a large manufacturer of high-tech photocopying equipment, where employees would have been familiar with the older methods of copying, this second, more prosaic theory seems the most sound.

CNN effect *noun*, loss of sales and profits in the travel, hotel, restaurant, and entertainment industries caused by mass viewer interest in and corporate alarm about an international combat incident garnering daily, real-time television coverage: "Some potential travelers are riveted to their TV sets, captivated by news reports about the [Gulf] war, a condition some are calling the '*CNN effect*'" (*Chicago Tribune*, January 28, 1991).

THE STORY: Ratings for CNN soared to a level five to ten times above pre–Gulf War levels, because people were "intensely interested in the first real-time war in history and [were] just planting themselves in front of the TV" (John J. Rohs, a lodging analyst at Wertheim Schroder and Company, *New York Times*, January 28, 1991).

The beginning of a recession, concern about the possibility of retaliative terrorism, and a reduction in corporate travel to the Middle East and other locales deemed dangerous resulted in the *CNN effect*, a new compound formed on the order of the preexisting term *January effect*, or *J effect*, defined by economist David L. Scott in *Wall Street Words* (1988) as "the tendency of stocks to perform better in January than at any other time of the year."

In an antonymic twist of meaning, the *CNN effect* denotes a *downturn* in profits in travel-related sectors. Even domestic vacations got canceled in the year of the word's coinage: "People [didn't] want to miss a single Scud," commented Tim Gallagher, a spokesman for Carnival Cruise Lines Inc., in Miami, to the *Times*.

Since that time, *CNN effect* has begun to take on yet another meaning. It now is used to denote the instancy of the electronic communicative media, a factor contributing to the flash proliferation of new words in the English language. And for more about the mind-set of those who didn't want to miss a single Scud, turn to *modem pilot*, which explores some hidden frustrations.

conversate *verb*, to engage in conversation: "He has made the tavern his regular watering hole since he moved to Dorchester from South Carolina last year. 'It's the only place where I can come and cool out. Everybody gets together and just *conversates*. Folks talk about sports, the news, general stuff'" (*Boston Globe*, March 20, 1989).

THE STORY: Here's a verb that rarely appears in edited prose—one that readers who abhor back-formations such as *commentate* will love to hate. (A *back-formation* is a new word, such as *televise, edit, diagnose, burgle, vacuum clean,* or *recreate,* that is created by removing an affix from a preexisting word, such as *television, editor, diagnosis, burglar, vacuum cleaner,* or *recreation,* or by removing what is thought to be an affix, such as *pea* from the earlier English *pease.*)

If *conversate* grates like a fingernail moving across a blackboard, consider the verb *visionate,* this one not a back-formation but an example of suffixation: *vision* plus *-ate,* where *envision* would certainly do. A citation from "Mighty Moment from Maui" by Kari Omar Sonne in the July 15–31, 1989, issue of the *Lahaina* [Hawaii] *Sun* brought the word to my attention: "If it is your dream, *visionate* it!" Still another such suffixation is *ethnicate* (*ethnic* plus *-ate*), used in the November 14, 1992, issue of the *Washington Post* in reference to "'*ethnicated*' [mailing] lists [sold to direct mailers by database companies] that strive to separate Americans by their racial or ethnic backgrounds for commercial purposes," created often by analysis of surnames and with input from linguists and sociologists. See also *informate.*

dual-channel person *noun,* one of the group of people, aged eighteen to thirty, who form their opinions and derive their television entertainment from only two networks, CNN and MTV: "The *dual-channel person* . . . wants a store with a corrugated cardboard business card and a philosophy, preferably an earnest one. . . . The *dual-channel person* cares mostly about clothes with a short life span . . . and music recorded yesterday. . . . He likes nasty black boots, beaded jewelry and boogie boards. And a florist called Weeds" (*New York Times Magazine,* October 9, 1994).

THE STORY: Shaheen Sadeghi, the builder of the Orange County, California, "anti-mall" officially dubbed "the Lab," used this term to denote his clientele, said the *Times Magazine,* which called those in it "the lost generation of mall rats." *Dual-channel people,* who, according to the *Times Magazine,* consider themselves "too cool for the food courts" and who are "too rumpled to appreciate Chanel or Nordstrom," can avail themselves of the clothing at Urban Outfitters, the recordings at Tower Alternative, and the comic books at the Collectors Library. Instead of the obligatory skylighted atrium, green plants, and concrete fountain that accent traditional malls, the anti-mall offers *dual-channel* shoppers an open-air living room accented with furnishings from thrift shops, burnt desert grass, facades of scaffolding, and an oil-drum fountain. Trucked-in urban grit and a rotating exhibit of accumulated debris complete the ambiance of this, a new niche-market retailing center, whose time may or may not have come (some *dual-channel people* think it is too in-your-face). See also *flyover people*, *Xer*.

edgy advertising *noun*, a risky, nonconformist approach to product promotion: "'The . . . theme exploits and celebrates individuals and celebrities—people willing to stand by themselves. It's *edgy advertising*'" (Bill Hamilton, *Advertising Age*, July 4, 1988).

THE STORY: *Edgy* with the meaning "risky" has been in use for a number of years in the car sales business, as in "That customer wants to buy the Corvette, but his credit's a little edgy." This sense of *edgy*, logically stemming from the established one, "nervous," is most probably the source of *edgy advertising*, although the influence of familiar idioms like *live on the edge* and *on the cutting edge* cannot be discounted. The term appeared again in the general media, this time in the March 31, 1991, edition of the *New York Times*, in a story headlined "Advertising's Antic Upstarts": "To do good work—Donnie Deutsch of the Deutsch Agency calls it '*edgy advertising*'—means finding clients who will take risks."

The technique so named is used chiefly by small, aggressive agencies attempting to build their reputations. Their clients are typically retailers and other small companies unconstrained by the preconceived, rigid ideas about advertising imagery and product positioning quite often held by corporate bureaucrats. Such small companies are also tightly run by their managements, who are courageous and willing to take risks in order to win. "Other types of clients are often not welcome," said the *Times*. In fact, such *edgy advertising* agencies have been known to fire their own clients.

flyover people *plural noun*, *slang*, the United States television-viewing population living between the East and West coasts, specifically, between New York–Boston–Washington and Los Angeles: "Out there among the *flyover people* . . . there may be some poor soul who does not instantly recognize that 'West 57th' is the Manhattan address of CBS News" (*Wall Street Journal*, June 2, 1986). "*Flyover people*, so dubbed by bicoastal network executives hurtling between Gotham and Los Angeles, live in the Out There. *Flyover people*, being the real arbiters of taste, circle something new and wonder whether it's agreeably fashionable . . . and ultimately make the decisions that determine its long-term failure or success" (*New York Times*, November 2, 1985).

THE STORY: *Flyover people*, the term of art for those the late Bishop Fulton Sheen once characterized as the "meat" between "the crusts on the great American sandwich," is interesting not because it is new but because it is old. According to E. M. ("Bud") Rukeyser, an executive vice president at NBC, whom I interviewed in 1987, *flyover people* came into use in the fifties. It was an industry term, one that never enjoyed wide use outside the business. In fact, its occurrence in general contexts was rare in the eighties, and remains so in the nineties.

Flyover in other combinations, forms, and uses appears from time to time in entertainment industry contexts. Consider these remarks by Dave Shiflett, the deputy editorial page editor of the *Rocky Mountain News*, taken from a book review he wrote in January of 1992 for *The American Spectator*: "The authors begin their study with a general survey of television's brain children, whom we can refer to hereafter as the *tubers*. Seventy-three percent live either in California or along the Boston-Washington corridor, a fact that immediately raises suspicions out here in the *Great Flyover*."

This *Great Flyover* is also called *flyover country*, according to the September 21, 1992, issue of *Insight*, in an article about the controversial book *Hollywood vs. America* by the equally controversial Michael Medved: "In tones of impassioned outrage and trenchant sarcasm, it amasses dozens upon dozens of examples supporting the thesis that Hollywood is out of touch with the rest of America ('*flyover country*' as industry execs have been known to call it)." Still another term for it is to be found in a piece by *New York Times* columnist A. M. Rosenthal, dated April 19, 1987: "You hear and read that in New York and on the West Coast, too. Perhaps it is also being said and written in the '*great overfly*,' as the rest of the country is sometimes called around Los Angeles."

Certainly these are terms to keep on the "Watch List," as is *Coaster*, the word for an executive who does the flying-over in the great commercial aviation *flyways*. See also *dual-channel person*.

hot button, *noun, slang,* something known to generate a strong, specific response, as: **a.** a key concern, factor, or interest known to influence decision-making: "Executives with sign-off power have nontechnology *hot buttons* such as market share, competitiveness, cost control, value added, new products and services or hiring and retaining good people. Read the business plan; find out what the executives want. . . . By learning about management's *hot buttons*, you have . . . now identified the 20% of the company's activities that account for 80% of management's attention, interest and the areas they are likely to fund money to improve" (*Computerworld Focus*, October 16, 1985). **b.** a specific approach or set of approaches known to trigger widespread consumer interest in and approval of a product and to motivate consumer spending: "Much . . . revolves around what Campbell marketing research director Tony Adams calls consumer *hot buttons*—buzzwords like 'fresh,' 'healthful,' and 'high quality'" (*Inc.*, August 1985). **c.** a product, service, discipline, or concept that generates widespread, intense interest or approval: "Artificial intelligence . . . has made the leap from an obscure, ivory-tower chimera to an industry *hot button*" (*Data Communications*, July 1986).

THE STORY: A very old meaning of *hot button* is vulgar. It was street talk for the clitoris (also called simply *button*). The term later came to be used in marketing, and citations for it in that area of usage go back at least to the early 1970s.

In 1981 a *Washington Post* article used the term with respect to motivating factors among voters. It has also been used in the contexts of sports medicine, food and food packaging, direct-mail book sales, and even art exhibits: "Today, museums are under attack for being hopelessly vulgar. If they're not being caught in manipulation of the art market . . . they're being accused of selling out—in both senses—with huge 'blockbuster' shows such as the roseate Renoir at the MFA or the kitsch of Andrew Wyeth's world. These are . . . *hot buttons*, and museums, once elitist, now frantic to be popular, can't help pushing them" (*New England Monthly*, January 1986).

Hot button, like *panic button*, also has a nonfigurative meaning. It can denote an actual button, attested by this entry in Jonathon Green's *Newspeak: A Dictionary of Jargon* (1984): "**hot buttons** (TV) those buttons by which a home viewer can 'vote' or otherwise participate in interactive . . . television." Green speaks of TV sets linked by a special handset to certain broadcast studios; participants in interactive programming can answer questions and render opinions, verdicts, and other reactions instantly by pressing the right buttons in response to the host's prompting.

infomercial *noun*, a consumer-specific, brand-specific, television semidocumentary, three to sixty minutes in duration, that imparts consumer information (for example, on health care, food shopping, finance, or a product) and also subtly invites viewers to buy the sponsor's product or service as depicted by a presenter, most often a celebrity: "Each program contains two *infomercials*, which identify the sponsor and explore a topic relating to child development such as play, imagination or language. There is no overt pitch for the product" (Associated Press, May 24, 1986). "By now we all know *infomercials*. . . . While *infomercials* are still largely the domain of kitchen gadgets, exercise machines and cosmetics, Fortune 500 companies have begun to take note of the format's power as a marketing tool" (*Washington Post*, October 30, 1993).

THE STORY: Why bother with this word if everybody knows it by now? The money involved, is why. Since the year 1984, when the FCC repealed its 12-minutes-per-hour restriction on television commercial airtime, *infomercials* have sustained steady gains. According to the National *Infomercial* Marketing Association (NIMA), in 1992 this genre of advertising generated $750 million in gross sales. Gross sales of a whopping $900 million were forecast for 1993. At the end of 1993, some industry analysts had predicted that *infomercials* would become a $1 billion-a-year business. Another reason to write about the word is its spelling: the variant is *informercial*, but it seems that the industry has settled on the non-*r* spelling. A third reason to talk about it is its etymology: "I take credit for coining [*infomercial*, a blend of *information* and *commercial*], even though everybody else has used it," said Michael E. Marcovsky, a cable TV consultant and the president of Marnel Associates, Ltd., in Los Angeles, during an interview on March 9, 1982, with United Press International. Said he, "When we were at QUBE, we had a form called the *infomercial*, and it was an information, or antiprogram, segment. . . . I never had one complaint from a consumer about an *infomercial*."

There have been some complaints, however. Most of them had to do with some sponsors' making unsubstantiated product claims or misleading claims. At one juncture, the industry was trying to find another term to use in place of *infomercial*—*program-length advertisement* being one suggestion. But the original blend has stuck in the language, and the format is still on the screen: viewers seem much more willing to watch *infomercials* than hard-sell commercial spots because the *infomercials*, a mix of subtlety and profundity, offer their audiences potentially useful information in a story or documentary format rather than being an annoying interruption to regular programming.

In 1993, for the second year, the NIMA awarded prizes to those judged the best in the *infomercial* industry. Among them? The Best *Documercial* (one cast in documentary format) and the Best *Storymercial* (one cast in fictional format). Regardless of the format, *infomercials* now "'identify the fact that they are a product pitch three times each half hour—at the beginning, middle and end,' said [Steve] Dworman [the publisher of *Infomercial Marketing*

Report]" (*Los Angeles Daily News*, November 9, 1993). That's really *mersh*. See also *advertising cinema*.

informate *verb*, to extract useful information from the successful performance of tasks; accomplish tasks and translate the results into useful information: "[Information technology] *informates* as well as automates. It 'textualizes' the production process" (*New York Times*, April 21, 1988).

THE STORY: "When the in-forms are mating, can the back-formates be far behind?" asked a Word Watcher in 1988, in a riposte to discussion in my column of *informate*. This verb, pronounced with primary stress on the first syllable, is, like the unexceptionable *automate*, a back-formation. (See also *incent*.) Coined roughly thirty years after the appearance of *automate*, *informate* is the creation of Shoshona Zuboff, a specialist in social psychology and the history of work. The *Times* noted that Zuboff coined the word "for what she finds to be the most far-reaching use of the new technologies: a process of continual learning that companies use to improve products or services and to enhance their production, distribution or marketing. . . . *Informating*—the smoothest way to computerize a workplace—collects data about those tasks to find greater efficiency."

Although *informate*, a creation of the late 1980s, certainly jars the sensibilities of linguistic conservatives, it is formed in exactly the same way as *donate*, a fixture in English since the year 1785. If you can bear the stress, see also *conversate*.

lunch lid *noun*, *slang*, an assurance given to White House journalists that no newsworthy events will occur during their lunch breaks, leaving them free to relinquish the pressroom: "The announcement at the White House that 'the *lunch lid* is on' means reporters are free to go to lunch knowing that war will not be declared while they're eating a corned beef on rye and, in fact, nothing newsworthy will happen until after 3 o'clock" (*New York Times Book Review*, May 11, 1986).

THE STORY: The term *lunch lid* is most probably derived from the turn-of-the-century American idiomatic expression *The lid's off*, which was discussed by William Safire in *Safire's New Political Dictionary* (1993). He gave us the pertinent citation: "'Commissioner of Police McAdoo,' wrote the *Philadelphia Public Ledger* in 1904, '. . . has taken frequent occasions to deny that the "lid" was off*, to use the slang definition of a lax administration.'" There it meant no-holds-barred activity, Safire said.

Yet another influence may be the American idiom *Put the lid on*, traceable at least to 1935. The sentence-idiom *The lid is on* is used by White House staff and the Secret Service to indicate that the president is unavailable and that no earth-shattering events are expected. Both expressions occurred in an August 1993 *Vanity Fair* piece titled "Protecting the president from pizza: how the U.S. Secret Service *puts the 'lid' on* 'Eagle' [the code name for President Clinton]." In the text, it was then stated that "the press would get the word—'*The lid is on*'—and take the low-salaried agents out for drinks." See also *Twinkie*.

media availability *noun*, an opportunity for a person of interest to the press to visit with and talk informally with representatives of the print and electronic media at a predetermined time: "Laura D'Andrea Tyson, chair of President Clinton's Council of Economic Advisors, will participate in a *media availability* at 3 P.M., Wednesday, Feb. 23, in the Music Room on the second floor of the Smith College Alumnae House. . . . Media representatives interested in attending the *availability* should contact the Smith News Office" (press release, Smith College Office of College Relations, February 21, 1994).

THE STORY: *Availability*, whose most commonly used sense is "the quality or state of being available," also has the less often encountered meaning "that which is available; an available person or thing," used in locutions like *We tried to furnish our French farmhouse using local availabilities*. It's idiomatic English in that example, but it does sound rather quaint. This somewhat rare sense goes back to the nineteenth century, these citations from the *Oxford English Dictionary* being typical: "His list of possible *availabilities* in the matrimonial line" (Oliver Wendell Holmes, *The Guardian Angel*, 1867); "Against the gate-post she settled her most substantial *availability*, and exerted it" (Richard D. Blackmore, *Cripps the Carrier*, 1876). Add now to this second sense a third, defined as "an act, instance, or time of being available or accessible to conversation with and questions from the press." Both the usage and the definition follow the pattern established by the American English compound *photo opportunity* and its British English cousin *photo call*.

According to Stacey Schmeidel, director of media relations at Smith, the difference between a *press conference* and a *media availability* is that the person of interest visits informally with the press at an *availability*; at a *press conference*, the person would issue a statement of newsworthiness to be followed by a formal Q&A session.

Media availability in and of itself is not a self-explanatory compound. For instance, in the sentence *Media availability in terms of coverage of the event was nonexistent,* the term means the availability of the media to reach and then cover the event. Therefore, care must be used in employing the compound in sentences.

With respect to *photo opportunity,* a much older compound (William Safire said that it goes back to a Ron Ziegler coinage during the Nixon administration), that term has now been clipped through long-term use to *photo op.* Will we ever get *media av?*

mersh *adjective, slang,* financially profitable: "If nothing else, 'Nick and Hillary' is not likely to be accused of being *mersh*" (*New York Times,* April 20, 1989).

THE STORY: This word, which can also be used as a noun meaning "a hit," is an example of the items in the lexicons of specialized languages, in this case, the in-language of Madison Avenue. It is particularly interesting from the viewpoint of linguistic process: *mersh* is a respelling representing the pronunciation of the second syllable of the word *commercial,* which, in the process, underwent clipping. In the *Times* citation, the reference is to an ailing television series from 1989.

The word also appeared as part of the title on the jacket of a punk-music album by the Minutemen, called *Project: MERSH.* The jacket depicted three record-company executives anguishing over the group's sales figures, with one of them exclaiming, "I got it! We'll have them write hit songs." For a discussion of another in-language word, this one indigenous to the New York garment industry, see also *garmento.*

muffin-choker *noun, slang,* a bizarre news story: "It's the end of the year, time to clear the computer of . . . *muffin-chokers,* as they're called in the newsroom" (*Boston Globe,* December 28, 1990).

THE STORY: This piece of journalistic slang, undoubtedly derived from a newsperson's early-morning reaction to the unpalatably unbelievable, joins several similar nouns ending in *-er* that have been used in journalism and in literary circles for years: *tearjerker, chiller, cliff-hanger, shocker, snorter, spinetingler, thriller, potboiler,* and *bodice-ripper.*

newszak *noun, slang,* a television entertainment show formatted in the manner of a news broadcast: "Steinem hasn't dimmed her feminist outlook for the sake of the columns or the morning *newszak*" (*New York*, August 25, 1986). "Transmitted by satellite to 128 stations, the flashy, staccato-paced 'Entertainment Tonight' has become the most popular new nonnetwork show on television. It is the latest example of a growing trend in television to use a news format for an essentially entertainment program, an amalgam that has been characterized in the industry as *newszak*" (*New York Times*, January 18, 1983).

THE STORY: *Newszak* is, of course, a blend of *news* and the *-zak* of the trademark *Muzak*. *Talkzak* is similarly formed: "The endless *talkzak* at the Knesset is a perfect counterpoint to the inescapable *muzak* that pollutes our daily lives" (*Jerusalem Post*, June 29, 1990).

Muzak goes back to 1938. It was formed from *Kodak*, then the best-known trade name, and *music*, with alteration of the *s* to *z*. So far, neither *newszak* nor *talkzak* has gained enough currency to warrant entry in most dictionaries. They may, however, establish themselves over time, in the manner of *newspeak* (thank you, George Orwell) and *factoid* (thank you, Norman Mailer).

numeronym *noun*, a telephone number that spells a word or words, typically the name of a product, company, or service: "It's not as easy as you would think, creating *numeronyms*. If there's a one or a zero in the number, you're out of luck" (*New York Times*, February 5, 1989).

THE STORY: According to this *Times* story titled "1-800-BAD-NEWS," the novelist Eric Kraft coined the word *numeronym*. It is formed of *numero-* ("number") plus the suffix *-onym* ("word; name"), the suffix coming from the Latin *-onymum*, from the Greek *-ōnumon*, from *onuma*, "name."

Dictionaries got into the *numeronymous* game back in 1992, when Sandra Goroff-Mailly, the publicity director of *The American Heritage Dictionary, Third Edition*'s launch, created *1-800-NEW-WORD* as part of the public relations campaign. Callers dialed the *numeronym* and listened to one of sixteen scripts about matters of language narrated by actor Tony Randall. The creators of *numeronyms* use an existing set of digits or a new array of them chosen in advance to fit letters into messages.

A similar process is in play in the creation of vanity-license-plate messages. For example, Judge Lance A. Ito of the O. J. Simpson case once, as a young lawyer, had "7 BOZOS" on his license plate (the reference was, it is said, to the California Supreme Court). Registries of motor vehicles, however, have to be on watch for potentially offensive messages. Consider, for example, one that slipped through the cracks in Virginia. According to a November 3, 1993, *Washington Post* story, GOVT SUX was the message on the license plate of a 1988 Toyota Land Cruiser. Even though the owner claimed a positive response from other motorists (thumbs-up signs, grins, waves, and so on), the Virginia Department of Motor Vehicles canceled the plates it had issued allegedly through "human error." Of course, the owner sued. During the course of the litigation, it was revealed that other numeronyms also on the hit list were WORK SUX, VA SUX, and I95 SUX. Language is personal and highly subjective, a truism also revealed in the same litigation: Virginia would accept BREAST if the applicant could prove convincingly that the reference was to chickens, not humans; THIGH, however, would be unacceptable. The legal bottom line in this, the case of "A Tag NOT2B4GOT-TEN," in the numeronymy of the *Washington Post*, was that the motorist won. A federal judge ruled in spring 1994 that criticism of the government is protected speech. The owner's lawyer did suggest, however, that his client obtain yet another set of plates, these reading "1ST AMEN." Amen, brother.

paper curtain *noun*, a complex of bureaucratic obstacles, such as documentation and regulations, that serves to conceal the true nature of an entity or operation or that obstructs free communication: "Fortunately, there are ways for well-informed investors to at least glimpse what lies behind the *paper curtains*. Banks are required to publish vast numbers, and from these it is possible to piece together a fair estimate of how sound or unsound . . . an individual bank is" (*Forbes*, July 1, 1975).

THE STORY: *Paper curtain*, also used in the eighties in reference to censorship in South Africa, goes back at least to 1960, evidenced by these remarks by presidential speechwriter Richard Goodwin, speaking on the subject of getting a candidate's views directly to the voters in a way other than by the print media: "In 1960 there was very little use of commercials [in the campaign], but television decided the election. I remember [John F.] Kennedy saying that television is the only way we can break through the *paper curtain*, the only way to get people to hear what we are saying" (*Life*, September 1988).

Twenty years later, the late president's brother, U.S. senator Edward M. Kennedy, used the very same term, but with a different meaning, during his own short-lived presidential campaign. In a speech criticizing Jimmy Carter's proposal to revive draft registration as a response to the Soviet invasion of Afghanistan, Kennedy said, "I oppose registration when it only means reams of computer printouts that would be a *paper curtain* against Soviet troops" (*Facts on File News Digest*, February 1, 1980).

The development of *paper curtain*—especially as used by John F. Kennedy—is doubtless influenced by analogy with *Iron Curtain* and *Bamboo Curtain*, both of which were well-established terms during the Cold War, the former going back as far as eighteenth-century France, where it was used to mean a fireproof curtain for theaters. (Other such terms are *sand curtain*, relating to Arab-Israel relations; *marble curtain*, Hubert Humphrey's term denoting press and government relations; *cobweb curtain*, a reference to press relations with Buckingham Palace; *lace curtain*, an inadvertent pun created by *Pravda* years ago with respect to the closure of New England to Soviet tourists; *Jim Crow curtain*, coined by Adam Clayton Powell; *nylon curtain*, a reference to corporate communications at E. I. du Pont; *Caribbean curtain*, used by the *Washington Post* in 1993 in an editorial referring to the Clinton administration's use of the U.S. Navy and Coast Guard off Haiti; *Blue Curtain*, used to denote the impenetrably tight-knit fraternity of U.S. Air Force senior generals; and *red-tape curtain*, used to describe the bureaucratic layers in Vietnam that serve to slow the development of international trade with that nation.)

Since its first use, *paper curtain* has continued in use in various contexts, among them references to forged bona fides and the use of paperwork to obstruct immigration into the United States of groups deemed undesirable. When Senator Edward Kennedy used the term, he, perhaps, was influenced also by the expression *paper tiger*, for a *paper curtain* of draft registration printouts at the time of the Afghanistan incursion would have been nothing more than a high-tech, bureaucratic bluff.

pipe a quote (*or* **a story**) *idiom*, to fabricate (a quotation or news story). Used even if the gist of what a person has said is reflected in the text: "Dr. Jeffrey M. Masson, a psychoanalyst, . . . accused Janet Malcolm, a writer for *The New Yorker*, of *piping quotes* that were damaging to his reputation" (*New York Times*, January 20, 1991).

THE STORY: The ultimate origin of *pipe a quote*, an idiom long in use within the Fourth Estate, is obscure. An obvious immediate influence might be the verb sense of *pipe*, "to utter shrilly," or the same word in its American-slang senses, defined variously by Harold Wentworth and Stuart Berg Flexner in their *Dictionary of American Slang* as "to send a message; to give information; talk or tell." Its most recent connection seems to lie with the modern communications sense of *pipe*, "to transmit sound; distribute a signal," so defined by Richard Weiner in *Webster's New World Dictionary of Media and Communications*. Weiner notes that "a recent slang use of *to pipe* is *to fake*, as with a rare journalist who *pipes a story* by making up characters or events." He went on to define a *pipe artist* as "a journalist who makes up quotations."

An element of hucksterism in the mystery shrouding the idiom was evident early on. A plausible origin, yet unproved, is that the idiom is circus argot, suggested by this passage from H. L. Mencken's *Supplement Two* of *The American Language*: "The street peddlers [following traveling shows], who call themselves *pitchmen*, frequently undertake independent tours, and not a few of them have covered the whole country. Their trade journal is the *Billboard* (Cincinnati), which also caters to all other outdoor showmen, and every week they contribute to it what they call *pipes*, *i.e.*, news reports from the field, describing business conditions and telling of the movements of pitchmen. . . . *To cut up pipes* is to gossip or boast."

Interestingly, a slang sense of *pipe* specific to cards points even more strongly to the idea of dishonesty inherent in the journalistic idiom at issue, though it seems to have very little direct bearing on that idiom from the semantic standpoint. The gerund *piping* is defined by Thomas L. Clark in his *Dictionary of Gambling and Gaming* as "a cheating method in which an observer of the game signals a confederate as to the value of cards held by an opponent," a sense traceable to another verb sense of *pipe*, "to watch," attested by the *Oxford English Dictionary* to as early as the year 1846.

schmooseoisie *noun*, the expanding class of people in the United States who make a living by talk, as on radio or television: "'Oprah's a member of the *schmooseoisie*. . . . Government is all *schmooseiocrats* taking trillions and giving back words'" (Paul Lewis, interview, *Boston Globe*, October 14, 1992).

THE STORY: Boston College English professor Paul Lewis, the coiner of *Frankenfood*, has given our language yet another colorful word, *schmooseoisie*, a double foreign borrowing from Yiddish and French, the two elements from the two languages having coalesced to form a blend. He coined it especially for *Globe* reporter Mark Muro during the interview cited above. Lewis, who said at that time that the *schmooseoisie* include "such traditional groups as teachers and therapists," added in a January 28, 1994, telephone interview with me that the word also encompasses those people who spend their lives calling in to talk radio. He believes that many members of the U.S. middle class are fixated on talking, and he uses the escalation in the popularity of phone sex as just one example.

Facts and figures of the radio broadcast industry validate the professor's assertions: News/Talk (N/T) captured, by the beginning of the first quarter of 1994, the largest share of total radio listeners of any format in the Top 25 markets. N/T also captured the biggest share of listeners aged twenty-five to fifty-four in the Top 25, powered, according to *Radio & Records*, by N/T vitality in listeners aged thirty-five to fifty-four. What is more, N/T attracts large numbers of highly educated, affluent listeners. More than 34.8 percent, or one third, of the N/T listenership have college degrees.

But who are some of the *schmooseoisie*, aside from Oprah? People like Al Gore, Bill Clinton, Janet Reno, and David Gergen. Excluded would be people like Michael Kinsley and Pat Buchanan, who have been dubbed *screaming heads* by Beltway pundits.

Spinnish *noun*, facile, ostensibly neutral language used to manipulate, slant, manage, or otherwise alter the public's perception of an event, a set of circumstances, or an opponent's record in favor of the speaker or of the speaker's political position or candidate of support: "He is speaking in a language that is most effective when those being addressed do not know what language is being spoken. It is the international language of political *Spinnish*. In fact, more than just a language, it is a camouflanguage" (Mark Alan Stamaty, "Washingtoon," *Village Voice*, August 18, 1988).

THE STORY: Lexicographers regularly read and mark the dialogue of cartoons. In this one, I found an intriguing spin on the now familiar noun sense of that word, denoting the activities of the spin doctors. Stamaty's dialogue went on thus: "Occasionally, someone like . . . a campaign manager speaks so much *Spinnish* that he completely forgets how to speak English." Here I spy a startling, though unproven, connection between *Spinnish* and the sense of *English* defined as "the *spin* given to a [billiards] ball by striking it on one side and releasing it with a sharp twist."

trawler *noun*, *slang*, a television viewer who uses a remote control to flip from broadcast to broadcast, sampling many programs but settling on few if any. Also called *channel surfer*: "*Trawlers*. One of the most-feared new phenomena in broadcasting" (*Columbia Journalism Review*, March/April 1992). "*Channel Surfers!* Catch the Big One: Tele-Communications Inc. announced this week it will offer 500 cable stations to its subscribers by 1994" (*Washington Post*, December 5, 1992).

THE STORY: This term and the activity it denotes may be obsolete by the end of the nineties or before, if John Sculley's predictions in the *Boston Sunday Globe Magazine* of March 1, 1992, are to be believed. Asked if he thought the age of *channel surfing* would end when 400–500 channel options open up, he replied: "It won't be very enjoyable to try to race through them all to see what's on. You're going to have to preselect for some of those channels." He added that multiple channels will be used at the same time to deliver a single program, such as a sports program viewable from many different angles, a concept that is markedly different from today's programming realities.

At the moment, however, *trawling* or *surfing* by inveterate *couch commanders* still presents some disturbing problems relating to public policy and marketing. During the Gulf War, for instance, commercial broadcasters noted with dismay that enormous segments of viewership would switch to CNN from the Big Three (CBS, ABC, NBC) just when a commercial break would occur: these *couch commanders* want, at all cost, to avoid even one second of advertising. *Trawling* is also disturbing in terms of public attention given to the serious issues facing today's society. Will the average viewer have the patience or interest to focus on programs addressing problems such as the economy, health care, violence, lawlessness, and the homeless when it is so easy and inviting to press a button and make the Whole Messy World Go Away?

As Howard Kurtz put it in the June 10, 1993, *Washington Post*: "At bottom, there is this: Can a complicated public issue be intelligently debated in today's sound-bite culture, where partisans must play their roles and score their rapid-fire points—*Anita Hill lied! No, Anita Hill was victimized!*—before the audience starts *channel-surfing?*" See also *elevator surfing, graze, shoulder surfing.*

Twinkie *trademark,* used figuratively to denote a television news anchor whose chief asset is a pleasing physical appearance as opposed to newsgathering experience and proven broadcast talent: "In the world of television news, *Twinkies* are the model-like anchormen and -women who read the news. But throughout her colorful broadcasting career, the iconoclastic [Linda] Ellerbee has never been called a *Twinkie*" (*US*, June 16, 1986). "In the TV news business the cute ones are called *Twinkies*. This is not a term of endearment; it is used to describe anchors whose most discernible talent is a pretty face" (*Washington Post*, October 18, 1983).

THE STORY: The proprietors of trademarks become understandably exercised when their carefully protected marks take on separate linguistic lives through figurative extensions. In the case of *Twinkie*, the mark has taken on pejorative meanings transcending the newsroom and moving into the courtroom.

Twinkie defense goes back to a 1979 murder trial in which Dan White confessed to the killings of San Francisco supervisor Harvey Milk and Mayor George Moscone, but asserted that his overconsumption of the sweet junk food had elevated his blood-sugar level to the extent that he had suffered diminished capacity at the time of the 1978 slayings. Though the jury found the defendant guilty of manslaughter, it did give consideration to his excuse. "That marked a change," wrote Chip Rowe in "The Age of Innocents" (*Playboy*, June 1994). "No longer was this simple homicide: It was killing with a qualifier, murder with a note from Mom. Since then, the change has accelerated. Defense arguments these days start with extenuating circumstances before spinning wildly out from there."

In these pejorative usages, *Twinkie* undergoes the same process experienced by other food trade names such as *Pablum* and *Oreo*. *Pablum* has spawned the entirely generic *pablum*, defined as "trite, insipid speech, conceptualization, or writing." *Oreo* is used pejoratively by some African Americans with respect to one whose values and behavior mimic those of the white community.

warmedy *noun*, a television comedy characterized by warmhearted, traditional family relationships among wholesome characters: "NBC demanded that the series be turned into another Eight Is Enough, a somewhat sappy but successful *warmedy*" (*Fortune*, December 31, 1979).

THE STORY: Warmedy is a B.M.B. (Before Murphy Brown) entertainment blend, formed, of course, from *warm*hearted and com*edy*. It joins other showbiz blends like *biopic*, *infotainment*, *simulcast*, *narrowcast*, *faction*, *docudrama*, and the trademark *Cassingle*, used since June 1982 as a proprietary name by International Records Syndicate. "Prince's 'Sign of the Times' and Bryan Adams' 'Heat of the Night' are the beginnings of what retailers concede is another ripple in the new wave—the 'cassette single.' . . . Industry pressure is pushing for the 'cassette single' moniker, but look for it to be shortened to '*cassingle*' by consumers who don't care that IRS Records has copyrighted that name," read a March 25, 1987, *Washington Post* citation.

Cassingle, obviously a blend of *cassette* and *single*, emerged in the early 1980s when the cassette boom was still in its initial stages. The popularity of cassettes was increased by the proliferation of the Sony Walkman and similar compact cassette players. At the same time, sales of 45 rpm records and LPs began their dramatic downward spiral to oblivion, though today the noun *record* is still used by many in the music business, with a new meaning: "compact disk." See also *infomercial, newszak.*

9

Word Perfect in the Nineties:
Hi-Tech, Hi-Sci

aerogel

agrimation

appeasement engineer

black mayonnaise

compunications

criticality 1

Deep Vision

digital money

Divorceware

elephant (*adjective*)

Exxon

fuzzy elevator

ghost net

glowboy

Goodyear

liger

modem pilot

morph

nacul

passion pop

Permaprose

quux

rockplow

teledildonics

terraform

thermagation

trojan horse

urban forest

virtual office

vog

WYSIWYG

Xeriscape

Science . . . cannot exist on the basis of a treaty of strict
nonaggression with the rest of society; from either side,
there is no defensible frontier.
—Don K. Price, *Government and Science*

Price penned those thoughts forty-one years ago. Even though the
metaphors recall the Cold War, the thoughts behind the words have been
validated by the crossover in the eighties and nineties of high technology
from the labs into business into law into entertainment into our most private
of private lives. Some of the words discussed in this chapter are totemic of
that permeation of undefendable frontiers: *virtual office*, *Divorceware*, *morph*,
Deep Vision, and *teledildonics*. From *compunications* and *agrimation* to *thermagation*—the hi-tech extermination of termites—the language is a leading indicator of the digitalization of society, right down to the advent in the
nineties of *digital money*.

It is not remarkable, then, that about half the words in chapter 9 are dedicated to high technology. In studying them as a group, the lexicographer acts
like the archaeologist in that he or she sifts through the words of various
worlds and tries to find out where everyone else has been. During this
process of "immediate archaeology," certain conclusions may be drawn. One
of them is that in trying to get beyond the now, we verge upon a big step beyond the screen into virtuality, carrying with us all the positive and negative
baggage of our own reality. Consider what happened to old friend Alice, in a
different time.

"How would you like to live in the Looking-Glass House?" Alice asked her kitten in *Through the Looking-Glass*. "I'll tell you . . . my ideas about Looking-Glass House," said she. "First, there's the room you can see through the glass—that's just the same as our drawing-room, only things go the other way. . . . The books are something like our books, only the words go the wrong way. . . ."

And so it goes when we look not at, but *through*, the screen into the world of cyberspace, or cyberland, which encompasses the Information Superhighway predicted by the coiner of *compunications* and a sector along that highway, the *virtual office*. The language beyond the screen is one of the fastest-proliferating sublexicons of twenty-first-century English. Once merely the private lingua franca of nerds and hackers, cyberEnglish—technical in meaning but with a deceptively ordinary-sounding overlay—has, in the past few years, become deprivatized: its expressions are fast becoming constants in mainstream English as a direct result of the new mass access to the nets.

In creating mass access to cyberspace and in developing the infrastructure of the Information Superhighway—complete with the visitor centers, shopping malls, and town squares advertised in 1994 by CompuServe, for example—we have, in effect, established a Second National Life, one in which all or most of the intellectual transactions of traditional, paper-bound life—even paper money and coin, now called in England *digital money*—can and do occur electronically with little or no face-to-face contact, often under screen names echoing the pseudonym *Lewis Carroll*. Further, in a development worthy of the imagination of an Orwell or a Koestler, anonymous net managers monitor the transactions taking place on the electronic interstate and international corridors of the nets. The anonymous monitoring the pseudonymous. How very nineties.

But monitoring and control are necessary, it seems. Aside from all manner of professional activities carried on in cyberspace, the people and organizations operating there bring with them the same array of talents, goals, problems, personal agendas, quirks, antics, and criminal intent or acts that are to be found in the physical workplace and in the home. Herein lies the danger of "going the wrong way." The impersonality of cyberspace offers some communicators much greater freedom of action and expression in a virtual world devoid, to some extent, of controls, the net managers notwithstanding. Using a screen name, you can stroll the malls, the highways, the byways, and the back alleys of cyberspace, entering various communities, being whoever you want to be (cross-dressing, too, for that matter), and chatting with others with the same interests, agendas, or proclivities. In terms of business, effective control and management of the transactions taking place in the virtual marketplace will be *the* major challenge facing decision-makers in the nineties and beyond. In terms of personal privacy and freedom of speech, the anonymity of information management and monitoring has serious implications.

Jim Manzi, the chairman and CEO of Lotus Development Corporation, has said that "technology . . . has a way of taking unexpected turns" (*New York Times*, February 6, 1994). Indeed it has: when we entered the Space Age in the late 1950s, it was predicted with some assurance that the second dimension of national life would be created in outer space, replete with space shuttles and permanent, crewed space stations. Instead, the very technology so essential to the success of an exploratory space program has created this Second National Life, not in outer space but in an "intermediate space" in which those empowered with access can operate instantly and globally.

Those empowerees—the members of a rather exclusive, and, yes, potentially exclusionary, class of people—could conceivably spend most of their working and playing hours on-screen—not a healthy scenario, as we saw in the late 1980s with the so-called Dungeons & Dragons syndrome that allegedly affected some children who played certain video games to such an extent that they lost touch with reality and became prisoners of virtuality. Consider *teledildonics*, also called *cybersex* and *virtual sex*. The terms convey the message.

In *Murder in the Cathedral*, T. S. Eliot wrote that "human kind cannot bear very much reality." If that be so, how much *virtuality* can human beings bear without becoming dissociated from reality, when the two become compressed into work and private life? This is the question posed by the words in the chapter having to do with the world of *trojan horses*, *quuxes*, and all the rest. And this is the question to be pondered by all of us at the dawn of the next century.

While computer science has been trying to move us beyond the now, ecology has been trying to preserve what was here before we arrived. That's the second major trend in nonmedical science that, through some of its key words, dominates chapter 9. Stewart Udall expressed the import of the ecological problems facing earth when he said in 1970 that "over the long haul of life on this planet, it is the ecologists, and not the bookkeepers of business, who are the ultimate accountants."

And when Jacques Cousteau told Congress a year later that "the sea is the universal sewer," he must have had in mind things such as *black mayonnaise* and *ghost nets*—things that so captured the national consciousness that the words denoting them eventually gained entry in some dictionaries well after they had been defined in "Word Watch."

This "chemical barrage [that] has been hurled against the fabric of life," a weapon "as crude . . . as a cave man's club," as Rachel Carson so aptly put it in *Silent Spring*, is captured in the verbed form of the trademark *Exxon*, a form that defies an expensive linguist-driven corporate program to create a name devoid of intrinsic meaning.

On the ecological upside, there are words like *nacul*, a genre of environmentally compatible architecture; *Permaprose*, a building material that redefines recycling; *urban forest*, not a contradiction in terms but an urban ecological asset finally meriting serious preservation attention; and *Xeriscape*, the cultivation of a dry environment.

But in all, if one word were to be chosen from the chapter 9 list that might evoke memories of an era, it would have to be *criticality 1*. That word appeared in my column during the first year of the column's life and it, like *grassy knollism*, is a traumatic flashback word, one that echoes with John Glenn's memorable statement of June 28, 1986: "This is a day we have managed to avoid for a quarter of a century." When the explosion of the *Challenger* spacecraft occurred, it was viewed in real time on the television screens of millions. *Criticality 1*, then, is itself a symbol of what can go wrong in a high-tech world. And the term is symbolic of the instancy of communications discussed at length in the preceding chapter. Yes, the boundaries have become irretrievably blurred; we have *morphed* into a Second National Life; and technology does have a way of surprising us. It is we who will have to manage it.

aerogel *noun*, an extremely lightweight, transparent, highly porous solid substance, one of the lightest known solids, with a density as low as 5 mg/cu cm, consisting of tiny spheres of bonded silicon and oxygen atoms joined into long strands randomly linked to one another with air pockets between the strands. Also called *frozen smoke*; *San Francisco fog*: "After more than 50 years in the laboratory, a class of materials known as *aerogels* is beginning to make its ghostly presence felt" (*The Economist*, October 8, 1988). "Check out silica *aerogel*. . . . It . . . may have applications in insulation or rocket fuel storage" (*Inside R&D*, January 31, 1990).

THE STORY: *Aerogel*, developed at the Lawrence Livermore National Laboratory, in California, is ten times lighter than any solid matter previously weighed. In its lightest form, it has the density that would result "if a teaspoon of water were to be dispersed uniformly throughout a volume of more than one gallon" (*New York Times*, March 6, 1990). According to the February 2, 1990, issue of the (London) *Daily Telegraph*, "NASA, which supported the work, plans to use the gel to trap cosmic particles in space. In an experiment on one of the next space shuttle flights, it will be ejected into space to collect micrometeoroids and very fine debris found in the tails of comets. The material is ideal for the experiments because it is so light that the tiny particles will not be burned up on impact. Because it is extremely pure, scientists will be able to examine the cosmic dust for carbon, the foundation of all life, without interference." See also *frozen rope*.

agrimation *noun*, automated farming, especially the use of supersmart robots to perform heretofore manual operations such as selecting and picking fruit and vegetables and milking cows—operations requiring acute vision, dexterity, and the ability to make choices: "A small band of researchers at a score of universities and companies around the world . . . are intent on putting robots down on the farm. Tireless and versatile, these mechanical migrants will do everything from harvesting artichokes to milking cows. The researchers have coined a new word for the move to automated farming: *agrimation.* . . . What makes *agrimation* feasible is a new generation of robot 'eyes'" (*Business Week*, September 8, 1986).

THE STORY: This quotation was a first citation for the word *agrimation* in a nontechnical publication, a factor closely watched by lexicographers when deciding whether or not a word is starting to enter the general parlance. *Agrimation* gained entry in the third edition of *The American Heritage Dictionary of the English Language*, published in 1992, on the basis of continuing occurrences in general and technical sources. The word, which also appeared in the February 25, 1985, issue of *ElectronicsWeek* with reference to "the world's first agricultural automation conference, *Agrimation I*," is a blend of the *agri-* in *agriculture* and the *-mation* in *automation*. This coinage signaled, at the time, the development and dissemination of still another high-tech language.

Two other entrants into that language were *video eyes*—the electronic eyes enabling a robot to perform delicate tasks, such as the picking of peaches, in varying degrees of light and shade; and *cowbot*—a robot capable of feeding a dairy herd, attaching and detaching milking equipment, and then cleaning the equipment. Cowhands even today need not fear outplacement, however: engineers have not yet developed *cowbots* capable of wrestling 800-pound steers to the ground for branding.

appeasement engineer *noun, slang,* an ineffective, inefficient, usually inexperienced and unknowledgeable computer field-service technician: "Because he's NEW and ALONE, he's what you call an *appeasement engineer,* the new guy they send so they respond within the 4 hour guaranteed response period. . . . Your average *appeasement engineer* is about as clued-up on computers as the average . . . 'hacker' is about B.O., and their main job is to make sure the power plug is in and switched on, then call back to the office for 'PARTS'" (Internet message, February 3, 1994).

THE STORY: No book on the language of the nineties would be au courant without a message from one of the on-line nets used as citational evidence in word development. This medium, and the genre it has spawned—*digital history*—is dominated by the *digerati.* Of course, the coiner of *appeasement engineer* is a member of this elite. The coiner is called the "Bastard Operator from Hell" on the full transmit, and is also known as "a net-legend."

A net-legend, that person is: early on in the message, the writer related a feeling of frustrated boredom in an office setting. To relieve the ennui, "[The person gets] some iron filings and pour[s] them into the back of [the] Terminal until it *fizzes out* . . . , then call[s] [the] maintenance contractors and log[s] a fault on the device." That's when the *appeasement engineer* enters, stage right. (Do these two deserve each other, or what?)

These types of documents in their totality constitute a new writing genre—a kind of *digital history,* as opposed to an *oral history*—a genre that records the views and mind-cultures of the inhabitants of cyberspace. These writings, IMHO (in my humble opinion), share certain identifying characteristics, regardless of subject matter: prolific use of abbreviations, acronyms, and jargon; loose, open-ended sentence structure and a certain laxness of syntax overall; misspellings and typos; a certain rambling stream-of-consciousness style in many instances; and more often than not, a bit of the snide, a bit of Attitude. Here, people can talk and write at the same time. On the nets, writers' efforts are not airbrushed by editors, so there is a certain unfinishedness to their pieces. When will we have the first CyberWriters' Awards for general excellence?

black mayonnaise *noun*, toxic sludge found on the bottoms of harbors, bays, oceans, and seas, formed of undecayed sediment, sewerage, and petrochemical waste, often extending for miles: "Dredging Baltimore Harbor to depths of 115 ft. has spurred measures to avoid stirring up harmful sediments. There's a 'whole list of chemicals on the bottom,' says . . . project manager Kenneth D. Merrill. The top 10 ft. of harbor material, '*black mayonnaise*,' will take the longest time to consolidate; the rest is better, sandy soil, he says" (*Engineering News-Record*, June 4, 1981).

THE STORY: Citations for *black mayonnaise* go back at least to 1978, with the most graphic one having appeared in the August 1, 1988, issue of *Newsweek*: "What is happening underwater . . . is not for the squeamish. Scuba divers talk of swimming through clouds of toilet paper and half-dissolved feces, of bay bottoms covered by a . . . sediment . . . appropriately known as '*black mayonnaise*.'" Our earliest evidence indicates that this form of sludge received its name from fishers and oceanographers.

Another interesting compound in this same lexicon is *toxic tort*, referring to environmental lawsuits: "The unique problem of *toxic torts* and their possible solutions currently are being studied by task forces appointed by . . . the National Association of Manufacturers, the Chemical Manufacturers Association, and the American Petroleum Institute" (*Legal Times*, January 17, 1983).

compunications *noun*, a coupling of the technologies for transmission and manipulation of information; the data and other information in such a system; the system itself or a network of such systems: "The notion of '*compunications*' was central to a fascinating seminar at the Aspen Institute" (*Washington Post*, September 15, 1986).

THE STORY: *Compunications*, a blend of *communications* and *computing*, was coined by Harvard professor Anthony G. Oettinger. Daniel Bell also used the word (which was deemed by *Washington Post* reporter T. R. Reid "a great new buzzword") in the foreword of his *Coming of Post-Industrial Society* (1976), where he focused on the major challenges facing this society: "The major problem . . . will be the development of an appropriate 'infrastructure' for the developing *compunications* networks . . . of digital information technologies that will tie the post-industrial society together." Bell went on to mention the infrastructures already in place—transportation, energy, and telecommunications. He then stated that "with the explosive growth of computers and terminals for data . . . and the rapid decrease in the costs of computation and information storage, the question of hitching together the varied ways information is transmitted . . . becomes a major issue of economic and social policy."

In 1986, the *Washington Post* reporter predicted "technical marriage[s]" between communicating tools and companies. Now consider these statements from the February 8, 1993, issue of *Time*: "Cyberpunk culture is likely to get a boost from, of all things, the Clinton-Gore Administration, because of a shared interest in what the new regime calls America's *'data highways'* and what the cyberpunks call *cyberspace.* Both terms describe the globe-circling, interconnected telephone network that is the conduit for billions of voice, fax, and computer-to-computer communications. The incoming Administration is focused on the wiring, and it has made strengthening the network's high-speed data links a priority."

Watching this progression of citations is the act of watching ideas take form in reality, Virtual Reality, even. Here we see a word, *compunications*, which denotes today's electronic networks, not sustain the wide use required to gain dictionary entry. Someday it will be looked at as a bit of lexical ephemera, perhaps, but it will always be remembered by those who study the history of the data highways as we know them and as they will be in the twenty-first century. Interested *compunicators* may wish to see also *virtual office.*

criticality 1 *noun,* an item of hardware or a system on a spacecraft, or on the rocket launching the spacecraft, for which there is no backup, the loss or failure of which will result in a catastrophic accident involving loss of crew, craft, and payload: "NASA and the commission have said the rubber O-ring seals in the booster rockets must be redesigned before another shuttle is launched. But these seals represent just one item on a list of about 900 'critical,' or *criticality 1* items, meaning they have no backups in case of failure, and whose failure would cause a catastrophic accident" (*Boston Globe,* March 10, 1986).

THE STORY: The word *criticality,* virtually unused in the general parlance before the space shuttle *Challenger* crash, is not new to English at all. Formed on the adjective *critical* plus the suffix *-ity,* the term was recorded for the first time in the year 1756 in the *Oxford English Dictionary* in a quotation from Thomas Gray, to wit: "I hope to despatch you a packet of my *criticalities* entire." In this context and at that time, the word simply meant "a critical remark; a criticism." In its early uses, the word also meant "the quality or state of being critical" and "a moment of crisis."

But by the late 1940s and the early 1950s, *criticality* had taken on an entirely new, technical sense, this one being "a critical condition," specifically that of fissionable material, illustrated in this citation from the December 14, 1980, issue of the *New York Times Magazine*: "It entails expertise in high explosives, *criticality* (bringing the nuclear material to the point of chain reaction), detonation systems and electromechanisms that are complex and potentially very dangerous."

More than 200 years after its first recorded appearance in English, *criticality* acquired a fourth meaning, one that caused the term to become a household word after millions of viewers watched in horror the television coverage of the *Challenger* disaster.

Deep Vision *trademark*, used for three-dimensional television technology, achieved without the employment of multiple cameras and special glasses: "Throw away the silly glasses. You won't need them for *Deep Vision*—the latest in 3-D TV" (*USA Today*, May 31, 1990). "In a new version of *Ben Hur*, the hero's chariot practically leaps off the TV screen. And when Charlton Heston's Moses parts the Red Sea, it looks miles wide. The secret: a new type of three-dimensional television called *Deep Vision*" (*Business Week*, June 18, 1990).

THE STORY: A small British company called Delta Group, consisting of a few postgraduate scientists from the Department of Physics, Imperial College, London, and some filmmakers developed this brain-interactive technology, which works like this, according to a Reuters story dated May 30, 1990: "*Deep Vision* makes a digital version of a film and inserts electronic cues that send slightly different images to each eye. When played through a decoder, it appears three-dimensional no matter what angle or distance the viewer is from the set." James Asheby, the inventor, and founder of the Covent Garden company Delta Group, said that the internationally patented *Deep Vision* should be inexpensive to produce, can be applied to any videotape or image—black or white—and should be useful in nonentertainment applications as well, such as medical training or military simulation.

digital money *noun*, cash that is transferred electronically via a cash card and terminal/modem, used instead of paper money and coins in all financial transactions: "In England, starting next year [1995], something called the Mondex system—*digital money*—is going to get a trial run. . . . *Digital money* is too grim not to become a terrific success. And when it does, it will threaten with extinction the pyramids with eyes on top of them, national mottoes, pictures of Presidents and queens and the delicate engraving of fine lines to stop counterfeiters" (*New York Times Magazine*, March 6, 1994).

THE STORY: In the past fourteen years, the noun *plastic* has taken on a new sense, that being "credit cards." Now comes *digital money*, one more step through the looking glass into the world of virtual reality. The *Times Magazine* pointed out that the British Mondex card works like the Metrocard now used to access the New York City subway system, a card that is supposed to have put the *token suckers* at a distinct disadvantage if not out of business. The Mondex card, like the Metrocard, stores cash. The card is worth exactly what the customer pays for it, and, when it is used at a special terminal, as in a store or elsewhere, the desired amount is deducted, withdrawn, transferred, or deposited—via phone hook-up.

The new *digerati*, the global users of the on-line networks, will, no doubt, find *digital money* anything but "grim." They are already engaging in all manner of on-line social and intellectual transactions on the Information Superhighway: "Some 20 million people worldwide use the Net, . . . a 'data grazing ground for budding *digerati*,' as [J. C.] Herz terms it" (*Publishers Weekly*, May 16, 1994). Herz uses the term *digital suburbia* to denote part of this Superhighway, of which she calls CompuServe "a subdivision." *Digerati*, used by Herz in her 1995 book *Surfing the Internet*, joins several others in a small set: *literati*, *glitterati*, *illiterati*, and *vulgarati*. See also *virtual office*.

Divorceware *trademark*, used for computer software intended for couples in do-it-yourself divorces: "'*Divorceware*' provides forms and instructions for everything from a property settlement to custody arrangements" (Lynchburg, Va., *News & Daily Advance*, April 5, 1992).

THE STORY: Before getting the *divorce jewelry* and the *divorce frame*, splitting couples need *Divorceware*. It was developed by Springfield, Virginia, engineer and software systems designer Howard Whetzel, who learned by experience that divorce is, by and large, a matter of reaching an agreement and filing court papers—steps that can be taken more economically without an attorney. Whetzel said that he coined *Divorceware* in February of 1992. His company, Avenue Software, began selling the $75 IBM-compatible package in March of that year. He said that *Divorceware*, not intended for "fractious" cases, "will work for any situation where the two parties can stay in the same room long enough to work it out." He advises taking the completed documents to an attorney for review. His primary customers to date: attorneys. See also *divorce jewelry*.

elephant *adjective*, of, relating to, or being an oil field or discovery having the potential to produce an enormous yield over time: "Originally, Hibernia was estimated to have reserves of 1.5 billion to 2 billion barrels. Further delineation of the field has knocked these reserves down to 525 million to 800 million barrels—still an *elephant* find in the oil trade" (*Christian Science Monitor*, December 9, 1985). —*noun*, such a field or discovery: "For Oil Industry, That Next '*Elephant*' Proves Elusive: Many searches for new reserves have failed. OPEC could be the beneficiary" (headlines, *New York Times*, March 20, 1994).

THE STORY: "It's not that the major oil companies aren't trying," said the *Times*. "ARCO drilled 13 wells and spent $163 million in Alaska in 1993, but it came up with only modest finds. British Petroleum made a large discovery in 1992 in Colombia, which for a while had the industry anticipating an '*elephant* field,' but that field fell short." This lack of new, immense discoveries could spell for us another oil shortage or, at the very least, higher prices because of renewed economic growth in many nations, itself causing an upswing in the demand for oil. And so the meaning of the adjective and the noun is important to those wanting to be au courant.

Linguistically speaking, *elephant*, as in *elephant field*, parallels similar use in the printing industry of the compound *elephant folio*, "a book or other publication measuring 60 centimeters, or 2 feet, in height." Not only that, the adjective *elephant* joins other established general-use, zoology-derived descriptors such as these: *monster, mammoth, mastodon, dinosaurian, dinotherian,* and, of course, *elephantine*.

Elephantine, a general term, has taken on a meaning specific not to oil drilling and exploration but to computer hackerdom. It denotes programs or systems "that are both conspicuous hogs . . . and exceedingly hairy in source form," says *The Hacker's Dictionary*, edited by Eric Raymond. "An *elephantine* program," the *Dictionary* informs us, "may be functional and even friendly, but (as in the old joke about being in bed with an elephant) it's tough to have around all the time (and, like a pachyderm, difficult to maintain)." The *Dictionary* notes that "in extreme cases, hackers have been known to make trumpeting sounds . . . at the mention of the offending program." See also *birdcage, hippo*.

Exxon *trademark*, used in lowercase as a verb in this citation, meaning to damage, especially by pollution: "Let's hear it for a new verb that, like the oil in the water, truly rises to the occasion: 'Get this rust heap off the reef, mate, before you *exxon* the whole harbor.' 'I'm all thumbs. I tried to change the oil in my car, and I *exxoned* the whole driveway'" (Bill Wilson, Vienna, Va., in a letter to the editor, *Washington Post*, April 28, 1989).

THE STORY: Well, Bill, this isn't the first time a corporate name has been verbed: another name, also formed with two *x*'s, immediately comes to mind—*Xerox*. According to J. B. Davis, coordinator of public affairs at Exxon U.S.A., to whom I wrote concerning your usage, that company began extensive studies in 1966 resulting in adoption of the word *Exxon* in 1972 for nationwide use. Experts in language, statistics, and design studied 10,000 candidate names generated by computer in order to find a replacement for *Esso*. Having narrowed this list to about 200 terms, the research group came up with *Enco* as well as *Exxon*. *Exxon* was finally selected because it was deemed easily recognizable and remembered, the double-*x* combination was regarded as distinctive and readily adaptable to a unique graphic design, and word-association research showed *Exxon* to be superior to the others in connoting the qualities of a progressive company.

Davis went on to say to me in a letter dated February 12, 1990, that "the name *Exxon* has no intrinsic meaning. In fact, besides making sure that everyone could say the word, the researchers took care to ascertain that it did not translate objectionably into another language. (For example, we had learned that the word *Enco* . . . translated into 'stalled car' in the Japanese language.) Linguistic studies were done in 55 of the world's principal languages, and natives of nearly every country in the world were interviewed." See also *Goodyear.*

fuzzy elevator *noun*, a smart elevator, whose computer-driven dispatcher uses artificial intelligence and fuzzy logic—the logic of approximate reasoning—in estimating the number and location of waiting people, the number of people in each car, and the proximity of the cars to various floors, so as to determine where and when an elevator should be assigned, thereby reducing passenger waiting time and controlling overloading and overcrowding, particularly at lunchtime, in high-rise office, hotel, and hospital buildings: "Even though Otis's first working *'fuzzy' elevator* is being installed in a new Japanese hotel, the company sees a big market for the technique in renovations of elevator systems in the United States and elsewhere. . . . Besides Otis, several Japanese companies . . . make *fuzzy elevator* dispatchers" (*New York Times*, September 22, 1993).

THE STORY: Lovers of fuzzy dice will adore this term, which is a media coinage derived by association with the preexisting compound *fuzzy logic*, itself not a contradiction in terms. Sources at Otis Elevator World Headquarters said in a January 26, 1993, telephone interview that insiders there have no generic descriptor for the smart elevator.

The mathematical theory of fuzzy logic has an interesting history, though. It was conceived as far back as 1965 by Lofti Zadeh, a professor of electrical engineering and computer science at the University of California at Berkeley. Fuzzy logic didn't become sexy in American technological circles until very recently; in Japan, however, the idea caught on and caught on fast in a culture driven by high tech for the sake of high tech.

It's easy to understand why the Japanese love fuzzy logic if you understand how fuzzy logic works: rather than enabling a computer to use reasoning based on typical, crisp, yes or no questions, fuzzy-logic software enables a computer to deal with gray-area decisions—the same kinds of decisions that confront the human brain every day.

In terms of elevator management, once the purview of human dispatchers, fuzzy-logic programming tracks human traffic patterns by compiling data relating to the time periods between stops at the same floor, the number of buttons depressed by boarding passengers, and changes in weight loads. The computer analyzes these data, integrates the answers to preprogrammed questions, and then arrives at a consensus decision determining which elevator should be assigned to what floor, and when, for maximum efficiency and speed.

Those readers who have lamented that they should have built elevator commuting time into their arrival, lunch-hour, and departure schedules will be glad to learn that *fuzzy elevators* can reduce the average waiting time by 15 percent, and the longest waiting time by a dramatically bigger factor. A simple scenario makes the point, operationally speaking: A passenger waits on the third floor to take an elevator to ground level. Two elevators are available—an empty one on the twelfth floor, and another on the seventh carrying five passengers. Though the car on 7 would get to 3 sooner using crisp yes/no logic, dispatching it to answer that ground-level call would actually delay the passenger's arrival at ground level, owing to the probability of intermediate stops generated by the five passengers already in the car, and to the crowding factor. Fuzzy logic will therefore send the empty car on 12 to pick up the passenger on 3.

Particularly in Japan, fuzzy-logic controls are to be found in a wide array of devices and machines: in electric rice cookers, in the speed controls of the Sendai subway trains, and even in electric shavers.

ghost net *noun*, an abandoned plastic commercial drift net, or a large fragment of one, that ensnares and kills marine life such as whales, turtles, seabirds, seals, walruses, porpoises, and fish: "Reports have been received . . . of entire nets cast adrift by Japanese fishermen. . . . These *ghost nets* fish around the clock, until they become laden with fish and other animals and sink. The loss of 50,000 fur seals each year is attributed to *ghost nets*" (*Christian Science Monitor*, March 21, 1986).

THE STORY: This relatively new compound is formed in the manner of the familiar *ghost ship*, *ghost town*, and *ghost hand* (in poker), and the less generally familiar *ghost band* (a musical group, especially one specializing in swing, that still bears the name of its deceased leader and continues to perform with a new leader and chiefly new members, in the manner of the Nelson Riddle Orchestra), *ghost rider* (a person who pretends to have been a passenger on a wrecked mass-transit vehicle in order to collect insurance money), *ghost train* (a convict-carrying train that travels only at night), *ghost surgery* (surgery performed by a physician on another physician's patient by arrangement with that physician but unbeknownst to the patient), and *ghost turd* (a vulgarism for *dust woolly*).

Ghost net attests to the proliferation of floating trash and garbage that continues to foul the world's waters, endanger its ecology, and destroy its marine life. A citation from a 1987 Greenpeace newsletter states that "annually, the driftnet fleets leave approximately 500–600 miles of net floating in the North Pacific. At present rates of fishing, in the year 2000, there will be enough *ghost nets* that, if lined up, would stretch one third the way around the world." Drift nets "range in length from 5 miles to 30 miles and hang from the surface to a depth of 35 feet, where they drift with the currents and are invisible to the fish" (United Press International, June 15, 1987). Paul Watson of Vancouver, B.C., a leader in the Sea Shepherd Conservation Society, said in the same UPI story that approximately 150,000 marine animals perish in *ghost nets* each year.

glowboy *noun*, *slang*, a radiation-control worker who repairs nuclear power plant equipment in hazardous areas and who is often exposed to very high levels of radiation: "An estimated 5,000 unskilled workers are hired by the [nuclear] industry each year as . . . *glowboys* to repair steam-turbine generators. They do manual jobs in which a few minutes of exposure puts them at the upper end of radiation limits set by the U.S. Nuclear Regulatory Agency" (*U.S. News & World Report*, November 12, 1984).

THE STORY: The few printed citations available for this nuclear industry jargon term indicate that *glowboys* travel from plant to plant, working on an as-needed basis. Another word for this kind of laborer is *jumper*: 'Jumper . . . is shoptalk for a temporary nuclear worker who hops into a plant's radioactive area and repairs what he can before exceeding his exposure limit to radiation" (Associated Press, June 25, 1984). Other synonyms are *fresh meat*, *minuteman*, *radiation sponge*, and *sponge*.

Goodyear *trademark*, used in this citation as a verb meaning to run over a live animal, reducing it to roadkill: "Early one summer morning several years ago I found an otter stretched across the shoulder of the road. She'd emerged from high grass, poked her head across the edge of the blacktop, and was *Goodyeared*" (Lionel Atwill, *Sports Afield*, April 1993).

THE STORY: Trademarks, which intrinsically have no part of speech, sometimes get verbed. In fact, it's a mark of pop culture to use figuratively catchy brand names even though they are clearly proprietary. And the trend has roots even further back: remember "Let's put the milk into the *Frigidaire*"? Had Lionel Atwill so chosen, he might have had the otter *BFGoodriched*, *Firestoned*, or even *Michelined*. When I asked him why not the latter, in an interview on July 8, 1993, he replied that the choice of wording "represents my own basic attempt to balance the trade deficit." He also pointed out that the choice was influenced by tire brand recognition dating to his youth. *Goodyear*, for which I have the single verbed citation, joins *Exxon* and others. Consider the usages of those writers who *Xerox* their manuscripts, *Clorox* their dirty linen, *Spackle* their walls, *Windex* their windows, *Jet Ski* on lakes, and *FedEx* or *UPS* materials to their publishers. And do not forget the president of the United States who was once described as having a *Chiclets* smile. He was followed by a *Teflon* president.

Now, if verbing a tire brand strikes some readers as stranger than using trade names adjectivally, consider what has happened with the trademark

Saturn, which has been -ized. Derived from the famously customer-friendly approach adopted by dealers of the GM *Saturn*, said to account for 75 percent of customer satisfaction after purchase of the car so named, *Saturnize* means "to train in auto-sales techniques intended to foster positive consumer attitudes toward the dealer and develop loyal, repeat customers."

A third, rather alarming, such functional shift is the verb use of *Uzi*, defined as "to shoot at with a machine gun." "Machine-gunnings occurred so frequently among [drug] traffickers that '*uzi*,' after the automatic weapon, became a verb, as in 'They'd just *uzi* the place up,' to quote a scarred drug pilot from Georgia with 16 years in the business" (Thomas E. Ricks, *Wall Street Journal*, June 30, 1986).

liger *noun*, an interspecies hybrid cat, with light ocher stripes and a mane in the male, produced by crossing a male lion with a female tiger: "The two young *ligers*, which are already larger than their lion father, may become the largest living members of the cat family" (Springfield, Mass., *Morning Union*, October 11, 1986).

THE STORY: Here is an example of word formation imitating life: in addition to the blend *liger*, there is *tiglon* or *tigon*, denoting a cross between a male tiger and a female lion. Backcrossing a *liger* with a tiger yields a *tili*. This sort of genetic manipulation of the big cats has occurred chiefly in circuses, according to Ulysses S. Seal, Ph.D., resident scientist at the University of Minnesota and the Minnesota species coordinator of the Tiger Species Survival Plan. For example, in an extensive breeding program, Josip Marcan, an animal handler with the Clyde Beatty–Cole Brothers Circus, produced a male *liger* weighing in at 900 pounds as well as a litter of *tilis*. It was Marcan who first named his "completely new species" the *liger*. He and other circus breeders managed to overcome the natural antipathy between lions and tigers by raising them together from birth, thereby facilitating the breeding process later on and avoiding the use of artificial insemination.

Zoo professionals, whose traditional responsibility has been to protect and preserve self-sustaining breeding populations of pure, often endangered species, object to genetic manipulation of the cat family. David Anderson, curator of the Audubon Zoo in New Orleans, said that such breeders treat the cats "like orchids" in a "totally irresponsible" effort to make money. He characterized *ligers*, *tiglons*, and *tilis* as "junk animals" during an interview. And Dr. Seal noted in a 1988 telephone interview that breeding experiments like these "reflect our age-old penchant for the freak, the sideshow, the deviant." But economic considerations could prompt a change in attitude among zoo officials about designer cats, according to Oliver Ryder, of the San Diego Zoo, who said in an interview with United Press International some years ago that "'many zoos, in order to function, are going to have to have something to do with attendance. . . . The common area of ground with the circus is showing something that is unusual.'"

This phenomenon has its linguistic parallel in the word *beefalo* (a hybrid resulting from a cross between the American buffalo, or bison, and beef cattle). And the phenomenon alluded to by Ryder has an analogue in the blockbuster shows mounted at certain art galleries to draw more crowds and more money. See also *hot button*.

modem pilot *noun*, a personal-computer operator who engages another operator in simulated aerial combat: "They're called '*modem pilots*' who sit in desk chairs and dogfight on personal computers. And since real fighting began in the Persian Gulf . . . more and more of them are realizing Walter Mitty fantasies from behind a desk" (Associated Press, February 3, 1991).

THE STORY: The Persian Gulf War brought forth a whole lexicon of jargon and doublespeak (for instance, *human remains pouch* for *body bag*; and *incontinent ordnance*, a warhead or weapon that strikes off-target, either prematurely or in a larger-than-designated area, often causing *collateral damage*—the injury or death of civilians—during *target visitation* or *suppression*), along with videotaped serial combat operations footage reminiscent of Nintendo. *Modem pilot* came to public attention at the same time, with sales of military simulation programs escalating for some makers by 35 percent after the United States and the Coalition forces began bombing Iraq.

Most buyers of aerial combat simulators are men between the ages of twenty-five and fifty-five. Mike Weksler, a consultant for CompuServe who arranges countrywide dogfights, said in the AP story quoted above that "flight simulators have replaced the golf putter in corporate America. . . . Guys take a lunch break, call up someone in New Jersey, blow them out of the sky and go back to work." See also *couch commander*, at *trawler*, *paintball*, *practical shooting*.

morph *verb*, to undergo transformation from one set of graphic characteristics into another on screen, by use of computer technology: "As the computer displayed several pictures of Marilyn Monroe *morphing* smoothly from one to the other, or a little girl transforming into a poodle—and back—the crowd oohed and aahed" (*Washington Post*, January 19, 1993). "The '*morphing*' technique used by filmmakers to great effect in 'Terminator 2' and Michael Jackson's 'Black or White' video has come to personal computers" (*Radio & Records*, July 30, 1993).

THE STORY: A fast car can turn into a bounding tiger on screen or the face of a former president of the United States can melt into that of his successor. The process by which this is accomplished, *morphing*, is hot but pricey: a single *morph* created for commercial reasons can run into tens of thousands of dollars. With the release in 1992 of a Macintosh-compatible software package called *Morph*, a version of the technology became accessible by personal computer for considerably less, however.

Morph in this new high-tech sense is a clipping obtained by extraction of the third syllable of *metamorphosis*, which came into English from Latin *metamorphōsis*, itself from Greek, from *metamorphoun*, "to transform," and made up of the prefix *meta-*, "meta-," plus *morphē*, "form." *Morph* in English has well-established senses going back to the mid-1940s. These are specific to linguistics and botany. The etymology of this *morph* is not certain, however. One theory has it that the word is a back-formation of *morpheme*, which came into English from French *morphème*, itself a blend of Greek *morphē*, and French *phonème*, "phoneme." Another possibility is that this *morph* is merely a freestanding, independent usage of the suffix *-morph*, meaning variously "form, shape, or structure," and "morpheme." The suffix in question goes back to Greek *morphos*, from *morphē*. Regardless of the most recent developmental stages of the high-tech *morph* and the linguistic-botanical *morph*—clipping, back-formation, or suffixal adaptation to freestanding form—one ancestor is known to be shared by all: *morphē*.

nacul *noun*, the concept and practice of designing and building dwellings and other structures so that their occupants are integrated harmoniously with the surrounding environment; socially responsible ecological architecture: "[Tullio] Inglese coined the term '*nacul*' . . . to represent the concept of building and living in harmony with nature" (Hatfield, Mass., *Valley Advocate*, May 16, 1988). "But if and when '*nacul*' becomes an accepted part of the English language, etymologists will trace its origins back to an architectural firm in Amherst [Massachusetts] and the company's philosopher/founder" (Springfield, Mass., *Union-News*, November 16, 1989).

THE STORY: Tullio Inglese, who is the director of an architectural firm in western Massachusetts, the *Nacul* Environmental Design Center, created this blend of *nature* and *culture* in the late 1960s. Building structures as efficient responses to environmental imperatives is the mission of environmental architecture. These imperatives include energy conservation and the efficient use of surrounding land. In this connection, Inglese was, in 1988, designing a multiunit, multifamily dwelling complex called Solstice 1, ideal for *intentional communities*, and created to house 120 people. Solstice 1 was modeled on his home village of Roccacaramanico, in central Italy, where all the houses were connected into a single complex. The thirty-six-unit Solstice 1, which includes common spaces as well, was designed for a fifty- to sixty-acre site, much of which would be used for farming and orcharding. As with Roccacaramanico, in which 1,000 people lived together in a single stone building while using the sparse surrounding land for vineyards, grazing, and gardening, the American complex, whose design is now complete, would make economical use of available land, materials, and energy.

Although there has already been a trend to clustering dwellings into multiunit complexes here, architects have resisted total relinquishment of the single, large, one-family dwelling. In 1989 Inglese stated that he believed world demographics would demand adherence to the *nacul* formula in the future. The future seems to be now, given the new conditions of families, ecological problems, and, more to the point, violent weather patterns in some parts of the country.

Inglese, prompted by the devastation created on August 24, 1992, by Hurricane Andrew as it leveled much of south Florida, developed a conceptual design for a sustainable community of 50,000 people, called "Orion," incorporating the principles of *nacul*, which would be impervious to flooding and would be hurricaneproof as well. In the design, land would be formed into a circular berm approximately one mile in diameter, thus elevating the building site well above the highest possible high-water mark in the wettest of seasons. Excavation would produce an interior pond and several interconnected, surrounding ponds, open for small-boat traffic and being an aquaculture for all kinds of water life—flora and fauna. An electric train, golf carts, bicycles, and elevators would provide intracommunity transport, with all motor vehicles of the conventional kind having been parked outside the complex at a designated terminal. The individual buildings constituting the single complex would all be built around columns housing stairs, elevators, and utilities—a design not at all unlike the "pole buildings" used by the Seminoles who once lived in south Florida. Rooftops would be flat, thereby providing space for gardens, greenhouses, walking paths, outdoor theaters, and so on. Places of worship, nurseries, schools, offices, stores, and the like would be included within the entire structure, allowing the environs to be used for agriculture. Specially designed wind generators would be used to convert the force of violent winds into electric energy stored in batteries and in the ponds. This is an interesting alternative to the conventional rebuilding that is in progress in south Florida right now, a rebuilding that may put residents back in harm's way if another killer storm strikes. See also *intentional community.*

passion pop *noun, slang,* used as a name for a newly developed cold-tolerant amphiploid derived from crossing *Passiflora incarnata* L. and *P. edulis* Sims: "One virtue of the *passion pop* . . . is that it grows as far north as Georgia and possibly farther north than that" (Associated Press, October 31, 1991).

THE STORY: *Passion pop* is a "barbarism," in the opinion of the one person who should know—Robert J. Knight, Jr., Ph.D., the research horticulturist in Homestead, Florida, who developed this new plant in 1988. When *passion pop* appeared in the February 1992 "Word Watch," Dr. Knight said this in a letter to the editor dated January 31, 1992: "It was appalling to find . . . that Anne Soukhanov's eagle eye had intercepted and recorded the barbarism that has been hung on my recent product. . . . As its daddy, . . . I firmly believe it deserves a name less suggestive of a failed orgasm than the one given it."

In 1994 I called Dr. Knight to find out what, if any, progress had been made in creating an official name for his botanical baby. In the spring of that year, he sent me the information: *Byron Beauty.* The *Byron* comes from Byron, Georgia, the site of the U.S. Department of Agriculture facility where the plant was grown and tested through 1993.

Byron Beauty is called "an ornamental passion vine." It has a perennial root, and begins flowering in Georgia between the third week of June and the first week of July. Its leaves are trilobed, are strongly denticulate, and range in size from 5.1 to 9.6 inches long and from 5.9 to 10 inches wide. The flower is a typical passionflower in structure. It has an inner disk of deep purplish-blue petals and filaments surrounded by an outer margin of lighter color. A unique characteristic is its crinkled fringe of white that marks the outer edge of an otherwise deep purplish-blue filamentous corona. Its fruit, which, like that of any passion fruit (*Passiflora*), is edible, may, it is hoped, become a useful crop for warm temperate climes.

How then, did *passion pop*, the spurious name, come about? Dr. Knight told me in a telephone interview that it was the creation of a public relations person. (It came from the *passion* in *passion fruit* plus the *pop* in *maypop*.)

Permaprose *trademark*, a semirigid, multicolored paper laminate constructed from old design magazines that have been internally bonded by an adhesive, used in interior applications calling for moderate strength, absorption of vibration, or insulation: "And in what may become the most useful new material of the decade, Arthur Apissomian, a designer in Wadena, Minn., recently invented Permaprose, a plywoodlike material derived from recycled design magazines" (*New York Times*, November 1, 1990).

THE STORY: It isn't often that a lexicographer has the opportunity to define a new word denoting a new thing while examining the weight, composition, and texture of that very thing. But such was the case with *Permaprose*, the last word, in a manner of speaking, in the art and craft of recycling. Samples of *Permaprose*, sent to me by the inventor/coiner, still repose in my files, much like the can of hominy once inserted into the citation files at Merriam-Webster, Inc., by the then pronunciation editor, the late Edward Artin, following a spirited and sportive discussion with another editor about the difference in consistency between hominy and grits. (As a southerner, I had been asked to referee the discussions.)

Permaprose, which undoubtedly has a longer shelf life than a can of hominy, can be used in constructing pedestals and pillars, as spacers and protective blocks, and in paneling and molding. It is a light, hard, tough, roughly textured material measuring 8.25 inches by 11 inches in its individual modules. Its multicolored stripes are narrow from compression. They are interspersed in some places by visible lines of typeset matter. "Color content is unpredictable. . . . Unpredictability is one of the fascinating charms of *Permaprose*," says the spec sheet accompanying the samples. In a telephone interview, Arthur Apissomian told me that he coined the word in 1990—the year he invented the material. The material resulted from an effort to create a totally new form from an existing form that itself would be reusable without undergoing major change or destruction. Apissomian added that the term itself is "a tongue-in-cheek reference to the deathless literary style of the design magazines."

quux *interjection, slang*, used as an expression of mild disgust: "*Quux* . . . is uttered mostly for the sake of it" (untitled, unpublished list of computer jargon at MIT, Stanford, and Worcester Polytechnic Institute, compiled by Guy L. Steele Jr., et al.).

THE STORY: Guy L. Steele Jr. is the coiner of *quux*, originally a "metasyntactic variable" like *foo* and *foobar*. A version of the citation shown above eventually made its way into *The Hacker's Dictionary*, edited by Steele, and published by Harper & Row in 1983. *Quux* reappeared in *The New Hacker's Dictionary*, edited by Eric S. Raymond with the assistance of and illustrations by Steele (a.k.a. "The Great *Quux*" Himself), published by the MIT Press in 1991. In the latest tome, a "mythical," if not downright mythic, etymology of *quux* is given, to wit: "from the Latin semideponent verb *quuxo, quuxare, quuxandum iri* [sic]; noun form variously *quux* (plural *quuces*, anglicized to *quuxes*) and *quuxu* (genitive plural is *quuxuum*, for four *u*-letters out of seven in all, using up all the '*u*' letters in Scrabble." (Foo! I say.)

This monosyllable ran twice in "Word Watch": once in January 1989 and again in February 1991. It ran the second time, in an updated version, by popular demand—not from the hacker subculture but from the subculture of people Out There who avidly collect words in English having double *u*'s. My original piece listed ten double-*u* forms; another twenty-five were added in 1991, thanks to a ream of letters and more research. Here's a master list of these words, to which readers are invited to add. (Acceptable additions cannot be first names, middle names, surnames, or geographic names. Furthermore, the words must have been in print in English-language sources. They may not be foreign words or phrases that never occur in English.)

Double *u*'s 4 U

vacuum, vacuumize, residuum, continuum, semicontinuum, duumvir, duumviri, duumviral, duumvirate, individuum, menstruum, intermenstruum, premenstruum, postmenstruum, paramenstruum, lituus, equus, muumuu, squush, squushy, aruugah, equuleus (a foal), *mutuum* (a type of loan under Roman law), *suaviloquus* ("Hee which speaks Rhetorically," from *Cockeram's English Dictionarie: or an Interpreter of Hard English Words*, 1623), *carduus* (a thistle), *commiscuum* (a division in taxonomy), *liguus* (a snail), *obliquus* (an oblique muscle), *praecipuum* (a term in Roman and Scots law), *Smectymnuus* (a fictitious name made out of the initials of five authors of *An Answer to a Book*), *suum* (a word imitative of the sound of the wind and used by Shakespeare), *triduum* (a period of three days), *suus et necessarius heres* (a family heir including a slave in Roman law), *suus heres* (a type of heir in Roman law), *Weltanschauung*, and *zuurveldt* (an African veldt poor for grazing). Oh yes, I almost forgot: the derived adjectival form *quuxy*, a word that both editions of the dictionaries of hacker language assure me is in use.

rockplow *verb*, to convert (seasonally inundated prairie wetlands) to cultivable fields by dragging a plowlike implement over the pinnacle rock surface, breaking it up and making the land smooth and level. Vegetable crops are then planted there during the winter dry season: "Proposals to *rockplow* wetland areas at ... three ... sites ... have been made. ... The crushed rock and other materials are used to fill the wetlands' characteristic solution holes" (*PR Newswire*, October 15, 1987).

THE STORY: An article in the January/February 1988 *EPA Journal* explained that *rockplowing* results in "the destruction of valuable wildlife habitat and major disruption of the food chain ... and water purification functions provided by the wetlands." When one considers the fact that about 55 percent of the wetlands of the lower forty-eight states that existed during colonial times have been destroyed by human hands, the word *rockplow* and its now more commonly occurring gerund form *rockplowing*, which developed in the manner of *snowplow, snowblow, sandblast, groundbreaking,* and *earthmoving*, take on an additional, ominous, dimension. The EPA reported in 1988 that in spite of increased public concern about environmental issues, about 300,000 acres of wetlands were being destroyed every year, with agricultural conversion accounting for the loss of 85 percent of our freshwater wetlands nationwide.

teledildonics *noun*, sexual activity conducted interactively in cyberspace. Also called *cybersex*; *virtual sex*: "[A] book by ... [Howard] Rheingold describes how you might one day slip on 3-D glasses, headphones and a lightweight bodysuit with a mesh of tiny tactile detectors coupled to stimulators. The gear is wired to powerful computers that record your movements and cause you to experience sounds, sights and the sensation of touching or being touched. ... Then you have the computer call up ... people wearing similar gear. 'You see a lifelike but totally artificial representation of your body and your partner's,' Mr. Rheingold writes. ... [It] is fairly easy to guess what people would do. ... Mr. Rheingold refers to it as *teledildonics*. Others ... call it *cybersex* or *virtual sex*" (*New York Times*, January 9, 1994).

THE STORY: *Teledildonics*, a tripartite compound used by author Rheingold in his book *Virtual Reality*, is just one of many neologisms proliferating in the lexicon of cyberspace. Just as the origin of the word's key constituent element, *dildo*, is uncertain, so too is the feasibility of the scenario given above.

The idea is not impossibly far-fetched, though, given current advances in virtual reality technology and a 4,000-year-old pornography industry consistently displaying innovatively resourceful use of "new media." As an example, in terms of technological advances, *virtual skiing* is expected to hit the markets in the next five years. (Participants wear head mounts simulating the visual effects associated with skiing and stand on metal foot plates simulating the feel of changing downhill ski terrain.) And *cybersex*, albeit in its rudimentary stages, is happening right now within the on-line adult *communities* (a new sense of that word) accessed by people on the *nets*: interested parties, typically using *screen names*, key their sexual fantasies into the system or load into it graphic erotica during *hot chats* or *TV* (transvestite) *chats*, already a matter of concern to parents of underage kids who have *strolled* off the beaten track of the *data highway* into the fleshpots of cyberspace.

CD-ROMs providing interactive graphic sessions with models who disrobe on command have been produced ("Tweak Out and Turn On, Daddy!"). *Videophone sex*, which redefines *teleconferencing*, is expected to take up, in the next two years, where *phone sex* left off. Finally, the demographics of the *teledildonic* consumer market are significant to its future: men, the chief consumers of pornography through the ages, also happen to be the chief purchasers of new electronic communicative devices. All these factors combine to make *teledildonics*, in the *Times*'s view, "the ultimate *killer app*," where *app* is a clipping of *application*, with the compound meaning the single characteristic function that accords a system or device extraordinary appeal.

I do have a problem with the concept of those bodysuits, however: fat people will need Stealth models to erase their moguls; thin people, especially women, will need *cyberaugmentation*. And then there's the Vice Squad. How will it cope? One thing is sure: the future is getting increasingly unreal as virtuality rather than reality governs thought, thence actions. Should the two converge on a broader scale within the data-highway populace, in the manner of the so-called Dungeons & Dragons syndrome that allegedly affected some youngsters in the eighties, we'll be confronted by the specters of *cyberadultery*, *cyberpederasty*, *cybervice*, *cyberviolence*, and, of course, the Thought Police—ever ready to abridge First Amendment rights.

terraform *verb*, to create, on another planet, a life-sustaining environment like that of Earth: "A handful of planetary scientists, aeronautical engineers and space fanatics have a dream. A gargantuan vision. The concept is *terra-forming*" (*New Scientist*, February 5, 1994).

THE STORY: The verb *terraform* goes back at least to the mid-1970s or before, for it is a fixture in the literature of science fiction. The big news in the nineties is that the idea behind the word is gaining ground in official NASA circles and elsewhere in the astronautical community. People are now having symposia on *terraforming*, and are starting to ask for funding for research.

One idea among the *terraformers* is to make Mars habitable, not a facile task, given that planet's environment of extremes. It has, for instance, temperatures that dip to a level below –100°C, a dust-laden atmosphere with violent winds that blow at speeds of up to 200 kilometers per hour, and an atmospheric pressure of less than one hundredth of Earth's. This atmosphere is so thin that exposure to it outside a pressurized environment or suit would cause human blood to boil.

Undaunted by these exigencies, however, the *terraformers* envision a two-phase project that will take about 100,100 years to bring to closure: In phase one, the temperature of Mars will be raised from its average surface reading of –60°C to 0°C, allowing water to exist as a liquid on parts of the planet's surface. To help raise the surface temperature, factories will be built in pressurized structures. These will be designed to emit greenhouse gases (chloro-fluorocarbons and perfluorides) at a rate of 900 tons an hour. (This we have experience with.) After about 100 years, this warmer, wetter, kinder, gentler Mars will have developed a thicker atmosphere. Phase two takes longer—at least 100,000 years. In this phase, water-living organisms and trace elements will use sunlight to remove the carbon dioxide (it's 95 percent on Mars) and boost the oxygen level in the atmosphere to a level that will sustain human life, or at least permit humans to breathe.

The morality of *terraforming* is at issue, of course: "The idea of trying to manipulate another planet, without first demonstrating that we can reverse the damage already inflicted on Earth, would . . . be . . . the height of arrogance," said Eugene Hargrove, the editor of *Environmental Ethics*, to *New Scientist*.

But why are we contemplating this manipulation of Mars in the first place? "One popular idea is that humans should start preparing another home, a kind of Noah's Ark, in case Earth becomes uninhabitable," said *New Scientist*.

thermagation *noun*, extermination of termites by use of high heat: "Then there's heat, in several forms of 'thermal' extermination, or '*thermagation*.' Either the whole house or a single area may be heated to 150 degrees or more. Or hot pads—'thermal blankets'—may be applied to the walls where termites live" (Washington Home section, *Washington Post*, November 25, 1993).

THE STORY: A blend of heat, cold, microwaving, and "guns" is the alternative methodology now being used in places like California by the so-called new wave exterminators whose challenge it is to avoid use of fumigants, some of which may be dangerous to human health.

Aside from the heat treatment, there's the *magnetron*, a device that beams microwaves through walls, killing the termites supposedly without scorching the wood. Going from one extreme to another, there's the *Blizzard System*, used by a Long Beach pest control company: liquid nitrogen is sprayed through small holes driven into wallboards, reducing the within-the-wall temperature to twenty degrees below zero. Finally, and this is really far-out, there's the *Etex Electro-Gun*, which looks like a gun hooked up to an electrical outlet. The operator scans the gun across a wall space; the device senses the presence of termites. The operator then hears a change in emitted sound from the gun and sees a change in the color and arcing pattern of the electrical emission as the gun is ready to zap the varmints.

All of these are "spot" eradication methods and devices; they depend, for efficacy, upon spot location of the pests. Improvements are under study. For instance, the University of California at Berkeley, which is studying both *electro-guns* and microwaving, is building a *Villa Termiti*, to be infested with the insects and then treated with various eradication, or termination, methods under scrutiny.

trojan horse also **Trojan horse** *noun*, a seemingly benign, but actually illicit, program, often inserted within a legitimate program, that is then introduced by hackers or others into another's computer or computer system, ostensibly as a standard feature or add-on, such as a directory lister, a game, an archiver, or a virus finder, but actually intended to carry out a secret function, such as total memory erasure, data scrambling, theft, or espionage. Also called *trojan*: "Known as *trojan horses*, the programs pretend to be something useful, like a word processor or game board. But they are electronic terrorists, ready to erase or scramble data stored in computers. . . . 'Now there are much shrewder *trojans*,' . . . [Eric] Newhouse said. 'One called notroj pretends to be a program that guards against *trojans*. It's actually a time bomb that will wipe out your hard disk after it's more than 70 percent full'" (*New York Times*, May 19, 1987).

THE STORY: This term, now familiar to all computer-literate Americans, is a sense extension first conceived by "MIT-hacker-turned-NSA-spook Dan Edwards," according to *The New Hacker's Dictionary*, published in 1991 by the MIT Press. An early printed use of it dates to a 1974 issue of *Datamation*. It has gained entry in most adult dictionaries of American English, not a gratifying thought, when one considers that such entry is predicated on long-term, wide, sustained use.

Evidence attests to the employment of *trojan horses* not only in the sabotage of computer bulletin boards but also in illegal funds transfer and military sabotage. Don Parker, a senior information processing officer at the Stanford Research Institute, was quoted in *American Banker* (April 11, 1979) as having said on *The MacNeil/Lehrer NewsHour* that "the computer is now the vault of today. And so what you [the computer criminal] want to do is get your *Trojan horse* in there so that it executes at the time at which there is the most money available and the perpetrator is in the safest position [to steal funds]."

Some *trojan horses* execute instantly; others function as legitimate software for weeks or months and then activate. Insecure password systems are often the reason for such system penetration. In terms of military sabotage—a context that harks back to references made to the infamous "wooden horse" of war in Homer's *Odyssey* (Book 8) and Vergil's *Aeneid* (Book 2)—Reuters of July 3, 1983, cited an article appearing in the July issue of *U.S. Naval Institute Proceedings* in which the authors, Lieutenants Peter Grant and Robert Richie, "warn that computer saboteurs could cause key information from a combat zone to be garbled in transmission and could make U.S. missiles explode prematurely." In an artful twist, bringing use of the term full circle to Agamemnon's ten-year siege of Troy, the authors added that "the careful insertion of . . . *Trojan horses* into computers sold to potentially hostile countries would be a reliable and virtually undetectable intelligence asset."

John P. Brennan, Word Watcher from Fort Wayne, Indiana, commented thus on this piece and its content in a letter to the editor of *The Atlantic Monthly* dated October 22, 1987: "What is most fascinating about Soukhanov's note on the term is her unintentional demonstration that the moral development of the species has not proceeded much beyond the level of 1184 B.C.E., the traditional year of the fall of Troy." Actually, that was my intent. Everything written in my "Word Watch" column is most certainly an intentional comment on the society that shapes the words of our lives.

urban forest *noun*, a usually dense grove of trees and other plants covering a city area; *also*: flora along streets and in yards: "Nationally, *urban forests* are estimated to number in the millions of acres. . . . Only recently have foresters paid much attention to the *urban forest* ecosystems, which can . . . provide a habitat for other plants and animals" (Hatfield, Mass., *Valley Advocate*, February 9, 1987). "Group to Focus on the Valley's *Urban Forest*: . . . The *urban forest* includes trees in residential yards or those growing along our streets, parking lots and parks, plus those left in natural forests adjacent to homes, offices and shopping centers" (*Roanoke* [Va.] *Times & World-News*, August 22, 1993).

THE STORY: *Urban forest* goes back at least to the seventies if not earlier. It is an important term, for trees cover about 30 percent of the land in the average U.S. city. Rowan A. Rowntree of the U.S. Forest Service has said that a typical American city appears to be one-third grass, one-third trees, and one-third pavement—cities in the Southwest excluded. Worldwide, about 60 to 80 percent of urban land in temperate climes qualified as forest land. Two of the most heavily forested cities in the United States are Birmingham, Alabama, and Cincinnati, Ohio. New York City has about 4,500 acres of hickory and oak forests, and the Forest Preserve District of Cook County includes 65,000 acres—within the city of Chicago itself. According to a 1979 citation from the Associated Press, Rio de Janeiro underwent severe ecological problems with its forest: a satellite study indicated that 40 square miles of Rio's urban forest—an area as big as San Francisco—was lost because of the activities of high-rise contractors, subdivision developers, and squatters, not to mention truck farmers. With an increased concern about the health of these forests, a new agent noun, *urban forester*, has entered the parlance, as has the discipline *urban forestry*.

A related compound of ecointerest to urban planners and dwellers is *urban wind*: a strong wind that hits the face of a high-rise building, sweeps downward, and curls up between the building and adjacent buildings, thereby creating a powerful vortex, strong updrafts, and great turbulence on the ground and at corners. "The study of *urban winds* generally began in the 1960s, when many . . . skyscrapers were built and people first noticed winds were a problem around them" (Springfield, Mass., *Sunday Republican*, March 6, 1986). Anyone who has tried in vain to walk against or escape an *urban wind* in Boston (also known as "The City of Derelict Umbrellas") or in places like the Windy City itself can attest to the problem, which is no *urban myth*.

virtual office *noun*, a style of chiefly off-site work in which mobile employees are linked by laptop computers, modems, E-mail, cellular phones, portable faxes, smart beepers, and personal digital assistants to one another, clients, and teamers located in a main office. Also called V.O.: "The goal is to create a *'virtual office'* without walls: although . . . employees . . . [can] drop in at the main office, they work mostly at home, in a client's office, a hotel lobby, even an airport lounge" (*New York Times*, October 28, 1993).

THE STORY: The adjective *virtual*, meaning "existing or resulting in essence or effect though not in actual fact, form, or name," has come a long way, semantically speaking, since it first appeared with that sense 340 years ago. Long used in the fields of optics and nuclear and particle physics, *virtual* penetrated the lexicon of computer science in 1959 with the meaning "not physically existing as such but made by software to appear to do so from the point of view of the program or the user." This sense presaged its later appearance as part of the compound *virtual reality*, which denotes, of course, a synthetic, artificially created, interactive, computerized environment. *Virtual reality* was mainlined into the national lexicon by the media in 1986, but it goes back at least to 1968, when computer graphics pioneer Ivan Sutherland built the first headmounted 3-D display system.

Not surprisingly, the term *virtual office* is derived by association with *virtual reality*. It is the semantic symbol of a major decentralizing, deconstructive, reconstructive trend in the physical workplace—one resulting from a major shift to a knowledge-based economy. Other contributing factors are corporate cost-cutting especially in physical plants and overhead, a perceived need for those in sales to spend more so-called face time with their clients, the escalation in the number of part-time and temporary workers as a result of early retirements and layoffs, the proliferation of consultants for the same reasons, the increased use of flextime in the workplace, and, of course, the very existence of the new communications technology. Some companies cite the Clean Air Act as a factor contributing to the advent of the *virtual office*: The Act requires major urban companies with 200 or more employees to reduce motor-vehicular commuting mileage by 25 percent by 1996.

Some employees, understandably nervous about the new work arrangements, associate the *virtual office* with what they call a *virtual workforce*, hired by what the November 14, 1994, issue of the *Wall Street Journal* called *virtual companies*, or *companies-in-boxes* (ones that will outsource all assignments to outside vendors, keeping only the *core business*). Potential side effects include the *second-class citizen phenomenon*, denoting a disparity between *teamers* and *mobiles* in this, a new state of *officelessness*, a state in need of a *virtual water-cooler*, or a fulcrum, such as a videophone, used to keep those working off-site linked to and plugged in to the goings-on in the main office. (It has long been noted that human interaction in an office environment is a requisite to cohesiveness and esprit de corps, if not to a strong work ethic.)

Finally, the concept of the *virtual office* brings with it a whole new sublex-icon to the language of the workplace: the *drop-in office*, a facility or room used in turn by many different employees who reserve it by way of an *electronic concierge*; *groupware*, software designed to permit many different people to work simultaneously on the same project, document, or database from varying locales; *hotelling*, the establishment of offices for temporary use only when needed; the *just-in-time office*, one set up and used only when necessary and typically at the last minute; and *villaging*, the creation of future new towns in which people will live, shop, and work in close proximity while engaged in transactions on the *information highways*.

vog *noun*, the humid, polluted haze resulting from continuous volcanic eruptions and the venting of lava and noxious gases: "Peter Young, president of the Kona-Kohala Chamber of Commerce, last week said the [Kilauea] volcano and its *vog* . . . have been a 'mixed blessing' for the Big Island. 'The positive benefits are that it is a draw for the visitor industry and provides recreational opportunities for residents. At the same time, environmentally it has had an impact on the sky and air. We can't rely on waking up in the morning and seeing clear skies anymore,' Young said" (*Pacific Business News*, January 8, 1990).

THE STORY: By 1990 over fifty citations for *vog* had accrued. Like *smaze* and *smog*, *vog* is a blend. It is formed of *volcanic* plus either *fog* or *smog*. *Vog*, thought to be composed of sulfur dioxide oxidized into sulfates, obstructs and reduces the sun's rays, produces a particularly strong type of acid rain, generates fly ash, and can be dangerous to the health of people, especially those already experiencing respiratory problems, and to animals: "Veterinarians . . . say 'vog' . . . appears to be causing unusually high numbers of stillbirths [and] stunted growth among calves. . . ." (*USA Today*, September 5, 1990).

In January of 1990 the Hawaii County Council formed the Hawaii County *Vog* Authority, a panel of medical and volcanic experts convened to deal with the severe problems engendered by the continuous eruption of Kilauea, which had caused *vog* to spread over the islands as far away as Honolulu, 150 miles from the eruption site.

WYSIWYG *acronym,* what you see is what you get. Used to refer to the user-friendly capability of a computer to screen an accurate rendition of a printed page, for example: "The new version [of a document processor] has page previewing known as *WYSIWYG* (pronounced wizzy-wig) . . . which displays on the screen a smaller, exact version of what the printed page will look like" (*New York Times,* November 4, 1986).

THE STORY: Good-bye, *QWERTY,* hello, *WYSIWYG,* was what I thought way back in the eighties, which seems a thousand years ago in terms of computer technology and lingo. In those days, it was Big News that a term like *WSIWYG* had appeared in sources such as *The Economist, Fortune, Financial Times, Byte, InfoWorld, ComputerWorld Focus, High Technology,* and *Data Communications.* Remember that in the eighties, desktop publishing was starting its emergence, and so reading a citation like this one from the February 24, 1986, issue of *InfoWorld* was tantamount to browsing through the *Ford Times* magazines of the fifties: "*WSIWYG* . . . has graduated from buzzword . . . to become an important factor in [this] rapidly expanding market."

Now, the expression "What you see is what you get" was popularized nationally by Flip Wilson and his creation "Geraldine" on the *Flip Wilson Show,* a television show of the seventies. (This nugget is directed to the teenysomethings who were too young then to remember the show now.) Other computer acronyms of potential reader interest are *WORM* ("Write once; read many"), *WIMP* environment (*window, icon, menu, pull-down menu*), *WIBNI* (hackerspeak for "Wouldn't it be nice if?"), and *WOMBAT* ("*waste of money, brains, and time*").

Xeriscape *trademark,* used for a drought-resistant method of landscaping achieved by using plants that require little water: "You won't find the word *xeriscape* in any normal dictionary. It was coined only recently to describe landscapes that are designed to be beautiful while using a minimal amount of supplemental water, fertilizer, and time" (*National Gardening,* August 1989).

THE STORY: The citation above gives the headword in lowercase because the word was not trademarked until 1991. Citations dated 1993 indicate the change in status, just another example of how words change over short periods. Pronounced [ZĒR-i-skāpe], the word is a blend, according to John and Adele Algeo of *American Speech*. Its components are *xeric* and land*scape*. *Xeric* comes ultimately from the Greek *xēros*, meaning "dry," according to Robert Kourik, the writer of the piece in *National Gardening*. Kourik, who engages in *Xeriscaping* himself, is thereby a *Xeriscaper*. Neither the word nor the concept is new, however. Citations go back to 1981. The concept has long been called *drought-resistant landscaping* in the trade. *Xeriscape* should not be confused with *zeroscape*, defined by *Avant Gardener* as a garden or other area landscaped totally with rocks.

10

Words for the Road
(and the Friendly Skies)

birdcage
Bosnywash
car bra
cruise (*noun*)
funny car
greenlock
land yacht

my-kah
pencil-whip
skycar
suitcase car
white knuckler
winter-beater
yestertech

Americans have always been eager for travel, that being how
they got to the New World in the first place.
—Otto Friedrich

Having arrived here on an excellent adventure, Americans came to be condemned to a life of endless commuting, whether by stagecoach, the IRT, the MTA, or the shuttle—that airborne ghetto, as it was once called—where, in the nineties, you sit, more often than not, next to the guy with the key-clicking laptop, the one who's always on the phone, the one with the beefy elbow that intrudes upon your space and your newspaper.

This commuting destiny is best represented by the word *Bosnywash*, denoting the Northeast corridor, one where, in Pat Buckley's opinion, you will inevitably experience "the worst excesses of the French Revolution." It's also been called by Robert Reinhold one of "the main . . . divorce routes" in the country, plied by unaccompanied children who shuttle in ever-increasing numbers between the homes of their divorced parents.

Certainly the stress of the workplace and endless commuting takes its toll on personal life, regardless of whether you own a *land yacht* or a *winter-beater*, a *skycar* or a *funny car*, a *suitcase car* or a *my-kah*. But Americans, in their never-ending love affair with wheeled transport, can always unwind at the end of the work week on a *cruise* in a local parking lot.

To get home to the *funny car* awaiting the next hobbyist drag race, you've sometimes got to endure a *white knuckler* in the *birdcage*. Though explicitly defined at its entry, *white knuckler* takes its meaning ultimately from pronunciamentos such as this one, published and distributed by Rumanian National Airlines in the eighties: "Exit according to rule, first leg and then head. Remove high heels and synthetic stockings before evacuation: Open the door, take out the recovery line and throw it away." Okay. At last I know just what to do with the stockings in an in-flight emergency aboard a *white-knuckler*. But what am I to do with the *car bra?*

Enter the lexical showroom and browse, but don't walk off with the *suitcase car.*

birdcage *noun, slang,* controlled airspace in the immediate vicinity of an airport: "An Aeromexico DC-9 and a private Piper aircraft collided in the congested *birdcage* . . . around Los Angeles International Airport" (*Time,* January 12, 1987).

THE STORY: This specialized use of *birdcage* is slang for the technical expression *terminal control area,* which itself is commonly abbreviated to *TCA,* according to James T. Murphy, a vice-president of the Air Transport Association. Still another term for the same thing is *upside-down wedding cake,* a word-picture in which the inverted top of the "cake" represents the immediate terminal area and the other layers, increasing in diameter, represent ever-widening areas of airspace in which aircraft are stacked. This use of *birdcage* is not new to the pilots and others concerned. Given that *bird* has been used for many years as a slang synonym for *aircraft,* the formative structure of the word is obvious. As an extended sense of the word denoting a structure for confining birds, *birdcage* in this use parallels other figurative senses of words denoting the dwellings and habitats of various animals. Consider, for instance, *pigpen, doghouse, chicken coop, rabbit warren, lion's den, tiger cage,* and *snake pit.* See also *beehive* at IC, *elephant, hippo,* MOOSE at IC.

Bosnywash also **BosNyWash** *noun,* the Boston–New York City–Washington, D.C., corridor: "Home, sweet *Bosnywash.* Governor Kean of New Jersey came to New York . . . to assure New Yorkers that they need not be so concerned over a loss of jobs to New Jersey, because . . . we are all residents of one big megalopolis, all of us dwelling in the land of *Bosnywash*—an 'economic belt' of 'shared problems' and 'shared hopes' stretching from Bos to Wash. 'New York is the knee in *Bosnywash,*' Mr. Kean asserted, 'and the kneebone undeniably connects to New Jersey.' 'Baloney,' responds Mayor Koch" (*New York Times,* March 27, 1984).

THE STORY: Pronounced [BOS-neh-wash], this abbreviated-acronym-turned-noun is also used as an adjective: "Business travelers on the *Bosny-wash* circuit appreciate the convenience," reported *Time* on April 4, 1988. *Bosnywash* goes back as far as the year 1969, according to the *Barnhart Dictionary of New English*. The Barnharts pointed out that "similar names have been proposed for other regions comprising several large metropolitan areas: *Chipitts* (Chicago to *Pittsburgh*) and *Sansan* (San Francisco to *San* Diego)."

car bra *noun,* **1.** a close-fitting cover to protect the front end of an automobile from insects, flying gravel, and the elements. Also called *front-end mask*; *sports-car snood*: "The third category of customers in the so-called performance market is interested in 'ground effect' items which make the car look as if it could go fast: spoilers and air dams. They are also big buyers of louvers for hatchbacks, sports *car 'bras,'* [and] sun roofs" (*Automotive Marketing,* October 1986). **2.** a radar-absorbing carbon-filter nose cap used on the front end of an automobile to resist and confuse police radar. Also called *nose bra*; *nose mask*; *stealth car bra*: "Required accessories: vanity license plates, sun roof, CD player, car phone—two lines, please—car fax, and . . . a *car bra*" (*USA Today,* February 11, 1991).

THE STORY: Citations date to 1986 for the first sense of *car bra*, but the item has been on the market for as long as twenty-six years. In a February 24, 1991, letter to the editor of the *Chicago Tribune*, Geoffrey Gerhard, sales manager of Colgan Custom Manufacturing in Costa Mesa, California, remarked that "anyone who has experienced the devastation caused by love bug season in southern California will verify the sensibility of using a *car bra*." The term acquired its second sense in recent years, after a carbon-nickel composition was incorporated into the original *car bra*'s foam center. The added compound absorbs radar microwaves until the vehicle comes within close range, thus giving the driver a chance to spot speed traps and slow down before being clocked.

cruise *noun, slang,* an organized gathering of specialty car owners, in which vintage and customized cars are parked and displayed in roped-off areas for interested passersby to admire: "The phenomenon is called the *Cruise* and it's the rage among mostly middle-aged men who gather in local parking lots to show off the dream cars they never could afford in their youth. Customized, polished and often sporting thousands of dollars' worth of vintage parts, hundreds of cars go on display at *cruises*" (*Washington Post*, June 22, 1993).

THE STORY: Although the gerund *cruising* in the automotive sense is not new, the enthusiasm of middle-aged baby boomers for specialty and customized cars has given new life and a new meaning to the base-form word. The *cruise* of the nineties, as opposed to the *cruising* of the kids of the fifties who drove their hot rods down the streets of Middle America, has specific, distinguishing characteristics that build a new sense of the word and set it off from its predecessor. For one thing, the cars are parked, not driven. No alcohol is allowed at *cruises*. And the *cruisers'* often expensive car stereos (some costing as much as $70,000) are not played. Some *cruises*, however, do feature fifties bands and dancing. Large *cruises* can attract hundreds of vehicles admired by thousands of fans.

Several reasons have been advanced for the growing popularity of *cruises*. The owners have great personal pride in their customized and rehabilitated creations, and showing them off is a major factor. Many *cruisers* relish the attention of crowds. Regardless, a lot of money—$10 billion a year—is being spent on these specialty cars, said the Special Equipment Manufacturers' Association in 1993. And many of the vehicles are structural blends of vintage car bodies and parts. For example, a *cruiser's* vehicle might be a hybrid of a 1940 Chevrolet with 1948 Pontiac taillights, a 1968 Chevelle steering column, 1938 DeSoto bumpers, a 1946 Chevrolet dash, and a 1974 Chevrolet 350 hp engine.

funny car *noun*, a drag-race-only vehicle with a customized fiberglass chassis that is a replica of a street car: "Those of you who regularly follow our drag race records know that the current 1/4-mile A/FC, or VW-powered *funny car* record is held by California's Bob Godfrey at 7.93—169.52 mph" (*Dune Buggies and Hot VWs*, March 1993).

THE STORY: The Volkswagen Beetle that disappeared from U.S. showrooms in 1979 now has a street-car descendant: the Concept I Cabriolet, expected to reach the markets in 1997. But in the meantime, the old Beetles have morphed into *funny cars*, at least in some amateur, hobbyist circles. These Beetles, reconfigured aerodynamically and reengineered for more power, represent a small subculture of the overall *funny car* phenomenon.

According to a spokesperson with the National Hot Rod Association, interviewed in April 1994, *funny car* in its primary sense denotes a 5,000 hp engine fueled with nitromethane, as opposed to gasoline or alcohol, and a popular street-car chassis, perhaps one customized from the Oldsmobile Cut-lass or the Pontiac Firebird.

The term *funny car* exemplifies items in the private languages spoken in the United States, ones the average reader would be unfamiliar with unless the reader were an aficionado of a particular hobby, sport, or other activity. The term, not yet entered in most general dictionaries, goes back to the six-ties and is bicoastal in linguistic reach. It evolved as a descriptor of the vehi-cle in question simply because the hybrid vehicle, after customization, "looked funny."

VW *funny cars* certainly live up to their etymological reputation: "To give Ken's *funny car* body a little more aerodynamics, the front nose was raked out and extended 5-inches along with the addition of a front spoiler . . . the four fenders were narrowed 2-inches and raised 2-inches. . . . The rear deck lid and apron were shortened and reshaped . . . to . . . cut down on wind resis-tance" (*Dune Buggies and Hot VWs*).

Funny car joins other compounds of the type already established in En-glish, some funny and others not: *funny bone, funny book, funnyman, funny pa-per; funny farm; funny business, funny money;* and *funny cigarette.* See also *half-Cab.*

greenlock *noun,* a massive traffic jam during peak season in national and state wildernesses and parks: "Public land managers have a name for the overcrowding of paradise. They call it '*greenlock*,' and it seems unlikely that it will release its hold on the great outdoors in the foreseeable future" (*Chicago Tribune*, April 21, 1991).

THE STORY: By the year 2010, an estimated 90 million people will have visited the already overcrowded major national parks and wildernesses, called by the *Tribune*'s headline writer a "trampled heritage." The problem extends from Acadia in the state of Maine to Yosemite in California. Visitors to the parks escape the pandemonium of urban life only to be confronted with it in the so-called wilds, even to the extent that reservations must be made for access to and camping in many of these locales. *Greenlock* has a sec-ond sense as well, this one sports related: "Most L.A. County [golf] courses are no less crowded, and private courses have occasional '*greenlock*'" (*Los Angeles Times*, November 1, 1986).

land yacht *noun, slang,* a large, elaborately styled automobile, typically one manufactured during the sixties or seventies. Also called *greaser yacht:* "The ride is padded, although not quite as plush as the billowing *land yachts* of earlier decades" (*Business Week*, January 9, 1989). "The sound of the enormous old car door opening and the sight of this little figure getting out were depressing. The judge . . . comes to work in a *greaser yacht* practically ten years old" (Tom Wolfe, *Bonfire of the Vanities*, 1987).

THE STORY: The term *land yacht*, which has three separate meanings, goes back as far as the year 1906 with reference to a three-wheeled vehicle having a mast and small sails, used to race with the wind on roads, beaches, and deserts. The term, along with a diagram of the thing, appeared in A. Russell Bond's *The Scientific American Boy* (Munn & Co.): "Only one thing of importance occurred between our Christmas holidays and Eastertide: this was Bill's invention of the *tricycle sailboat* or *land yacht*. . . . Our *land yacht* proved to be quite a successful craft in the flat country around the school."

The term can also mean a motor home or a mobile home, and one of the earliest citations for that sense is to be found in Preston Sturges's screenplay for the film *Sullivan's Travels* (1941) in which a *land yacht* constructed from a bus follows the protagonist, a film director, on his journey on foot down the back roads of America. A more recent citation for this sense comes from the April 21, 1983, issue of *Machine Design*: "These 20 to 35 ft. *land yachts* are mostly self-contained—with an independent power source and water- and sewerage-holding tanks."

The word *land* is an essential element in many other compounds classed as slang and having a nautical flavor: *land crab* (a landlubber), *land navy* (pretended sailors or vagabonds), *land pirate* or *land rat* (an unscrupulous land speculator or a highwayman), *land-shark* (a land-grabber; a lawyer; a usurer; a customs officer), and *land-swab* (an incompetent sailor).

my-kah *noun*, a privately owned motor vehicle in Japan: "To assure that the *my-kahs* will be legally parked at least part of the time, the government now requires proof of a permanent garage or parking space before it will issue license plates" (*Washington Post*, July 16, 1991).

THE STORY: Here is yet another example of a Japanese borrowing from English, that is to say, a Japlish word or phrase. (Others are, for instance, *man-shon* for apartment-condominium and *aisu-kurimu* for ice cream.) It is estimated that more than 20,000 such borrowings have been created.

Another term of interest seen in the weekly Tokyo magazines is *homeless car*, this referring to vehicles without permanent garages, or, in police parlance, vehicles of no fixed address. Entrepreneurs are trying to cope with the parking problem by designing and building car elevators and stacking carousels. The top fine for a parking violation rose in 1991 to 200,000 yen, or $1,449.28, an amount that, in 1991, was more than two weeks' pay for the average worker. See also *skinship, skycar, suitcase car.*

pencil-whip *verb*, *slang*, to conceal (the nonperformance of a required procedure or the existence of a structural fault, for example) by falsifying documentation, usually in order to save time and in the belief that the data are too routine and unimportant to be double-checked: "A number of pilots put off the regulatory biennial flight review . . . to the last weekend before the 24-month deadline, during which all topics are crammed-in, glossed-over and *pencil-whipped* just to squeak by. . . . Talk about an accident waiting to happen!" (*Business & Commercial Aviation*, June 1988).

THE STORY: This, the primary sense of *pencil-whip*, is deeply rooted in the lingo of the aircraft, air transport, radar, and nuclear power sectors. Its emergence was probably associated with the structure of the preexisting terms *pencil-push* and *pencil-pusher*, but the influence of *penciler*, "an inexpert forger," cannot be totally discounted.

And there is another sense, this one more closely linked to words like *pistol-whip* and *horsewhip*: "to issue a scathing written critique of." A September 12, 1988, Associated Press story quoted Tony Dorsett, of the Denver Broncos, as follows: "I've seen one of the greatest quarterbacks of all time . . . get torn up (in the media). . . . I know you guys are going to get me. Maybe you guys won't *pencil-whip* me this week, but I know it's coming."

skycar *noun*, a lightweight one- to four-passenger car-sized aircraft capable of vertical takeoff from a standing start, motionless mid-air hovers, and vertical landing, having a cruising speed of about 326 mph, able to get about thirteen miles per gallon of fuel, and designed for commuting: "A *skycar*! The car-sized aircraft was modelled at the Essen Motor-Show . . . yesterday. . . . The *skycar* . . . is designed to take off and land vertically—handy for those tight parking spots" (*Toronto Star*, November 26, 1991).

THE STORY: The idea of the *skycar* goes back to the late 1950s, when Paul Moller, formerly an aeronautical engineering professor at the University of California at Davis, first thought of it as a vehicle capable of rising above traffic jams. Moller has spent the past twenty-six years and many millions of dollars transforming an almost unthinkable notion—one that is said to have inspired George Jetson's flying car in the Hanna-Barbera cartoon series—

into reality. According to a January 27, 1991, article in the *Chicago Tribune*, the *skycar*, which "looks like a cross between a Corvette and a fighter jet," is officially designated by Moller the M400 Volantor (*Volantor* being derived from the French word for *flight*).

Among the *skycar*'s characteristics are eight air-cooled rotary engines, each generating 150 hp, and each having two rotating pistons, two of the engines, weighing 70 lbs. apiece, mounted on each of four nacelles, or "powering ducted fans"; a set of movable deflector vanes configured to focus the thrust of the fans downward during takeoff and then retracting into horizontal position as the *skycar* gains altitude; engine antinoise capability; and foldable tips on the high wing tail for easy garage parking. Cockpit equipment includes computerized in-flight stability devices, simplified controls—one joystick for altitude and climb and another for direction, two video screens for flight control and navigation, and a ballistically ejectable parachute for use in case of "catastrophic engine failure."

In 1991, seventy-two orders for the *skycar* had been placed, with a $5,000 deposit required for each. The projected cost per aircraft was $800,000—in the Neiman Marcus Christmas catalog range—with consumer pricing forecasted to drop to affordable middle-class range when high-volume production starts up, a discomforting scenario indeed. Looks like the country's really going to need those air traffic controllers Clinton rehired. See also *mykah, suitcase car.*

suitcase car *noun*, a three-wheeled motor vehicle capable of speeds of up to 18 mph and foldable into a sixty-six-pound, suitcaselike, portable package: "The 'Suitcase Car,' a mere 32 in by 24 in by 10 in when folded, opens to a length of 46 in, width of 41 in, and height of 16 in" ([London] *Daily Telegraph*, May 9, 1991).

THE STORY: For those who don't relish standing on line for a taxi at LAX, Logan, O'Hare, Heathrow, or Orly, here's a stocking stuffer for your Gladstone bag or the overhead bin—Mazda's *suitcase car*, exhibited in prototype in 1991 at Matsuda's Fantasiad.

The designers hope that the prototype, albeit not scheduled for production anytime soon, will someday metamorphose into a mass-produced portable car that can be stored in the baggage bay of an aircraft on, say, an overseas trip, so that its owner can simply unpack and unfold the car and drive away from the airport upon deplaning.

If you think that the idea of a *suitcase car* is so crazy as to be unworthy of notice, let me say that it's already been done—and done back in the early 1960s. At that time, an acquaintance of mine stationed with the army in Germany dismantled his tiny Messerschmitt car (of German manufacture, by the same folks who brought us the ME-109 at twelve o'clock high in the Un-friendly Skies of Europe), a car shaped like a cockpit on wheels with a Perspex canopy that hinged up and down for driver entry and exit. He then packed the pieces of the car in a standard-issue footlocker for shipment as hold baggage back to the States. The last we heard of him, he was seen driving away from Brooklyn Army Terminal. See also *my-kah*, *skycar*.

white knuckler *noun*, *slang*, a short-haul commuter airline flight: "The crash of [a commuter aircraft] outside [a Minnesota community] revives a long-running debate over the safety of regional airlines, the fastest growing part of the nation's airline industry. Nicknamed '*white knucklers*,' by frequent fliers, the short-haul flights attracted 48.9 million passengers in 1992, more than four times the number when the U.S. airline industry was deregulated in 1978" (Knight-Ridder, December 3, 1993).

THE STORY: Anyone over five feet nine inches tall who has had to crawl on hands and knees down the aisle of a small commuter aircraft and then shoehorn his or her body into a small, hard, straight chair will appreciate the appellation *white knuckler*, for just getting to and into one's seat can be an example of adventure travel. Next come the frequently heard remarks about the two sewing machines powering the craft, and the straight chair lashed to the port wing for overbookees. Then comes the flight. This writer, who has flown millions of air miles in such aircraft, has experienced violent thunderstorms, snowstorms, ice storms, and downdrafts—not pleasant in any aircraft, but particularly unnerving in small planes highly sensitive to midair turbulence.

In all seriousness, *white knuckler* refers to passenger anxiety over four major concerns that have been voiced about regional airline accidents: problems in pilot training and judgment, alleged in a U.S. congressional aviation subcommittee hearing in 1992 as "a cause or contributing factor in approximately two-thirds of all commuter accidents historically"; high turnover among pilots and managers; problems involving FAA oversight and scrutiny; and equipment problems, an example being a lack of ground-proximity warning devices on some regional aircraft.

Etymologically, the term *white knuckler* derives from the preexisting, now established slang adjective *white-knuckle*, which means "apprehensive; nervous" and "scary." *White knuckler* joins a host of similarly formed compounds whose constituent elements are color terms plus anatomical names, these being typical: *bluenose, blue blood, yellow-bellied, black-hearted, silver tongue, red-neck, red-handed, red-faced,* and, more to my point, the *red eye.*

With respect to meaning per se, *white knuckler* joins these lexicoanatomical terms: *teeth-chattering, bone-crunching, back-breaking, stomach-churning, hair-raising, weak-kneed, heart-pumping, gut-wrenching,* and *heart-stopping.* Certainly this list could be used to describe a friend's experience somewhere over the Midwest when a fistfight broke out between the pilot of such an aircraft and a fellow passenger.

winter-beater *noun, slang,* an old, cheap, dilapidated car with a good engine and heating system that is used only during the winter months, the owner's regular car having been put into storage. Also called *beater; rat; rat car; winter wreck:* "'Only certain cars qualify as *winter-beaters.* It has to be a piece of junk with a defroster and one hell of a heater. It has rust from the front bumper to the back and looks like a goat's been eating on it'" (Minnesota resident Kathy Ashby, *Los Angeles Times,* November 8, 1987).

THE STORY: Though Michael Linn, a professor in the English and linguistics department at the University of Minnesota, Duluth, has said that *winter-beater* is a "local regional expression" indigenous to the Minneapolis–St. Paul area, a great deal of commentary from Word Watchers in the Middle West, Northeast, and Canada attest much wider linguistic distribution. The term connotes both a *beat-up* car and the *beating* the car has to take from the winter elements, plus the effects of road salt and the winter driving techniques of other motorists. And, of course, the term can be construed as "an automobile that *beats* the winter." *Winter-beaters* are owned primarily by smart people who do not want to subject their luxury cars to the 120,000 tons of salt deposited by some states on their roads in winter. *Winter-beaters* can sell for as low as $100 apiece; many owners simply throw them away at the end of the season.

I could end the story here, but that's impossible, given the letter I received from Michael A. Green, of Calgary, dated March 26, 1988—a letter that depicts the lifestyle and the culture of those who rely on *winter-beaters:*

> Had [you] visited the geographical center of winter, which is situated here, [you] would have discovered not only *winter-beaters* but also *summer-beaters.* People here drive *beaters* all year long. We don't

even have garages for our regular cars, our *beaters* are our regular cars.

Our *winter-beaters* come equipped with ... *block-heaters*. This is not an option, it is a precondition on all vehicle purchases. ... Attached to this *block-heater* is a regular electrical cord which pokes out of the front of yer wreck. ... It resembles a miniature toast-r-oven. This cord is plugged into your house. Some of our local wrecks may even have 15 to 20 feet of this cord poking out from between the grill. So it doesn't get caught up in the [rear wheels] many drivers wrap it around their side mirror[s] 15 or 16 times [while driving].

It gets so cold here that most *beaters* are plugged in when you aren't driving them. Which means about 16 hours a day. ... What I like to do is stroll down our lane-way about two in the morning, when it's minus 30 Celsius. It's real quiet at that time. All you can hear, besides the crunching of snow under your boots, is the hum and gurgle of all those little toasters working overtime, protecting the motor liquid from freezing and cracking your [engine] block.

So as you can see *winter-beater, wreck* or *beater* is not indigenous to the Minneapolis–St. Paul area; in fact those words originated here along with *summer-beater* and *block-heater.*

The *regional* label originally attached to *winter-beater* has been removed. This proves that responsible opposing views are always welcome.

yestertech *adjective,* of or relating to the technology of the past, especially the technology predating the eighties and the nineties, typically excluding such features as digital readouts, and, in the case of motor vehicles, air bags, air-conditioning, power windows, and cruise control: "We needed another Cobra-type vehicle, that was air-in-the-face, *yestertech,* with no digital instruments and, powertrain-wise, outside of the fuel management computer, something the average shade-tree mechanic could service—and the computer ought to last forever, except that people will be changing chips" (Carroll Shelby, *AutoWeek,* May 27, 1991).

THE STORY: *Yestertech* is used here with reference to the Dodge Viper, a sports machine with an 8-liter, 488-cubic-inch, 400 hp V-10 engine—a car with more than 450 foot-pounds of torque that accelerates from 0 to 60 mph in 4.5 seconds and whose top speed is 165 mph—a vehicle called by the October 22, 1991, London *Sunday Telegraph* "[the] ultimate hairy-chested sports car." Certainly in an era of *green cars* and electric cars, this piece of *Vanishing Point* nostalgia stands out as one more instance of sixties retro in the nineties.

Although the word *yestertech*, the descriptor of such technological nostalgia, sounds as new as the vehicle it modifies, it isn't. Citations for it go back to 1987 at least. Here's one from the *Playboy* of October of that year, this for the noun, and used to refer to business, not road, machines: "This old dog . . . get[s] a little nostalgic for all that *yestertech* now and then. You know the stuff I mean: those old clunkers that you don't have to plug in, the ones that give you a print-out on a piece of paper exactly as you hit the keys."

11

Man Does Not Live by
Words Alone...There's Food

appliance garage
blaff
canola
FlashBake
Frankenfood
gastroporn
golden banquet
graze

impitoyable
olestra
powdered water
Quorn
toy food
triticale
Zip Code wine

Food is history.
—Giuliano Bugialli

The history of the eighties was marked by greed and conspicuous consumption—in this case, the consumption of expensive, exotic food, food that had been infantilized to the extent that it was more fit for custom-framing than for serving.

"Poor darling fellow—he *died* of food. He was killed by the dinner table," said Diana Vreeland of Christian Dior in 1986. The same might be said of those who went home hungry after an exorbitantly expensive nouvelle-cuisine meal, written up on the menu in the language called *gastroporn*.

But times change, and here's a quote that exemplifies Giuliano Bugialli's statement. Said Jeff Smith of nouvelle cuisine, "I don't go for the nouvelle approach—serving a rabbit rump with coffee extract sauce and a slice of kiwi fruit. . . . The way I feel about it is this: Beat me or feed me, but don't tease me. It's *toy food*: who needs it? Serve it to toy people" (*Boston Globe*, January 11, 1987). When you turn to the entry for *toy food*, you will see that it refers, in the nineties, to cooking-by-the-numbers kits for the culinary illiterati who dominate the landscape once populated by well-to-do yuppies whose consuming passion included all manner of kitchen gadgets housed in *appliance garages*. Good-bye, kitchen cookbook libraries and food processors. Hello, food *assemblers*. And by the way, what do we mean by "Hard-cook the egg"? Do it in a microwave, or what?

The eighties was also the era of nonsmoking, of fitness, of the anticholesterol obsession, and of the beginnings of genetically engineered foodstuffs. All these trends have continued, to a great extent, into the nineties. They are to be seen with *canola, triticale, olestra,* and *Quorn.* And genetically engineered foods like the first two have been dubbed *Frankenfood* by the same Boston College English professor who gave us *schmooseoisie.*

Probably the most important trend word in this chapter is the trade name *FlashBake*; it represents the biggest change in stove technology since the microwave was introduced. It's a device fit for the nineties and beyond, and should help from-scratch as well as by-the-numbers *assemblers* in their culinary engineering. *Qu'ils mangent de la brioche—avec, naturellement, le vin de Zip Code.*

appliance garage *noun,* a built-in countertop kitchen cabinet often having a roll top, in which small appliances can be stored while hooked up, ready for immediate use: "Great things have been happening in kitchens lately. The sine qua non is the *appliance garage,* the built-in unit that keeps the blender, the toaster, the mixer and the food processor out of sight but not out of mind or out of reach" (Springfield, Mass., *Union-News,* June 11, 1987).

THE STORY: The *appliance garage* is just one of many convenience features included in new and remodeled kitchens as a response to the needs of two-career couples who enjoy cooking, who are spending more and more time in the kitchen possibly as part of the *cocooning* trend begun in the eighties; who, at the time of this writing, had enough money to Hammacher Schlemmer themselves to surfeit on all manner of new kitchen gadgets; and who want exceptional kitchen organization, efficiency, storage space, and work space. The term goes back at least to 1981 when the craze for cooking often exotic food became evident. Other words related to the serious kitchen are *island* (affording countertop and storage space) and *peninsula* (a cooking center housing the grill and range). And the walk-in pantry has returned to popularity.

blaff *noun,* a West Indian stew consisting of various ingredients such as fish or pork and seasonings such as lime or garlic, and often containing fruits and vegetables: "Stuffed crabs, crayfish dishes, a fish stew called *blaff,* and acras, or hot fish fritters, are among the specialties served in the Creole restaurants [of the Caribbean]" (*New York Times,* March 25, 1984).

THE STORY: In pursuit of the facts about *blaff,* I spent an evening at Yvonne's Caribbeana on Route 9 in Hadley, Massachusetts. There, I learned that, in the manner of borscht, every lady's *blaff* is different, and that's all I learned while eating fried plantain and Jamaican curried goat (the soup du jour was not *blaff*). It remained to get in touch with Richard Allsopp, the coordinator of the Caribbean Lexicography Project and compiler of the *Dictionary of Caribbean English & Usage* at the University of the West Indies at Cave Hill, Bridgetown, Barbados, in order to get to the bottom of this linguistic pot.

Blaff is of special interest not only because it has begun to appear on American menus but also because it illustrates the dangers inherent in basing etymological judgments solely on printed citational evidence. Our citation from the *Times*, and another from the *Washington Post*, suggest that the word, used chiefly but not exclusively in Guadeloupe (French West Indies), is "imitative"—that is, it is spelled to reflect the sound made when a fish is plunged into boiling water or hot oil.

Professor Allsopp set the record straight. He responded:

> *Blaff* is likely formed from *braff* by way of a shift from *r* to *l*, a common linguistic occurrence. *Braff* is the form that occurs in Dominica, a neighbor of Guadeloupe—a country with a strong French Creole history and culture, originally British but now an independent state. In Dominica *braff*, pronounced [braaf] but seldom written, is a heavy mixture of fish, dasheen, green bananas, and seasoning with plenty of liquid to make it souplike. Instead of fish there may be (and more often is) pork or smoked manicou [a small arboreal opossum of the genus *Marmosa*]. In Grenada the same is called *fish-broff* and is usually done with red snapper, ketchup and tomatoes, to make it red, or else it is made gray by eliminating the ketchup and tomatoes, and by using fish other than ones with red flesh but with the same or similar vegetables. Both . . . *braff* and *broff* derive from English *broth*, the first reflecting a British English dialectal vowel as in *brath*, a form noted in the speech of Dorset and Devon, and both showing the influence of London cockney (i.e., the shift from *th* to *f*), of which some examples occur in Dickens.

Those disappointed that the imitative etymology is incorrect will be glad to know that another food word, *shabu-shabu* (a Japanese dish consisting of a simmering pot of broth, vegetables, and noodles in which thinly sliced beef or chicken is quickly cooked at the table and then dipped into a flavorful sauce), is, in fact, imitative: *shabu-shabu* reflects the sound made by bubbling water.

canola *noun*, a genetically engineered variety of rapeseed, used to produce a vegetable oil lower in saturated fats than all others and high in monounsaturates: "You can grow . . . *canola* most places wheat is grown. The plant's oil is all but tasteless, and perfect for a cholesterol-obsessed country—only 7% saturated fat, compared with 15% for soybean oil . . . and 51% for palm oil" (*Forbes*, October 16, 1989).

THE STORY: The word *canola*, etymologized in two current dictionaries as "origin unknown," is not a mystery at all. It began as an acronym for "*Can*ada, *o*il *l*ow *a*cid," and it was coined in 1978 by the Canadian seed-oil industry when a variety of the rape plant low in heart-damaging acids and glucosinolates was developed.

Canola, constituting Canada's second-largest cash crop and grown on 9 million acres there as of 1989, stands three feet tall and sprouts dozens of oblong seedpods, each containing a half-dozen or so small seeds. During the harvest, mowers cut the *canola*, which is then dried. After drying, combines separate the seeds from the pods and the seeds are then crushed to yield *canola oil*. This oil, now a familiar sight on U.S. supermarket shelves, was first approved in 1985 by the FDA and became available here the next year. Industry analysts forecast that by 1995 the United States will have 5 million acres of *canola* fields, a figure expected to double by the year 2000.

FlashBake *trademark*, a computerized lightwave oven that uses bursts of highly concentrated visible and infrared light from quartz bulbs to cook food almost instantly from the inside out and brown it from the outside in: "Steak and salmon cooked in the *FlashBake* in less than two minutes and were well seared and exceedingly juicy" (*New York Times*, June 9, 1993).

THE STORY: In 10,000 B.C. we had the hot rock. In 2,500 B.C., we got the first convection oven. In 1946 A.D. the first microwave appeared. Now comes *hypercooking* via the *FlashBake* lightwave oven, developed in Fremont, California, by high-tech Silicon Valley entrepreneurs and researchers after seven years of R&D. (The developing company, Quadlux, is named that because the four entrepreneurs starting it had a sense of Latin etymology: *quad* for "four"; *lux* for "light.") This high-tech hot flash of theirs will probably revolutionize cooking in the next century.

With the *FlashBake*, the brevity of cooking time is extraordinary: 20 to 30 seconds for bagels and quesadillas, 40 to 50 seconds for a crisp-crusted, juicy pizza, 60 to 70 seconds for cheese omelets, 90 seconds for salmon fillets, and 110 seconds for chicken breasts. The stainless steel oven, accessed like a CD player, is programmable for fifty recipes and cooking times. It is controlled by push buttons. Food rotates on a carousel, and the 5,500°F heat is controlled by circulating, vented cool air. The oven, which does not have to be pre-heated, uses less electricity than a conventional one. Welders' glass is used in the food-viewing window.

The *FlashBake* brings with it a whole new menu of culinary vocabulary: Food can be cooked *differentially*—for instance, the top can be cooked less than the bottom. The 112-pound model has an *oven footprint* of less than four square feet. The oven's *brain remembers* recipes and cooking times. And a verb *FlashBake* has evolved, not through general usage, as is usually the case, but through Quadlux's own advertising. "You can '*FlashBake*' dozens of delicious foods faster and better," says the brochure "Cooking at the Speed of Light." Who was *FlashBaking* in 1993, the year the product was first introduced? Hotels, hospitals, and some commercial eateries. The current price is a bit steep: $7,500 to $10,000—but Quadlux plans to market a home consumer model forecast to retail at about $1,000.

Frankenfood *noun*, genetically engineered plant and animal foodstuffs: "'*Frankenfood*' ... summed up nicely the monstrous unnaturalness of such controversial new products as genetically enhanced tomatoes and chromosome-tinkered cows" (*Boston Globe*, October 14, 1992).

THE STORY: Here's an etymologist's delight: a new word whose coiner and date of coinage are known without question, a word that gained immediate, widespread currency through the electronic media, and one that has potential staying power. The coiner is Paul Lewis, an English professor at Boston College. He coined *Frankenfood* in the second week of June 1992. It first appeared in print in a letter he wrote to the editor of the *New York Times* dated June 28, 1992. A few days later, the term appeared again in the Sunday *Times*, this time in a headline that read: "Geneticists' Latest Discovery: Public Fear of '*Frankenfood*.'" The neologism was soon picked up by *Greenwire*, the *Los Angeles Times*, and even the London *Daily Telegraph*.

The speed with which the word took hold exemplifies the supersonic velocity with which a hot new term can soar into the Gulf Stream that is English today in our electronic, uplinked, downlinked age.

How does the coiner feel about his lexical success? "I'm proud of this word," Lewis said to *Globe* reporter Mark Muro. "It has a phonetic rhythm, it's pithy, and you can use the 'Franken-' prefix on anything: 'Frankenfruit' ... 'Frankenair' ... 'Frankenwater' ... [or] 'It's a Frankenworld.'" When he heard his coinage used on NPR's "All Things Considered," it was, of course, a very special treat, but not nearly as special as hearing his daughter running about, shouting, "Daddy's word was on the radio!" A great moment for a scholar of our marvelous, robust native tongue. A great moment for a father. And a great moment for lexicographers to chronicle and preserve.

gastroporn also **gastro-porn** *noun, slang,* precious language and luscious photographs used, as in gourmet cookbooks or on the menus of expensive restaurants, to depict recipes or meals in the most mouthwatering manner: "This [book] may be the greatest example to date of what some wags call '*gastroporn.*' The eyewatering portrayals of food are so stimulating that you may actually confuse your eyes with your mouth" (*Newsweek*, December 16, 1985). "Fantasy takes over. I am having sensual experiences just thinking about eating. This is *gastro-porn* ... a constant titillation where most of the action takes place inside one's head" (Martin Walker, *Manchester Guardian Weekly*, April 29, 1990).

THE STORY: Ten years' worth of citations exist for *gastroporn*, found in sources like *Food and Wine* and *The New Republic*. The most illuminating one, however, was in a March 11, 1990, story in the London *Sunday Times*. The writer, Dominic Lawson, explained that at Miller Howe, John Tovey's luxurious gourmet hotel on the northeastern shores of Lake Windermere in the Lake District—a place where five-course meals including seven vegetables with the main course are de rigueur—reprints of Brillat-Savarin's 1825 classic *Physiologie du goût* are left on the bedside tables in each of the fourteen guest rooms.

Lawson, while staying at the hotel, opened his copy of the book at random, and found this passage, which he described as "*Gastro-porn*, really, but with a message":

> Following an admirable first course there appeared, among other dishes, a huge Berbezieux cockerel, truffled fit to burst, and a Gibraltar rock of Strasbourg foie gras. The sight produced a marked, but almost indescribable effect on the company ... all conversation

ceased, for hearts were full to overflowing, and the skilful movements of the carvers had every eye; and when the loaded plates had
been handed round I saw successively imprinted on every face the
glow of desire, the ecstasy of enjoyment, and the perfect calm of utter bliss.

golden banquet *noun*, a sumptuous meal, the various courses of which are
sprinkled with flakes of gold: "The order [interdicting the use of gold on food
chosen by officials of state-run companies] came down from Beijing recently
to the famous Guangzhou Restaurant, a palatial state enterprise and former
Taoist temple in downtown Canton that specializes in '*golden banquets*'"
(*Chicago Tribune*, September 17, 1993).

THE STORY: In China, where about 70 million people still live in poverty
and over 1 million country laborers wander the urban streets in search of jobs
paying $2 a day, high-ranking members of the Communist nomenklatura
were, as late as 1993, living like the mandarins of old, dining on such delica-
cies as stewed deer's tail, twice-fried crocodile's feet, honeyed wild duck's
tongue, and sautéed head of snake—all sprinkled with helpings of gold powder, with the price range for the sprinkles going from as low as $17 to as high
as $1,000 per person.

The nomenklatura have surpassed their mandarin predecessors in this
use of gold: the mandarins were known to use the gold in soups and in tea,
chiefly as a means of balancing the male and female principles of the human
body (the yin and yang) and as a way of calming unruly temperaments and
driving evil humors from the body. Gold has also long been a symbol of power
in China. The irony is that the gold sprinkles are now imported to China
from Japan because the Chinese goldsmiths seem to be unable to produce
shavings of the fine quality needed for these gustatory delights. (Rich Japanese have been having *golden banquets* for years; they got the custom from the
Chinese.)

graze *verb*, **1.** to eat various appetizers (such as guacamole, goat cheese mar-
inated with herbs and oil, sushi and sashimi, and Korean beef short ribs) as a
full meal: "Making a meal of appetizers is a popular sport these days (some
people call it *grazing*)" (*Food and Wine*, April 1986). "The most important
trend in American restaurant dining seems somehow un-American. These

days, a whole meal often consists of a series of little dishes brought to the table, one or two at a time, for everyone to share. Called *grazing* or 'modular eating,' this new trend is a far cry from having one's own slab of meat, some vegetables and a fork and a knife in each fist to fend off stray intruders" (*New York Times Magazine*, September 7, 1986). **2.** to allow (a child) to sample food products in a supermarket and then return the products to the shelf: "When a term fits, we borrow it. I first read about *grazing* in a magazine article lamenting the decline in public morality. *Grazing*, the outraged author explained, is what supermarket managers call the behavior of certain mothers with small children who frequent their stores. As the mother herds the children along, she stops long enough to open a box of cereal or crackers, and sneak the kids a quick 'wad.' Then she replaces the box on the shelf before moving on" (*US Air*, February 1986). **3.** To sample various television programs in succession, using a remote control: "Between videos, and other TV shows they *graze* with their clicker, Beavis and Butt-head have mundane adventures" (*Washington Post*, October 10, 1993).

THE STORY: New sense development is clearly in action with the monosyllable *graze*. The first two caught on, and so are entered in most dictionaries of the nineties. The third is still emerging.

The verb *graze* ordinarily brings to mind grass, herbage, cud, and perhaps compartmented stomachs, not trendy restaurants, the decline in parental morality, grubby little hands, and—in the third sense—the imagery of an impatient, information/entertainment-overloaded, sound-bitten culture.

An article in the Health extra of the *Washington Post*, dated March 9, 1993, attested the trend toward *grazing* at cocktail parties: "Bipartisan *Grazing* Without Regrets: Capitol Hill Receptions Require Disciplined Eating Habits." In the piece, the writer offered various suggestions for coping night after night with high-caloric intake at these occasions. One was this: if the *grazer* plans to substitute party fare for a full dinner, he or she should plan to *graze* through a well-balanced medley. Avoid, for example, selecting fifteen fried chicken wings as your main course, supplemented with ten fried zucchini sticks as a surrogate side dish. And for more information about television *grazing*, see also *trawler*.

impitoyable *noun*, an extremely large, typically lead crystal wine-tasting glass configured so as to enhance taste and amplify aroma: "The new *impitoyable* . . . lead crystal glasses are weirdly shaped indeed. At a recent private tasting nearly half the guests showed up with *impitoyables*" (Hatfield, Mass., *Valley Advocate*, February 23, 1987).

THE STORY: For those who are ruthlessly honest in their judgments about wine, this French borrowing is particularly apropos. In French, the adjective *impitoyable*, from which the English noun is borrowed, is pronounced [ăN-pē-toi-ä' blə]. The French adjective means "pitiless; unpitying; unmerciful; unsparing." It can also be used as a noun in French: "You'll want *Les Impitoyables* ('the pitiless'), designed to concentrate odors" (*New York Times*, December 14, 1986).

Richard M. Gold, Ph.D., wine adviser for the *Advocate*, explained in the 1987 piece that the glasses are made in four shapes for four kinds of wine: a giant brandy snifter enhances the flavor and aroma of young red wines; an enormous tulip-shaped glass is for old red wines; a flute with ripples on the interior surface stimulates the formation of bubbles in champagnes; and a tall chimney-shaped glass is for white wines. The great size of the glasses allows more oxygen to reach the wine when it is swirled. All the glasses have narrow mouths to concentrate aroma during tasting.

In July 1987, when the word appeared in "Word Watch," it had not been fully naturalized into English: most often, it appeared in italics with parenthetical textual glosses. Since then, however, its currency has broadened sufficiently for it to have gained entry in the 1992 third edition of *The American Heritage Dictionary of the English Language*.

olestra *noun*, an organoleptic, fat-mimicking, fat-replacing noncaloric compound made of sucrose and six to eight fatty acids from vegetable oils such as soybean and corn oil, bonded into a molecule too large for the digestive enzyme lipase to break down, intended for use in cooking, frying, and baking. *Olestra* acts as a cholesterol absorber by trapping the cholesterol in ingested food while it is still in the digestive process, thereby preventing absorption of the cholesterol through the mucosa of the small intestines. Serum cholesterol level is thus reduced by at least 20 percent. Also called technically *sucrose polyester* (SPE): "Procter & Gamble took the current American obsession with health, mixed it in with the country's passion for cooking, and came up with what could be the product of the future—a fat-free cooking oil substitute called *olestra*" (*Forbes*, January 11, 1988). "*Olestra* . . . looks like fat, cooks like fat, and gives foods . . . the taste and mouth feel of ordinary fat. . . . It performs the same as fat, because it is *made* from fat. . . . It differs from ordinary fats and oils in one important respect: it is not digested or absorbed, so it contributes no fat and no calories to the diet" ("Olestra: Questions & Answers," Procter & Gamble, 1993).

THE STORY: Fat-fighters take note: in 1987 a senior vice-president at Drexel Burnham Lambert predicted that *olestra* had the potential of becoming a $1 billion product. To date, *olestra* hasn't hit the markets. Its discoverers are still awaiting FDA approval, said a Procter & Gamble spokeswoman interviewed in November 1993.

Olestra, not a trade name, is a clipped blend of *sucrose polyester*. The word was first used publicly on May 11, 1987. The substance was developed in 1968 in P&G's labs by Dr. Fred Mattson. *Advertising Age*, which listed *olestra* as one of "10 categories that will make news in 1988," ran a contest in its December 28, 1987, issue, in which readers were asked to coin new names for the product, ones with a bit more oomph and pizzazz than *olestra*, which conjures in the layperson's mind visions of *oleo* and, of course, *polyester* (very Middle America). Some of the submissions were: *Frequent Fryer, NutraSuet, Petrole-Yum, Fatsimile, Oh! Cal-cutter!*, and *Fry-o-nara*.

powdered water *noun*, dried vegetable fat that encapsulates water and releases it upon application of heat: "*Powdered water* is about ready to burst upon the public consciousness" (Associated Press, October 28, 1991).

THE STORY: *Powdered water* is listed in Kim Long's *American Forecaster Almanac 1992* as one of the big new items for that year and afterward. *Powdered water*, not the contradiction in terms it may seem to be at the outset, was developed for use in microwavable baked goods, which in the past have been regarded as inferior to oven-baked pastries because of their dryness.

Quorn *trademark*, a mycoprotein vegetable alternative to meat that is high in protein, high in fiber, low in fat, and devoid of cholesterol: "For Europeans in search of low-fat, no-cholesterol alternatives to meat, *Quorn* is hot news. Introduced in 1985 to British consumers, this fungus-based food is now available in much of Western Europe, with an application pending for its export to the United States" (*Cook's*, June 1990).

THE STORY: "Discovered in 1980 [after nearly twenty years of research] by Rank Hovis McDougall [the British food conglomerate], *Quorn* is a mycoprotein made by fermenting a microscopic fungi [*sic*] called *Fusarium graminearus* in a liquid solution of sugars, vitamins, minerals and ammonia. . . . It has a fibrous texture similar to meat, and tastes rather neutral, but soaks up the flavour of sauces it is cooked in," said the June 10, 1990, issue of the London *Sunday Times*.

With a texture similar to tofu, *Quorn* is used as a beef or chicken substitute chiefly in potpies, stews, stir-fry dishes, and curry recipes prepared commercially. Eventually it will be sold in blocks like tofu in food stores' refrigerated cases. In the parlance of the British food industry, items such as *Quorn* are classed as so-called food novelties, or novelty foods. "Like it? Good heavens, that wasn't the idea when the Methodist miller Lord Rank ordered his scientists to find a new protein in the Sixties, when there was the promise of a desperate world food shortage ('Eat up your *Quorn*, there are plenty of starving children who would be grateful for it.' 'They can have mine, Mummy.')" (*The Independent* [London], June 3, 1990). *Quorn* is also the name of a Leicestershire village, now called Quorndon, the site of a famous hunt. Before the product bearing this same name is launched in the United States, better get a team of linguists or some imaginative people from *Adweek* to concoct a new trade name. *Quorn* just isn't sexy, cousins.

toy food *noun*, a dish, such as fajitas or even beef burgundy, whose ingredients are premeasured, premixed, preprepared, packaged in numbered containers, and sold as a cooking kit, to which items the assembler may add merely one ingredient: "The cooking-by-the-number chefs . . . stir just enough and add just enough of a personal touch at the last minute to make it seem . . . their own creation. . . . 'It's truly *toy food*,' says Martin Friedman, editor of *New Product News*. 'You get a little piece of this, a little of that, put it all together and make something, just like . . . an Erector Set'" (*Washington Post*, August 5, 1992).

THE STORY: *Toy food*, used by Marty Friedman in association with the old Shelley Berman joke routine about airline food, brings into sharp focus some personal-life trends typical of the so-called Nanosecond Nineties: hassle and avoidance of it, time and a lack thereof, changing domestic roles, *assembly* as opposed to *cooking from scratch*, and culinary illiteracy, not to mention the importance of appearances as opposed to reality.

In a spring 1994 interview, Friedman said that *toy food* is a "very nineties word." Not only that, he pointed out that in this, the *era of assembly*, family-meal *assemblers* will soon be able to purchase entire *meal kits* containing the ingredients for all courses of, say, a French dinner, perhaps coq au vin—the French onion soup mix, a caesar-salad dressing mix (of course, the salad itself will have been bought already prepared from a grocery deli), the sauce mix for the entrée, the side-dish mixes, and a dessert mix. The *assembler*, having picked up the salad at the deli counter, need only buy the bird. *Assemblers*, who have rather sophisticated notions far surpassing prepackaged comfort food, want sophisticated dinners without any of the effort involved in shopping for ingredients and food preparation. Into this group of people fall those who are too tired or busy even to study recipe books and learn cooking techniques, seniors who have cooked for thirty or forty years and are tired of doing so, people who have had their fill of microwaving and take-out, two-career couples, singles, and single parents. Others are youngsters assigned to prepare the evening meal. A subcategory includes those who lack basic culinary skills because, according to Friedman, Caroline Mayer (the editor of the *Washington Post*'s Food section), and Marcia Copeland (an executive with General Mills), their parents never took the time to impart those skills.

Finally, some consumers simply do not comprehend the most basic language of *from-scratch cooking*; hence, the advantage of the numbers. Judy Lund, the supervisor of editorial services at Betty Crocker, has pointed out that "several consumers . . . called our 800 number to ask what *knead* means. . . . And we learned that . . . *hard-boiled egg* is . . . easier to understand than *hard-cooked egg*. People didn't know how to cook the egg. Should they do it in a microwave, or what?" (*Betty Crocker 1990 Food Issues Forum*). Another hard word? *Cream*, said Lund in the same *Forum* transcript, as in the instruction "*Cream* [the] butter and sugar."

triticale *noun*, a high-protein, high-lysine cereal-grain hybrid that is a cross between wheat and rye: "Many types of grains can be added to our diets, some as familiar as rye, barley and oats, others more obscure but no less valuable, from a nutritional perspective: Job's tears, *triticale*, amaranth, quinoa, millet, spelt and teff, to name a few" (*Chicago Tribune*, February 22, 1990).

THE STORY: The word *triticale*, pronounced [trih-ti-KAY-lee], is doubly interesting—in terms of its etymology and in terms of its agricultural history, a long one indeed, punctuated by prognoses of spectacular success, flops, and finally a new, genetically engineered life. The word is a blend of the botanical nomenclature of the plant's parents—wheat (*Triticum*) and rye (*Secale*).

Originally developed in Sweden in the 1800s and bred by the Germans, it was found growing wild in Scotland at about the same time. Because of some technical difficulties, it was produced only on an experimental basis for many years. In the sixties experimenters predicted great things for *triticale*, one being that by the nineties, it would be a prime competitor worldwide of wheat. That just didn't happen. Technical difficulties persisted: The yield was poor, for starters. Additionally, the grain failed to set enough seed. It shriveled easily. It proved to be much less adaptive to cold and heat than had been predicted. When it did grow tall, it fell over. It also sprouted green shoots from its seeds whenever the weather became humid. The ripening cycle was overlong. Finally, when baked, it caused the bread to be heavy.

Researchers went to work to improve the grain. They overcame the sterility problems that had caused the poor seed. They managed to eradicate the shriveling. They raised the level of gluten to enhance rising in bread. They shortened the maturation cycle.

Genetically speaking, the most common varieties of today's *triticale* are engineered by crossing tetraploid wheat with diploid rye to yield a hexaploid. This crop, ideal for locales with poor soil, is grown in the United States in Nebraska, Minnesota, and the Dakotas; and in Europe, chiefly in Poland.

Nutritionally speaking, *triticale* provides the high-protein content of wheat and the high-lysine content of rye. (The amino acid lysine, essential in good nutrition, is often lacking in the diets of people from Third World nations.) Flour made of *triticale* now works well in other foods besides bread: pasta, pancakes, and tortillas, among many others. And so we have a word, a plant, and a grain that have together risen like the phoenix.

Zip Code wine *noun*, an inexpensive French wine having as its sole appellation of origin a postal code, and often being a blend of several different wines: "Much of the U.S. wine industry blames the Europeans for its woes—particularly the low-priced French *Zip Code wines*" (United Press International, December 2, 1984).

THE STORY: "American merchants would often tell customers that so-and-so's *vin blanc* was really excess production of his Puligny-Montrachet or whatever. The French government wisely put a stop to this labeling practice a few years ago by ordering bottlers and shippers to delete their exact addresses from labels of non-*appellation* wine, though they were allowed their postal code in conjunction with their name" (*Food and Wine*, November 1986). The article went on to say that "American wags quickly named such bottlings ZIP-code wines, and the name has stuck." *Zip Code wines*, which constituted in the mid-1980s approximately half the gallonage of imported

French wines in the United States, have been described variously by tasters in California as "soapy . . . acidic . . . banana oil . . . cut-grass . . . tobacco . . . aldehydes . . . acetate . . . iodine . . . medicinal" (*Los Angeles Times*, October 20, 1985). These wines, which were priced as low as three dollars a bottle or even five to six dollars a case in 1984, often come to market in "slope-shouldered" bottles.

12

Working Out
with Words

aquarunning
black-water rafting
buildering
Exerlopers
extreme skiing
fitness walking
foot tennis
half-Cab
heli-hiking
in-line skate
kickboxing
mudwalking
orbiteer

paintball
playtza
practical shooting
pulk
river rider
sabermetrician
snow skate
spinning
SSAWS
swim spa
Urban Yoga
zone

Sports is the toy department of human life.
—Howard Cosell

The vast majority of the words here relate not to our traditional national pastime, spectator sports, but to individualized sports, particularly those targeted to personal fitness. The vocabulary therefore represents the single most important shift in sports during our time: activities like jogging, *fitness walking*, *aquarunning*, *orbiteering*, *snow skating*, *in-line skating*, *heli-hiking*, *mudwalking*, cycling, power walking, and *kickboxing* compete on a level playing field with sitting in the bleachers or in front of the television, watching others sweat it out.

"Many manufactures are competing for your foot," wrote Sybil Robinson in 1986 about running shoes. The shod human foot has indeed been put through its paces in the past two decades, as people pound the pavement, *blade* along in locales from Santa Monica to Manhattan, run in their tubs, circle mountains, climb buildings and other obstacles (*buildering*), *snow-skate* down mountains, take treks after being off-loaded from choppers, slog through the mudflats of Holland, *kickbox* their frustrations away, engage in *foot tennis*, and buy *Exerlopers* to experience a new, third dimension to running. In fact, exercise centered on the human foot took off so fast that I was overtaken by events in the year 1986 when *fitness walking* was rejected as a "Word Watch" entry owing to its instant recognizability. In 1994, the same was true of *snow skate*: With the appearance of *snow-skating* Norwegian soldiers at the winter Olympics, the term and the sport were globally understood within minutes, and sales soared.

If the human foot has become central to this, the new national sporting life, as never before, adventure travel is an equally important trend, also begun in the eighties. Adventure travel, or vigorous vacationing, is nontraditional, strenuous outdoor vacationing, chiefly to wilderness areas famed for their natural beauty and involving activities such as trekking, mountain climbing, rock climbing, and white-water rafting. Hence, the chapter discusses *black-water rafting, heli-hiking, orbiteer, river rider,* and *mudwalking*—words that take you along the dark rivers of New Zealand caves, to the tops of Canada's spectacular mountains, *around* some equally spectacular mountains, down rivers—in cars, yet, and through those mudflats mentioned earlier. Most of these vacations of vigor require not only physical conditioning but also the money to pay for them. That is the hidden theme of this aspect of the new sporting life: it derives from an eighties culture of money and a desire for the new, the unusual, the healthy, an escape from the workplace and the city.

A subplot to the sporting life of individualized vigor is a trend among some toward risk-taking, in the manner of the arbs and junk bond traders of the eighties. If you want to live on the edge, try *extreme skiing* and the *half-Cabs* of snowboarding, or perhaps *buildering* your way up the World Trade Center. But if something snaps, don't blame this author.

"Sports is like a war without the killing," said Ted Turner, who, of course, got that from George Orwell ("[Sports] is war minus the shooting"). In so speaking, both men identified the *hot buttons* that provoke some of us to seek tension reduction and frustration relief not by becoming *modem pilots* but by becoming game-players at physical combat when we seek to engage every weekend in *paintball* or *practical shooting.*

If "sweat is the cologne of accomplishment," as Heywood Hale Broun once said of rodeos, then the rodeo of American sports and fitness has been, and continues to be, a succès fou. Read on and let the games begin.

aquarunning *noun,* a fitness exercise that combines elements of running and swimming in rather deep water, often used as therapy for sports-related injuries: "*Aquarunning* combines the cardiovascular benefits of running with the safe buoyancy of swimming. By simulating the running motion while submerged in water, the *aquarunner* gets a great workout" (*Boston Herald,* September 26, 1988).

THE STORY: The object of this exercise is to keep yourself moving rapidly enough in water to maintain great buoyancy. Anyone who has ever played water polo knows the exertion factor. According to Patrick Mooney, cross-country coach at the Northfield Mount Hermon School in Gill, Massachusetts, "You're running and with the proper motion you're running on top of the water. The arms and legs should be moving rapidly enough to keep you afloat. So if you don't pump your knees and your arms, you sink." Some *aquarunners* wear a flotation device called a *wet vest*, which is wrapped snugly about the body like a life preserver.

Fitness exercises can also be done in the bathtub. Barbara Pearlman, director of exercise at Elizabeth Arden Salons, recommends bathtub exercises called *tub toners*, especially for travelers who can find no exercise facilities at their hotels. *Tub toners* include "leaning back on the elbows and doing easy bicycle movements with one knee to the chest as the other leg is extended forward, flexing and pointing the feet, and doing alternate leg lifts," according to a *New York Times* interview dated May 15, 1984. A second, equally unlikely, exercise site is the airline seat: Scandinavian Airlines has developed its own in-flight exercise program, which includes *stationary jogging*.

black-water rafting *noun*, the sport of exploring caves by riding inner tubes on rivers and streams flowing through them: "Welcome to the flip side of white-water rafting, New Zealand–style. *Black-water rafting* takes place underground, with wet suits and headlamps" (*Washington Post*, October 4, 1992).

THE STORY: If you're not afraid of jumping off underground waterfalls, caving in general, or experiencing the possibility of hypothermia, this adventure-travel sport is the one for you. *Black-water rafters* typically proceed through the underground watercourses by *eeling* (a word often used by them interjectionally)—each grasping the legs of the person ahead—with their headlamps turned on. This keeps the group safely together while the *rafters* view the caves and their features—for example, the masses of glowworms within. If this sport lacks appeal, turn to *mudwalking*. It's done in the Netherlands.

buildering *noun*, the sport of climbing human-made structures, such as the facades of tall buildings, often without the use of climbing equipment: "Bob Barton has a fantasy. He someday wants to climb the 64-story U.S. Steel

Building. Barton said his art [is] dubbed *buildering*" (United Press International, December 6, 1981).

THE STORY: *Buildering*, which denotes one of several spin-offs of rock climbing, occurs in *The Night Climbers of Cambridge*, published in the late 1930s. (The book describes the creative scaling techniques used by curfew-breaking undergraduates.) The linguistic formation of *buildering* was without doubt influenced by the existence of the word *bouldering*. *Bouldering* is a sub-sport of rock climbing in which the *boulderer* climbs on natural boulders, low outcroppings, or short cliffs, practiced without the backup support of ropes and anchors, for example, that climbers usually employ. (*Bouldering* was recorded in print as early as 1920.)

According to a May 3, 1978, story in the *Washington Post*, "*Builderers* prefer older, stone structures to *builder* on," because they have more *jamcracks* (tiny openings into which a *builderer* can jam a knuckle, a finger, or a toe) than the sleek-skinned modern high-rises do. Diehard *builderers* prefer extemporaneous climbs. Said George Willig, famed for having climbed the World Trade Center in 1977, "Very often you walk down the street, see a building that looks interesting and decide to give it a try" (*Washington Post*).

"Word Watch" reader Hinder Gonchor, a New Yorker, added a personal view from the top in a letter to the editor of *The Atlantic Monthly*, published in the May 1988 issue: "High up in our apartment building it is not unknown for someone to '*builder*' his way into an open window for the purpose of making off with some loot. '*Buildering* & entering,' I think we'll call it now."

Exerlopers *trademark*, used for impact-lessening running boots mounted on elliptical springs that increase energy expenditure in a more efficient workout than conventional running shoes do, and that decrease stress impact: "The first thing you notice when wearing *Exerlopers* is that you bound along like an astronaut on the moon when you're running" (*Fortune*, May 5, 1993).

THE STORY: A nonnative speaker of English had to consult an English-Russian/Russian-English dictionary when coining *Exerlopers*, the word denoting his invention. The inventor of *Exerlopers*, Russian-born neurophysiologist Dr. Gregory Lekhtman, said in an interview in August of 1993 that he coined the word in 1976 or shortly thereafter. He sought an English word that would best denote the idea of exercise by long-stride running. A dictionary entry for the verb *lope* gave him the second element of this blend, the other two elements being, of course, the *exer* in *exercise* and the *-er* agent-noun suffix. He did not release the name publicly until 1982.

Exerlopers, described variously in the citations as "futuristic," "high-tech," and "space-age," look like in-line skate boots mounted on springs instead of blades or wheels, and the springs are very bright in color. The wide rubber sole, the strong ankle support afforded by the laced-up high-tops, and the low center of gravity on the weight-bearing foot provide safety and stability. A more beneficial gait pattern requires the user to flex more at the hip, resulting in a lengthened, heightened stride. The springs, when absorbing the shock of contact with the ground, release it gradually—good news for joggers, whose feet, during runs, hit the ground fifty to seventy times a minute, each step carrying a force of three to eight times the jogger's body weight. *Exerlopers*, which should be used only on dry, flat surfaces, are distributed by NordicTrack and sell for $199.95. They are available in all sizes for all ages. Dr. Lekhtman said that women are big buyers of the product; they seem to be quite receptive to new ideas. See also *in-line skate*.

extreme skiing *noun*, the sport of skiing typically involving runs down rugged, previously unskied, steep terrain, dropping down narrow couloirs, and jumping long vertical distances, as off ridges and cliffs: "Enter *extreme skiing*. The jumps, the leaps, the flights, the crashes, the stuff that makes today's skiers catch their breath" (*Boston Globe*, November 21, 1991).

THE STORY: In April 1991 the first World *Extreme Skiing* Championship was held in Valdez, Alaska. During the three-day competition, thirty-six stars of the sport, called *extreme skiers* or *skiing extremists*, were judged on style, line of descent, number of turns, and speed. They downed slopes fifty-five degrees steep and negotiated vertical drops measuring 2,600 feet. Since it is all but impossible to observe such a competition in person, the sport is captured for ordinary folk by films such as the Warren Miller production *Extreme Winter*, featuring Dan and John Egan, called "The Wild Boys of Skiing" by *Skiing* magazine.

According to an interview in the November 1991 *Campus Calendar*, Dan Egan said that "[the sport] is an extension of the freestyle in the '70s. . . . People have been jumping cliffs a long, long time. With the lack of U.S. ski racers' success on the world cup, the industry was starving for celebrities. For the first time, in the early '80s, they [the ski industry] became willing to accept skiers from a non-traditional background as ski heroes." He went on to say that the acrobatics on the slopes seen during the seventies "kind of changed skiing from the racing mind to wildness."

fitness walking *noun*, the aerobic sport of brisk, vigorous walking, usually at speeds ranging from three and one-half to five miles an hour, intended to improve cardiovascular efficiency, strengthen the heart, reduce the risk of developing osteoporosis, burn calories, depress the appetite, aid weight loss, maintain a high metabolic rate, reduce stress, and improve the mood and mental functioning. Also called *exercisewalking; power-walking; speed-walking; striding; walking*: "Fitness walking, or *striding*, offers virtually injury-free conditioning" (*New Age Journal*, September/October 1986).

THE STORY: *Fitness walking* was rather new back in 1986 when I first wrote about it; it exploded in popularity before we at *The Atlantic Monthly* got around to printing the piece, so this term, one might say, was overtaken by events. It's useful to include it in this book, though, because no record of the major words of our lives during the mid-1980s would be complete without some mention of it. I live in a Virginia town that has a 2.5-mile "loop" of sidewalk that is crowded with walkers of all ages, even at eleven o'clock at night during the steamy southern summers. From octogenarians to one-year-olds in carriages vigorously propelled by striding parents, they're all out there.

Walkers might be interested to learn that the term *fitness walking* was coined in 1984 by Adrienne Ingrum, the executive editor of The Putnam Publishing Group, and James Rippe, M.D., attending cardiologist and the director of the Exercise Physiology Laboratory at the University of Massachusetts Medical School in Worcester, during work on a book about the sport. Dr. Rippe explained that *fitness walking* should not be confused with *race walking*, the Olympic sport characterized by a very distinctive gait intended to maximize speed to an exceptionally high degree. The *fitness walker's* gait is closely akin to that of the ordinary walker: the 25 percent increase in pace over that of ordinary walking does not appreciably alter the walker's posture and style of movement. And in *power-walking*, the walker wears or carries weights. A verb *fitness walk* emerged during the mid-1980s: "*Fitness walk* through the day," advised a brochure by the Rockport Company, the manufacturer of walking shoes.

foot tennis *noun*, a game played on a doubles tennis court by three or four people on a side who use their feet, knees, heads, or shoulders to bat a slightly deflated volleyball back and forth across the net until one team scores 21, to win: "It may not yet be as popular as, say, arena football, but . . . you can bank on it: *foot tennis* is coming to your neighborhood" (*New York Times Magazine*, May 28, 1989).

THE STORY: *Foot tennis*, similar to four-person volleyball and scored in a manner similar to Ping-Pong, appears to have originated in Eastern Europe, where it is extremely popular. The game is played professionally in Hungary and informally in other countries, including the United States. Most of the players are athletes, especially soccer enthusiasts, who want to stay in prime physical condition. Said Tony Vee, a computer analyst and *foot tennis* player, "The game is good for tension [reduction]. . . . If you have a lot of tension, this game will get rid of it" (*Los Angeles Times*, August 26, 1987).

half-Cab *noun*, a move in snowboarding that involves a 180-degree spin while board and rider are airborne: "Approach the obstacle fakie, with a moderate amount of speed. Just before reaching the obstacle, bust a *half-Cab*. Land in a five-0-grind, leaning back slightly to maintain balance on your tail. When you have reached the end of the obstacle, continue rotation with a backside revert" (*Snowboarding*, March 1993).

THE STORY: Big airs . . . sky off . . . fakie . . . pipe, half-pipe, quarterpipe . . . Cab, half-Cab . . . carving . . . Euro-carving . . . jibbing . . . gnarly . . . Indy nose bonk . . . endless wave . . . Sound like a blabalanche? The answer is yes only if you're unfamiliar with the private language of snowboarding, one that takes its linguistic cues from its antecedents, skateboarding and surfing. If you're not one of the 1.8 million people who snowboard—eighteen-year-old males constitute 88 percent of the group—you'll understand virtually nothing in a snowboarding 'zine.

Before getting into the story behind *half-Cab*, readers and writers must first explore the character of this sport; otherwise, the history of the term onto which this piece is hung will be meaningless.

Snowboarding is not just a sport; it is an experience challenging nature and gravity, and its practitioners are noted generally in the industry as risk-takers. The language used reflects these facts. Snowboarding, which involves descending a snow-covered slope while strapped to a board bigger than a skateboard but smaller than a surfboard, requires balance, coordination, and sheer in-your-face audacity. Its genesis is rooted in controversy: two claimants vie for the title of progenitor. Sherman Poppen of North Muskegon, Michigan, constructed an early prototype of today's snowboard. It was called a *snurfer*. The first *Snurfing* Race took place in 1967. But Tom

Sims, a New Jersey snowboard manufacturer, claims that he made skateboards for use on snow as early as 1963.

Having said all that, let's talk about things like *Cabs* and *half-Cabs*. *Cab* is of interest because it involves not only athletic prowess but also three linguistic processes: clipping, blending, and eponymy. *Cab* is a clipped form of the noun *caballerial*, itself a blend of the surname *Caballero* and *aerial*. A man named Steve Caballero devised the move that now bears part of his name.

But what about some of the other terms in this lexicon? *Fakie*, which, like *grind* in *five-0-grind*, comes from skateboarding, denotes the process of riding backward with the right foot forward. A *grind* involves sliding on a bar—an obstacle—with the board parallel to the bar. And the *five-0* is unrelated to *Hawaii Five-0*; it means fifty-fifty. The various *pipes* denote ditches in the snow, shaped like full, half, and quarter sections of real pipe. Each side of the pipe is a wall, or a *hit*, with the *hit* being the place where you jump. A *big air* is the degree of elevation the boarder gets when he or she *skys off*. *Jibbing* is riding the board over something that is not snow—for instance, a picnic table or the top cover of a snowblower. *Gnarly*, a surfers' term, means "excellent." *Endless waves*, also from surfing, are endless expanses of snow-covered terrain on which the boarding is great. A *nose bonk*, as in *Indy nose bonk*, is grabbing your toeside edge, extending the front leg, and *kissing* (touching) the side of a *hit* but not colliding with it. Finally, from rap, snowboarders have taken a few linguistic items: *bust* ("to do; perform"), as in *bust a half-Cab*, and *going fat* (from *one fat dude*), meaning to perform a move really well. For those of you over thirtysomething, don't try to do any of this at home. See also *funny car*.

heli-hiking *noun*, transport by helicopter to otherwise inaccessible points of natural interest, such as glacial ice fields or high alpine meadows, where one is dropped off for recreational short hikes and exploration, and then picked up by the helicopter for the return to a base lodge: "For the less ambitious, *heli-hiking* in the mountains is a popular means of scaling the peaks without the perspiration" (*Newsday*, May 7, 1989).

THE STORY: Thanks to Charles B. Sweningsen of Edina, Minnesota, I was able to get the real story behind *heli-hiking*, a story that was not told in the original "Word Watch" entry because of a lack of accurate citational evidence, the bane of the lexicographer's existence. Here's the real background: *heli-hiking* is linguistically derived from *heli-skiing*, the latter having been invented as a sport and coined in 1963 by Hans Gmoser, then the director and owner of Canadian Mountain Holidays in Banff, Alberta.

Heli-skiing allows helicopter-borne skiers to access ordinarily inaccessible wilderness areas with thousands of square miles of deep powder in places sustaining at least 60 feet (18 meters) of dry snowfall annually. In 1965, only 18 passengers engaged in *heli-skiing,* as opposed to 4,500 in 1993. *Helihiking* began in 1978, again founded by Canadian Mountain Holidays but in conjunction with Tauck Tours of Canada. Arthur Tauck, the president of that company, had been a *heli-skiing* client of Gmoser. He asked Gmoser to permit Tauck Tours clients to use Gmoser's lodges in the summer for heliborne hiking treks. According to Marty von Neudegg, the marketing manager for Canadian Mountain Holidays, whom I interviewed in September of 1993, *heli-hiking* is a joint coinage of Tauck and Gmoser's. Von Neudegg said that *heli-hiking* "can be done by anybody who can walk down the street," and he added that "many people have never left the pavement." Now these city-bound folk can stand 9,000 feet up and watch a sunset, and in so doing, view "what had been the unattainable." In 1978 only 800 passengers engaged in *heli-hiking;* in 1993, as many as 2,700 did it.

in-line skate *noun,* a roller skate with a boot mounted on a line of three or four narrow wheels configured to simulate an ice-skating blade, the back of the right skate having a rubber brake pad as opposed to the front bumpers on many conventional roller skates: "The *in-line skate* looks like a hockey skate mounted on . . . wheels" (Springfield, Mass., *Sunday Republican,* October 30, 1988).

THE STORY: This citation marks the early introduction of a product that has swept the country since then, now more often than not called by the trade name *Rollerblades. In-line skates* were first developed in 1980 by two Minnesota brothers for ice-hockey players to use during off-season training. But the concept of such a skate goes back to the early 1700s, when a native of Holland nailed wooden spools to strips of wood and attached the strips to his shoes. It was only in 1863 that an American inventor modified the original configuration by placing the wheels in pairs side by side, one pair under the ball of the foot, and another under the heel.

In-line skates, the latest development in this historical progression, are "more fun than running, more challenging than roller skates, and [provide] a great body workout too," said the April 1988 issue of *Triathlete.* They have sustained wide, continuing appeal—to fitness enthusiasts, the weight conscious, joggers desiring a low-impact alternative to running, serious athletes desiring new cross-training options, trendy fun-lovers, and families seeking group entertainment for all ages.

The activity of *in-line skating* is now embedded in American recreational culture, but the term for it is not. Instead, as I have already suggested, the brand name for the product took hold in the public mind to such an extent that we have not merely derivative forms such as the verb to *Rollerblade*, the gerund *Rollerblading*, and the agent noun *Rollerblader* but also clipped forms like to *blade*, *blading*, *blader*, and the compound of the nineties *blading date*. See also *Exerlopers*.

kickboxing *noun*, the martial art and sport of attack and defense, practiced in a twenty-by-twenty-foot boxing ring, that combines elements of karate and boxing. Also called *full-contact karate*: "[Maine] Gov. Joseph E. Brennan wants the state to regulate *kickboxing*, but followers of the sport said . . . that bureaucrats will only ruin it" (United Press International, December 9, 1985).

THE STORY: Kirik Jenness, holder of a black belt in karate and co-owner of the Karate Health Fitness Center in Amherst, Massachusetts, explained in a 1988 interview that *kickboxing*—a U.S. adaptation of a Thai and Burmese fighting style that permits vicious groin kicks, elbowing, and kneeing—first surfaced here in January of 1970 under the sponsorship of Joe Lewis, a black belt in karate and a champion *kickboxer*.

The sport failed to win any measure of popularity until September 14, 1974, when Tom Tannenbaum, president of Universal Studios, staged a *kickboxing* spectacular on a major television network. Since then, as Anthony Elmore, world heavyweight champion of the Karate International Council of *Kickboxing*, remarked to United Press International, the sport has been on a "roller coaster ride" of popularity, with the peak reached in 1984.

The rules of the sport are essentially like those of boxing, but kicks and a more varied array of punches and strikes are permitted. (The dangerous moves used in Thai and Burmese *kickboxing* are prohibited in the American version.) *Kickboxers* also don padded gloves and padded footwear for the ring.

mudwalking *noun*, the sport of trekking for miles through muddy tidal flats on the North Sea coast of the Netherlands: "Over the past 25 years, *mudwalking—wadlopen*—has become a popular pastime in the northern province of Friesland. While the Swiss scale the Alps and the Norwegians crisscross their mountain ranges on skis, the Dutch are busy walking in the *wad*. *Wad* is Dutch for tidal flat" (*Washington Post*, August 23, 1992).

THE STORY: So much for Hans Brinker and the silver skates. *Mudwalking*, the practitioners of which have redefined *quagmire*, is virtually unheard of outside Holland. It is also called *horizontal mountain climbing*. Clearly, it is not for the prissy, the pristine, the weak-kneed, or the fearful. Guides are required to shepherd their *mudwalker* charges through hazards such as quicksand pits (long sticks are used for this) and to ensure that everyone has vacated the flats before the North Sea tide turns. Walks usually last several hours. By the end of about four and a half hours one is expected to have established one's *mud legs*.

Tried-and-true techniques of *mudwalking* are walking on one's tiptoes, taking wide Nestea plunges and hoping for the best, and attempting to "skate." *Mudwalking* tours are scheduled in July, August, and September. Each tour is limited to 140 people, so sign up early for next year. "Before You Go," as the headline for the above citation read, what's to know? It is pointed out that people who are shorter than five feet will have to swim through the channels of water that are present here and there, so they should not forget a change of clothing.

Why do people do it? For the challenge. For the differentness. Maybe as an antidote to the "almost clinical cleanliness of the Netherlands." And maybe because most of us still like to play in the mud. See also *black-water rafting*.

orbiteer *verb*, to go around high mountains instead of scaling them: "To *orbiteer* Mt. Everest, [Ned] Gillette, with longtime friend and accomplished adventurer Jan Reynolds, lived at between 17,000 and 24,000 feet for months and crossed six Himalayan mountain passes more than 20,000 feet high" (*US*, December 15, 1986).

THE STORY: According to *US*, Ned Gillette coined the word *orbiteering*: "The term 'mountain climbing' is self-explanatory; Gillette dubbed the concept of going *around* mountains 'orbiteering.'" The word is of special interest because it employs the suffix *-eer*, which occurs with relative frequency in English. It is used chiefly to form nouns, and it means "one associated with, concerned with, or engaged in."

Most nouns formed with *-eer* are animate (*balladeer, cannoneer, targeteer,* *missileer, auctioneer*), but a few have inanimate senses (*gazeteer*). In the latter part of the seventeenth century, gerunds and participles with *-eer* as a constituent element began to appear. In some instances the gerund and participial forms actually predate infinitive or finite verb forms. The noun *engineer*, for example, goes back to the fourteenth century. The participle *engineering* appeared in 1681, and the gerund in 1720, but a finite verb form *engineered* appeared only in 1781.

Many *-eer* words also have pejorative denotations and connotations: *conventioneer* (of Tailhook scandal notoriety), *privateer, picketeer, pamphleteer, pulpiteer, imagineer, sloganeer, electioneer, black marketeer, racketeer,* and *profiteer* are typical examples (but not *mutineer*, which came from the obsolete French word *mutinier*). *Orbiteering*, however, has no such negative overtones. Formation of the word may have been influenced by the existence of related terms such as *mountaineering*, the sport or technique of climbing mountains; and *orienteering*, an English modification of the Swedish word *orientering*, influenced by *-eer*, and defined as the sport of cross-country racing in which the contestants, equipped with maps and compasses, negotiate checkpoints on an unfamiliar, predetermined course.

paintball *noun*, a strategy survival game, based on Capture the Flag, played on indoor or outdoor courses by teams armed with air guns that shoot cartridges of water-soluble paint. Also called *splatball*: "*Paintball* is . . . similar to the popular laser tag that lured even professional men and women out of their offices in recent years" (*Indianapolis Business Journal*, September 5, 1988).

THE STORY: Attired in black SWAT suits or camo fatigues, protective helmets, and goggles, close to three million people had played *paintball* by 1989. Also referred to as the Game, the War Game, the Survival Game, the Adventure Game, the Ultimate Game, Pursuit, Skirmish, and Strategy, *paintball* was created in 1981 by George "Pumping Iron" Gaines and two of his friends. Franchised as the National Survival Game, by 1989 it was being played on about 100 courses throughout the United States, Canada, and Europe, not to mention countless unfranchised courses in southern California, where an estimated 100,000 people were participating in it each week.

The courses feature special effects such as fog and smoke, simulated combat conditions, and varying terrain. According to the rules, a player who is hit with paint is "dead." That player must leave the course until the next round (a round typically lasts one hour; three rounds usually make up a game). Points are scored for every "kill"; if no one captures the flag or other trophy, the game can still be won on the strength of individual points scored. *Splatmasters*, or dedicated players of *paintball*, say that they enjoy the game because of its tension-reduction value. The game also allows one to undergo the intense, heightened experience of war in the sense identified by Hemingway and others—yet under safe conditions.

In a September 22, 1987, article in the *Whole Earth Review*, Rick Fields posited "a world in which the indirect 'ritual' of war games—with *paintballs* or laser guns or flour pellets or bamboo swords, for that matter—[would be] employed in place of the unspeakable weapons we pay our best scientists to produce." Drawing upon neo-Jungian psychologist James Hillman's thesis that it is vital for us to "deconstruct war" by moving "the martial away from direct violence toward indirect ritual," Fields expressed the hope that "if we take our spirit of play and imagination seriously enough, . . . the Game, in one form or another, may blossom into something the world could use—if not a moral then at least a playful alternative to war." Tell that to the warlords of the nineties, whose agendas are less than playful. See also *modem pilot, practical shooting*.

playtza *noun*, a method of body toning and relaxation in a sauna whereby a person is beaten gently with oak leaves, usually followed by a few minutes of steam and then the bath: "After a Turkish bath, have any remaining cares driven away by a Shiatsu massage, a Swiss needle shower, or the Bulgarian oak *playtza* (a gentle beating with oak leaves)" (*Business Week*, October 6, 1986).

THE STORY: As is the case with *mahosker* and *mamou*, the story behind *playtza* is complex. The word appeared twice in "Word Watch," once in March 1987 and again in April 1988, because the information originally at hand was misleading, skimpy, and incorrect. Early on I suggested a Bulgarian connection, and was set straight by a pile of letters. A number of readers suggested (correctly) that *playtza* comes from a Yiddish word meaning variously "shoulder," "the shoulders," and "the upper back." Still others suggested Polish or Russian etymologies. And so I asked Marvin Herzog, the editor in chief of *The Great Yiddish Dictionary*, to adjudicate the matter. Herzog, a professor at Columbia University and one of the specialists who contributed information about *mahosker*, replied thus about *playtza* in a letter to me dated May 28, 1987:

The word *playtza* is surely derived directly from Yiddish *pleytse*—"back," "shoulder." The Yiddish word, in turn, is derived from the Polish plural form *plecy*, meaning i) "back," "shoulders," and ii) "protection" (i.e., "pull") and "patronage."

What of possible Slavic sources other than Polish? Most, or perhaps all, of the Slavic languages have a form cognate with Polish *plecy*. They are all presumed to derive from the reconstructed Common Slavic *pletje*. [The asterisk is a linguistic notation for a reconstructed form.] Nevertheless, Bulgarian is the least likely source of Slavic influence on Yiddish and an unlikely source on the word in English, as well. Russian influence on Yiddish is relatively late and really quite meager. It's no rival for Polish.

The Yiddish expression *untershteln a pleytse* means "to lend a hand." I'm pleased to have been able to do that in this case.

Indeed, Professor Herzog did lend a much-needed hand: the situation with *playtza* points up the imperative of having specialist-consultants at hand when studying the English language and the diverse, complex strands that make it what it is. And a helpful Word Watcher contributed a Yiddish sentence in which our word is key: *Git mir a playtza*, which is a polite way of asking a companion in a Turkish bath to "please lend me a hand by scrubbing my back."

practical shooting *noun*, an activity in which a marksman tests his or her ability and reaction time in a staged criminal or terrorist situation by firing a gun at human-silhouette targets that suddenly appear along a prescribed course on a range. Points are awarded for shooting the "perpetrators"; penalties are imposed for shooting "innocent bystanders" or "hostages": "The targets this summer afternoon at the Gilbert Small Arms Range . . . have heads and shoulders and kill zones. They are supposed to look like people. That's why it's called *practical shooting*, the fastest growing handgun sport in America" (*Washington Post*, July 11, 1985).

THE STORY: One hundred thousand people engaged in *practical shooting* in 1985, according to a 1986 *Newsweek* story. The activity has been described variously as a sport, a game, and a "new American martial art," according to Michael Bane, the editor of the magazine for the U.S. *Practical Shooting* Association. Changing scenarios on the ranges are employed (for example, "Sunday in El Salvador" and "McDonald's Lobby" were featured on some ranges in the eighties). Quite often substantial purses are awarded to winners of competitions. Although law enforcement officers have been competing on such ranges for years in order to improve, maintain, and test their marksmanship and reaction times in stressful situations, the activity became popular among civilians much later. An *-er* agent noun, *practical shooter*, has also evolved. See also *modem pilot, paintball*.

pulk *noun*, a sled about 4 feet in length and 1¾ feet in height, shaped somewhat like an elongated dish with runners, typically constructed of fiberglass-reinforced polyester with a cover and a seat protected with a windshield and sunlight filter, used with tow shafts to pull a small child behind a cross-country skier or hiker: "This children's *pulk* provides the method of transportation considered by ski experts to be the best, most enjoyable way to take small children over ice and snow" (Hammacher Schlemmer catalog, Winter Supplement, 1988).

THE STORY: Here is an example of an old word with an interesting history that denotes an old means of transportation now enjoying a new, updated use. (This new use has spawned a new word, *sit-skiing*.) *Pulk*, also spelled *pulka*, is a word whose ultimate roots lie in the Lappish language. It came into English as early as 1796 via Finnish *pulkka*, with the meaning "a Lapland traveling sledge." *Pulk* is also an element in the Norwegian term *Fjellpulken*, wherein *fjell* means "mountain," *pulk* means "sled," and the *en* is the definite article for use with a masculine noun.

According to Sara Garnes, Ph.D., an associate professor of English at Ohio State University and a specialist in Icelandic, Norwegian, and Swedish, the Lappish word *bulkke*—the ancestor of *pulk*—has an analogue in *bulke*, a word used in north Norway dialects as a disparaging term for "a small, poor, and ugly pulk." Specifically, in the Kautokeino area, this word was used chiefly in jokes. A related Norwegian word, *bulkur*, meant "a draught-sledge for transporting manure." None of these rather obscure, negative nuances come to light in the *Oxford English Dictionary*'s definition for *pulka*, where one nineteenth-century citation describes the sled as being about five feet long, eighteen inches wide, one foot deep, and canoe shaped: "You sit upright against the stern-board, with your legs stretched out in the bottom," said a writer in 1858, using language more nautical than alpine. Other early citations indicate that the sled, sometimes without runners, was pulled by reindeer or dogs.

The modern *pulk* "became popular in European and Scandinavian countries following World War II, when disabled veterans needed a way to get around in snowy terrain," said the *New York Times* of March 5, 1985. This type of sled is still used by ski troopers in Norway and neighboring countries to transport tents, sleeping bags, and other supplies across snowy terrain— usually one *pulk* per pair of troopers. In a 1987 *New England Monthly* article, *pulks*, which were recommended for infants aged six months or older, were deemed a splendid substitute for the "less-than-foolproof rigs [made] out of Snuglis, sleighs, backpacks, and bicycle helmets" used by an ever-increasing number of cross-country skiparents.

Still other evidence in the saga of the *pulk* indicates it has been adapted and reconfigured in the United States for use by physically disabled people who want to ski downhill. In this application, the *pulk* undergoes a name change: it is called a *sit-ski*. The *sit-ski*, shaped generally like a kayak, is guided by the rider who uses small, ten-inch poles for the purpose. A rubberized blanket is fitted snugly over the rider to preclude falling out.

The *sit-ski* is shepherded from behind by *tetherers*, people who ski without poles and are prepared at any moment to stop the *sit-ski* in an emergency by pulling on a trailing tether line. According to a March 5, 1985, *Los Angeles Times* story, the sport of *sit-skiing* was developed in 1978 by a Santa Cruz sportsman. Today, the *sit-ski* is the sole vehicle in which a wheelchair-bound person can enjoy downhill skiing.

river rider *noun*, one who engages in the sport of driving an all-terrain vehicle, such as a four-wheeler, a dune buggy, or a converted van or pickup truck, down a river: "For two years the Missouri Legislature has debated grounding . . . *river riders*. But until it acts, relaxing along parts of the Black River remains . . . as appealing as pitching a tent along an L.A. freeway" (*Newsweek*, June 29, 1987).

THE STORY: The Germans had a more sedate, civilized way of *river riding*: a Berlin manufacturer built a small convertible car (now antique), that was amphibious. You simply pulled up to the edge of a lake, river, or canal, turned a few knobs to make the vehicle watertight, and drove in. A small propeller at the back of the *water-car* drove it along, and you navigated with the steering wheel.

As might be expected, however, we Americans do things in a more rough-and-tumble manner. This sense of *river rider* (it has two other meanings) probably derives from the sport of *Texas mud-racing*. In that sport, cars, pick-ups, and so-called *high-riders* (compact trucks with raised suspensions)—all equipped with powerful racing engines—are driven through shallow, flooded trenches about 200 feet long and 75 feet wide. The activity is supposed to have originated years ago when folks staged impromptu races on squishy river-bottom roads. Relocation of the sport to shallow rivers was the next logical step.

According to the June 29 *Newsweek* citation, "The six-mile stretch of river near Lesterville, Mo., . . . was overrun by 6,000 ATVs . . . last Memorial Day." In the process, canoeists were driven aside (run off the road, so to speak), the waters muddied, and the fish-spawning beds disturbed.

The second sense of *river rider* is a bit more prosaic: it denotes one who floats down rivers on unpowered craft like tubes, canoes, and air mattresses. In the early 1980s, interest in this sort of *river riding* surged as an adjunct to the adventure-travel craze. People were willing to pay about $600 for a week-long trip and about $1,250 for one lasting nineteen days on rivers like the Colorado. This sport is still very popular.

A subspecies of such *river riders* is, however, less than genteel. The prime objective is to organize *river-riding* beer busts. An August 23, 1982, *Newsweek* story described the horror of New Braunfels, Texas, residents when 60,000 *river riders* in fleets of inner tubes, rafts, canoes, and "tugboat" floats loaded with beer, invaded the Guadalupe River.

A third sense, the most unusual of all, denotes a horseback-mounted tick inspector. This use of the term seems to be restricted more or less to those inspectors patrolling the Rio Grande border, where they round up tick-infested stray cattle, sometimes in the process encountering violence from smugglers, illegal aliens, and rustlers.

sabermetrician *noun*, a mathematician-statistician who uses computers, sophisticated statistical formulas, and enormous files of accrued data to measure the abilities of baseball players and teams and to predict future performance of both: "Today *sabermetricians* and other game analysts have replaced . . . index cards [showing individual players' statistics] with microchips. . . . *Sabermetricians* are also helping teams sharpen their offense, developing formulas that combine the best of batting average, on-base average, and slugging percentage—to provide—at last—an accurate measure of not just how hard a player hits but how well he contributes to his team's run production" (*Discover*, October 1987).

THE STORY: *Sabermetrician* is derived from *sabermetrics* (the mathematical and statistical analysis of baseball), a word coined some years ago by Bill James, the author of *The Bill James Baseball Abstract*. In coining *sabermetrics*, James altered the initials of the Society of American Baseball Research (a 6,000-member organization founded in 1971 to promote historical-statistical study of the game) and then combined them with the suffix *-metrics*, intended to denote the sense of measurement. James has said of baseball that "there may well be no other facet of American life, the activities of laboratory rats excepted, that is so extensively categorized, counted, and recorded" (*Discover*, June 1982).

Some big-league teams still do not take *sabermetrics* seriously, however, a skepticism perhaps heightened by the innate unpredictability of the game. And Thomas Boswell, writing in the April 12, 1987, issue of the *Los Angeles Times*, lamented the shift from the sense of play to the world of cold numbers-crunching, a lament that is as apropos to the nineties as it was to the eighties: "These days, lawyers run rotisserie league teams and *sabermetricians* cross swords with 500-page tomes, debating the exegesis of comically obscure stats. How can the game be dragged back to the state of ramshackle disrepute where it belongs, thrives, and merits the love of children?"

snow skate *noun*, a boot similar in configuration to a downhill ski boot, but roomier and without the arch-compression and ankle-shackling characteristics of a downhill boot, that tapers to a flat, three-inch-wide strip of slippery plastic running the length of the sole and that has a raised toe for kick starts and walking up hills. Also called *SnowRunner*, a trademark: "When 110 Norwegian military officers swept down the ski slope and off the Olympic Nordic ski jump . . . as they were scheduled to do at the [1994 winter] Games' opening ceremonies . . . the world . . . may have thought they forgot their skis. Indeed, they threw them away, along with their poles and those tight-fitting boots—in favor of *snow skates*, the newest gear to hit the hills since snowboards" (*Washington Post*, February 13, 1994).

THE STORY: The sport is emerging, and so are the names for the footwear making it possible for just about anyone, regardless of age, courage, or athletic ability, to hit the downhill slopes, even the hills ominously marked with the big black diamonds (expert trails).

Though *snow skates* had been in use in Europe for about eight years prior to 1994, they reached the United States only in 1991. Interest soared by way of the 1994 Olympics coverage and the article cited here from the *Washington Post*, according to a spokesman from SnowRunner, Inc., the St. Paul, Minnesota, proprietor of the trademark.

It's easy to learn how to *snow-skate*, to use the new verb. A two-minute lesson converts you into an agent noun, a *snow skater*: you learn to keep your weight over the middle to the back of the skates, keep the tips up, and turn uphill to slow down or stop. Getting out of a scary spot no longer involves sweats, chills, and an iron will: You can just walk away from it. It is possible to "dance" down a slope, to jump and pirouette in midair—the works. This promises to be the winter craze of the nineties, and some advocates go further: they are already working to get *snow-skating* dance and speed events incorporated into the next winter Olympics.

spinning *noun*, the fitness exercise of working out on a stationary bicycle in the manner and posture of a racing cyclist. Also called *RPM*: "*Spinning*—or *RPM*, as it is sometimes called—is done on a sleek stationary cycle . . . modeled after a real racing bike, usually to throbbing dance music" (*U.S. News & World Report*, May 16, 1994).

THE STORY: If the eighties to the nineties was the heyday of the spin doctors, surely the nineties will be, in terms of fitness, the decade of the *spinners*, especially since *spinners* for home use hit the market in 1994.

In classes lasting at least forty minutes in health clubs, the person *spinning* spends half the time pedaling while standing, and most of it in racing-cyclist posture—doubled over the handlebars with abdominal muscles tucked in, torso arched. This posture forces the *spinner* (note the second sense of the agent noun) to work not just the leg muscles but the lower abdomen and upper body. The rest of the body moves with freedom, permitting the person to "almost dance on [the] bike." This new type of exercise can burn several hundred calories per session.

"Created in Los Angeles by former bike racer Johnny G., *spinning* is quickly becoming the most popular—and crowded—class at gyms on the Right and Left Coasts" (*Details*, June 1994).

SSAWS *acronym*, Ski Summer, Autumn, Winter, Spring: "You'll see a 25-story-tall metal box on stilts . . . ; that's the ski resort. Specifically, that's 'LaLaPort SkiDome SSAWS,' the biggest indoor ski resort on earth, with a slope 240 feet high and 1,500 feet long, covered with a fairly powdery man-made snow that has the same constituency year-round. . . . The basic lift ticket at SSAWS, covering two hours of skiing, is $54 for adults and $41 for children" (*Washington Post*, January 2, 1994).

THE STORY: Japan is the mecca of *indoor skiing*—is that a surprise? SSAWS, which the Japanese pronounce [zouse], not only denotes the trans-seasonal nature of the new skiing of the nineties, but also refers to the facility in which the sport is enjoyed. In response to a ski craze that began in Japan about five years ago, the Japanese have constructed eight human-made ski areas called *jinko sukii-jo* in the central part of the country, with the biggest two a few minutes by train from downtown Tokyo. SSAWSes were created to satisfy the needs of the so-called can't-wait ski crowd—chiefly young people aged eighteen to twenty-eight, who just can't wait for the first seasonal snowfall to jump onto the slopes.

When you engage in indoor skiing at a SSAWS, you rent your equipment there. Having passed through two air locks, you enter the slope arena, cooled to a perpetual 32°F. High-speed quad chairlifts convey skiers to the top of the single, large hill (it is about as wide as the length of a football field). One side of the hill is "advanced"; the other, "intermediate." The terrain often features moguls. When you fall, you know it: the undersurface is concrete. Après-ski features include a restaurant, sauna, health club, and shops.

swim spa *noun*, a usually prefabricated fiberglass pool measuring about eight by fourteen feet, having an adjustable current allowing the user to exercise by swimming in place, thereby eliminating the need for a larger pool: "Not every backyard has room for a 70-foot lap pool. Those who are short on space but long on energy might consider *swim spas*" (*Boston*, March 1988).

THE STORY: This type of pool has a hydrotherapy spa at one end and the swimming area at the other, with the artificial current driven by a built-in jet. The *lap pool*, preferred by serious swimmers with a lot of space, is long and narrow, measuring about six or ten feet wide and forty or seventy feet long. In addition to the characteristic lane markers, a *lap pool* can have little *swim-outs*, small alcoves with benches for swimmers who wish to stop and take a break.

Urban Yoga *noun*, a new, nineties yoga that mixes stress-relieving stretches with strenuous aerobics and muscle toning set to music, and intended to work out every muscle in the body. Also called *Power Yoga* and technically,

Ashtanga yoga: "The number of yoga classes being offered in gyms and health clubs is at an all-time high. Many carry decidedly unmystical names like *Urban Yoga* and *Power Yoga*" (*U.S. News & World Report,* May 16, 1994).

THE STORY: About 4 million people in the United States practice yoga, which is about twice the number of four years ago. *Urban Yoga,* effective in offsetting the effects of stress and useful in post-heart-attack recuperation, is a hybrid of aerobics and the poses of "traditional" yoga. *Urban Yoga* is also used in treating chemical addictions and some obsessive-compulsive behaviors, because it instills in the practitioner the self-discipline requisite for enhanced self-control.

"The *Urban* and *Power* types who really want to get their heart rates up will be performing an offshoot of *hatha yoga* [which is over 6,000 years old] called *Ashtanga yoga,* which uses the same poses but links them rapidly to one another," *U.S. News* reported.

Workouts typically last ninety minutes, starting with ten to fifteen minutes of highly focused breathing exercises. A thirty-minute period of sitting poses that stretch and strengthen the muscles is followed by another thirty minutes of standing poses. Classes end with fifteen minutes of relaxing poses.

Urban Yoga joins a number of other compounds of which *urban* is a key first element: *urban guerrilla, urban homesteading, urban myth, urban renewal, urban sprawl, urban wind, urban forest,* and *urban contemporary* (the music genre).

zone *noun, slang,* in world-class champion athletes, a level of mental concentration so intense that the brain functions at its peak, the player's sense of time is distorted and elongated, a feeling of effortlessness and certain victory prevails, and euphoria is experienced; a state of altered consciousness that enables such athletes to achieve peak, winning performance. Also called *flow state:* "Studies by sports psychologists . . . are taking . . . the mystery out of why Ivan Lendl or Boris Becker or the world's other great players always seem to win the big points. The answer . . . lies . . . in the *zone,* as the players call it. 'Becker's in the *zone,*' they say, or Becker's *zoning* it.' . . . But how . . . does a player get into the *zone.* . . ? It is not a simple step, but rather a long, complicated process. It builds not over the course of a match or single tournament, but rather over the course of several years" (*New York Times,* September 5, 1986). "Mike Csikszentmihalyi, a psychologist at the University of Chicago, directed a research team that studied basketball players, chess players, surgeons and others. . . . One element almost always mentioned was this moment or moments of special absorption, which Csikszentmihalyi calls a *flow state*" (*New York Times*, September 5, 1986).

THE STORY: This use of *zone* as a noun, as well as other uses of it as a verb—*zone* (out), for instance—and as an adjective derived from the verb collocation, come directly from the television show *Twilight Zone*, and ultimately from *ozone*. The first extension involved drug use, and, in fact, a *zone* or *zoner* was "one stoned on drugs; a space cadet." *Zoned out* meant "spaced out; zonked out." The expression *lost in the twilight zone* means "tuned out of what is going on around one." When the public became aware of the ozone layer, the verb *zone* (out) gained wide currency, perhaps influenced by the song title "Lost in the Ozone Again." Only later did the nondrug sense develop.

The term *twilight zone*, like *catch-22*, has become generic in the sense that it has taken on separate lexical identity. *Twilight zone*, so used in a broad array of printed sources over time, gained sufficient currency to be entered and defined in the third edition of *The American Heritage Dictionary of the English Language*. It is an ambiguous area between two distinct states or conditions. Development of these words and their changing meanings illustrate the conjoint power of the electronic entertainment media, the drug culture, and pop culture in shaping the English used in America in this generation.

13

Words from an Exhibition:
But–by Definition–Is It Art?

airy-fairy
blendo
blood culture
Boweryphone
chopsocky
dollar house
ear candy
egoboo
electromythic
genocide pop
graphic novel
Harold

informance
McWhirtle
Mondegreen
noirish
octoplex
outsider art
plop art
plutography
shanté
undertoad
'zine

Individuality of expression is the beginning and end of all art.
—Goethe

But the Devil whoops, as he whooped of old:
"It's clever, but is it Art?"
—Rudyard Kipling

The words discussed in this chapter are representatives of some of the artistic and social trends in the past decade; whether or not each lexical item denotes true art or truth is for you, the reader, and not the Devil, to determine.

It is appropriate to conclude a book about the words of our lives with a discussion of vocabulary rooted in the arts, for here the art and craft of the lexicographer conjoin with the art and craft of the writer, the cinematist, the musician, the painter, the sculptor, the dancer, and the poet. Literature, and, more generally, oral and written text, is the expression of knowledge. As such, it forms the body of evidence used in lexicographic reportage—investigative reportage, really—of language and of the thoughts and acts of those using it. Art is the expression of the tensions and conflicts involving the artist's world—the outside world and the interior world. And so the imperatives of language and life expressed in varying media come together for lexical and linguistic analysis and commentary.

In terms of subject matter, literature and the cinema compete for the most entries, and it's a tie. Art and the decorative arts have the fewest entries, but that's not the point. In one instance, the group with the fewest entries addresses by itself one of the major issues facing our society today—the chasm between the advantaged and the disadvantaged, discussed at some length in the Introduction.

Seven key themes emanate from the list. Not surprisingly, AIDS is in the forefront at *blood culture*. Nihilism and the despair of Generation X are evident at *noirish* and *Harold*. A sharply shifting U.S. economy has dictated the advent of the *dollar house* in the nineties, as opposed to the *octoplex* of the eighties. The effects of desktop publishing are evident at *egoboo* and *'zine*. The pared-down nineties style is previewed at *blendo*.

But two of the most important trends—the failure of parents and schools to impart a strong grounding in the liberal arts to American youngsters, and the disparity between rich and poor—are to be confronted in two small word sets here. "Achilles exists only through Homer. Take away the art of writing from this world, and you will probably take away its glory," wrote François-Auguste-René de Chateaubriand 170 years ago. He must have been worried about the decline in the public school system in France, but he, at least, didn't have to deal with such things as "the New Literacy," also called "media literacy," and "critical-viewing skills." These kinds of issues are addressed at *genocide pop*, an entry that really asks, Are we to educate our children merely through television and the cinema, when universal ethical and moral problems are at issue? And *graphic novel*, another example of the pervasive penetration of pictures as opposed to text into the national mind, denotes an item of literature that Chateaubriand probably wouldn't have touched with a ten-foot pole.

"Art derives a considerable part of its beneficial exercise from flying in the face of presumptions," or so Henry James believed. He might have liked *plop art* in its second (not first) sense—the unauthorized art that is exhibited in public places, often as a means of revolting against one's fate (with apologies to André Malraux). And no doubt James and Malraux would have enjoyed viewing examples of *outsider art*, the highly expressive work of untrained, nontraditional artists using highly unexpected combinations of materials to express their inner feelings about the outside world.

"Great nations write their autobiographies in three manuscripts—the book of their deeds, the book of their words, and the book of their art." John Ruskin's opinion draws together the strands that unite the words in chapter 13, and indeed all the chapters in the book.

The autobiography of the twentieth century is close to completion. It is too late in the production schedule for major revisions. Now it will be left to critics in the next century to judge us. Perhaps the totality of this book will hint at the nature of that judgment, with respect to the end of the century.

But Earth's last picture has not yet been painted, and the autobiography of our society has not come close to its ultimate conclusion. We are the writers. We are the wordsmiths. Clearly, there is much left for us to do.

airy-fairy *noun, British slang,* an intellectual, especially one in the foreign office: "They'd wanted him for Ambassador in Paris but he'd turned it down; he'd no patience with the *airy-fairies*" (John le Carré, *A Perfect Spy*, 1986).

THE STORY: In the citation, John le Carré, known for using the language of *espiocrats, lamplighters,* and other fixtures in the *overworld* of the secret services, engaged in the linguistic process of functional shift, in which he took a relatively old adjective and turned it into a noun. The most current adjectival meaning of *airy-fairy* is this: "so speculative or visionary as to lack all purpose, substance, and practicality." A citation from the *Manchester Guardian Weekly* makes the point: "The issue . . . is largely obscured by an increasingly unreal debate about *airy-fairy* constitutional modalities."

Airy-fairy at first glance looks like a reduplication such as *teeny-weeny* or *itsy-bitsy* (a *reduplication* being a new word formed by doubling the initial syllable or all of a root word or by doubling all or part of another word). It's not. Its history involves variously the work of Britain's most influential poet, the creator of *H.M.S. Pinafore,* and the writer of *Lady Chatterley's Lover.*

Airy-fairy derives from Tennyson's "Lilian," written in the year 1830:

> Airy, fairy Lilian,
> Flitting, fairy Lilian,
> When I ask her if she love me,
> Claps her tiny hands above me,
> Laughing all she can;
> She'll not tell me if she love me,
> Cruel little Lilian.
>
> . . . .
>
> Praying all I can,
> If prayers will not hush thee,
> Airy Lilian,
> Like a rose-leaf I will crush thee,
> Fairy Lilian.

In its first recorded use thereafter, dated 1869, *airy fairy*, now used as a compound modifier, meant "delicate or light as a fairy," so used by W. S. Gilbert in *Bab Ballards*, called that because these comic verses, originally sent to *Fun*, were signed by him under the pseudonym "Bab":

> *No* airy fairy *she,*
> *As she hangs in arsenic green*
> *From a highly impossible tree*
> *In a highly impossible scene.*

It was left to D. H. Lawrence to use the word, now hyphenated, in the sense "fanciful," with disparaging connotations. The key citation, dated 1920, derives from his novel *Lost Girl*: "He had already an *airy-fairy* kind of knowledge of the whole affair."

blendo *noun*, a style of interior decoration that mixes high-tech, Eurostyle, and antique furnishings into an integrated, individualistic whole: "One style . . . is . . . commonly called *blendo*. It's getting a lot of play" (Hatfield, Mass., *Valley Advocate*, October 5, 1987).

THE STORY: According to Gary A. Marker's article "Help! Somebody Get Me an Ambience!" from which the citation is derived, *blendo* is achieved through the interplay of vivid colors, different textures, and radically opposed materials and forms such as "marble against stainless steel and brass, soaring arches jammed up against rectangles, metal pipes and mesh." (High tech is characterized by the use of traditional industrial products such as baked enamel factory lampshades and plastic-coated grid-mesh. Eurostyle employs clean, lean, modular furniture made of synthetic materials.)

The word *blendo* is a good example of the productivity of the suffix *-o* in forming imaginative new words. This suffix, often used in Australian English, can be appended to nouns to form other words like *bucko*, *kiddo*, and *boy-o*. Used with adjectives, it produces terms like *cheapo*, *deado*, *pinko*, *nutso*, *weirdo*, and *wacko*. It also can be employed in the formation of interjections, such as *cheerio*, *righto*, and *blasto*. When *-o* is applied to clipped forms, one gets *aggro*, *ammo*, and *combo*, for example. This suffix does not come into play in the formation of words such as *gonzo*, *condo*, and *retro*, however. The English word *gonzo* comes from an Italian word of the same spelling meaning "idiot," itself perhaps a clipped form of *Borgonzone*, meaning "Burgundian," or it may come from the Spanish word *ganso*, meaning "dullard; goose," of Germanic origin. *Retro* and *condo* are simply clipped forms of *retrospective/retroactive* and *condominium*, respectively. See also *garmento*, and, at *octoplex*, use of *pep-u-uppo*, a Briticism, of course.

blood culture *noun*, reaction of pop culture to the implications of AIDS, triggered by an obsession with and a fixation on the connection between sex and death as depicted by the imagery and symbolism of body fluids in some artistic genres, such as film and literature; that segment of the populace so affected: "'Bram Stoker's "Dracula,"' a movie that was ridiculed in advance by much of Hollywood and the press as a certain flop, a 'Bonfire of the Vampires,' was an unexpected sensation in its opening weekend, selling $32 million worth of tickets. . . . 'Bram Stoker's "Dracula"' is an orgy of blood-sucking, bloodletting and blood poisoning. It's beyond Grand Guignol: it's opera for the new *blood culture*" (*New York Times*, December 6, 1992).

THE STORY: In its inevitable imitation of life, art has confronted the Prince of Our Disorders—AIDS. Films and books go about their mission of expressing the fears, fantasies, and concerns—if not the pathologies—of the society in which they reside by triggering reactions from viewers and readers. In this instance, as Frank Rich, a *New York Times* writer, put it, our *blood button* has been depressed by certain art forms (compare *hot button*). The Dracula film and Anne Rice's *Tale of the Body Thief* are examples.

AIDS, Rich said, has replaced the threat of thermonuclear war as *the* obsession of the general populace in the post–Cold War era. AIDS, he said, "does to the bloodstream what Communists and other radicals were once rumored to do to the nation's water supply."

In much of the art of *blood culture*, the message is this: sex and death are irrevocably linked, because of the undiminished threat of the AIDS virus. The linkage and the threat have, of course, irrevocably changed the conduct of private life.

"Blood is too precious a thing in these times," to quote a line from the Dracula film spoken by the Count himself, as he leaves one of his victims, a Victorian English girl, to whom he has bequeathed a "disease of the blood unknown to all medical theory," according to her doctor. Rich said that "the AIDS invocations [like this one in the film] are so unsubtle that it is hard to understand how Hollywood, which is nothing if not cynical, failed to realize what 'Bram Stoker's "Dracula"' was and how it might play to an alarmed public."

At that time (1992), Hollywood had not produced a serious work focusing on AIDS (*And the Band Played On*, for example, was released a year later in 1993). And so the Dracula film and other similar works played to sensation in a pop culture ill read and ill informed, a culture lacking the intellectual grounding to accept it as cinematic art, just that. Along with sensation, of course, went titillation, triggered by subtexts suggestive of violent sex, sadomasochism, and homoeroticism.

Socioerotic spin-offs include what Rich called a "fetishization of the condom, the blood's ubiquitous defender," and "the new pop porn," the former represented in the Mylar shrink-wrap that encased Madonna's book *Sex*, and the latter seen in advertisements for certain brands of clothing. See also *genocide pop*.

Boweryphone *noun*, an idiophone, or struck instrument, that has a consistently sharp, relatively high timbre, that is randomly tuned to different pitches, and that is constructed from an array of empty wine bottles: ". . . he has used trash to build 200 instruments, some of which have been displayed at the Smithsonian. . . . The percussion creations include . . . the *Boweryphone*—a set of empty bottles of cheap wine" (*Wall Street Journal*, September 1, 1986).

THE STORY: Were it not for a definition of *Boweryphone*, the uninitiated might reasonably assume it to be a tough-New-York-City telecommunications device (in serviceable black, please) with rotary-dial digits limited to the numerals 9-1-1.

Although the earliest citation for it, taken from the March 8, 1983, issue of the *Washington Post*, said that the *Boweryphone* is "koto-like," and that it is made from "a half-dozen tuned (and empty) Thunderbird wine bottles," I needed to consult with its inventor, Princeton graduate Skip LaPlante, in order to find out when he constructed it ("Sometime between 1977 and 1978," he said in a telephone interview), what it really sounds like, and how it is played. LaPlante, whose words are directly reflected in the definition given at the outset, noted that the wine bottles found in the Bowery produce a good sound; hence the name. He pointed out that the genre "music for homemade or found instruments" (also called "trash music" by others) has flourished for thousands of years. The modern form of such music as played by LaPlante has existed since about 1974.

Boweryphone, exemplifying some of the words of this genre, took ten years to work its way into mainstream print publications outside the field of music. So far, it has not achieved the wide general currency of a word like *glass harmonica* that is requisite for entry in a general, adult dictionary.

chopsocky *noun, slang,* a low-budget martial-arts film characterized by violent fights involving kung fu: "The *chopsockies* present a poor image of martial arts, with the lead actor provoking violence. The character I play always acts in self-defense" (Chuck Norris, quoted by the Associated Press, August 20, 1982).

THE STORY: *Chopsocky* (traceable to 1978), like *kidvid* and *kideo* (television programming and home video for children), *oater* (a Western movie), *celeb bio tuner* (a film about a show business personality), and, years ago, *baloney, payola,* and *sitcom,* was either coined or popularized by *Variety. Chopsocky,* in the manner of other terms in the fields of broadcasting and film, appears to be a blend, this time a mix of *chop* (the martial-arts striking move), *sock* (a punch), and the noun suffix *-y* (meaning "activity or an instance of it"), although the influence of *chop suey* cannot be discounted.

dollar house *noun,* a movie theater, independently owned, that charges modest admission to pictures run several months after their national release: "He is negotiating to build a 10-screen '*dollar house*' in Northern Virginia" (*Washington Post Business,* March 28, 1994).

THE STORY: For those viewers who like the conviviality of going to the movies but who don't want to pay first-run prices and who are tired of renting videos, here's the ticket. With the big chains buying up most of the local, independently owned theaters, many of the remaining independents are letting viewers have it both ways—they're turning their operations into what's called in movie-industry jargon *dollar houses.* This format permits the locals to sidestep David-and-Goliath competition with the Big Boys and at the same time charge from $1.00 to $1.75 for admission. In this respect, the trend parallels the surging success of the factory-outlet stores in a society now obsessed with the economy and joblessness. And from the viewpoint of the locals, the idea is sweet: *dollar-house* operators pay their distributors only about one third of the receipts (they call it the *gate*), in comparison with the 90 percent usually charged by the distributors in the first weeks after the opening of a major movie. Conveniently enough, the distributors typically leave a few months between the end of a first run and the start of its rerelease on video, thereby providing a *dollar-house* operator a window of opportunity to step in with the movie before its video release date.

Some *dollar houses* double as small cafés, with waiters selling beer and sandwiches to viewers seated in comfortable chairs around tables. In a business in which "people vote every day with their feet and their wallets," as

Cineplex senior executive Howard Lichtman put it to the *Washington Post*, the time seems to have come for the niche market represented by this emerging new form of movie theater.

ear candy *noun*, a light, often short piece of music considered pleasing to the listener: "Cuts like the title track . . . are the sure-fire *ear candy* he's grown adept at churning out since his solo career and his Hollywood 'Love Theme' chores . . . caught fire" (*Musician*, October 1986). "She opened with the obscure but charming Sonata in D Major by Baldassare Galuppi, which functioned mostly as a warmup piece, a bit of *ear candy*" (*Washington Post*, March 11, 1985).

THE STORY: Coincidence of word choice among pop/rock and classical music critics is rare. An exception is *ear candy*, denoting a choice aural morsel. Unlike *ear music* (improvisational music), which, according to Clarence Major's *Dictionary of Afro-American Slang*, goes back to 1917, *ear candy* seems newer. Its formation parallels that of *nose candy*, a slang term for cocaine. A direct association between the two has not been proved, however.

Other terms used to characterize light music with instant, widespread appeal are sweets-related: *bonbon* (so used by Sir Thomas Beecham), *lollipop*, and *confection*—this according to Robert J. Lurtsema, the host of "Morning Pro Musica," produced by the Boston NPR station WGBH. In an interview, Lurtsema said that he considers Luigi Boccherini's minuet *ear candy* but Richard Wagner's prelude to *Die Meistersinger* a very large *lollipop*. What on earth might we call Gustav Mahler's Symphony No. 8, a.k.a. the *Symphony of a Thousand*? *Jawbreaker*, perhaps.

egoboo *noun*, *slang*, recognition or praise for one's activities as a science-fiction fan or professional science-fiction writer, and the gratification so derived: "Someone who's into fanac [fan activities] contributes a lot of . . . time to working on fanzines, organizing conventions, etc. One of the rewards is *egoboo*" (*Washington Post*, March 28, 1986).

THE STORY: *Egoboo*, probably a blend of *ego* and *boost*, is still used just about exclusively in the realm of science fiction. Harry Andruschak commented thus in *s.f. chronicle* (May 1988): "I cannot tell you . . . what gratification, what *egoboo*, I would derive from having a . . . coinage of mine incorporated into the English language. I had forgotten, once upon a time, that I invented it [the word *egoboo*]; my authority for authentication is

Charles Burbee." The citation from the Washington Post went on to say that "over the years a vast number of fannish locutions have come and gone," but that fanzine, 'zine, fanac, and egoboo are still being used. So is cyberpunk, a movement among some young writers (and now, computer wizards) who have a penchant for razor-edged, futuristic visions of a world dominated by drug use, computer technology, and cybernetics. Although it is true that few such terms ever emerge from their subcultures to penetrate the linguistic mainstream, it does happen. Fanzine, fanac, 'zine, and cyberpunk have gained entry in dictionaries of the nineties, helped along, no doubt, by the explosion in desktop publishing.

Said a Washington Post story datelined January 29, 1993: "People create zines not with an eye toward profitability, but rather toward the modest fame that comes from having a steady readership of in the hundreds of thousands." Typical titles of these 'zines? Consider Black Leather Times, Teenage Gang Debs, Strange, Rub-a-Dub-Dub, Virgin Meat, Synth-Pod Review, Uno Mas, Shattered Wig Review, Gulp, Take This, Jack Ruby Slippers (surely a venue for entrepreneurial edgy advertising), Unshaved Truths (good for Congress), Chokehold, and Worm. Whatever they are, they're aggro and rad. For still more on this, turn to 'zine.

electromythic adjective, of, relating to, or being a style of furniture sculpture in which elements of the present (such as electricity and neon) and a sense of the past (such as details of styling reminiscent of ancient Egypt and Rome) are combined in the form of giant chairs: "Sculptor Christopher Sproat builds chairs that have been categorized as electromythic, although he prefers the term Gothic futurism" (Smithsonian, April 1986).

THE STORY: In an interview, Christopher Sproat told me that the term electromythic, formed of the prefix electro-, referring to electricity, and mythic, was coined by the painter Paul Shapiro in 1979 or thereabouts, with reference to Sproat's eight-foot-tall chairs. These chairs are decorated with neon, gold leaf, and elaborate carvings. Sproat's larger-than-life furniture represents to him the acute sense of absence he first felt as a youth upon the death of his father. The scale of the chairs, which are so tall that a person must climb the legs in order to reach the seats, might suggest other things to other people: "People who sit in his chairs, he says, 'will look like little children, or Lilliputians on someone else's throne'" (Smithsonian). The term Gothic futurism, the name of Sproat's genre, is his own coinage.

genocide pop *noun*, materials, such as films and exhibits, intended to elicit mass interest in the Holocaust, that de-emphasize to some degree the nature of the people and the cultures so destroyed and the nature and the amorality of the perpetrators of the destruction, and that concentrate instead on the spectacle of the slaughter; *also*: mass-culture interest in and understanding of these materials—often simplistic and superficial in scope and depth—at a time when the true nature of the Nazi war against humanity is being sub-jected to skepticism, revisionism, and even denial: "*Genocide Pop*: Between the Holocaust Museum and 'Schindler's List,' the spectacle of mass murder has permeated mass culture. But both tell us far more about present ambigu-ities than about past truths" (*Washington Post* headline, January 16, 1994).

THE STORY: The term *genocide pop* introduced a major, and controversial, story in the *Washington Post* by Philip Gourevitch, a contributing editor to *The Forward*, a Jewish weekly. The story, which appeared at the time of the opening of the Oscar-winning Steven Spielberg film, generated a great de-gree of reader interest and responses, pro and con. But the story was not so much a critical review of the film as it was a critical commentary on the ways by which the horrors and complexities of human history are presented to and assimilated by this culture.

Gourevitch articulates the problem denoted by the term *genocide pop*: "Critics have hailed the [Holocaust] museums [in the District of Columbia and Los Angeles] and the movie as windfalls for the moral education of the nation. Despite daily dispatches from Bosnia, where nationalistic genocide appears to be the law of the land, reviewers have acted as if opposing the Holocaust 50 years after the fact can save the world from shame in the pres-ent and future. . . . 'Schindler's List' has been treated less as a Hollywood movie than as a work of documentary history that will instruct audiences on the nature of good and evil." He went on to say that a cinematic mystifica-tion of Schindler's wartime career only serves to promote a simplistic under-standing of morality. He added that, in forcing "absolute good and absolute evil to occupy the same body," moral ambiguity as exemplified by Schindler and others like him is replaced with "moral incoherence." The result is that this movie "tells us much more about the confusions of our time than about the realities of the past."

First of all, in an era in which mass-market audiences study pictures and images more than text and assimilate ideas in sound- and view-bites, it is highly disturbing but totally unsurprising that the moral ambiguities and the deep contradictions in the character of the real man Schindler may have been blurred, compressed, suppressed, or even erased in and from the screen Schindler. Of course, Gourevitch was entirely correct when he asserted that the result is the conception of Schindler as "a good Nazi," an impossible combination in terms of ethics.

Genocide pop represents exposure of the fallacy of some reviewers' belief that a nation can be educated, or reeducated, in matters of complex human history through the compressions and license of art without prior grounding in scholarship. See also *moral panic*.

graphic novel *noun*, a paperback book in a trim size typically 7 by 10 inches or 8½ inches by 11 inches, illustrated usually in full-color panels with dialogue balloons and other text, encompassing a minimum of 64 pages but occasionally extending over 100 pages, designed to combine the power of prose and the physical artistry of illustration in treating adult themes, and often created by a single artist-author: "*Graphic novels* are not comics or magazines. *Graphic novels* are books. Period. By virtue of format, however, they use artwork in a comic medium" (*Publishers Weekly*, November 6, 1987). "The old literary guard may see the advent of *graphic novels* as an onslaught of 'visual noise,' but can't it just as easily be seen as part of the development of a universal, visual language? Picture-communication is a democratic form, crossing language barriers, reaching people with marginal reading skills, and, at its best, attaining the highest artistic standards" (Lance Hidy, interview, January 21, 1988).

THE STORY: The subject matter treated in this, a genre popularized in the eighties in the United States, is diverse: fantasy, the superhero, science fiction, and the classics have defined its focus.

M. Thomas Inge, a humanities professor at Randolph-Macon College and a Fulbright lecturer with doctorates in English and American literature, commented on that focus in a *Roanoke Times & World-News* piece dated March 24, 1993: "Recently, several people have thoroughly demonstrated that they can write . . . *graphic novels* . . . which are in their own way as complex as James Joyce's and William Faulkner's novels."

The genre can be traced at least to the thirties, according to Lance Hidy. During those years, Lynd Ward produced novels heavily illustrated with wood engravings and short stories in illustrative form without words. And in the sixties, Eugène Ionesco's *Bald Soprano*, published by Grove Press with typographic interpretation by Massin and photographic interpretation by Henry Cohen, became an example of what Hidy called "*ink theater*," wherein "the page becomes a stage, usually with the actors presented in full figure." *The Bald Soprano* featured photographs of the actors in the Nicolas Bataille Paris production, with the typeface "modulated to create the illusion of vocal sounds."

Still other examples are, according to George Beahm, who was quoted in *Publishers Weekly*, "Art Spiegelman's *Maus* [which] anthropomorphizes cats and mice to make a statement about the horrors of the Holocaust, Kay Reynolds's *Fortune's Friends* [which is] a contemporary detective story with atypical characters, and Harlan Ellison's *Demon with a Glass Hand* [which is] a contemporary fantasy." Readers of *graphic novels* tend to be baby boomers, members of a generation steeped in visual pop culture.

The production of these books is now economically feasible because of advances in printing technology and desktop publishing that allow affordable color illustrations on every page of a volume. Reference points for the artwork can range from the movie or television screen to the computer screen: full-color action frames can be frozen onto the printed page and bonded with dialogue in a series of enticing panels. Cinematic *graphic novels* have long been popular in Japan. In Italy, black-and-white illustrated adult stories are treated in what Hidy calls *fumetti*. And in Mexico and Latin America, the genre is called *fotonovela*.

Harold *verb, slang,* to frequent cemeteries in order to witness and contemplate the passage of life into death: "From the ages of 18 to 21, I *Harolded* away almost weekly at the Capilano View Cemetery [in West Vancouver], sitting on its benches, strolling among its neatly mowed stones, seeing who had died, when and at what age" (Douglas Coupland, *The New Republic*, February 21, 1994).

THE STORY: Douglas Coupland, wordsmith of the *Xers*, provided citational evidence for this interesting cinematic given-name eponym, which also functions as a noun: "In Britain there is a subgroup of citizens called train-spotters who spend their afternoons sitting on railway embankments clocking the passage of local trains. In North America there is a similar subgroup, comprised almost entirely of teens, obsessed with hanging about cemeteries. . . . They are called 'Harolds.'" The word comes from the cult-film classic of 1971 entitled *Harold and Maude*, starring Ruth Gordon and Bud Cort. In the movie, a deadpan twentysomething, who is acutely disillusioned and obsessed with suicide, meets an eighty-year-old lady at a funeral—attendance at which is a mutual hobby—and in the ensuing relationship they explore the meaning of life.

The defining characteristics of a true *Harold* are, in Coupland's view, a hubristic notion of one's own immortality, laughing in the face of death, and deriving adolescent pleasure from the knowledge of the existence of death yet having no fear of it.

If *Harolding* has no appeal, try *Gumping* through life. In a manner similar to that of *Harold and Maude*, the 1994 summer movie hit titled *Forrest Gump* has been verbed. The usage is attested in this citation from a piece by Michael Douglas of the *Akron* (Ohio) *Beacon Journal*, dated August 4, 1994: "Are we going to '*gump*' our way through Bosnia, running, running, running until Serbs and Croats and Muslims live together in peace?" In this and another of his usages ("A year of debate over health care, and one can't help but wonder whether Americans are waiting to '*gump*' our way to reform"), Douglas uses the verb to mean "to muddle though with complaisance, trusting that it'll all work out well in the end." My definition is derived from the thesis of the movie, which related the life and times of a rather "slow" Alabama boy who managed to progress upscale to football star, war hero, even millionaire business executive—by dumb luck and through acts of God, not by effort, drive, and ability.

Called the *Forrest Gump factor* by Michael Lerner, the editor of *Tikkun*, this factor is explained by him in the August 14, 1994, issue of the *Washington Post* ("In 'Gump' We Trust"): "[The movie] offers a new redemptive vision of American history and a reconstructed image of [the American people who made the film so successful at the box office]." *Gump* the movie, Lerner believes, reconstructed the myth that the 1960s had shattered—that America, always well-intentioned, could, by dint of luck or an act of God, muddle through. The header to his piece said it all: "The Summer's Hit Movie Says a Lot About the Soul of America—and Gives Me the Willies." See also *genocide pop*, *undertoad*.

informance *noun*, an informal recital or a presentation of an artistic work in progress during which a spokesperson, such as the composer, the choreographer, or a performer, addresses the audience about matters such as the structure and meaning of the piece, or the artistic goals and the problems in achieving them: "The word *informance* is intended to integrate the informal and the informative aspects of a performance, with a suggestion of intimacy thrown in. The *informance* is supposed to be a sharing of the artist's professional world with the audience" (*New York Times*, November 16, 1986).

THE STORY: Every now and then, dictionary editors encounter a word, the coinage of which is disputed. Such is the case with *informance*, designating an art form that is essentially a mix of interactive artistry and oral program notes intended to break down the barrier between audience and artist. According to David Staples, audience development director at Jacob's Pillow in Becket, Massachusetts, whom I interviewed in the summer of 1988, *informance*—a blend of *inform* and perform*ance*—was jointly coined in 1986 by Trisha Brown, a choreographer, and Liz Thompson, the artistic director at the Pillow. A citation from the July 6, 1987, issue of the Hatfield, Mass., *Valley Advocate* had alerted me to the existence of the word, and on that basis I had called the Pillow: "New music, new dance, modern dance, nouvelle, dining al fresco, dialoguing with the arts, *informances* with the artists—it's all happening at the Pillow." The dancers and the spokesperson narrating the *informances* are called *informers*, according to the same article: "There is opportunity for audiences not only to see but to dialogue with the *informers* in a question-and-answer period afterwards."

More research, however, revealed that *informance* was actually coined in 1970 by singer Judith Allen of Affiliate Artists, Inc., in New York City, the group that pioneered this art form. According to an Affiliate Artists spokesperson, whom I interviewed, Allen exclaimed one day to Richard Clark, president of the organization, "I've *got* it!" with regard to finding a name for the artistic activity they were engaged in. Allen's coinage is a blend of *informal* and *informative perform*ance, characteristic of the Affiliate Artists' recitals, which can occur anywhere, chiefly in nontraditional settings across the country, such as factories, church basements, and prisons. The group's performers and narrators, many of whom are soloists and all of whom require extensive training before giving such recitals, are not called *informers*.

McWhirtle *noun*, a light-verse form of two four-line stanzas, each stanza consisting of an initial iambus, seven anapests, and an optional terminating unstressed syllable, with the rhyme usually on the last words of the stanzas and rhymes elsewhere optional: "The *McWhirtle* is a variation on the double dactyl" (E. O. Parrott, editor and compiler, *How to Be Well-Versed in Poetry*, 1990).

THE STORY: The meaning here was written by Bruce E. Newling, of New Brunswick, New Jersey, who coined the word in 1989 when he attempted to write a double-dactyl tribute to his friend Harry "Skip" Ungar. In doing so he inadvertently devised another verse form having a pleasing rhythm similar to that of everyday speech. He named the form *McWhirtle*, after the protagonist Myrtle McWhirtle in a verse of his entitled "Dear Ann Landers." Here is the double-dactyl variation, the inspiration for the newly coined word, entitled "The Piano Player":

> I read in the papers
> That Harry F. Ungar
> Performs in a night spot
> Near soigné Scotch Plains,
> Caressing the keyboard
> While affluent yuppies
> Are eating and drinking
> Their capital gains.

When the coiner brought his word to my attention, I was struck by the similarity in form of *McWhirtle* to *MacGuffin*, a term that Alfred Hitchcock used to denote any person or element giving spurious meaning to a plot.

Mondegreen *noun*, a mishearing and misrepeating of a popular saying, a proverb, or the lyrics of a song, typically going back to one's childhood: "Christmas songs are good sources of *Mondegreens*, like 'Chipmunks roasting on an open fire . . .' or 'Get Dressed, Ye Married Gentlemen'" (*San Francisco Chronicle*, August 10, 1992).

THE STORY: Sylvia Wright introduced the term *Mondegreen* to English when she wrote an article in *Harper's* about the phenomenon. As a child in England, Wright loved the ballad "The Bonny Earl of Murray," and her favorite stanzas went like this, at least to her ear:

> Ye Highlands and Ye Lowlands,
> Oh, where haw ye been?
> They hae slay the Earl of Murray,
> And Lady Mondegreen.

Poor Lady Mondegreen, slain with the gallant earl. Or so Wright thought. Only many years later did she learn the real wording:

> They hae slay the Earl of Murray,
> And laid him on the green.

Other, more contemporary *Mondegreens* are "There's a bathroom on the right" for Credence Clearwater Revival's "There's a bad moon on the rise," "While shepherds washed their socks at night" for the line in the famous carol that really goes "While shepherds watched their flocks by night/All seated on the ground," and "Gimme the Beach Boys, free my soul" for the Dobie Gray lyric "Gimme the beat, boys, free my soul."

noirish *adjective*, projecting an aura suffused with disillusionment, pessimism, despair, mystery, and often a dark sexuality: "[The] performers seem self-conscious and arty rather than boldly parodistic when they strike their sinister poses in [the] dim, *noirish* lighting" (*San Francisco Chronicle*, May 31, 1990). "He and his fine cinematographer . . . have created a . . . *noirish* mood—not quite menacing but not exactly comfortable either" (*Time*, October 23, 1989). "This *noirish* existential stuff is cleverly laid out with excellent, believable chase footage" (*Car and Driver*, January 1989).

THE STORY: Given the ample spread of printed citational evidence for *noirish* in the literature of the cinema and in sources such as the *Boston Globe*, the London *Sunday Times*, *Newsweek*, the *Washington Post*, and the *Los Angeles Times*, it is surprising that the adjective has not gained entry in some dictionaries of American English. *Noirish* is the second element of the compound *film-noirish*, itself spun off from the French borrowing into English, *film-noir*. The French compound, meaning literally "black film," gained currency in the mid-1950s or 1960, according to *The Random House Dictionary of the English Language, Second Unabridged Edition*.

Noirish by definition denotes the negatives shown above. However, writers who use this adjective often feel compelled to gloss it with a redefining English adjective, most often the redundant word *dark*. This fact is even more reason to enter the word in the dictionary. Still other terms co-occurring quite often in the same contexts as *noirish* are these, gleaned from the citations: *bleak; menace; dislocating; erotic obsession; concealed truth; grainy black-and-white; a prismatic fable of greed and vengeance; a seamy life that leads to murder; a rich, shady Texan; moody; sultry; torrid; funky; seedy backdrops for tawdry affairs*—a list that in itself creates a mind-picture of the word under discussion.

Noirish, in addition to being an extracted element of a compound, is a double-adjectival formation. To the French adjective *noir*, English has added the qualifying adjectival suffix *-ish*, here meaning "characterized by," but primarily "somewhat," as in "somewhat bleak, black, or dislocative." The borrowing *noirish* also exemplifies the reverse of linguistic change in France, a country whose literary academy and government are attempting to curb by legislation the importing of non-French, especially English, words into the national language. *Noirish* is an example par excellence of the receptiveness of English to diversity. However, to date, English has not taken to other well-known French adjectives in this manner: there are no parallel formations derived from *blanc* (white), *vert* (green), *jaune* (yellow), or *rouge* (red).

octoplex *noun*, a building with eight small movie theaters inside it: "'There will be duplexes, triplexes, quadruplexes and *octoplexes*. There will be no end of darkened closets in the basements of . . . buildings'" (Kent L. Barwick, president, Municipal Art Society, *New York Times*, July 26, 1987).

THE STORY: Spurred perhaps by the tradition of *cinoplexes* in shopping malls and multiplex cinemas elsewhere, some builders began in the eighties to convert large old buildings into multiple small cinemas in an effort to offer viewing audiences more choices within a single facility.

The word *octoplex* first surfaced in this sense during the late 1980s, evidenced by this citation referring to Margaret Thatcher, taken from an article by Alex Heard in the August 23, 1987, issue of the *Washington Post*: "Was there an upheaval in the world's geo-politico-stylo hierarchy that put us in the position of having to listen to condescending pep-u-uppo talks from the leader of a country that doesn't even have one *octoplex* SuperCinema or Dinosaur Putt-Putt?"

This compound is purely Latinate, and the *-plex*, meaning "fold," goes back 6,000 years to the Indo-European root *plek-*, a root shared by other modern English words like *plait*, *complex*, *perplex*, and *display*, the latter defined as an image displayed on a movie screen.

outsider art *noun*, a work of contemporary art created by an untrained, non-traditional artist using highly unusual media such as wire, bones, buttons, pebbles, tin sheets, or pieces of concrete to externalize his or her visions, view of life, and dreams, with the results being eccentrically original and usually abstract, raw, primitive, and sometimes frightening: "The French call it *art offshore* or *art brut*, and in English it is known as *outsider art*: works by unschooled visionaries . . . who know nothing of mainstream art" (*New York Times*, January 6, 1991).

THE STORY: The *outsider* in *outsider art* refers to the untrained, naively appealing quality of the artistic creations and to the venues of the creators—

typically isolated locales far from established art centers. *Outsider artists* are often country folk, the elderly, the very young, or sometimes the mentally ill.

This genre has existed for many years, going back at least to 1950, when a rather unorganized group of people, *outsiders* to mainstream art, split from a larger whole, commonly called folk artists. These *outsiders* "display total independence and [their] creations have no traditional roots but spring often from visions and dreams," according to Roger Ricco and Frank Maresca, the owners of the Ricco/Maresca Gallery in New York City and the writers of the 1988 book *American Primitives, Discoveries in Folk Sculpture*, which devotes a chapter to the genre.

Because of skyrocketing costs associated with established art, collectors have started scrambling for the work of unknowns; hence, the five figures that can be gotten for the work of some *outsider artists*. *USA Today* reported on August 7, 1991, other reasons for the growing popularity of this art: "Collectors, bored with establishment art, are seeking something different. And a renewed respect for handcrafted items fits the back-to-basics mood of the '90s."

plop art *noun*, **1.** a subgenre of public art, specifically an artwork chosen for and placed by a corporation in an otherwise bland or utilitarian public space in order to improve or obscure it: "[The] bust of Moscone is something Michelangelo could have recognized as a work of art—although he might have been puzzled by its lack of dignity and its forthright acceptance of the ugly. It could exist . . . in a public space. (Which was its fate—after its rejection by the Arts Commission it was bought by an art dealer.) . . . Such works of art have been derisively termed '*plop*' *art*, or, in the case of [another artist's] ubiquitous sculpture, 'the turd in the plaza' [the latter expression having been attributed to the American architect James Wines]" (*San Francisco Examiner*, December 15, 1991). **2.** unauthorized art exhibited in public places, or the alteration of existing or approved art; unauthorized art sneaked into and displayed without invitation or permission in a museum, or art left at random in a gallery, restaurant, or private home, also without the permission of the owner or proprietor: "In a *plop art* display last year, [Richard] List covered a campus statue of The Golden Bear in Lower Sproul in a plastic tarp to promote safe sex" (Berkeley, Calif., *Daily Californian*, February 27, 1991).

THE STORY: If art imitates life, then the two very discrete senses of one term, *plop art*, make a strong statement about the corporobureaucratic and the less privileged sectors of our society, and about public and private concerns. *Plop art* in its first sense is so named chiefly because in most instances the artworks are afterthought add-ons to an already finished public space, placed there only after somebody suddenly realizes that a critical piece of the ensemble is missing. As *Examiner* art critic David Bonetti has said, "A humane environment is what is usually missing—something no work of art can satisfactorily remedy, any more than an asprin can cure cancer." Clearly, then, the effect is Let's Just Dump It There. Also falling into this genre are official bronze commemorative monuments, called *off-the-rack sculpture* by insider wags, according to a citation gleaned from the July 18, 1992, issue of the *Washington Times*.

The term *plop art* in its second sense goes back at least nine years, according to *plop artist* Richard List. Writing in the Fall/Winter 1991 issue of the Berkeley, California, *Homeless Voice* (volume 3, number 3), List explained some of his work: "During the summer of 1991 came the confiscation of Gilda, the property of one of Berkeley's most creative and illustrious individuals—the Hate Man. . . . I started posting information on a tossed away rug I hung on the chain-link fence there surrounding the vacant lot. I also took Gilda Radner caricatures, which I photocopied and stapled onto rugs and other recycled items in a style reminiscent of Andy Warhol. I labelled the work '*plop art*' and the vacant lot was referred to as 'The New Sense Art Museum' which was colorfully advertised." List has explained in other writings that *plop art* does not damage any existing structure or the surrounding land, and that graffiti is definitely excluded from the genre.

What are some of this famous *plop artist's* other creations? One exhibit consisted of fifty-seven television sets, painted in fluorescent colors with sayings and poems and pieces of bread and pizza attached to them, placed on Mount Tamalpais one Sunday afternoon. (The attachments harken back to Picasso, who, in the year 1912, pasted a shard of oilcloth to a still life.) Another construction was a Styrofoam form of a homeless man called "Art," attached in cruciform position to a chain-link fence along with a sign reading "Don't Crucify the Poor."

This type of *plop art* first appeared in 1986, according to Gene Turitz, chair of the Berkeley Arts Commission, with a statue by Fred Fierstein called "The Guardian." The sculptor got tired of waiting for the city to approve installation, and so he went ahead and installed it himself on his own. This sculpture of a figure that is half man, half tiger, became the centerpiece of controversy after installation. Fierstein was first issued with a citation for littering. That was eventually retracted. Then, when the piece was about to be removed, Fierstein obtained sufficient signatures to put the whole issue onto a ballot for the voters. In the end, the voters sided with Fierstein and the piece remained in place—"a clear triumph of art over bureaucracy," in the opinion of the October 18, 1991, *East Bay Express*. And so credit for the first example of *plop art* is Fierstein's, but credit for the new sense development of the term itself is List's.

But is any of it art? you might ask. If it is true that, in the words of William Saroyan, "the role of art is to make a world which can be inhabited," then *plop art* in its second sense, at least, does that, because it makes us think, particularly of the ways in which society has evolved for better or for worse, and it forces the viewer to confront that worse, to help better it, perhaps.

plutography *noun*, the practice of writing books and articles about the very rich, their lifestyles, and their private lives: "It is the age of *plutography*, where the acts of the rich turn them into great stars" (Tom Wolfe).

THE STORY: Tom Wolfe is the coiner of *plutography*. The *pluto-* goes back to the Greek *ploutos*, "wealth," and the suffix *-graphy* to the Latin *-graphia*, itself from the Greek *graphein*, "to write." Both *plutocracy* and *plutography* share the same Indo-European root *pleu-*, "to flow." A derived form also exists: "Curiosity has grown more shameless and more feverish—more *plutographic*, in fact" (*New York Times*, March 31, 1986). Interestingly enough, Wolfe, a writer known for his apt assessments of various elements of the national character in an array of novels, has not only contributed a new word with staying power, he has also contributed one that, by its very constituent elements, takes us back 6,000 years to the reconstructed ancestor of English, Indo-European. Here's a coiner who definitely has the right stuff.

shanté *interjection*, used as a theater direction to a performer, indicating that the performer should behave in such a way as to create an enchanting aura on stage: "On her dance-floor hit 'Supermodel,' RuPaul commands, 'Turn to the left! Now turn to the right! Sashay! *Shanté!*'" (*Details*, February 1993).

THE STORY: This interjection, used by the seven-foot-tall drag queen, is most certainly a borrowing. It may be a clipped, respelled form of the French boulevardier's greeting, *enchanté*, meaning "enchanted" or "delighted" (to meet or see you). Or it may be a borrowed respelling of the plural imperative of the French verb *chanter*, spelled *chantez*, and meaning "sing." (When used in the transitive, *chanter* can also mean "to celebrate.") Still another theory holds that *shanté* is derived from or otherwise related to the Sanskrit word *shantih*, repeated three times in the T. S. Eliot poem *The Waste Land*, and glossed there as "the peace which passeth understanding."

All of which brings to mind a new word, *girlingo*, discussed by Jason Reeves in the May 1994 issue of *Genre*, to wit: "As soon as *gender illusionist* Girlina hit New York City, the nights in Manhattan were filled with a whole new sound. It's referred to as '*girlingo*.' So what is this strange new tongue? Well, you know . . . when you're feeling '*swirly*' and '*all that way*,' then you go '*ki-ki*' with friends. Huh? Listen for more '*girlingo*' on Girlina's first dance mix, OK, sugar?"

undertoad *noun*, fear of the forces of doom and of the unknown, coupled with an anticipation of mortality, often symptomized in people by acts of violence and cruelty and in displays of personal weakness and excess: "It scares me sometimes, the state of things in the world right now. . . . My ultimate fear is the annihilation of nuclear war. I mean, that's the real *undertoad*" (Robin Williams, *Washington Post*, July 23, 1982). "If the prospects of fleeting fame and penury, whether real or imagined, trouble [Canadian writer Timothy] Findley periodically, his genuine self-doubt is forever near the surface, threatening to pull him down, and if not destroy him, silence him for good. This is his personal *undertoad*" (*Quest*, October 1982).

THE STORY: John Irving, in introducing *undertoad* to the general parlance by way of a child character in *The World According to Garp* (1976), followed the examples of Lewis Carroll, the coiner of *chortle*; Horace Walpole, the coiner of *serendipity*; Gelett Burgess, the coiner of *blurb*; Anthony Hope, the coiner of *Ruritania*; and Joseph Heller, the coiner of *catch-22*. In *Garp*, the boy Walt, having been warned many times by his elders about the dangers of an undertow, utters the term *Under Toad* in this sequence of dialogue set on a New Hampshire beach:

"What are you doing, Walt?" Helen asked. . . .
"I'm trying to see the *Under Toad*," Walt said.
"The what?" asked Garp.
"The *Under Toad*," Walt said. "I'm trying to *see* it. How *big* is it?"
And Garp and Helen and Duncan . . . realized that all these years Walt had been dreading a giant *toad*, lurking offshore, waiting to suck him under and drag him out to sea. The terrible *Under Toad*. Garp tried to imagine it. . . . Would it ever surface? Did it ever float?

Walt worries that the "vile *Under Toad*" might always stay submerged, all-seeing and "bloated" and "slimy." This term, which became a code word for *anxiety* in the novel, is attributed by Irving to his own son Brendan, "who [had] once misunderstood a warning about swimming in the ocean" (*Time*, August 2, 1981). Since the time at which the book appeared, a number of citations for the word have surfaced, most of them styled in the solid form—these being from *The Sciences*, the *Washington Post*, *People*, *Time*, *Quest*, and the *New York Times*. *Undertoad*—a word that reflects the pervasive anxiety of people in an uneasy world and a world fraught with change—is most certainly worth watching for some time to come.

'zine or **zine** *noun*, *slang*, a special-interest, usually amateur-published, magazine, idiosyncratic in style, that is targeted to readers sharing that interest: "It's good to see that *'zines* in this class—including *K.D.S.*, *Geek Attack*, *Freezine*, *Rag Read*, *Spunk*, *Crank*, *Joke*, and others—don't take their scene or themselves too seriously" (*Thrasher*, May 1986, a skatezine quoted in *Harper's*, October 1986). "Welcome to the highly irregular world of *zines*, the magazine equivalent of public-access television" (*New York Times*, November 8, 1993).

THE STORY: The word *'zine*, like its linguistic bedfellows *'cuda* (from *barracuda*), *'roid* (from *steroid*), *'lude* (from *Quaalude*), *'burb* (from *suburb*), and *'hood* (from *neighborhood*), is a clipped form. *'Zine*, now more often being styled without the apostrophe, is ultimately, if not directly, derived from the last syllable of *magazine*. That syllable came to be used in the last twenty-nine years as an element of other coinages such as *fanzine*, *amazine*, *skatezine*, *newszine*, *freezine*, and *prozine*—all of them *'zines*. *'Zine* as a freestanding form emerged from these other forms, popularized in the early 1980s by Mike Gunderloy, it is said. He is the founder of *Factsheet Five*, itself a *'zine* that reviews other *'zines*. Originally the *'zines* were produced with stencils or photocopiers. Today they are produced with desktop publishers. The number of *'zines* in circulation has markedly increased in the past two years, and from 1980 to 1993, the number escalated from a mere 5,000 to about 20,000. See also *egoboo*.

End Points, Starting Points: The Processes Behind the Evolution of Language

"Language changes every eighteen or twenty miles," or so goes the Hindi proverb. The thought is particularly apt with respect to the English language, specifically American English.

The forces of change that affect English-speaking society forge changes in the language, as we have seen just in the few hundred words discussed in this book. Parallel forces—various recurring linguistic developmental processes—work to alter the architecture of English, more often than not intersecting with social processes. These linguistic forces of change deserve brief discussion.

The seven processes occurring most often in the development of the words chosen over the years for the column "Word Watch" are, in order of frequency, these: compounding, derivation-by-association, eponymy, coining, trademarking, borrowing, and blending. Following are descriptions of these and other common linguistic processes.

Compound Assets

A great many, if not a majority, of the new terms in American English these days are construed as compounds—open, hyphenated, or closed. For our purposes, a compound is a term composed of two or more once-separate words that coalesce to accord the new term a unitary meaning of its own, a meaning not derivable by analysis of the separate meanings of its constituent elements. Thus we consider as "non-self-explanatory" compounds like *universal reactor* (unrelated to nuclear power), *category killer* (not a serial murderer), *blood culture* (not that which is drawn from a patient's vein and then analyzed in a lab), *influence mine* (not a treasure trove for Beltway influence peddlers and lobbyists), and *outlaw party* (not mounted men in black on the way to Dodge City). Into this set fall terms like *private bank*, a compound with two discrete, very different, and highly technical meanings in high finance.

English is as elastic as spandex in its compounding methods. A mere handful of examples appear in this book, but some of them bear mention. Verbs, for instance, can be formed by compounding a noun with another verb, as in *death qualify* (and things like *judge-shop* and *window-shop*). Verbs plus adverbs can yield nouns like *go-fast*, and the same process can generate adjectives like *go-slow*. In a similar manner, prepositional phrases can become set compounds that function as adjectives: *at-risk*, *on-site*, *offscreen*, and *online* are examples. The adjective *beyond risk*, discussed in this book, is in the process of solidifying into the same type of adjective as *for-profit*, as in *for-profit hospitals*.

Speaking of health care and medicine, that field has generated all manner of compounds, from things like *bursa musculi bicipitis femoris superior* to *Fick's halo*. In this book, two types of noun compounds seem to proliferate. In one set, a noun (the producer or the cause of the condition) combines with another noun (the site of the condition or its effect) to yield a name for a condition: *casino feet*, *'roid rage*, and *holiday heart* are illustrations. Medicine also uses a "false possessive" in related compounds, where a "possessive" noun (often but not always the one experiencing a condition) fuses with another noun (the condition, expressed in terms of its site, signs, or symptoms), to produce a new term like *pizza-cutter's palsy* or *jogger's paw*.

Guilt by Association

Derivation of a new term by association with a high-profile, preexisting term is a central process in the changing English of the nineties. The velocity of the process is driven by the media, fueled by the immediacy of information access. Here we see the *couch people*, urban refugees whose very name derives from others such as the Vietnamese (and more recently, the Haitian) *boat people*. *Computer literacy* has spawned many derivatives—one of them, *emo-*

tional literacy. White Iraqi takes its text from *White Russian. Virtual office* is clearly derived by association with *virtual reality*, and the same holds with *virtual sex. Greenlock* was influenced by *gridlock*, itself a relatively recent entrant into English.

Some derivations-by-association are extremely prolific. Take *blue-* and *white-collar*, for instance. After them came *pink collar*, followed over the years by a small army of copycats: *bright-collar*, *gold-collar worker*, *open-collar worker*, *green collar* (fraud), even *no-collar*. Terms in which *mafia* is the key second element have proliferated, with *atomic mafia* and *train mafia* two of the latest. Similarly, *iron curtain* has been the linguistic muse for newer forms like *paper curtain*, *blue curtain*, and a host of others.

But there's more. *Heli-hiking*, we now know, was coined in direct association with a predecessor adventure-travel sport, *heli-skiing*, up in Banff, Alberta. *Carjacking*, the term, imitated *hijacking* and all the other *jackings* perpetrated by terrorists in our time. *Club Fed* takes off on *Club Med. Garage hopping* is associated with things like *table hopping*, linguistically speaking; and there the resemblance ends, with the click of a door opener. *Sudden sniffing death*, the possible result of *huffing* (discussed at *glading*), has a structure very similar to the preexisting *sudden infant death syndrome. Smoking bed*, and more recently, *smoking memos*, have nothing to do with "Smoking or nonsmoking, sir?" Rather, they go back to the *smoking gun* of Watergate. Similarly, *grassy knollism* derives from repeated media references over the years to a *grassy knoll* along an infamous Dallas roadway in November of 1963 when the unthinkable happened.

Terms such as *smoking bed* and *grassy knollism* demand a certain level of political and historical literacy from their users, and so they mark an accentuated trend in the use of English toward the literacy of the twentieth century, as opposed to the literacy associated with The Greats.

Name-calling

Eponymy, the process by which the name, as of an era, a place, or a thing, is derived from that of a person, is especially powerful today, because this is the era of plutography, pathography, and obsession with the acts and antics of the Rich and Famous. Thus, *imeldific* and the verb *marcos* strut across the linguistic stage, hand-in-hand, hand-in-glove, along with other verbs derived from surnames, such as *Krone*, *Lerach*, and *Rembrandt*. (Remember that at

Rembrandt you met five other verbs: *Bork*, *Thomas*, *Souter*, *quayle*, and *Norville*.) First-name verbs, like *Barbara*, and first-name nouns, like *georgi*, *Bernie*, and *Nancy*, fill out this wild and crazy bunch, followed close behind by the newer *Stephanopouli*.) Add to these the *half-Cab*, denoting a spectacular snowboarding move devised by one *Caballero*, whose surname has been clipped.

Taking off on the established patterns of medical eponymy (*Thucydides syndrome*) are *Begin amputation* and *Paula Jones Disease*, the latter bringing to the fore political-sexual scandal (*Hart Rule*), law (*Chip Smith charge*), and convenient amnesia (*Waldheimer's disease*).

Geoeponymy, involving the names of the peoples of countries and the names of countries and places, is to be seen at *Iraqi manicure* (patterned after such things as *Chinese water torture*), *New York barricade*, *full Cleveland*, *Paris Lip*, *Boweryphone*, and the phonetic-dialect respelling *Guyland Defense*.

A subset is a sort of renaming, a *Jurassication*, by which process the titles of films, the names of networks, and the names of people (real or fictional) take on linguistic lives of their own in a pop cultural shorthand. Joining this group are *dance with (the) wolves*, *Schindler defense*, *CNN effect*, *Lake Wobegon effect*, *Kojak Liberal*, the noun and verb *Harold* (at the entry for which *gump* appears), and *zone*. From print we get *vogueing*, *Penal Michelin*, and the new *Fagins*.

Coining: Strong Linguistic Currency

Coinages in this book fall into two major categories: personal and corporate. Personal coinages are those created by individual writers to fill a professional need or just for the sheer fun of it. Corporate coinages are words created as an adjunct to a product-development or business strategy. Corporate coinages are also closely tied to the creation of trademarks, a separate process.

Anticipointment, a coinage of some note and a blend as well, exemplifies how, in an era of heightened information access, the name of the real coiner (advertising executive Ray Jacobs) can slip through the cracks and go unnoticed as others pick up on the usage and are erroneously accorded credit for creation of the term. *Firp*, the creation of Jonathan Kellerman, is an example of a word made up just for kicks. And the sci-fi community, prolific in its coinages just like the computer hacker community is, has given us *egoboo*, courtesy, we are told, of Harry Andruschak. As for *dracontologist*, a monk did it (with help from his knowledge of the classical languages).

Greek and Latin variously assisted coiners such as Ike's adviser Somerset Waters with *emporiatrics*; Joseph J. Tecce of Boston College with *hedonia hypothesis*; Paul D. MacLean, M.D., with *isopraxis* (a word now being altered with a fake *-ism*); William H. Riker of the University of Rochester with *heresthetic*; Tom Wolfe with *plutography*; painter Paul Shapiro with *electromythic*; Jack Lessinger, emeritus of the University of Washington (Seattle), with *penturbia*; and so on.

While Madonna and her graffiti-artist friends gave us *boy toy*, Jean-Jacques Rousseau gave us *civil religion* in *The Social Contract* (1762)—that pair, a study in contrasts. Thomas Hine, architecture critic at the *Philadelphia Inquirer*, contributed *populuxe*, and, like columnist Ed Shamy of the *Roanoke Times & World-News* did with his word *jantakinzillion*, added a letter or two to make it sweet.

Sylvia Wright gets credit for *Mondegreen*, but John Irving, who gave us *undertoad*, had his youthful character commit a *Mondegreen* when first using *undertoad*. Al Neuharth of *USA Today* engaged in homography when he created *bumbo*, a word that joins three others of the same spelling and pronunciation but with very different origins.

Bruce E. Newling came up with the poetically quirky *McWhirtle*, and told me how he did it. Another Boston College professor, Paul Lewis, coined *Frankenfood*, an example of a coinage that gained instant currency via the media. He also coined *schmooseoisie*, and he told me how these new creations came to mind. The fact that lexicographers can talk to coiners about their word creations is, in itself, exciting. Would that we could have spoken to Lewis Carroll about his plays on words.

In the business world, Gifford Pinchot gave us *intrapreneur*, trend analyst Faith Popcorn contributed *decession*, and Carnegie-Mellon University professor Robert E. Kelley created *gold-collar worker*. Corporate coinages include *snow skate* and *olestra*, the latter standing for sucrose *polyester*, with an *a* added at the end. Peter Barnes and his colleagues, then at Working Assets, thought up *greentapping* to name their concept. And the people at the Softgel Association were responsible for mainstreaming *softgel* into the medical, pharmaceutical, and consumer lexicons as a nonthreatening substitute for *capsule*, a word tainted by association with the tamperings of the eighties.

Trademarking

Trademarks are generated individually, as is the case with *Permaprose*, and by group or corporate efforts, as is true of *Shelter-Pak* (created by students) and *Exxon* (created by corporate effort via a large team of linguists). *Cassingle*, a blend like *warmedy* (at which it is discussed), is important because it is associated with the point at which the beloved 45 rpm record disappeared. *Deep Vision* marked a big step forward in advanced electronics in the entertainment industry. *Xerocracy*, derived, of course, from *Xerox*, represents the nonfreedom of speech in Iran. *Xenomouse*, which draws on classical antecedents, brings to mind genetic engineering and the ethical controversies surrounding that field. *FlashBake* represents probably the most signal advance in cooking since the introduction of the microwave.

As seen at *Xerocracy*, trademarks have a way of taking on figurative lives of their own. In so doing, through popular usage, they often undergo orthographic and structural alteration: the verbed form of *Exxon*, the nouned and suffixed form *Velcroid*, and the compound form *Twinkie defense* are examples.

Trademarks can become symbolic of the public's fascination with diverse product lines and specific activities, attested by the popularity of the trademark *Rollerblade* alone, in the plural, and in derivative forms like *Rollerblading*, *Rollerblader*, and so on, as opposed to *in-line skate*—all this because of writers' and speakers' usages. Will *SnowRunner*, as opposed to *snow skate*, exhibit this kind of behavior? And what of *Exerlopers*, the mark coined by a Russian doctor who had to consult an English-language dictionary to name his product?

Borrowing from Peter to Name Paul

"The English language is the sea which receives tributaries from every region under heaven," wrote Emerson. How right he was: borrowing words from foreign languages has always marked the multicultural identity of the mother tongue. A few borrowings among the many in this book are *fruppie*, which combines the *fr* in Yiddish *fromm*, "religious," and the *uppie* in *yuppie* to yield a new word. A quick but inexhaustive sampling of direct borrowings discussed in the book includes these: from Lappish, *pulk*; from Japanese, *sukoshi*, *skosh*; from Italian, *wallyo* and *agita*; from Zulu, *lobola*; from Russian, *Sovok*; and from Portuguese, *lambada*.

A subset of borrowing is what is called the loan-translation. This is the process by which the semantic constituents of one term are translated literally into their equivalents in the borrowing language, as is the case with *superman* from *Übermensch*. Two examples of loan-translation at work in this book are *Wall in the Head*, from German *die Mauer in den Köpfen*, and *fifth disease*, from French *cinquième maladie eruptive*.

Once in a while a term or expression will enter English two times (or more) from two (or more) different source languages at two (or more) times in history. *Typhoon*, with its variously Arabic, East Indian, Greek, and Chinese roots and its background involving two separate points of entry into our tongue—India and then China—at two separate times—the sixteenth and seventeenth centuries, respectively—is the exemplar of this double- or multiple-entry phenomenon. Such may be the origin of *mahosker* (possibly a double borrowing from Irish Gaelic and Yiddish), in the manner postulated by some of *kibosh*. Similarly, the noun compound *wolf ticket* may be a loan-translation of a Russian expression, while the idiom *sell wolf tickets* may have its roots in Black English.

The complexities of etymological development often prove too much for the inexpert, as was the case with *blaff*. A major newspaper categorically stated that *blaff* was an imitative term, when in point of fact, it came into mainstream English (cuisine English, actually) by way of Caribbean English, where it had probably been formed on a preexisting English word *broth* by way of consonantal shift.

Word Processing: The Blends

Blaff and the language of cuisine bring us to the blends—words resulting from a prolific process, especially in the media and entertainment (*anticipointment, informance, infomercial, chopsocky,* and *warmedy*), psychology and sociology (*affluenza*), high technology (*digerati, compunications*), and science (*liger, triticale, agrimation, vog,* and *thermagation*).

Those who are dumbfounded by the sheer number of blends in today's English and who chortle about their slangy, breezy register or even lambaste dictionary editors for including so many blends in their word lists ought to remember that *dumbfound*, *chortle*, and *lambaste* are blends.

Less Is Sometimes More

Getting into some of the other language processes at work in this book, let's turn to abbreviations and acronyms. Acronymy is a highly prolific process in science, the military, politics and government, and pop culture.

WYSIWYG is a pop cultural antiquity—yes! an antiquity—which, when juxtaposed with *WIBNI* and *WOMBAT*, shows just how fast the language-that-can't-stand-still has moved along the digital highways. Other acronyms, such as *LUG*, signify the freedom of personal choices now accorded today's youth.

Acronyms have a way of nouning themselves in the manner of *radar*, *sonar*, and *snafu*. Such is the case with *dink*, *NIMBY*, and many others entering English in the eighties. *Canola*, the noun formed from *Can*ada, *o*il, *l*ow *a*cid, is yet another.

Abbreviations that reflect events of our times are *IC* (innocent civilian)—a Vietnam War item—and *TLB* (tough little broad)—used in terms of the Tonya Harding incident prior to the 1994 Winter Olympics.

Acronyms and abbreviations can be verbed, as we have seen with the British verb *sug*, and they can combine to form highly individualistic noun expressions such as *Bosnywash*.

The Quick Affix

Prefixation and suffixation serve at once to construct and deconstruct. With the latter, both *-ism* and *-phobia* have shed their hyphens and morphed into nouns. And the entries at *non-ism*, *laughism*, and *gephyrophobia* illustrate the richness of suffixation both as a tool for word building and as a sign of the social times.

Some conservatives believe that English is being *-ized* to death; no doubt they have recoiled at *incentivize*, the double whammy at *incent*. Another prolific verb suffix, *-ate*, is differentiated from back-formation at *conversate* in discussion of *visionate* and *ethnicate*.

O-suffixation (as with *cheapo*) is discussed at *garmento* and *blendo*. And we saw an interesting use of *-eer* (often pejorative) at *orbiteer*, which included references to others in the set like *mountaineer* and *orienteer*.

Dysfunctional Shift

Functional shift, often decried by purists (who wouldn't be able to *telephone* anybody without it), is the change in grammatical function of a word from one part of speech to another, exemplified by the verb *contact*. In this book, the street-gang verb *mad-dog* and the verbs *office* and *wife* exemplify that controversial process.

A political operative in the Clinton administration takes *there* and, in the manner of Gertrude Stein, uses it as a noun, but with a new meaning. And by way of a reference to Bob Dole, we were introduced to the noun *snide*.

Looking Back-formed in Anger

Back-formation is yet another process often glared at by purists, many of whom couldn't *edit* a manuscript or have their maladies *diagnosed* without it. Aside from *conversate*, words illustrating this process—the formation of a new word by removal of an existing true affix or element erroneously thought to be an affix—are *incent* and *informate*.

Clipping

Clipping is big these days, whether you're from the *'hoods* or the *'burbs*. From *metamorphosis* comes *morph*; from *magazine*, *'zine*; from *steroid*, *'roid*. Not to be omitted are *dis* and *suss*, illustrating the reduction of a word to its initial syllable.

Shoulda, Coulda, Oughta

Contractions, best illustrated in the general parlance by *wannabe*, which functions as both noun and adjective, are covered here at *gimme cap* (a compound dating at least to 1941), where we move from the seat of a tractor back to the Roaring Twenties to the vamp called the *Gimme Girl* in discussion of a commonly heard term rarely occurring in print.

Hide-Me Words

Euphemism, called a sign of the hidden insecurities of any era, is discussed at length at *food insecurity*; it is also to be seen at *constant whitewater*, well hidden by a sports overlay. It is exemplified at the innocuous-sounding *insurance technician*. *Delta-hedging*, a new term used in place of *portfolio insurance*, is still another example of packaging the unpalatable in fancy wrappings.

Idioms

Idioms, defined as set phrases with intrinsic meanings of their own that are not deducible from the sum of the meanings of their constituent word elements, are represented by *off the grid, pipe a quote, crash and burn, dance with (the) wolves, sell wolf tickets,* and *walk the cat back.* Though idioms per se don't constitute *process*, the formulation of idiomatic expressions does. American English is especially rich in this arena, as is the Russian language. And both languages draw heavily on zoologic imagery in many of their idiomatic expressions.

Intentional Rhymesters

Madonna and Imelda Marcos engaged in intentional rhyming when they brought *boy toy* and *hotsy-potatsy*, respectively, to the fore. Intentional rhyming is the process by which two rhyming words are juxtaposed, with one in the compounded set used in a figurative or exaggerated way. Marcos's term also involves a bit of reduplication, the repetition of an element within a word, often involving slight variation in the initial consonant or the medial vowel (*footsie-wootsie*).

The Numbers Game

If you're a *212* who plays the *88* and has seen someone get *86'd* from a bar or restaurant, then you know exactly how arabic numerals can be used in English as parts of speech. A prime example is *24/7*, followed by *9*.

Add to those the compounds formed of ordinals and words—*16th republic*, for instance—and compounds formed of spelled-out numerals and words—*million-dollar wound*, for example.

Related to the subject are the *numeronyms* you often dial when using *800* numbers. A subset is the combination of numbers plus letters and sets of often respelled words appearing on many license plates. All of which proves that language isn't the preserve of scholars alone.

Respellings, Reentries, Portmanteaus, and Mysteries

From respellings like *mersh*, *myc*, and *shanté*, to portmanteau words like *narcokleptocracy*, on down to formerly rare words such as *viatical* and *swive*, which are trying for comebacks, the English language, called by Emerson "a city, to the building of which every human being has brought a stone," unfolds. Sometimes those bringing the stones have gone unknown, as is the case with *mamou*, *grapho-therapy*, *hubba*, *skel*, *erk*, *smoodge*, *toyi-toyi*, and *tsotsie*, but here the theories surrounding these mystery words have been given.

Sense Development

It is in the area of sense development that we can get a take on what people are thinking and doing. A good example aside from the "innocent victim" sense of *mushroom* (one that may derive from a video arcade game) is the verb *graze*, which has taken on, in just the last decade or so, three new senses—to sample foods illegally in a supermarket, to dine on hors d'oeuvres or tiny samplings of food and make it a meal, and to engage in TV channel switching. Most recently, a fourth sense has developed: to sample the electronic networks and their various neighborhoods. *Graze* exemplifies in its sense development our personal dietary habits and our markedly decreased attention spans. Another word, the adjective *serious*, took on, in the eighties, a number of new senses emblematic of the Zeitgeist of a conspicuously earnest, yet commercially consumptive, period.

One process involved in sense development is a narrowing in meaning, also called specialization. It is evident at the noun *cruise* in its automotive-hobbyist sense; at *trojan horse*, where the idea of enemy infiltration from within narrows to the entrails of computers; and most particularly at *inoculation*, where the word takes on a preemptive politically defensive posture. (The opposite of specialization is generalization, a process not observed in the words under scrutiny here.)

Other examples of the range in which sense development can occur are melioration, or elevation, and pejoration, or degeneration. Melioration is the process by which a word, originally negative in meaning, takes on a positive or neutral meaning. *Prestige* once meant "a conjuring trick; a deceptive act or an imposture." It is a big semantic leap from there to "eminent, influential status." (Or is it, given the imperatives of power and politics in today's world?) *Fizzle*, once meaning "to fart," is no longer regularly associated with that physiological process. Its most common sense, clearly neutral, is an example of melioration. But *nice* is undoubtedly the exemplar of the process: It began in the thirteenth century, meaning "ignorant; foolish; stupid." From the fourteenth century it took on the sense "wanton; lascivious," an obsolete meaning today. Through centuries of varied change, *nice* developed the senses we know and use today, some of them "pleasing and agreeable," "attractive in appearance," "courteous and polite," and so forth. (There are no instances of this process in this book.)

Pejoration, or degeneration, is the process whereby a word with a neutral or positive meaning goes the other way and takes on a decidedly negative meaning. *Silly*, for instance, once meant "blessed; innocent; helpless." Over time, however, it eventually took on the meanings "foolish" and "frivolous" with which readers are familiar today. A *knave* in old English meant simply "a boy"; now it denotes a crafty, unprincipled person. And *minion*, at one time used without disparagement to mean "a highly favored person; a darling," has taken on the most often sought sense involving sycophancy and obsequiousness.

Pejoration has occurred in the sense development of Rousseau's term *civil religion*, a term in which that development moves downscale from an awareness that the United States was founded on the belief in a higher judgment to which the nation and the leadership are still held accountable, to a slang sense—an activity, interest, or set of principles to which faddish devotion is accorded, with the quoted illustration evoking the making of money as the *civil religion* of our time. Trademarks, created for positive results, can be particularly vulnerable to pejoration. This pejoration of trademarks is a double irony when one realizes that the marks, not being parts of speech in their inception, therefore are supposed not to have intrinsic meaning to begin with.

Melioration and pejoration—two opposing linguistic forces in the development of a changing language that has a starting point but has no real end point—are together a metaphor for the tension between the good and the bad, the laudable and the deplorable, and the beautiful and the ugly of our society and the lexicon it is busily amending.

The eminent language historian George Harley McKnight, whom I have quoted before, has said this about that: "It should be held in mind . . . that the two reverse processes balance each other. By degeneration, on the one hand, and elevation, on the other, language attains the expression, not only of the depths of human contempt, but of the ideal heights which are the goal of human endeavor."

Index

Terms in boldface are main entries. The page numbers on which to find them are also in boldface.